The editors and authors of the present volume decided to ask important and vital questions concerning an (alleged) crisis of multilateralism. Using the Covid pandemic as a starting point, they covered by their analyses different fields of international relations and international law, sometimes far away from classical areas of interest. They discussed new processes and try to give answers to a basic question: do we face a new development leading to the dusk of the multilateral and liberal international order, and what is the future of the international community. Fascinating questions, and more fascinating answers.

Prof. Władysław Czapliński, PAS Institute of Law Studies, Poland

Many have argued that multilateralism is in crisis. This book digs deeper by asking how and why multilateralism is in crisis. Combining theoretical reflections with case studies in specialized areas, it sheds new light on the nature, dynamics and implications of the crisis in multilateralism. The book also points to possible new ways ahead for international cooperation.

Prof. Wouter Werner, Centre for the Politics of Transnational Law, Vrije Universiteit Amsterdam, The Netherlands

This is a very timely book because it goes beyond the mere deploring of the crisis or multilateralism which is popular in international organizations such as the UN, and gives us food for thought on the questions 'how?', 'why?' but also 'what to do?'

Prof. Lauri Mälksoo, University of Tartu, Estonia

This erudite volume manages to chart the field of multilateralism's purported demise approaching the issue in a heterogenious yet coherent way. The good news is that the starting question "is multilateralism on the way out yet?" does not have a simple answer, as the splendid mix of contributing scholars shows

Prof. Dimitry Kochenov, Central European University, Hungary

This thought-provoking and timely collection will make a substantial contribution to the debate surrounding the crisis of multilateralism and the related transformation of the underlying international legal order. Featuring a mix of well-established and rising scholars, the volume combines theoretical and more general analysis with individual case studies focusing on developments in specific fields of international law. The collection is comprehensive and covers various fields of international law, allowing readers to get a complete picture of the complex reality of international relations as reflected in public international law.

Prof. Bryan Mercurio, The Chinese University of Hong Kong

The Crisis of Multilateral Legal Order

Multilateralism has served as a foundation for international cooperation over the past several decades. Championed after the Second World War by the United States and Western Europe, it expanded into a broader global system of governance with the end of the Cold War. Lately, an increasing number of States appear to be disappointed with the existing multilateral arrangements, both at the level of norms and that of institutions. The great powers see unilateral and bilateral strategies, which maximise their political leverage rather than diluting it in multilateral fora, as more effective ways for controlling the course of international affairs.

The signs of the crisis have been visible for some time – but recent crises indicate an acceleration of the on-going disintegration of the multilateral system, such as Brexit, growing resistance on the part of States to international monitoring of compliance and the radical change in the US foreign policy during the presidency of Donald Trump which saw the US withdraw from several multilateral agreements (e.g. the Iran Nuclear Deal and the Paris Agreement), some international organizations or bodies (e.g. the United Nations Human Rights Council or the World Health Organization) or paralyze some others (e.g. the World Trade Organization (WTO)).

Tackling the debate surrounding the crisis of multilateralism and the related transformation of the underlying international legal order, *The Crisis of Multilateral Legal Order* analyses selected aspects of the current crisis from the perspective of public international law to identify the nature of the crisis, its dynamics, and implications.

Lukasz Gruszczynski is Associate Professor (dr. habil.) of International Law at Kozminski University, Poland, and a Research Fellow at the Centre for Social Sciences – Institute for Legal Studies, Hungary. He earned his PhD from the European University Institute in Florence. In the past, he was a visiting researcher at the University of Michigan Law School, the Lauterpacht Centre for International Law at the University of Cambridge (as Winiarski Fellow) and Pazmany Peter Catholic University, as well as an intern at the Legal Affairs Division of the World Trade Organization. He regularly teaches EU law, public international law, and international economic law at various Polish and foreign universities. Professor Gruszczynski is the author of more than 50 publications, including two monographs: *Regulating Health and Environmental Risks under WTO Law* (OUP, 2010) and *Deference in International Courts and Tribunals: Standard of Review and Margin of Appreciation* (OUP, 2010). He is also a Managing Co-Editor of the *Polish Yearbook of International Law*, Editor of the *European Journal of Risk Regulation* (CUP) and a member of the Scientific Committee of gLAWcal – Global Law Initiatives for Sustainable Development (UK).

Marcin J. Menkes is Associate Professor (dr. habil.) and Head of post-graduate studies of Law and Economics of Capital Markets at Warsaw School of Economics, Poland, a Research Fellow at Michigan Law School, and Of Counsel in Quertius. In the past he has been a Visiting Fellow or lecturer at Lauterpacht Centre for International Law at the University of Cambridge, Cornell Law School, the Università di Torino, the Università di Bologna, and the Università degli Studi di Firenze. He is a member of the International Law Association Committee on the Rule of Law and International Investment Law and the ISDS Academic Forum. He is the author of over 90 publications, including monographs on *Economic Governance in Public International Law* (2016) and *Economic Sanctions in International Law* (2011). His research focuses on international investment and financial law, economic sanctions, and economic governance. He practises law in the area of international arbitration and litigation.

Veronika Bílková is Professor in International Law at the Faculty of Law of the Charles University in Prague, the Czech Republic, and serves as Head of the Centre for International Law at the Institute of International Relations in Prague. She graduated from the Law and Philosophical Faculties of the Charles University and obtained the European Master's Degree in Human Rights and Democratisation. She is the holder of the Diploma in International Law from the University of Cambridge. She is a member of the European Commission for Democracy Through Law of the Council of Europe and is on the Managerial Board of the EU Fundamental Rights Agency. In the past, she was a Visiting Researcher at the University Paris II Panthéon-Assas, Northumbria University in Newcastle, the Max Planck Institute for Comparative Public Law and International Law in Heidelberg, and the Columbia Law School. She is the author of five books and more 100 book chapters and articles in Czech, English, and French on international law (mainly the use of force, international humanitarian law, international criminal law, and human rights) as well as on international relations (mainly security topics and the UN).

Paolo Davide Farah is an Associate Professor (with tenure) at West Virginia University, USA, the Eberly College of Arts and Sciences, the John D. Rockefeller IV School of Policy and Politics and the Coordinator of the Eberly College Interdisciplinary Research Collaborative on Global Challenges and Local Response Initiatives. He is the Founder, President, Director, Principal

Investigator and Senior Research Fellow at gLAWcal – Global Law Initiatives for Sustainable Development (www.glawcal.org.uk), Researcher at the Center for Law & Development (CLD), Qatar University, Distinguished Professor of Law at Beijing Foreign Studies University (BFSU), Law School (China), and Senior Research Fellow at the Institute of International Economic Law (IIEL), Georgetown University Law Center, Washington, DC, USA. In the past, he has been an International Consultant and Legal Advisor for projects implemented for the United Nations Development Program (UNDP), for the Italian Ministry of Economic Development and Commerce and for the OECD. He has previously worked in the Legal Affairs Division of the World Trade Organization in Geneva and was an Associate Lawyer in the Baker & McKenzie Law Firm, Milan, Italy. He was a Visiting Scholar at Harvard Law School, the East Asian Legal Studies Program. He has more than 60 articles or book chapters, 9 books and 6 journal special issues published or forthcoming in English and 20 additional publications in Italian, French, Spanish, and Chinese, including a book published by the Law Press China.

Transnational Law and Governance

Series Editor: Paolo Davide Farah, West Virginia University, USA and gLAWcal – Global Law Initiatives for Sustainable Development, UK

In recent years the concepts of "transnational law" and "governance" have been explored by both scholars and practitioners with the terms taking on new meaning and significance, particularly in light of the ongoing economic crisis and a corresponding critical reappraisal of global institutional structures and governance. This multidisciplinary series aims to provide a home for research exploring these issues.

Transnational law covers a broad theoretical definition which includes studies emerging from disciplines such as international law, comparative law, international economic law and administrative law undertaken by legal scholars but also features extensive research undertaken by scholars from other disciplines, including but not limited to, political sciences, international relations, public administration, sociology, history, philosophy and geography. Governance in particular is now seen as important when we refer to the general stability of the markets, to good faith and other key principles which are fundamental to the notion of a fair market which is responsive to the needs of governments and citizens as well as businesses.

This series features cutting-edge works which critically analyse the relationship between governance, institutions and law from a variety of disciplinary perspectives.

Available titles in this series include:

The Transnationalization of Anti-Corruption Law
Edited by Régis Bismuth, Jan Dunin-Wasowicz and Philip M. Nichols

Global Values and International Trade Law
Edited by Csongor István Nagy

The Crisis of Multilateral Legal Order
Causes, Dynamics and Implications
Edited by Lukasz Gruszczynski, Marcin J. Menkes, Veronika Bílková and Paolo D. Farah

The Crisis of Multilateral Legal Order

Causes, Dynamics and Implications

Edited by
Lukasz Gruszczynski, Marcin J. Menkes, Veronika Bílková and Paolo Davide Farah

Routledge
Taylor & Francis Group
LONDON AND NEW YORK

First published 2023
by Routledge
4 Park Square, Milton Park, Abingdon, Oxon OX14 4RN

and by Routledge
605 Third Avenue, New York, NY 10158

Routledge is an imprint of the Taylor & Francis Group, an informa business

British Library Cataloguing-in-Publication Data
A catalogue record for this book is available from the British Library

Library of Congress Cataloging-in-Publication Data
A catalog record has been requested for this book

ISBN: 978-1-032-11663-1 (hbk)
ISBN: 978-1-032-32105-9 (pbk)
ISBN: 978-1-003-31285-7 (ebk)

DOI: 10.4324/9781003312857

Typeset in Times New Roman
by Taylor & Francis Books

Contents

Contributors

Sean Butler is Lecturer in Law at University College Cork (UCC), Ireland. His PhD, undertaken in UCC under an Irish Research Council Government of Ireland Scholarship and entitled 'Examining the Impact of the R2P Doctrine on State Sovereignty in Contemporary International Law', was awarded in 2016. His current research focuses on how the ongoing shift towards 'multipolarity' will impact the structure and functioning of the international legal system. His work has been published in a number of peer-reviewed journals, including *Irish Studies in International Affairs* and the *Journal of Conflict and Security Law*.

Malgosia Fitzmaurice is Professor and Chair of Public International Law at the Department of Law, Queen Mary University of London. In 2019, she was elected an Associate Member of the Institut de Droit International and, in 2021, was awarded the Doctorate Honoris Causa of the University of Neuchâtel. She specialises in international environmental law, the law of treaties, and indigenous peoples. Professor Fitzmaurice has been invited as a Visiting Professor by numerous universities, including IMO International Maritime Law Institute in Malta, UC Berkeley School of Law, University of Paris 1 Panthéon-Sorbonne, and University of Kobe.

Mary E Footer is Professor Emerita of International Economic Law at the University of Nottingham and former co-director of the Nottingham International Law and Security Centre. She previously taught at the University of Amsterdam, the Erasmus University Rotterdam and University College London. She was also a full-time Senior Program Legal Counsel at IDLO, Rome. She has been visiting faculty at various universities, including Università di Bologna, the World Trade Institute, Peking (Beida), and Tsinghua Universities, Beijing. Professor Footer holds a JD in civil law (UNA), an LLM in Public International Law (UCL) and a PhD cum laude (Erasmus).

Patrycja Grzebyk (dr. habil. iur.) is Associate Professor in the Faculty of Political Science and International Studies, at the University of Warsaw. She has been a visiting scholar at the National Taiwan University, the University of Cambridge, the University of Geneva, and the University of

Bologna. She is the author of numerous publications, including monographs: *Human and Non-Human Targets in Armed Conflicts* (2022) and *Criminal Responsibility for the Crime of Aggression* (Routledge 2013). Her main fields of research are international humanitarian law, international criminal law, use of force, and international jurisdiction.

Jessica C Lawrence (JD, PhD) is a Senior Lecturer in Law at the University of Essex in the UK. Her research applies insights from critical legal studies, governmentality studies, and contemporary social and political theory to analyse the relationships between transnational economic law and other areas of governmental responsibility, such as human rights, environmental protection, and migration law. Dr Lawrence has previously held research and teaching positions at the Central European University, the Vrije Universiteit Amsterdam, Amsterdam University College, and the UN-mandated University for Peace in Costa Rica. She is also a visiting lecturer at the Universidad de Los Andes in Bogotá.

Christopher Lentz has worked for more than a dozen years in international tribunals, where he has gained experience in international criminal law and procedure, public international law and diplomacy, and related fields of international law. Currently he serves as a Legal Officer in the Office of the President of the United Nations International Residual Mechanism for Criminal Tribunals. He holds a Doctor of Law degree from the University of Chicago.

Margherita Melillo is an Associate at the O'Neill Institute for National and Global Health Law of Georgetown University, USA, where she works on research, training, and advocacy for non-communicable diseases policies. She completed her PhD at the European University Institute, where her research focused on the role of evidence in the international law on tobacco control. Her thesis was awarded the 2021 Cassese Prize. Before her current position, she was a Research Fellow at the Max Planck Institute Luxembourg for Procedural Law.

Agnieszka Nimark holds a PhD in Law from the European University Institute in Florence, and a Master's degree in International Public Law and International Organizations from the University Paris I-Panthéon-Sorbonne. Since 2009, Dr Nimark has been affiliated with the Barcelona Centre for International Affairs (CIDOB), first as Associate Researcher based in Barcelona (2009–2014), then as Associate Senior Researcher based in the USA (2014–present). She is a visiting scholar at the Reppy Institute for Peace and Conflict Studies at Cornell University, Ithaca, NY. Her research focuses on nuclear disarmament movements and includes archival and oral history and documentary projects.

Vassilis Pergantis is Assistant Professor of Public International Law in the Law Faculty, Aristotle University of Thessaloniki, Greece. His fields of interest focus on general international law, specifically the theory of international law and sources doctrine, the law of international organizations, and the law of international responsibility, as well as human rights. He has published extensively in English, French, and Greek and is the author of two monographs: *The Paradigm of State Consent in the Law of Treaties* (2017) and *The Human Dimension of Diplomatic Protection* (2017, in Greek).

Ernst-Ulrich Petersmann was Professor of International and European law at the Universities of St. Gallen, Fribourg, Geneva, the Geneva Graduate Institute of International Relations, and the European University Institute in Florence. His almost 400 publications focus on international law, European law, and comparative constitutional law. He worked for the German government representing Germany in European and UN institutions (1978–1980), and as legal counsel in GATT and as a consultant for the WTO (1981–2021), as secretary, member, or chairman of GATT and WTO dispute settlement panels, and as chairman of the International Trade Law Committee of the International Law Association (1999–2014).

Maria Varaki is a Lecturer in International Law at the War Studies Department, King's College London. Before moving to the United Kingdom, she held research and teaching positions with the Erik Castren Institute of International Law and Human Rights in Helsinki, the Law Faculty of Hebrew University in Jerusalem, and Kadir Has University, Faculty of Law in Istanbul. She holds a PhD in International Criminal Law from the Irish Centre for Human Rights in Galway, Ireland, and two LLM degrees in International and Comparative Law, one from Tulane University, School of Law, and one from New York University, School of Law.

Oleksandr Vodiannikov, LLM, PhD (CEU), is an expert in the areas of international law and institutions, Ukrainian and comparative constitutional law, judiciary, and human rights. He is a legal advisor to the OSCE Project Co-ordinator in Ukraine and consultant for the Ukraine's Law Reform Commission. He also served as a member of Ukraine's Judicial Reform Council (2014–2019) and Constitutional Commission (2015–2019). He has authored more than 40 publications and has lectured widely on his diverse research interests.

Karolina Wierczyńska (dr. habil. iur.) is Associate Professor of Public International Law at the Institute of Law Studies of the Polish Academy of Sciences (PAS), Poland. She is a vice-president of the Committee on Legal Sciences of PAS (term 2020–2023), Deputy Editor-in-chief of the *Polish Yearbook of International Law*, Head of a Research Centre on International 7Criminal Law at ILS PAS, and a member of the ILA Committee on Complementarity in International Law.

Szymon Zaręba, PhD, is Assistant Professor in the Institute of Law Studies of the Polish Academy of Sciences and the Head of the Global Issues Programme at the Polish Institute of International Relations, Poland. He serves as an expert in the Warsaw Process Working Group on Human Rights and is a participant and leader of several research projects funded by the EU Justice Programme, the Polish National Science Centre, and the Polish Ministry of Science and Higher Education. He is also a former exchange student at the University of Manchester Law School, UK. His research interests include the responsibility of States and international organisations, human rights, as well as law and practice of international organisations such as the UN, the WHO and the Council of Europe.

Ewa Żelazna, PhD, is a Lecturer at the University of Leicester, UK. Her research interests are in the field of the EU external economic relations and her current work focuses on the EU's comprehensive international investment policy, as well as issues concerning the democratic accountability of the EU's external actions. She was a Visiting Research Fellow at the Max Planck Institute for International Public Law and Comparative Constitutional Law in Heidelberg and the Centre for the EU External Relations Law, T.M.C. Asser Institute in the Hague. She has also completed internships at the CJEU and the British Institute of International and Comparative Law.

Preface and Acknowledgements

The idea for this book was born during the conference, 'The Crisis of Multilateral International Order: Causes, Dynamics and Consequences', jointly organised in November 2019 by the European Society of International Law, Warsaw School of Economics, Kozminski University and the Institute of Law Studies of the Polish Academy of Sciences. Later it turned out that this was one of the last meetings before the whole world closed down due to the COVID-19 pandemic (at least for us – the editors and speakers). Reality, as we knew it, disappeared. National lockdowns, travel restrictions, facemasks in public spaces have become the new normal.

Despite these difficulties, we decided to continue our work on the project. The selected presenters were asked to prepare longer papers that would be included as chapters in the edited volume. This group was also complemented by two keynote speakers and a number of invited authors. The underlying idea was to produce a comprehensive work that would systematically address different aspects of the current crisis of multilateralism. Considering the failures in the global management system during the pandemic, this task has appeared to us more important than ever. Eventually, after two years of intense work, the manuscript took its final shape.

The preparation of this book would not have been possible without the financial support provided to Lukasz Gruszczynski by the National Science Centre in Poland as part of the OPUS programme (the project, 'The crisis of the multilateral trade system: gradual disintegration or natural evolution?', UMO-2018/31/B/HS5/03556).

We would also like to acknowledge the editorial assistance provided by Gautam Mohanty – a PhD researcher at Kozminski University. Excellent language correction was done by James Hartzell and Susan Dunsmore (editors).

Foreword

This is an important book. Not only does it have to be read more than once, international law and institutional scholars will actually find it helpful to read the editors' introductory and conclusion chapters first – before delving into the contrasting treatments of the other individual contributions in between.

The themes of trust, legitimacy of international laws and institutions, citizens achieving maximum individual freedom within national governments and international commitments, resilience and security, and sovereignty require knife-edge balancing in order to achieve what most contributors seem to desire – *liberal* multilateralism. While not explicitly addressed, *conservative* multilateralism is a stand-in for sovereignty and for going it alone on human rights, environmental and global climate protection, energy independence, the arms race, national security, and autocracy. Going it alone can dampen – or defeat – the concerns of many others, especially those dominating the international liberal order. However, denying or ignoring the power of the tendency towards conservative multilateralism may leave us powerless to change it. Forces representing both kinds of multilateralism co-exist, conflict, and demand the attention of people who disagree. To the extent that international law and principles can rescue any particular nation from its 'natural momentum' in any period of time is one of the greatest challenges of our time. The analyses and narratives in this book should open one's eyes to the difficult task lying ahead. It is a must read.

The book provides interesting and thought-provoking insights on non-trade concerns (NTCs) that could open up a larger discussion on the role of these concerns in the international arena in times of crisis of the multilateral legal order. These issues have become particularly important in the context of globalization and fit perfectly into the broader discussions related to the necessary changes and improvements of the international legal norms and systems of governance towards the protection of NTCs. These topics are constitutive and pivotal of the gLAWcal book series on 'Transnational Law and Governance' and 'Global Law and Sustainable Development', published by Routledge. In fact, gLAWcal – Global Law Initiatives for Sustainable Development, an independent non-profit research organization and think tank (http://www.glawcal.org.uk/) – through research, policy analysis, and advocacy, attempts to shed new light on NTCs issues, such as good and global governance, human rights, the right to water, rights to food, social, economic and cultural rights, labor rights, access to knowledge, public health, social welfare, consumer interests and animal welfare, climate change, energy, environmental protection and sustainable development, product safety, food safety and security. All these values are directly affected by the global expansion of world trade and should be upheld to balance the excesses of globalization.

Nicholas A. Ashford, PhD, JD
Professor of Technology and Policy,
Massachusetts Institute of Technology (MIT)
Member of the Scientific Committee, gLAWcal – Global Law Initiatives for Sustainable Development (UK)
Co-author of Technology, Globalization, and Sustainable Development: Transforming the Industrial State (Routledge, 2018)

Foreword

The present book brings together some of the papers presented at a conference held in Warsaw in 2019 on the topic: 'The Crisis of Multilateral International Order: Causes, Dynamics and Consequences', co-organised by the European Society of International Law, the Warsaw School of Economics (SGH), Kozminski University (KU), and the Institute of Law Studies of the Polish Academy of Sciences (ILS PAS). By posing some underlying questions: Are we indeed witnessing a crisis of the multilateral order?; What is its nature and its impacts?; the individual chapters revisit multilateralism and its 'discontents', not only from the perspective of general public international law, but also relating to specific areas of international law. They address the concept itself, as well as its dynamics in an ever-changing multilateral legal order.

Many thanks are due to the local organizers of the conference and to the editors of this volume, which will certainly be of interest to all those readers focusing on the contemporary challenges to multilateralism.

Photini Pazartzis
Professor of International Law
Athens Public International Law Center
Faculty of Law of the National and Kapodistrian University of Athens
Former President of the European Society of International Law (2019–2021)
September 2021

Abbreviations

AB	Appellate Body
ABNJ	areas beyond national jurisdiction
ACT	Access to COVID-19 Tools
ADM	automated decision-making
AFSJ	Area of Freedom, Security and Justice
ARSIWA	Articles on Responsibility of States for Internationally Wrongful Acts
ASEAN	Association of Southeast Asian Nations
ASP	Assembly of States Parties (of the ICC)
AU	African Union
BIT	bilateral investment treaty
BLM	Black Lives Matter
BRI	Belt and Road Initiative
CAI	China-EU Comprehensive Agreement on Investment
CBD	UN Convention on Biological Diversity
CCP	Chinese Communist Party
CCPR	Covenant on Civil and Political Rights
CEND	Creating an Environment for Nuclear Disarmament
CEPI	Coalition for Epidemic Preparedness Innovations
CETA	Comprehensive Economic and Trade Agreement
CFR	Charter of Fundamental Rights of the European Union
CFS	FAO Committee on Food Security
CJEU	Court of Justice of the European Union
CoE	Council of Europe
CPTPP	Comprehensive and Progressive Agreement for a Trans-Pacific Partnership
CPVAX	Covid Vaccine Access
CRPD	Convention on the Rights of Persons with Disabilities
CSM	Civil Society and Indigenous Peoples' Mechanism
CSO	civil society organisation
DSB	Dispute Settlement Body
DSU	Understanding on rules and procedures governing the settlement of disputes

EAW	European Arrest Warrant
ECB	European Central Bank
ECHR	European Convention on Human Rights
ECI	European Citizens' Initiative
ECT	Energy Charter Treaty
ECtHR	European Court of Human Rights
EEA	European Economic Area
EEZ	exclusive economic zone
EIA	environmental impact assessment
EU	European Union
FAO	Food and Agriculture Organization
FCC	Federal Constitutional Court of Germany
FDI	foreign direct investment
FTA	free trade agreement
GATS	General Agreement on Trade in Services
GATT	General Agreement on Tariffs and Trade
GAVI	Global Alliance for Vaccines and Immunisations
HRC	Human Rights Committee
HRL	human rights law
IACtHR	Inter-American Court of Human Rights
IAEA	International Atomic Energy Agency
ICC	International Criminal Court
ICCPR	International Covenant on Civil and Political Rights
ICESCR	International Covenant on Economic, Social and Cultural Rights
ICGC	International Climate Governance Coalition
ICJ	International Court of Justice
ICSID	International Centre for the Settlement of Investment Disputes
ICTR	International Criminal Tribunal for Rwanda
ICTY	International Criminal Tribunal for the former Yugoslavia
IEL	international economic law
IHL	international humanitarian law
IHR	International Health Regulations
IIA	international investment agreement
ILC	International Law Commission
ILO	International Labour Organization
IMF	International Monetary Fund
INB	Intergovernmental Negotiating Body
INF	Intermediate-Range Nuclear Forces Treaty
IO	international organisation
IOM	Independent Oversight Mechanism
ISA	investor-State arbitration
ISA	International Seabed Authority
ISDS	International State Dispute System
ITLOS	International Tribunal for the Law of the Sea

IUCN	International Union for Conservation of Nature
JCPOA	Joint Comprehensive Plan of Action
JEEPA	Japan-EU Partnership Agreement
LOSC	the Law of the Sea
MEA	multilateral environmental agreement
MFN	most favoured nation
MNC	multinational corporation
MS	Member State
MSI	multistakeholder initiative
NDCs	nationally determined contributions
NGO	non-governmental organisation
NNWS	non-nuclear-weapon State
NPT	Non-Proliferation of Nuclear Weapons Treaty
NTC	non-trade concern
NWS	nuclear-weapon State
ODA	Official Development Assistance
OECD	Organisation for Economic Co-operation and Development
PACE	Parliamentary Assembly of the Council of Europe
PCIJ	Permanent Court of International Justice
PGs	public goods
PHEIC	Public Health Emergencies of International Concern
PSPP	Public Sector Asset Purchase Programme
RCEP	Regional Comprehensive Economic Partnership
SAPs	Structural Adjustment Programs
SC	Security Council
SDG	Sustainable Development Goal
SOE	state-owned enterprise
TEU	Treaty on European Union
TFEU	Treaty on the Functioning of the European Union
TPNW	Treaty on the Prohibition of Nuclear Weapons
TTIP	Transatlantic Trade and Investment Partnership
UDHR	Universal Declaration of Human Rights
UN	United Nations
UNCAT	UN Convention against Torture and Other Cruel, Inhuman or Degrading Treatment or Punishment
UNCITRAL	UN Commission for International Trade Law
UNCLOS	UN Convention on the Law of the Sea
UNCLOS Optional Protocol	Optional Protocol of Signature concerning the Compulsory Settlement of Disputes
UNCTAD	United Nations Commission for International Trade Law
UNESCO	UN Educational, Scientific and Cultural Organization
UNGA	UN General Assembly
UNTC	United Nations Treaty Collection
US	United States of America

USTR	United States Trade Representative
VCCR Optional Protocol	Optional Protocol to the Vienna Convention on Consular Relations concerning the Compulsory Settlement of Disputes
VCDR Optional Protocol	Optional Protocol to the Vienna Convention on Diplomatic Relations, concerning the Compulsory Settlement of Disputes
VCLT	Vienna Convention on the Law of Treaties
WHA	World Health Assembly
WHO	World Health Organization
WTO	World Trade Organization

1 Introduction

Mapping the crisis of multilateralism

Paolo D Farah, Lukasz Gruszczynski, Marcin J Menkes and Veronika Bílková

In December 2019, the first cases of COVID-19 – known at that time as 'severe pneumonia of unknown cause' – were identified in Wuhan, China. The local Chinese authorities disregarded information about the outbreak, silenced the whistleblowers, including the now-famous Dr. Li Wenliang, and made numerous calming and misleading public pronouncements (e.g. as to the size of the outbreak or the absence of human-to-human transmission).[1] It was only in the second part of January 2020 that the true picture began to emerge, with thousands of patients storming the local hospitals. Wuhan soon went into the full lockdown, but the damage was already done, and the virus spread to other parts of China and beyond.

The World Health Organization (WHO) received their early information about the outbreak from the Chinese authorities at the beginning of January 2020. The situation was not considered to be particularly serious. On 21 January 2020, when individual cases of COVID-19 were already detected in several countries of Southeast Asia, the WHO eventually acknowledged that limited human-to-human transmission was possible. However, it took the organization some time to declare COVID-19 as a public health emergency of international concern, and then as a pandemic (30 January 2020 and 11 March 2020 respectively). This delay was partially caused by poor cooperation on the part of China, and partially by the lack of enforcement tools on the part of the WHO. At the same time, the WHO did not remain idle. It adopted a number of health guidelines but some of them proved later to be controversial (e.g. not urging the use of facemasks in public places, proposing loose travel restrictions with relatively open borders), and many countries decided to impose stricter measures, frequently in clear contradiction to the WHO's recommendations.

The domestic responses, however, were far from perfect as well. Most countries turned out to be completely unprepared for the pandemic. Governments frequently relied on unilateral measures with little coordination

1 Dali L Yang, 'Wuhan officials tried to cover up Covid-19 — and sent it careening outward' *Washington Post* (10 March 2020) <https://wapo.st/3hcJBqG> accessed 30 April 2022.

DOI: 10.4324/9781003312857-1

between each other. Many responses simply came too late or were poorly designed. For example, some European Union (EU) Member States decided to unilaterally close their borders, including those with other Members. This was done despite opposition from the European Commission, which saw such restrictions as premature.[2] All of these domestic actions led to considerable chaos and undermined rather than reinforced an effective response to the pandemic. Simultaneously, national egoisms were on the rise. Many countries introduced export controls over certain medical products in the form of temporary export bans.[3] Others imposed export restrictions on specific agricultural products, fearing disruptions in the existing supply chains. Again, such measures were often taken unilaterally, without consultations with their trading partners.

To make matters worse, the WHO – which was supposed to serve as a coordination centre – was transformed into a battleground between the United States (US) and China. The situation became so tense that the US first decided to freeze its financial contributions to the WHO, and later withdrew from the organization.[4] Although the WHO did make some mistakes early in the pandemic, it nevertheless seems that the organization has served primarily as a scapegoat for domestic policy failures. The World Trade Organization (WTO) – badly weakened even before the outbreak – was also side-lined, as pandemic-related trade restrictions were taken with the little regard for international trade rules. The same was true for the United Nations, which only played a marginal role in the pandemic, despite being (still) the most important international political institution. But many other international organizations were marginalized or have not delivered as they should have. For example, a recent study pointed out that the International Monetary Fund (IMF) was hesitant to provide the much-needed liquidity to developing countries. As bitterly concluded by the authors of the study, 'The world community is failing to deliver its own assessment of current gaps and is falling far short of doing "whatever it takes".'[5]

2 See e.g. Michael Peel, Richard Milne, and James Shotter, 'Denmark, Poland and Czechs seal borders over coronavirus' *Financial Times* (13 March 2020) <https://www.ft.com/content/4e89ec5c-6565-11ea-b3f3-fe4680ea68b5> accessed 30 April 2022. As summarized by the President of the Commission Ursula von der Leyen in her speech on 12 March 2020, 'certain controls may be justified, but general travel bans are not seen as being the most effective by the World Health Organization … Moreover, they have a strong social and economic impact, they disrupt people's lives and business across the borders.'

3 World Trade Organization, 'COVID-19: Trade and trade-related measures' (as of 14 April 2020) <https://bit.ly/3hk85P0> accessed 30 April 2022.

4 These decisions were subsequently reversed by the new American administration (see Jamey Keaten, 'Biden's US revives support for WHO, reversing Trump retreat' *APNews* (21 January 2021) <https://bit.ly/3xBm1cX> accessed 30 April 2022.

5 Thomas Stubbs et al., 'Whatever it takes? The global financial safety net, Covid-19, and developing countries' (2021) 137 World Development 105171, 6. Note,

The arrival of COVID-19 vaccines brought with them a promise to end the pandemic, but it also created its own problems. Governments from developed countries secured sufficient supplies by concluding early deals with pharmaceutical companies that prioritized their orders over those from developing countries. For example, the EU has reserved many times more vaccines than its entire population.[6] As a consequence, most developing states have been left behind, with the result that at least 90 per cent of people in lower-income countries was not vaccinated by the end of 2021.[7] Wealth and power, rather than actual needs, have again served as a primary allocation criterion.[8]

In order to address this problem, the so-called COVAX programme has been launched by the WHO. It brings together governments, intergovernmental organizations, civil society, and private sectors in order to provide equitable access to COVID-19 vaccines. Although almost 1.5 billion doses of vaccines have been delivered through this framework,[9] the overall success of the programme remains limited as its implementation is lagging behind, with developed countries unwilling to increase their commitments[10] or opting for a bilateral approach as part of their vaccine diplomacy policy. Paradoxically, such a situation will most likely prolong the pandemic, as many parts of the world will continue in the foreseeable future to be reservoirs of the constantly mutating virus.

Equally disappointing have been developments within the WTO. Several developing countries have been seeking the temporary waiver of certain obligations of the Agreement on Trade Related Aspects of Intellectual Property Rights (TRIPS), a move which would facilitate the production of COVID-19 vaccines and COVID-19-related drugs. Although developed countries, after initially blocking the proposal, eventually decided to consider it, the work in the TRIPS Council got stuck over the exact scope and specific conditions of the waiver.[11] In addition, even if it succeeds the logistics of producing generic

however, that more recently the IMF Board approved a plan to distribute $650 billion in reserve funds to help poorer nations with their vaccine rollouts and pandemic recovery efforts, Alan Rappeport, 'I.M.F. Board backs $650 billion aid plan to help poor countries' *The New York Times* (9 July 2021) <https://nyti.ms/3r5mu4T> accessed 30 April 2022.

6 EU Commission, '3rd contract with BioNTech-Pfizer for 1.8 billion doses', European Commission (20 May 2021) <https://ec.europa.eu/commission/presscorner/detail/en/ip_21_2548> accessed 30 April 2022.

7 Owen Dyer, 'Covid-19: Many poor countries will see almost no vaccine next year, aid groups warn' (2020) 371 BMJ m4809.

8 Lukasz Gruszczynski and Chien-huei Wu, 'Between the high ideals and reality: managing COVID-19 vaccine nationalism' (2021) 12(3) EJRR 711.

9 See <https://www.gavi.org/> accessed 30 April 2022.

10 Dalia Elkady, 'COVAX delays: A moral failure in full swing', SYNERJIES: Center for International & Strategic Studies (9 May 2021) <https://synerjies.com/covax-delays-a-moral-failure-in-full-swing/> accessed 30 April 2022.

11 Andrew Green, 'WTO council offers hope for TRIPS vaccine proposal', *Devex* (10 June 2021) <https://bit.ly/3yHMRAm> accessed 30 April 2022.

vaccines casts doubt on the sincerity of political statements about the willingness of developed countries to limit intellectual property protection.[12]

The COVID-19 pandemic and the reaction to it provide a good illustration of not only the importance of a well-functioning multilateral order, but also of its current crisis. Of course, we are not claiming here that the crisis of the multilateral international order is a simple result of the pandemic. As discussed below, the crisis had been already unfolding for some time and seems to be rooted in the geopolitical reconfiguration(s) taking place on the world scene, the rise of (inward-looking) nationalism, growing disappointment with liberal ideas, and structural problems in the existing international arrangements. The pandemic, however, has highlighted several important aspects of the crisis and perhaps has accelerated the whole process.

First, it has clearly shown that unilateral actions alone are insufficient to address the challenges relating to the global public goods, such as public health. Pandemics, similar to environmental degradation, climate change, or the arms race, know no borders and can only be effectively managed by coordinated actions on the part of the international community rather than through piecemeal national responses. As eloquently noted by the UN Secretary-General António Guterres, 'in an interconnected world, none of us is safe until all of us are safe.'[13]

Second, the response to the pandemic also confirms that international organizations remain heavily constrained in their activities by the Member States of such organizations, which frequently show little appetite for sharing with them their sovereign powers. In addition, they need to rely on the Members' resources and cannot perform their functions properly without States' engagement.[14] On top of this, international organizations can become relatively easy targets for States that want to shift the responsibility for their domestic failures. They may equally become hostages in the geopolitical struggles among their Members. Obviously, all of these factors have a negative impact on their effectiveness and demonstrate the overall weakness of the currently-existing arrangements.

Third, in times of global crises, such as the COVID-19 pandemic, instead of showing solidarity, States may actually turn inward, focusing on their national priorities (even if they are only short-term) rather than looking for common long-term solutions. In other words, the key tenets of multilateralism – trust,

12 Enrico Bonadio and Filippo Fontanelli, 'Push for COVID-19 vaccine patent waiver isn't a panacea: but it could nudge companies to share', City University of London (19 May 2021) <https://bit.ly/3rgpUC1> accessed 30 April 2022.

13 'None of us is safe until we all are, says UN chief at EU push to end COVID-19 pandemic', UN News (4 May 2021) <https://news.un.org/en/story/2020/05/1063132> accessed 30 April 2022.

14 Lukasz Gruszczynski and Margherita Melillo, 'The uneasy coexistence of expertise and politics in the World Health Organization: Learning from the experience of the early response to the COVID-19 pandemic', IOLR (published online ahead of print 2022), https://doi.org/10.1163/15723747-20220001.

cooperation, and transparency – may become rare during such periods; while antagonism, secrecy, and distrust – elements that characterize unilateralism – can dominate international relations.

Fourth, events such pandemics have the potential, due to their enormous political and economic impact, to reconfigure the existing balances of power in international relations, including in multilateral institutions. This seems to be the case for the COVID-19 pandemic, which has accelerated the process of a power shift from the West (as broadly understood) to the East, with China playing an increasingly important role. It has not only managed (at least for now) to regain control over the pandemic on its territory, but also has recovered from the economic crisis much faster than the US or any EU country.[15] The 'soft power' traditionally wielded and enjoyed by the West also seems to be fading away. Effective governance, rationality in decision-making, collective problem-solving, and global leadership have been the characteristic features of the West and broadly appealing to the rest of the world. This image has, however, received a serious blow during the pandemic, as many non-Western countries have done a much better job in controlling its progression.[16]

***

Before we proceed further, it is worth defining 'multilateralism' – the key concept of this volume – and explaining why we think that it is in crisis. Multilateralism is normally opposed to the unilateralism and bilateralism that dominated international relations in the pre-First World War period. The term literally means 'many-sided' and comes from the Latin words '*multus*' (many), and '*latus*' (side). Its etymology would suggest that it is simply about 'the practice of co-ordinating national policies in groups of three or more states, through *ad hoc* arrangements or by means of institutions' (understood as 'persistent and connected sets of rules, formal and informal, that prescribe behavioural roles, constrain activity, and shape expectations').[17] There are, however, other definitions of multilateralism which concentrate not so much on its quantitative aspect but shift their focus towards the qualitative dimension of the phenomenon. For example, Ruggie defines multilateralism as a process of organizing relations among three or more states on the basis of certain generalized principles of conduct, understood as 'principles which specify appropriate conduct for a class of actions, without regard to the

15 Françoise Huang, 'The world is moving East, fast', Allianz Research (18 January 2021) <https://bit.ly/2U6HCvk> accessed 30 April 2022.

16 John R Allen et al., 'The world after the coronavirus', *Foreign Policy* (2 January 2021) <https://bit.ly/3xAd1Vy> accessed 30 April 2022. See also Khan Sharun and Kuldeep Dhama, 'COVID-19 vaccine diplomacy and equitable access to vaccines amid ongoing pandemic' (2021) 52(7) Arch Med Res 761.

17 Robert Keohane, 'Multilateralism: An agenda for research' (1990) 45 Int J 731, 733.

particularistic interests of the parties or the strategic exigencies that may exist in any specific occurrence'[18] (e.g. the most-favoured-nation treatment in the area of international economic law). According to this view, multilateralism cannot be reduced only to the number of participating countries but is also about the indivisibility of interests among participants, a commitment to diffuse reciprocity, and a reliance on certain generalized principles of conduct. More recent definitions emphasize that multilateralism does not necessarily need to be limited to States, as non-state actors are actually playing an increasingly important role, either by pushing States to make multilateral commitments or laying the groundwork for new arrangements.[19] Also, as the liberal international order has dominated the world since the end of the Cold War, over time, multilateralism came to be equated with a certain vision of the world that is based on respect for:

- a shared system of norms and values;
- the promotion of open markets;
- international institutions;
- common security;
- progressive change;
- collective problem-solving;
- shared sovereignty;
- the rule of law.[20]

While the term 'multilateralism' is relatively new, the roots of the concept can be traced back to the Vienna Congress of 1814–15 and the geopolitical order that was subsequently created in Europe. This period, conventionally known as the Concert of Europe, was characterized by coordinated efforts of the Great Powers (initially Austria, Prussia, Russia, and Great Britain, later also France and the Ottoman Empire) aimed at avoiding wars and preventing revolutions, and by doing so maintaining the territorial and political status quo in Europe and abroad. Of course, this cooperation was not institutionalized and it excluded smaller states, which remained objects rather than subjects of international relations. At the end of the nineteenth century, one could also witness the emergence of various bureaus and unions which were supposed to help the States in coordinating their activities in the fields of transport and communications (e.g. the Universal Postal Union of 1874).

18 John G Ruggie, 'Multilateralism: The anatomy of an institution' (1992) 46 Int Organ 561, 571.

19 See Phillip Jones and David Coleman, (2005) *The United Nations and Education: Multilateralism, Development and Globalization* (Routledge 2005); Ramesh Thakur, 'Security in the new millennium', in Andrew F Cooper, John English, and Ramesh Thakur (eds), *Enhancing Global Governance: Towards a New Diplomacy?* (United Nations UP 2002).

20 G John Ikenberry, 'Liberal internationalism 3.0: America and the dilemmas of liberal world order' (2009) 7(1) Perspectives on Politics 71.

Although the First World War interrupted these processes, multilateralism as a way of arranging international relations made a comeback with the creation of the League of Nations.[21] Interestingly, the Covenant of the League of Nations not only created a multilateral institution but also included a set of the basic principles underlying the collaboration between States, such as collective security, the peaceful settlement of disputes, international cooperation in economic and social affairs, disarmament, and open diplomacy. As we all aware, this system turned out to be very fragile and eventually collapsed.

It was only in the post-Second World War period that multilateralism fully flourished, becoming a foundation for international cooperation. Initially it was a hybrid creature, consisting of a series of overlapping formal and informal frameworks (e.g. international security, trade, global health, or human rights) and 'combining universal aspirations such as human rights with a more prosaic system of managed competition in which major powers – including non-democratic and authoritarian ones – exert a prepondering influence.'[22] Championed by the US and Western Europe, it ultimately expanded into a broader and more uniform global system of governance with the end of the Cold War.

Lately, however, an increasing number of States seem to be ever more disappointed with the existing multilateral arrangements, both at the level of norms and of institutions. The most powerful States – both established and emerging – apparently see unilateral and bilateral strategies, which maximize their political leverage rather than diluting it in multilateral fora, as more effective means of controlling the course of international affairs. Paradoxically, many of the smaller nations, which are supposed to be clear beneficiaries of the multilateral system,[23] have also become very critical of it. They seem particularly frustrated by the functioning of various international organizations and the operation of international multilateral arrangements,[24] which they believe have failed to deliver on their declared goals[25] and/or suffer from geopolitical biases that are embedded in their institutional structures.[26] Indeed, power dynamics, as well as specific ideologies underlying the

21 Mario Telò, 'State and multilateralism: History and perspectives', in Mario Telò (ed.), *State, Globalization and Multilateralism* (Springer 2012) 7–44.

22 'Multilateralism is in crisis – Or is it?', in *Global Challenges: Global Governance in Peril* (Graduate Institute, Geneva 2020) <https://bit.ly/3qEWxsK> accessed 30 April 2022.

23 As famously stated by Kagan, multilateralism can be considered a 'weapon of the weak'. Robert Kagan, 'Power and Weakness', *Hoover Institution, Policy Review* (1 June 2002) <https://www.hoover.org/research/power-and-weakness> accessed 30 April 2022.

24 See e.g. Gregory Chin and Ramesh Thakur, 'Will China change the rules of global order?' (2010) 33(4) The Washington Quarterly 119.

25 Amitav Acharya, *Constructing Global Order. Agency and Change in World Politics* (CUP 2018).

26 Joint Meeting of ECOSOC and the GA's Second Committee, 'The changing political economy of globalization: Multilateral institutions and the 2030

current multilateral system and its components, play an important role in shaping it.

These critical convictions are also shared by many civil society groups from different sides of the political spectrum. Left-leaning movements have for years been raising issues of fairness and the protection of important non-economic values[27] which, they believe, have been forgotten by the international institutions. At the same time, right-wing groups have been advocating for tightly-controlled borders, self-sufficiency, protectionism, and prioritization of the national interest (as narrowly understood) over common international interests. In many countries some of these demands have eventually entered mainstream politics through the re-emergence of populist parties and movements.

Although the signs of the crisis already were visible for some time – even before the 2007–08 global financial crisis – the process has accelerated in recent years. Notable examples of the on-going decline of the multilateral system include the decision of the United Kingdom to leave the EU, withdrawals by various States from international agreements and institutions, or the growing resistance to international monitoring of compliance and the contestation of judgments of international courts (particularly as compared to the first two decades following the end of the Cold War). However, the most prominent signal so far has been the radical change in US foreign policy under President Donald Trump. During his presidency, the US decided to withdraw from several multilateral agreements (e.g. the Iran Nuclear Deal and the Paris Agreement), and leave some international organizations and bodies (e.g. the United Nations Human Rights Council and, as already mentioned, the WHO) or paralyze others (e.g. the WTO). It also pursued a unilateral foreign policy,[28] relying on its real (and perceived) political and economic strength, questioning the existing alliances, and turning its prime attention to internal affairs.[29] It remains to be seen to what extent the current American administration under President Biden will be able and willing to reverse these decisions and whether such reversals will be a permanent change or just a break in the rebirth of American unilateralism and isolationism.

Considering the above developments, it is hard to disagree with the diagnosis of the Secretary General of the United Nations, who said in his 2019 address to the General Assembly:

agenda – background note' (7 October 2016) <https://bit.ly/3wcEUBF> accessed 30 April 2022.

27 See generally Paolo D Farah and Elena Cima, *China's Influence on Non-Trade Concerns in International Economic Law* (Routledge 2016).

28 Marcin J Menkes, 'The legality of US investment sanctions against Iran before the ICJ: A watershed moment for the essential security and necessity exceptions' (2019) 56 Can Yb Int L 328.

29 For more details, see Reuben Steff, *US Foreign Policy in the Age of Trump: Drivers, Strategy and Tactics* (Routledge 2020).

> [w]orld order is increasingly chaotic. Power relations are less clear. Universal values are being eroded. Democratic principles are under siege. The rule of law is being undermined. Impunity is on the rise, as leaders and states push the boundaries at home and in the international arena. We face a set of paradoxes. The world is more connected. Yet societies are becoming more fragmented. Challenges are growing outward, while many people are turning inward. Multilateralism is under fire precisely when we need it most.[30]

Overall, there seems to be a growing consensus among experts and politicians that we are experiencing a crisis of multilateralism and the legal order that underlies it in terms of institutions, norms, and new initiatives.[31] We tend to agree with this assessment.[32]

Having said the above, one can also witness the emergence of new coordination and governance formats, which – unlike the post-Second World War arrangements – are often regional rather than universal, initiated without US leadership (or more generally outside the Western sphere of influence), and based on unusual alliances or undertaken by non-state actors (e.g. international courts, cities, multinational companies).[33] Examples of such projects include the continuing implementation of the Chinese 'One Belt, One Road'

30 'Secretary-General's address to the General Assembly', UN (25 September 2018) <https://bit.ly/3hy0F9T> accessed 30 April 2022.

31 See e.g. Jutta Brunnée, 'Multilateralism in crisis' (2018) 112 Proceeding of the ASIL Annual Meeting 335; Gro Harlem Brundtland, 'The UN @75' (2020) 26(4) Global Governance: A Review of Multilateralism and International Organizations 545; Council of Europe, 'Multilateralism 2020 – Annual Report of the Secretary General of the Council of Europe' (2020); G John Ikenberry, *A World Safe for Democracy: Liberal Internationalism and the Crises of Global Order* (Yale UP 2020); G John Ikenberry, 'The end of liberal international order?' (2018) 94(1) Int Aff 7; Mette Eilstrup-Sangiovanni and Stephanie C Hofmann, 'Of the contemporary global order, crisis, and change' (2020) 27(7) J Eur Public Policy 1077.

32 Note, however, that there are those who believe that multilateralism has been in continuous crisis for most of its existence (see e.g. Miles Kahler, 'Multilateralism with small and large numbers' (1992) 46(3) Int Organ 681; José E Alvarez, 'Multilateralism and its discontents' (2000) 11(2) EJIL 393; Bruce Jones and Susana Malcorra, *Competing for Order. Confronting the Long Crisis of Multilateralism* (Editorial Instituto de Empresa and Brookings 2020)) or that the claims of the severity of the current crisis are greatly exaggerated (see e.g. Richard Gowan, 'Multilateralism in freefall?' (United Nations University Centre for Policy Research, 30 July 2018) <https://cpr.unu.edu/publications/articles/the-multilateral-freefall.html> accessed 30 April 2022. At the same time, it is difficult to find scholars/experts who would dismiss the idea of the crisis entirely.

33 Angelica Bonfanti (ed.), *Business and Human Rights in Europe: International Law Challenges* (Routledge 2019); Alyssa Ayres, 'The new city multilateralism', Council on Foreign Relations (27 June 2018) <https://www.cfr.org/expert-brief/new-city-multilateralism> accessed 30 April 2022.

initiative; the successful conclusion of the Comprehensive and Progressive Agreement for Trans-Pacific Partnership (without the US); the possible multilateralization of the international investment dispute settlement process, and the establishment of multi-party interim appeal arbitration arrangements in the WTO; or the creation of the Rockefeller Foundation's 100 Resilient Cities network or the Global Parliament of Mayors. Emerging economies, especially China, are not only increasingly taking the lead in these initiatives but they also create and promote parallel multilateral institutions/arrangements over which they can exercise greater control (e.g. the Shanghai Cooperation Organisation, or the BRIC bloc). All these developments confirm that every crisis – rather than being a simple step backwards (i.e. to unilateralism or bilateralism) – can also create opportunities for radical reforms of the existing governance structures.

***

The above discussion brings us to the content of this edited volume, which should be seen as our contribution to the debate surrounding the current crisis of multilateralism and the related transformation of the underlying international legal order. In particular, this volume analyses selected aspects of the crisis from the perspective of public international law, both at the general level as well as within its specialized areas. To this end we have formulated two sets of broad research questions and asked the contributing authors to address some or all of them in their chapters. The questions relate to the nature, dynamics, and implications of the crisis, as follows:

1 *Nature of the crisis*: What is the nature of the current crisis of the multilateralism and what are the reasons behind it? Is it predominantly a result of various political changes currently taking place at the national level, a reflection of some deeper international geopolitical reconfiguration, or a result of the dysfunctionalities that exist within the multilateral system?
2 *Dynamics and implications of the crisis*: How is the crisis manifested in the specific areas of public international law and what is its dynamic? If no crisis is visible in a particular area, how can this fact be explained? What are the implications of the crisis for the selected specialized fields of international law or the global order as a whole?

The above two sets of questions also determined the structure of the entire volume, as the book has been divided into two parts, each of them focused on one set of research problems. Part I, entitled 'Conceptualizing the crisis', is composed of four chapters and offers some more theoretical and general insights into the reasons behind the crisis of multilateralism and the legal order behind it as well as the nature of the crisis as such. Part II of the book, entitled 'Dynamics and implications of the crisis', builds on the previous discussion and explores whether and how the crisis has manifested itself in selected specialized areas of public international law, and what its implications are for a respective legal regime. Of course, there are overlaps between these two parts. On the one hand, some general chapters do look at specific areas of international law in order to substantiate their claims. On the other hand, the authors contributing to Part II also attempt to address more general questions and in their analyses use the relevant findings made in Part I. In particular, they discuss the role of trust in building a multilateral order; the tension between sovereignty and multilateralism; normative and structural biases embedded in multilateral arrangements; shifts in geopolitics (i.e. power reconfigurations between the US, the EU, China, and Russia); and the existing dysfunctionalities of the current arrangements.

It is worth noting that when selecting the contributing authors, we aimed at maintaining a healthy balance between senior scholars and younger researchers. Consequently, the group of authors includes leading academics in the field, mid-career researchers, as well as those who are at the beginning of their academic adventure. Such an allocation of available space was a conscious decision, as it creates a multi-generational dialogue between the scholars. It is also important to highlight that while the scope of this edited book is comprehensive, it does not pretend to exhaust all relevant issues (which in any case would be an impossible task for a single monograph tackling such a complex problem). The final content of the book is therefore a compromise between the specific aims that we set out, the need to ensure sufficient coherence of the volume, and the research interests of the individual authors invited as contributors.

Last but not least, considering the existing wide variety of understandings of the term 'multilateralism', rather than imposing on the contributing authors one uniform definition, we decided to ask them to include a short explanation of how they understand this term for the purpose of their chapters. This decision has allowed us to preserve a sufficient flexibility, providing at the same time signposts for readers to facilitate them in navigating throughout the book.

Part I starts with Chapter 2 by Oleksandr Vodiannikov ('The Crisis of Trust in Contemporary Multilateralism: International Order in Times of Perplexity'), which looks at the crisis through the lens of the ideological systemic underpinnings of the international order and the historical and societal dynamics that have forged it (and which are now challenging it). In this context, the chapter explores the sources of that challenge, the role of trust in the multilateral order, and the concept of 'crisis' as such, including its three key indicators, i.e. money, decision-making, and compliance.

In Chapter 3 ('Believing Is Seeing: Normative Consensus and the Crisis of Institutional Multilateralism'), Sean Butler, drawing on the work of Paul Diehl and Charlotte Ku and their distinction between normative and operating systems of international law, highlights that the crisis is inherent in the current system and in its relation to sovereignty. He argues that the retreats are driven both by the operational logic of the institutional multilateral system and by an evolution in how the principle of State sovereignty is interpreted. In this context, he also notes that because of the power of the US normative hegemony in the post-Cold War era, the first of these drivers has been comparatively ignored. As pro-sovereignty actors gain greater power at the international level, the lack of understanding of the restraints imposed by the institutional multilateral system will lead either to a necessary adaptation on their part, an enduring frustration with the system that will hamper its efficacy, or an attempt to re-order the international system that will lead inevitably to dysfunction.

In her provocative Chapter 4 ('Revisiting the "Crisis" of International Law'), Maria Varaki explores to what extent different actors in international law can operate in a cathartic way with respect to normative and structural biases, and thus preserve the 'innocence' of international law while balancing between faith and critique. In this endeavour, she uses the Aristotelian concept of virtue – 'phronesis' or practical wisdom – to shed more light on the importance of human agency for the future of international law, using examples from the areas of international criminal justice and forced displacement/migration.

The final contribution in Part I is by Mary E Footer (Chapter 5: 'The Multilateral International Order: Reports of Its Death Are Greatly Exaggerated'). The author skilfully summarizes how the rise of emerging economies, in particular, China,[34] coupled with the ascent of authoritarianism, the growth of algorithmic governance, and the failure of the State-based international community to cooperate effectively on climate change and governance of the oceans are undermining the current multilateral international order. Yet she claims that alternatives to the existing system, such as 'multi-stakeholderism', are more mature now and can be used to address the existing challenges. According to Footer, a more pragmatic and action-oriented form of multilateralism, if properly arranged, can help to reinvent and reinvigorate the concept and practice of multilateralism.

Part II opens with Chapter 6, Christopher Lentz's cross-cutting empirical chapter ('State Withdrawals of Jurisdiction from an International Adjudicative Body'), which addresses one of the most serious expressions of the crisis of multilateralism. In this context, the author examines the extent of such withdrawals and the reasons motivating State denunciations, by examining inter-State disputes, international human rights law, international investment law, and international criminal law. His comparative analysis reveals that there are three primary reasons why a State chooses to follow this course of action and that, to date, the withdrawal of one or more States has been counteracted by the subsequent commitment of other States. He also submits that the likelihood and impact of a State's withdrawal could be reduced if

34 For an overview on the role of China in global governance, see Paolo D Farah, 'Trade and progress: The case of China' (2016) 30 CJAL 51.

international agreements conferring jurisdiction also provide for an appropriate time period between a State's notification and the withdrawal of jurisdiction from the adjudicative body in question.

Malgosia Fitzmaurice, in her Chapter 7 ('Multilateralism, Community of Interests and Environmental Law'), expertly addresses the historical evolution of the concept of communitarian interests and its relationship to multilateralism. The main quest for her is how to bridge and find effective ways and tools to raise the standard of protection of the environment in the clash between individual rights and social responsibilities. In this context, Fitzmaurice scrutinizes the issue of *locus standi* with respect to the protection of communitarian interests relating to protection of the environment, at both the international and national levels. She concludes that, at a practical level, international and national jurisprudence related to cases involving the protection of the communitarian interest has not flourished as much as was expected. In her view, a more promising way of protecting such communitarian environmental interests would be based on a human rights approach. In particular, the synergy with human rights norms gives the ill-defined environmental principles more substance and fleshes them out in terms of their content.

The issue of trust is also central for Vassilis Pergantis, who in Chapter 8 ('The Advent and Fall of Trust as a Cornerstone of Judicial Cooperation in Multilateral Regimes in Europe: A Cautionary Tale') seeks to understand whether and how the complex web of interconnected bodies and institutions in Europe rely on this concept for their legitimacy and effectiveness. Judicial cooperation serves as a testing ground for his analysis. He notes that trust as a cornerstone of multilateral cooperation in Europe is facing serious challenges, particularly in the area of human rights/rule of law. Pergantis argues that, given these circumstances, the European Court of Human Rights must rethink the way it employs trust if it wants to fully defend the Convention standards against authoritarian tendencies, as trust can become an impediment to the Court's proper functioning as a defender of multilateral collective guarantees. In contrast, the way the Court of Justice of the European Union (CJEU) uses trust is more multi-layered. On the one hand, mutual trust hinders national authorities' attempts to better defend the rule of law against defiant States by prioritizing the survival of multilateral cooperation. On the other hand, trust – as a cornerstone of the preliminary ruling mechanism and an expression of the principle of loyal cooperation – might be crucial to extending the legal bite of the European Union values set out in Article 2 of the Treaty of European Union, which might in turn allow the CJEU to hold backsliding States accountable for measures which undermine the rule of law and, consequently, the process of integration.

Agnieszka Nimark, in Chapter 9 ('The Nuclear Non-Proliferation Regime at 50: A Midlife Crisis and Its Consequences'), analyses the crisis of multilateralism in the sphere of nuclear non-proliferation. She looks at the potential consequences of the failure of this regime as well as possible ways it can regain its credibility. The old safeguards negotiated between the US and Russia under the Treaty on the Non-Proliferation of Nuclear Weapons are lapsing, and nations are starting to advocate for a change. Non-nuclear States are taking a more proactive approach to the control of nuclear weapons; an approach that has not been accepted by the major nuclear powers like the United States. For Nimark, the new approach of non-proliferation is interesting because it shifts the focus from national security to human security in order to move away from the mindset of the Cold War and offer an emerging role in this area for civil society organizations.

Chapter 10 by Patrycja Grzebyk and Karolina Wierczyńska ('The Crisis of Multilateralism Through the Prism of the Experience of the International Criminal Court') confronts the concept of multilateralism with the international criminal justice system, in which the International Criminal Court (ICC) plays a pivotal role. The authors focus their critical analysis on elements of the definition of multilateralism and how it is mirrored in the structure and practice of the ICC, specifically how it is institutionalized and whether the rules and obligations are held in common and equal for all States and are equally applied. Taking such a perspective makes it possible to show that the ICC – as a product of multilateral cooperation – plays a twofold role in international relations. On the one hand, it is an international organization enabling discussion via the Assembly of States Parties on international criminal justice, which thus strengthens multilateral cooperation and supports the idea of fighting against impunity. On the other hand, as a result of its specific role as a criminal court struggling against impunity for international crimes, the ICC usually acts as a supplicant requesting a State's cooperation and broader national engagement, thus reflecting the weaknesses of multilateral collaboration.

Ernst-Ulrich Petersmann, in his Chapter 11 ('Global Governance Crises and Rule of Law: Lessons from Europe's Multilevel Constitutionalism'), presents a compelling account of the problem that is faced by anyone trying to coordinate international actions to advance the goals of the international community. He notes that the rule of law – while an essential building block of multilevel governance in very different fields, such as health, trade, investments and environmental protection – is under fire worldwide, in some cases by the very promoters of the concept. Petersmann highlights the importance of supporting the multilevel judicial protection of the rule of law within trade and investment institutions in order to meaningfully address global challenges.

Jessica C Lawrence, in her provocative Chapter 12 ('We Have Never Been "Multilateral": Consensus Discourse in International Trade Law'), questions the widely held assumptions about the multilateral nature of the WTO regime. She argues that to refer to the present moment as a 'crisis of multilateralism' does more than simply describe the collective political and economic forces that are buffeting the organization. It is also a discourse that actively works to shape our understanding of the world, depicting the WTO as the institutional embodiment of an imagined past in which there was a broad consensus on how to manage the international economy for the good of all (i.e. a past in which 'multilateralism' existed); in contrast to a present in which fragmentation reigns, rogue actors flout collective norms in pursuit of their own self-interests, and the WTO is ineffective in reining in their behaviour. She highlights the political effects of such a discourse and challenges the implied narrative. In this context, Lawrence argues that the 'crisis of multilateralism' narrative evokes a universalist rhetoric that obscures the strong disagreement that has always existed regarding the substantive content of international economic norms, and throws a cloak of legitimacy over rules designed to further particular and contestable interests.

As demonstrated by Ewa Żelazna in Chapter 13 ('The EU's Reform of the Investor-State Dispute Resolution System: A Bilateral Way Towards Multilateral Solution?'), bilateralism does not in all cases imply working against multilateralism. The EU-sponsored reform of the investor-State dispute resolution system is seen by her a particular bilateral way towards multilateralism. In this context, Żelazna critically evaluates the EU's recent strategy of influencing a multilateral reform in international investment law through bilateral treaties, and examines the extent to which such an approach can be conducive to a gradual constitutionalization of international economic law.

Margherita Melillo, in her very timely Chapter 14 ('Challenges to Multilateralism at the World Health Organization'), concentrates on the challenges inherent in global health multilateralism. She argues that the crisis of legitimacy currently experienced by the WHO was not so much related to the magnitude of the challenge that the organization had to face during the COVID-19 pandemic, but was rather a consequence of the structural problems pre-existing within the WHO, that is: the lack of necessary resources; its contradictory mandate; and limitations arising from its over-emphasis on technical and medical expertise. The author concludes on an optimistic note by observing that, despite all the recent failures of the organization, States have not lost faith in global health multilateralism and are interested in learning and understanding how cooperation can be improved to prevent, or at least better manage, a future pandemic.

The text that concludes Part II is Chapter 15 by Szymon Zaręba ('The Council of Europe and Russia: Emerging from a Crisis or Heading Towards a New One?'). It discusses the importance of legitimacy for multilateralism and the functioning of international institutions, based on a case study of the crisis which ensued over the participation by the Russian delegation in the works of the Parliamentary Assembly of the Council of Europe, and its aftermath. The author argues, using the conceptual framework of the late Thomas Franck, that while solving one crisis (i.e. a political and financial one), the Council of Europe has plunged into a crisis about its own legitimacy and the legitimacy of its system of enforcement. In this context, he notes that the problem is particularly acute if the interests of a major power versus less powerful States are involved and in opposition. The result may be a feeling of injustice on the part of the smaller nations and an increased scepticism towards multilateralism as a way of addressing the challenges they are facing. This may in turn lead to various adverse consequences, such as reduced compliance with the rules set by a given organization or recourse to methods other than multilateral ones for resolving disputes. To prevent such crises, multilateral institutions must ensure equal treatment of both the powerful and those less so.

The volume ends with the Conclusion, in which we try to summarize the main findings of the contributing authors and make some general remarks on the factors that stand behind the crisis, their dynamics, and potential implications.

Post-scriptum

The manuscript of this book was handed to the publisher in September 2021. At that time the COVID-19 pandemic, together with its economic and geopolitical implications, was the main issue preoccupying scholars, politicians, and the general public. Obviously, it was also an important point of reference for many of our contributing authors as well as for us as editors. The Russian aggression against Ukraine has changed that picture. While the pandemic is far from over – as new variants emerge regularly and the winter season in the northern hemisphere most probably will be difficult – the world attention has switched to the problem of international security. The discussion seems to be dominated now by the idea of a new Cold War between the West and the East; remodelling of the international legal order by the emerging powers (such as China) and old hegemons (such as Russia); or the resilience of democracies in key countries to withstand the existing global authoritarian tendencies (with all their consequences for the international liberal order).[35]

The war between Russia and Ukraine, as well as the developments that have accompanied it, are very relevant to this book. For example, the launch of the war crimes investigation by the International Criminal Court (and the Russian reaction to this decision) are clearly pertinent to the analysis in Chapter 10, which specifically deals with the crisis of multilateralism through the prism of the ICC's experience. Similarly, the analysis in Chapter 9 on the current nuclear non-proliferation regime, or in Chapter 15 on Russia and the Council of Europe, will all definitely require an update once the dust created by the war finally settles.

35 Note that epidemics and international security have a long and close history, going back at least to the Plague of Athens in the fifth century BCE. See, for example, Giuseppe Paparella, 'What political psychology tells us about the likelihood of war post-pandemic', paper presented at King's College London (24 July 2020) <https://bit.ly/3L1oWBT>; Stephen M Walt, 'Will a global depression trigger another world war?' *Foreign Policy* (13 May 2020) <https://bit.ly/37GIfCQ>; Colin H Kahl and Ariana Berengaut, 'Aftershocks: the coronavirus pandemic and the new world disorder' *War on the Rocks*, 10 April 2020 <https://bit.ly/3yEvmUG> all accessed 20 May 2022.

Having said the above, it also seems to us that all the chapters remain highly relevant to the current situation, identifying and analysing issues that are perhaps more visible now (for example, the discussion in Chapter 2 on the role of trust in contemporary multilateralism or on the global normative consensus in Chapter 3). This is also true for those chapters that have been most impacted by the recent developments. Let us give two examples here. While Chapter 6 does not discuss the expulsion of Russia from the Council of Europe (which came before Russia's formal decision to withdraw from the organization), the main argument of Lentz still holds insofar as this has not provoked other States to leave the jurisdiction of the ECtHR. In a similar vein, Zaręba's Chapter 15) can be seen as an early warning of the potential consequences that may result from unprincipled approaches taken by multilateral institutions towards persistent violators of international rules.

The current situation will clearly influence the evolution of multilateralism: the processes taking place will be accelerated and reinforced by new dynamics. Although it will be worthwhile making another diagnosis in a few years' time, we believe the considerations in this volume remain useful as a guide for navigating this volatile period.

Part I

Conceptualizing the crisis

2 The Crisis of Trust in Contemporary Multilateralism

International Order in Times of Perplexity

Oleksandr Vodiannikov

1 Introduction

Something is going wrong with the multilateral international order. This sentiment underpins the growing debate as many scholars try to conceptualize various recent developments in the context of the crisis/no crisis divide. The point that seems to be shared by most is that multilateralism is at least contested.

When I started writing this chapter, two critical developments occurred – the COVID-19 pandemic, with States resorting to drastic lockdowns and social distancing measures, and the Black Lives Matter (BLM) movement. The pandemic has turned our world upside down, causing tragic loss of life and disrupting our social and economic order, while in the future this experience will affect our perception of normality and destabilize our cognitive mapping of the social order. The tectonic forces unleashed by the pandemic have reinvigorated and brought to the fore various anti-elitist protest movements across the globe, with BLM being the most vivid example, and their genuine appeals against discrimination, injustice, and inequality have the potential to crash the existing legal (including international) order. At least a part of the political and social elites have eagerly embraced the genuinely anti-elitist BLM agenda.[1] As a consequence, the BLM is becoming mainstream in politics, both internal and international. Some intellectuals toy with the BLM appeal; some accept it as a demand for policy change; others warn about its militancy, moral attitudes, and the political commitments that tend to weaken norms of open debate and toleration of differences in favour of ideological conformity.[2] But what is apparent is that the BLM movement is much more than a social protest against racial profiling and police violence, and at the same time much more than an anti-colonial or anti-discrimination movement. It entails a radical rupture with the past and a bulk rejection of normativity and the prevailing social order.

1 See Jose A Del Real, Robert Samuels, and Tim Craig, 'How the Black Lives Matter Movement Went Mainstream' *The Washington Post* (9 June 2020) <https://wapo.st/3wuInfA> accessed 30 April 2022.
2 'A Letter on Justice and Open Debate' *Harper's Magazine* (7 July 2020) <https://harpers.org/a-letter-on-justice-and-open-debate/> accessed 30 April 2022.

DOI: 10.4324/9781003312857-3

The COVID-19 pandemic and the BLM movement are both within the logic of the crisis of the post-modern State, and their consequences are still ripening, giving rise to a two-prong question: Why and how will the normalcy and normativity flux and the growing consensus in the media, upper-crust society, and political circles reshape the organization of international affairs?

International organization[3] and its institutions and regimes have historically revolved around a club model.[4] The club model of multilateralism generates efficiency, but societies usually face done deals. This club model reinforces the elitist nature of the international civil service and international diplomacy. International organizations (IOs) remain elitist in terms of both quality and their ways of operation. Club model IOs find it challenging to manage network problems.[5] Also, in globalization, the distinction between domestic and foreign becomes blurred, giving birth to transnational clusters and a growing pluralization in rulemaking. Therefore, multisectoral networks bypass established IOs.[6] Today these networks have become the vehicle to advance new normalcy perceptions and the anti-elitist agenda of the BLM and its progenies.

This moment of rupture that we are witnessing now in Western societies offers a new insight, free of status quo bias and the competency trap. In historical terms, it greatly resembles the Scientific Revolution, which itself developed amidst a 'General Crisis' of the seventeenth century[7] and gradually but steadily generated modern society and the modern State.

3 In this chapter, the term 'international organization' in the singular is used to denote the process in which relations among players in the international environment are arranged. That process is governed by 'international order' – the body of rules, norms, and institutions. See G John Ikenberry, *After Victory: Institutions, Strategic Restraint, and the Rebuilding of Order After Major Wars* (Princeton UP 2001) 23.

4 Robert O Keohane and Joseph S Nye Jr, 'Between Centralization and Fragmentation: The Club Model of Multilateral Cooperation and Problems of Democratic Legitimacy' (2001) KSG Faculty Research Working Papers Series RWP01–004 <https://bit.ly/3bPH2b5> accessed 30 April 2022.

5 For more on the hierarchies and networks conundrum, see Niall Ferguson, *The Square and the Tower: Networks, Hierarchies and the Struggle for Global Power* (Penguin Books 2017).

6 Networks in this chapter refer to one of the axes of human interactions as per Niall Ferguson's reflections:

> Networks are the spontaneously self-organizing, horizontal structures we form, beginning with knowledge and the various 'memes' and representations we use to communicate it. These include the patterns of migration and miscegenation that have distributed our species and its DNA across the world's surface; the markets through which we exchange goods and services; the clubs we form, as well as the myriad cults, movements, and crazes we periodically produce with minimal premeditation and leadership.

See Niall Ferguson, 'Networks and Hierarchies' (*The American Interest*, 9 June 2014) <https://bit.ly/3hORqDY> accessed 30 April 2022.

7 See Niels Steensgaard, 'The Seventeenth-Century Crisis and the Unity of Eurasian History' (1990) 24(4) Mod Asian Stud 683; JB Shank, 'Crisis: A Useful Category of Post-Social Scientific Historical Analysis?' (2008) 113(4) AHR 1090.

A retrospective look at the recent histories of discourses, be they political, scientific, or media, shows that the critical target of COVID-19's social or anthropologic effects – and even more so of BLM attacks – is the grand narrative of post-modern society and its rigid 'cosmology'. But the COVID-19 and the BLM phenomena were not the first: it is technological progress and its by-product – the post-truth condition – that eroded previously indisputable social axioms, principles, and values. The COVID-19 response, the BLM movement, and the post-truth condition constitute a critical continuum that has emerged out of several long-cycle trends and now controls how we make sense of the world around us. The pandemic and the BLM unclothe many uneasy and delicate issues that have been hidden under the general scientific and political consensus that has served as a bedrock of the international order. They have made apparent the fragility of multilateralism and globalization and re-conceptualized the striving for social justice and post-colonialism.

In this chapter, I focus on the current state of multilateralism and the broader analytical perspective of how international organization and order are changing. To what extent does the current turn in societies affect the international organization? How strong is the resilience of multilateralism, and why has critical discourse become a mainstream in IOs' communications? The forms and channels of transformations, habitually categorized in the scholarship as *the* crisis of multilateralism, are difficult to anticipate with certainty. Still, I attempt to look at and conceptualize those drivers that are shaping them now, including power constellations and societal contexts.

This chapter consists of three parts. Section 2 outlines the analytical framework of the inquiry, particularly the conceptualization of multilateralism, the role of trust, and communicative actions as its essential elements. Section 3 examines the theoretical concept of crisis, including its indicators, which are summarized in three key groups (money, decision-making, and compliance). It further conceptualizes the concept of 'crisis' in a more analytical sense. Section 4 applies the analytical framework to understand the crisis through the lens of the ideological system underpinning the international world order, particularly the 'cosmological consensus'. It looks at the historical and societal dynamics that forged the consensus and now challenge it. In this context, it proposes to look at COVID-19 and the BLM agenda as fitting into these dynamics.

2 What is multilateralism?

The first element of the analytical framework comprises the theoretical ramifications of multilateralism. When speaking of a 'crisis of multilateralism', do we mean features/characteristics of the current world order, multilateral institutions, or the institution of multilateralism itself?

There is a general consensus in the scholarship on several features of multilateralism as a social phenomenon in international relations. According to Ruggie, multilateralism refers to coordinating relations among three or more

States in accordance with certain principles.[8] Keohane defines it as 'the practice of coordinating national policies in groups of three or more States, through *ad hoc* arrangements or by means of institutions'.[9] Kahler posits that multilateralism is international governance of the 'many', as opposed to the bilateral and discriminatory arrangements that were believed to enhance the leverage of the powerful over the weak and to increase international conflict.[10] Caporaso observes that the term suggests more a belief or ideology than a straightforward state of affairs.[11]

Thus, first of all, multilateralism relates, in theory, to States and other subjects of international law. Second, multilateralism presupposes many actors, not necessarily 'all', but in any event more than two. Third, it also presupposes co-operation or coordinated actions. Fourth, it entails a belief or assumption that such concerted efforts are the optimal way to achieve international public goods, to ensure their unrestricted growth,[12] and to identify and incorporate core values. Some authors distinguish between multilateral institutions and the institution of multilateralism.[13] The former refers to designated IOs, while the latter operates via less formal, less codified habits, practices, ideas, and norms of international society.[14]

This scientific consensus, such as it is, poses several analytical difficulties. First, the term 'multilateralism' is not easily distinguishable in numerical terms. Though it does not presuppose any particular number of actors (States or IOs), it neatly fits into the continuum within the range of unilateral, bilateral, trilateral, multilateral, and universal. Second, the term falls short of encompassing all actors, whereas along with States and IOs other transnational networks and entities operate on the same footing with them in multilateral arrangements. International theorists have coined a separate term to cover such non-standard arrangements – multistakeholderism[15] – a term

8 John G Ruggie, 'Multilateralism: The Anatomy of an Institution' (1992) 46(3) Int Organ 561, 568.
9 Robert O Keohane, 'Multilateralism: An Agenda for Research' (1990) 45(4) Int J 731, 731.
10 Miles Kahler, 'Multilateralism with Small and Large Numbers' (1992) 46(3) Int Organ 681.
11 James Caporaso, 'International Relations Theory and Multilateralism: The Search for Foundations' (1992) 46(3) Int Organ 599, 601. Similarly, Ruggie argues that the definition of multilateralism should not miss the qualitative dimension of the phenomenon that makes it distinct (Ruggie (n 8) 566).
12 This belief in multilateralism as a powerful vehicle to generate economic growth effectively links it to (neo)liberalism as an ideological underpinning. See Luke Amadi, 'Globalization and the Changing Liberal International Order: A Review of the Literature' (2020) 2 Research in Globalization 1; G John Ikenberry, 'The End of Liberal International Order?' (2018) 94(1) Int Aff 7.
13 Caporaso (n 11) 602.
14 Ibid.
15 See Mark Raymond and Laura Denardis, 'Multistakeholderism: Anatomy of an Inchoate Global Institution' (2015) 7(3) Int Theory 572, 574. See also Chapter 5 in this volume.

which has become current with the advent of the UN Sustainable Development Goals. Third, multilateralism is perceived as having a clear ideological underpinning.

To remedy this analytical difficulty, the prevailing notion of multilateralism should be re-conceptualized. Indeed, multilateralism is not a thing in itself – it is a characteristic of the modern international organization. We need to look at it via the lenses of the systems theory.[16] Second, we need to revisit the prevailing analytical framework in contemporary scholarship that treats nation-states as compartmentalized units of analysis or elemental actors.[17] The difficulty posed by such an assumption has generated a number of new terms, such as 'global governance', 'international governance',[18] and 'transnational networks' to capture the complexity and interdependence between various actors on various levels (local, domestic, transnational, international). A systemic analysis requires that these units be disaggregated in order to pierce the corporate veil of a modern State and IO, and to look instead at vehicles and channels of power that influence and often shape the communicative actions within the system.[19]

While this argument conveys a sense of the complexity of global authority, it should not be taken to stretch the international system analysis beyond the realm where communicative actions occur. What is meant is a conceptual framework to account for the myriad of ways in which such actions are generated, frames articulated, ideas exchanged, and discourses directed. This makes it possible to study and analyse the external factors (environment) that

16 This 'systems' terminology is employed across virtually all scientific disciplines. See Wendell French, 'Processes Vis-A-Vis Systems: Toward a Model of the Enterprise and Administration' (1963) 6(1) Acad Manag J 46, 49. According to von Bertalanffy, the originator of the general systems theory, a system may be defined as 'a set of elements standing in interrelation among themselves and with the environment' (Ludwig von Bertalanffy, *General System Theory* (George Braziller 1969)). Skyttner defines a system as 'any structure that exhibits order, pattern and purpose', and maintains some constancy over time (Lars Skyttner, *General Systems Theory Problems, Perspectives, Practice* (World Scientific 2005) 57).

17 David A Lake, 'The State and International Relations' in Christian Reus-Smit and Duncan Snidal (eds), *Oxford Handbook of International Relations* (OUP 2008) 62, 83 *et seq.*

18 See Tanja Brühl and Volker Rittberger, 'From International to Global Governance: Actors, Collective Decision-Making and the United Nations in the World of the Twenty-First Century' in Volker Rittberger (ed.), *Global Governance and the United Nations System* (UNUP 2001) 1, 47 *et seq.*

19 As early as Robert Putnam's influential work, there appeared a number of studies to overcome this State-centered bias. However, while Putnam's framework (the 'two-level game' where Level II captures domestic political dynamics, while Level I represents the international area where governments act to satisfy domestic pressures) neatly fits into the 'club model' of international organization, it appears less reflective of the new reality of international networks, information flows, and the proliferation of new unconventional actors in world politics. See Robert D Putnam, 'Diplomacy and Domestic Politics: The Logic of Two-Level Games' (1988) 42(3) Int Organ 427.

help maintain and perpetuate the system, as well as the root causes, consequences, and drivers of change. And this crucial issue is often overlooked. What is the environment of the international system? The right answer could fuel further investigation into the forces that shape the current state of international organization, as well as unveil both constructive and destructive forces.

Multilateralism, as a systemic quality of international organization, operates both via symbols (rules, norms, principles, i.e. elements of international order) and communicative actions.[20] What is specific to multilateralism as compared with other systemic qualities (e.g. bilateralism, unilateralism/sovereigntism, universalism, reciprocity, etc.) is that: (1) multilateralism is not neutral towards social values and ideologies and operates in the form of institutionalized actions and communications; and (2) multilateralism is premised on trust.

Thus, multilateralism's essential elements are (1) communications, and as such, it fulfils the fundamental condition of autopoiesis,[21] namely, recursive self-(re)production; and (2) trust that increments in the history of such interactions and enables such (re-)production.[22] As such, it shapes, mediates, and constrains the goals, opportunities, and actions of actors co-operating within international organization. To understand how multilateralism constructs and constrains such co-operation should be viewed within a historical process, i.e. its timing, sequencing, outcomes (both intended and unintended), shocks, and disruptions. This facilitates or limits the actions of engaged actors, as it interacts with other factors of the environment, such as societal interests, culture, ideology, new ideas, and discourses.

2.1 Trust and international order

International organization is a heterarchical system, premised on the idea of co-operation, and co-operation demands trust.[23] There are many

20 This characterization of multilateralism accommodates its three primary forms: (1) formally institutionalized (IOs and institutions); (2) informally institutionalized (international regimes); and (3) non-institutionalized (ad hoc arrangements). These three forms can also be conceptualized as three stages of institutionalized multilateralism dysfunction.

21 *Autopoiesis* means 'self-renewing', i.e. the capacity of a system that allows it to be autonomous. See Skyttner (n 16) 60.

22 In Niklas Luhmann's terms, multilateralism could be perceived as a system with temporalized complexity. Its elements – communicative interactions – are unstable and endure only for a certain, often very short, time. They are, therefore, nothing more than one-time events that produce networks (i.e. a constellation of elements that is actual at any given moment). But such networks, although composed of unstable events, reproduce these elements in the autopoietic process of their disintegration and reproduction (i.e. the system's operation), thus constituting emergent orders of temporalized complexity. See Niklas Luhmann, *Social Systems* (John Bednarz, Jr, Dirk Baecker tr, Stanford UP 1995) 47–49.

23 As Niklas Luhmann observes, cooperation is possible when the level of trust toward the other exceeds a minimum trust threshold for each party (Niklas

definitions of trust which have been proposed in various fields of academic research[24] and borrowed or transplanted into the theory of international law and international relations, such as:[25] a rational process; a psychological mechanism; or a constructivist concept.[26] Classical social theory assumes that trust is a key ingredient of social capital and is required for societies to function properly, as it produces co-operation.[27] Recent academic research advances new critical elements in trust studies: shifting the focus from trust to trustworthiness;[28] rejecting the postulate that trust is the only source of co-operation in society; recognizing that trust is no more than one of many potential elements of cooperative behaviour;[29] and exploring the social role of scepticism and distrust[30] as a better option in strategic settings.

These recent developments in scientific research can be explained by the simple reason that trust escapes the calculus of rationality, as it is something more than confidence and predictability.[31] Haukkala and Saari claim that 'trust begins where knowledge ends' and that uncertainty – a leap of faith – is

Luhmann, *Trust and Power* (Howard Davis, John Raffan, Kathryn Rooney tr, John Wiley and Sons 1979) 73).

24 See Onora O'Neill, *A Question of Trust: The BBC Reith Lectures 2002* (CUP 2002); Russell Hardin, *Trust* (Polity 2006); Olli Lagerspetz, *Trust: The Tacit Demand* (Springer 1998); Diego Gambetta (ed.), *Trust: Making and Breaking Cooperative Relations* (Basil Blackwell 1988).

25 For a structured overview of trust research in international relations, see Jan Ruzicka and Vincent C Keating, 'Going Global: Trust Research and International Relations' (2015) 5(1) J Trust Res 8.

26 See Hiski Haukkala, Carina van de Wetering, and Johanna Vuorelmaat, 'Introduction: Approaching Trust and Mistrust in International Relations' in Hiski Haukkala, Carina van de Wetering, and Johanna Vuorelma (eds), *Trust in International Relations: Rationalist, Constructivist, and Psychological Approaches* (Routledge 2018) 1.

27 Robert D Putnam, 'Tuning in, Tuning out: Strange Disappearance of Social Capital in America' (1995) 28(4) PS: Political Sci Politics 664, 665; Francis Fukuyama, *Trust: The Social Virtues and the Creation of Prosperity* (New York Free Press 1995) 26.

28 Matthew R Cleary and Susan C Stokes, *Democracy and the Culture of Skepticism: Political Trust in Argentina and Mexico* (Russell Sage Foundation 2006) 11; Russell Hardin, *Trust and Trustworthiness* (Russell Sage Foundation 2002).

29 See Karen Cook, Russell Hardin, and Margaret Levi, *Cooperation Without Trust?* (Russell Sage Foundation 2005) 1.

30 Karen Cook and others, *Trust and Governance* (Russell Sage Foundation 1998); Cleary and Stokes (n 28).

31 It would be wrong to equate confidence and trust. Confidence predominantly relates to rational calculus and means foreseeability and predictability. As Haukkala and Saari observe, 'Confidence-building tools – such as increasing transparency and assurance mechanism – are, in reality, instruments to manage mistrust and to prevent conflict' (Hiski Haukkala and Sinikukka Saari, 'The Cycle of Mistrust in EU–Russia Relations' in Hiski Haukkala, Carina van de Wetering, and Johanna Vuorelma (eds), *Trust in International Relations: Rationalist, Constructivist, and Psychological Approaches* (Routledge 2019) 110, 112).

the essence of trusting relationships.[32] This conjunction of ignorance and faith makes trust an elusive concept. But this elusiveness brings the analytical framework closer to reality.

These new insights offer another perspective on trust: its primary role is at the interpersonal level. In order to produce a micro-level social order, trust can play a role in the regime of informal social exchange, where it decreases the need for regulation by State and other institutions.[33] But with the advent of atomized individuals, with the scrapping of small communities and further urbanization and social mobility, the actual role of trusting relationships has declined, and the importance of State regulation has increased.[34] Trust, therefore, is generally possible in stable social networks with history (ies), and the disintegration of such networks causes a decline in trusting relationships and increases the demand for more formal regulations and more legal rules.

Viewed from this perspective, with the increased complexity of international organization, the role of trust in making it function productively and effectively decreases. So trust plays a role in the relatively small communities of international actors, where it reduces the transaction and monitoring costs. But the number of community members is not enough to produce 'a leap of faith' and forge trusting relationships. The key here is the community: a network of actors sharing a history, identity, interests, traditions, sentiments, and values. The larger the community gets, the more attenuated these common denominators become, and so less room remains for trust. The formation of a community indeed requires social capital in Putnam's and Fukuyama's sense (social connections and the attendant norms and trust).

So international communities as stable networks can be formed around a normative consensus forged under the club model of multilateralism, where a diplomatic corpus, government officials, and leaders of various nations are in constant and intimate interaction. In communities that have evolved along these lines, even if a member 'defects' in a certain cause, it does not break the trusting relationships.

Despite the eloquent rhetoric in diplomatic fora about *the* international community, there are no real indicators that such a community exists and is even feasible in the nearest future. In many respects, the crisis sentiments and dismay over the crisis of trust stem from the apparent failure to stretch the community of Western societies into 'the international community'. So when we speak of the crisis of trust in multilateralism, we are effectively exploring the natural limits of multilateralism in its current form.

32 Ibid 113. See also Ken Booth and Nicholas Wheeler, *The Security Dilemma: Fear, Cooperation and Trust in World Politics* (Red Globe Press 2007) 230.

33 Cook, Hardin, and Levi (n 29) 1.

34 Ibid.

2.2 Communicative actions and frames of crisis

Words trigger actions. This idea is even more relevant with respect to international relations, as international order operates via symbols (rules, norms, principles) and communicative actions. Here, words are the predominant form of action. Hence in order to deconstruct the driving forces behind multilateralism, its evolution and demise, and to identify those fundamental sources that affect international co-operation and interaction, we need to look at these symbols and communicative actions in their broader societal context. We need to go beyond the abstract notions of institutions, organizations, and States. As multilateralism operates via communicative interactions that constitute self-(re)producing networks, we need to look at the cognitive structures that govern the perception and interpretation of reality, at Goffman's frames[35] that are generated within communicative processes and unconsciously adopted.[36]

So the focus should be on the crisis discourses that dominate the media and narrow communicative interactions within international fora, which both reflect crisis frames as well as contribute to their creation and perpetuation. Diplomatic discourse here plays an important role. On the one hand, it adds its frames into general media discourses, invents its own semantic units, and draws on popular cultures. So diplomatic narratives are part of the general process of producing frames of crisis. On the other hand, they import and borrow frames from other discourses (public media, social media, popular cultures). The issues in diplomatic narratives are framed by various actors (institutions, States, political and social leaders, ideologies, etc.), who struggle over the definition and construction of the social reality of international relations. There is currently no clear boundary between diplomatic discourses and public discourses in our media-saturated internationalized societies.

Such a frame analysis[37] is apt not only for sociology, but also for conceptualizing multilateralism's communicative actions. So I will use the term 'frames of crisis' to refer to the beliefs that certain actors spread with the aim of legitimizing and justifying unilateralism (as an antithesis to multilateralism) to protest against multilateral institutions and to coat over their bias against multilateral actions. Deconstructing these frames is especially

35 See Erving Goffman, *Frame Analysis: An Essay on the Organization of Experience* (Northeastern UP 1974) 10.

36 Gitlin has summarized frame elements: 'Frames are principles of selection, emphasis and presentation composed of little tacit theories about what exists, what happens, and what matters' (Todd Gitlin, *The Whole World Is Watching: Mass Media in the Making and Unmaking of the New Left* (University of California Press 1980) 6).

37 There is a wide range of approaches under the heading of frame analysis. See Robert A Benford and David A Snow, 'Framing Processes and Social Movements: An Overview and Assessment' (2000) 26 Annu Rev Sociol 11.

important, as they include basic questions that mobilize people – diagnosis of a situation as unfair[38] and construction of an aggrieved identity.[39]

Framing theorists Gamson and Modigliani define a frame as 'a central organizing idea … for making sense of relevant events, suggesting what is at issue'.[40] They distinguish between framing devices that suggest how to think about the issue at hand and reasoning devices that justify what should be done about it.[41] According to Maher, 'framing implies relationships among elements in a message, because those elements have been organized by a communicator (rather than by a communication researcher)'.[42]

Frames theory elegantly explains both the post-truth phenomena and the self-fulfilling crisis discourse in international relations. Communication/communicative actions in the multilateral setting of international organization entail the self-reproducing exchange of frames that define, construct, and adjust social reality. These exchanges, however, do not go through closed channels; they operate as an inclusive system, open to the intrusion of other frames generated in public discourse and lending and inserting these frames into such discourses.

This is precisely illustrated in the case of frames of crisis. They were coined in international scholarship long ago.[43] Critical discourses in the public media have also been prevalent before. These frames migrated into diplomatic discourses, became embedded into cognitive settings to interpret social reality, and now permeate political discourses in world politics: 'We live in an era of doubts and questions about the global order. We have seen an erosion of trust in bedrock institutions – at the national, regional, and global levels'.[44] A similar frame manifests itself in the UN Secretary-General's remarks:

38 See Kelly Bergstrand, 'The Mobilizing Power of Grievances: Applying Loss Aversion and Omission Bias to Social Movements' (2014) 19(2) Mobilization 123, 142.

39 See Bernd Simon and Bert Klandermans, 'Politicized Collective Identity: A Social Psychological Analysis' (2001) 56(4) Am Psychol 319.

40 William A Gamson and Andre Modigliani, 'Media Discourse and Public Opinion on Nuclear Power: A Constructionist Approach' (1989) 95(1) Am J Sociol 1, 3.

41 The five framing devices are: (1) metaphors; (2) exemplars (ie historical examples from which lessons are drawn); (3) catchphrases; (4) depictions; and (5) visual images (eg icons). The three reasoning devices are (1) roots (i.e. a causal analysis); (2) consequences (i.e. a particular type of effect); and (3) appeals to principle (i.e. a set of moral claims) (ibid 3–4).

42 T Michael Maher, 'Framing: An Emerging Paradigm or a Phase of Agenda Setting' in Stephen D Reese and others (eds), *Framing Public Life: Perspectives on Media and Our Understanding of the Social World* (Routledge 2001) 83, 86.

43 See Caporaso (n 11) 600; Inis Claude Jr, 'The Balance of Power Revisited' (1989) 15(2) Rev Int Stud 77, 86; Thorold Masefield, 'Co-prosperity and Co-security: Managing the Developed World' (1988) 65(1) Int Aff 1.

44 David Lipton, 'Trust, and the Future of Multilateralism. Introductory Remarks for the Eurofi High Level Seminar' (IMF, 30 April 2018) <https://bit.ly/3ve4kiL> accessed 30 April 2022.

> If one looks at today's governance problems at the country level, between countries or at multilateral governance in the world, we face a terrible lack of trust. Lack of trust between peoples, between Governments and political establishment. Lack of trust between countries and lack of trust in relation to governance in global multilateral institutions.[45]

The OSCE Secretary-General also observed that: 'We see increasing polarization between States but also within our societies. Predictability in international affairs is decreasing. There is little trust left between key players.'[46] Thus, the frames of crisis acquire additional legitimation and validation via the authority of the speakers.

I offer these citations (out of many) to illustrate the internal dialogism and dialogic orientation in this critical discourse: the uttering authorities are forthright in their orientation towards 'already said', 'already known', 'common opinion'. even while couching the statements as their own.[47] This is important to bear in mind, as these frames of crisis contribute to the identity elements constructed and re-constructed by the utterers within the discourse practice. As 'identity elements are not constructed by a single social actor but are always constructed by a participant in unison with other social actors and the environment',[48] we need to differentiate between frames of crisis as an identity claim, advanced in dialogic response to the social environment, and *the* crisis as a *process* within the international organization.

3 Crisis and its dynamics

In 2016, Eilstrup-Sangiovanni observed that: '[I]f the second half of the 20th century was the age of integration – of nations coming together and pooling sovereignty in pursuit of common goals – the 21st century looks increasingly as an age of drifting apart.'[49] Multilateralism, previously conceptualized as a 'weapon of the weak',[50] is under assault by many of those States that should be benefiting from multilateral arrangements.

45 António Guterres, 'Opening Remarks at the World Government Summit' (United Nations, 13 February 2017) <https://bit.ly/3oTFa6J> accessed 30 April 2022.

46 Thomas Greminger, 'Keynote address' by OSCE Secretary-General Thomas Greminger at the Basel Peace Forum 2019 (OSCE, 13 January 2019) <https://www.osce.org/secretary-general/409371> accessed 30 April 2022.

47 This brings us to Mikhail Bakhtin's critical theory of dialogic imagination. See Mikhail Bakhtin, 'Discourse in the Novel' in Michael Holmquist (ed), *The Dialogic Imagination: Four Essays* (University of Texas Press 1981) 269, 275, 300.

48 Sigrid Norris, 'Some Thoughts on Personal Identity Construction: A Multimodal Perspective' in Vijay Bhatia, John Flowerdew, and Rodney Jones (eds), *Advances in Discourse Studies* (Routledge 2007) 132, 134.

49 Mette Eilstrup-Sangiovanni, 'The Global Crisis of Multilateralism' (E-International Relations, 3 December 2016) <https://www.e-ir.info/2016/12/03/the-global-crisis-of-multilateralism/> accessed 30 April 2022.

50 Robert Kagan, 'Power and Weakness' (Policy Review, 1 June 2002) <https://www.hoover.org/research/power-and-weakness> accessed 30 April 2022.

Several telling indicators of the current crisis of multilateralism have become apparent over the last decade. They can be summarized in three key groups: (1) money (budget and financial resources at the disposal of IOs/multilateral arrangements); (2) decision-making (the ability to reach agreement/consensus); and (3) compliance with international law. They deserve to be looked at more closely.

Financial and other resources are critical to any IO. Complaints about the mismatches between IOs' mandates set by member States and the available resources are not new.[51] This goes hand in hand with the repeated funding crises that reoccur in some IOs.[52] What is new about the last decade is the phenomenon of a zero nominal growth budget – a target successfully bargained for by the member States of many IOs.

The member States' austerity policy towards IOs served to incentivize alternative modes of IO funding and IOs' growing appetite for resource diversification. This leads to imbalances, as in the case of the WHO, where the zero nominal growth approach resulted in voluntary contributions by member States and large private donors, accounting for 79 per cent of its budget[53] and giving rise to allegations that external donors, not member-States, dictate the priorities and action agendas of IOs.[54] This became acute in the US withdrawal from the WHO, as one of the critical claims advanced by President Trump's administration was 'the World Health Organization's alarming lack of independence'.[55]

The decision-making indicator embraces the lifespan of negotiations. The time needed to reach substantive agreements in IOs and multilateral

51 Quincy Wright, 'The Mode of Financing Unions of States as a Measure of Their Degree of Integration' (1957) 11(1) Int Organ 30; Klaus Goetz and Ronny Patz, 'Resourcing International Organizations: Resource Diversification, Organizational Differentiation, and Administrative Governance' (2017) 8(5) Glob Policy 5.

52 For the African Union, see Ulf Engel, *The African Union Finances: How Does It Work?* (Leipziger University Verlag 2015). For UNESCO, see Klaus Hufner, 'The Financial Crisis of UNESCO after 2011: Political Reactions and Organizational Consequences' (2017) 8(5) Glob Policy 96. For the UN, see Simon Duke, 'The UN Finance Crisis: A History and Analysis' (1992) 11(2) Int Rel 127. On the current liquidity crisis of the UN, see 'United Nations in Severe Financial Crisis, Secretary-General Tells Fifth Committee Meeting on 2020 Budget, Stressing Our Work and Our Reforms Are at Risk' (UN Press Release, 8 October 2019) <https://www.un.org/press/en/2019/sgsm19797.doc.htm> accessed 30 April 2022.

53 Lawrence O Gostin, 'The Future of the World Health Organization: Lessons Learned from Ebola' (2015) 93(3) Milbank Q 475, 478. See also Chapter 14 in this volume.

54 See Karolin Seitz and Jens Martens, 'Philantrolateralism: Private Funding and Corporate Influence in the United Nations' (2017) 8(5) Global Policy 46, 48 ('Private funding runs the risk of turning UN agencies, funds and programmes into contractors for bilateral or public-private projects, eroding the multilateral character of the system and undermining democratic global governance').

55 'Letter from the US President Trump to the Director-general of the WHO' (*Twitter*, 18 May 2020) <https://twitter.com/realDonaldTrump/status/1262577580718395393> accessed 1 January 2021 (now inaccessible).

arrangements steadily increases.[56] The recent history of multilateral negotiations abound with examples: negotiations on the Law of the Sea (1973–1982); the Uruguay Round of trade negotiations (1986–1994); the most recent Doha Round of trade negotiations (since 2001), and climate change negotiations, to mention just a few.

The final indicator (i.e. compliance with international law) encompasses the real motivation of States in choosing to comply with international norms, and the general perception of power, interests, and obligations. In other words, the focus here is on the legitimacy of multilateral institutions, multilateral co-operation, and their normative order. It reflects the tilting balance between rational/irrational choices to comply or not. The issue of compliance reframes the question of the legitimacy of multilateral institutions and the international normative order. It effectively calls into question the moral force of international law, i.e. to the extent that international law is legitimate, there is a moral duty to obey.[57]

In the scholarship, there is a consensus that compliance with international law is high.[58] However, recent developments raise questions about this belief. The first dynamic worthy of mention concerns the blows that came from several constitutional courts with their unequivocal refusals to give domestic effect to international obligations.[59] Another crucial development relates to

56 For more on an analytical framework of prolonged international negotiations, see Christian Downie, 'Toward an Understanding of State Behavior in Prolonged International Negotiations' (2012) 17 Int Negot 295.

57 Mattias Kumm, 'The Legitimacy of International Law: A Constitutionalist Framework of Analysis' (2004) 15(5) EJIL 907, 908.

58 See Jacob Katz Cogan, 'Noncompliance, and the International Rule of Law' (2006) 31(1) Yale J Int L 189, 190.

59 The Italian Constitutional Court in its seminal Decision no 238/2014 declared that the rule of international customary law on jurisdictional immunities of States never entered the Italian legal order, since it runs counter to the fundamental rights enshrined in the Constitution. The Court implicitly attacked the ICJ ruling in the *Jurisdictional Immunities* case on substantive grounds and blocked its enforcement. See Cesare Pinelli, 'Decision no. 238/2014 of the Constitutional Court: Between Undue Fictions and Respect for Constitutional Principles' (2014) 1 Quest Int L 33; Paolo Palchetti, 'Judgment 238/2014 of the Italian Constitutional Court: In Search of a Way Out' (2014) 1 Quest Int L 44. In 2015 the Russian Constitutional Court rejected the long-standing principle of the supremacy of international law and affirmed the priority of the national constitutional order. See Lauri Mälksoo, 'Russia's Constitutional Court Defies the European Court of Human Rights: Constitutional Court of the Russian Federation Judgment of 14 July 2015, No 21-П/2015' (2016) 12(2) EuConst 377. Later the same Court, under its new competence to declare 'impossible to implement' judgments of a human rights body, refused execution of the ECtHR judgments in the *Anchugov and Gladkov* case. See 107th Plenary Session Venice Commission, Final Opinion on the Amendments to the Federal Constitutional Law on the Constitutional Court CDL-AD(2016)016 (European Commission for Democracy Through Law, 11 June 2016) <https://bit.ly/349RaXX> and the *Yucos* case, Constitutional Court of Russian Federation, Decision of 19 January 2017 (in Russian) <https://bit.ly/3vJg8ZC> both accessed 30 April 2022.

the increasing resistance of national judiciaries to enforce judgments of international human rights courts and adjudicative bodies,[60] and the general reluctance of State-parties to implement such judgments.[61] We can also point to the recent paralysis of the WTO Appellate Body due to the blocked appointments of new members as falling within this category.[62] The third dynamic, even more highlighted in the media, pertains to withdrawals from multilateral arrangements and treaties.[63]

These compliance issues indicate a troubling shift in the perception of the legitimacy and moral force of multilateral institutions and the multilateral normative order. Investigating the causes and transformation trajectories under this indicator can be of particular help to understand the construction of legitimacy in the international normative order and identify the future power constellations in the international organization as an inclusive field of power with multiple competing authorities.

The above-discussed indicators focus on policy choices between multilateral, bilateral, and unilateral actions and reflect power relations in international organization. In the recent scholarship, many of these phenomena are characterized mainly as manifestations of *the* crisis.[64] But the question remains: should we conceptualize these developments as manifestation of *the* crisis, or are there other 'non-critical' explanations behind them? Are multilateralism and its institutions losing legitimacy and normative justification? And if *the* crisis is real, what will be its consequences and how will they reshape the international organization?

Thus it is pertinent to look at the concept of 'crisis'. The term 'crisis' in European languages originates from Greek 'κρίσις', where it generally designated

60 For more on Russian case, see (n 59). In 2008, the Venezuelan Supreme Court accused the Inter-American Court on Human Rights (IACtHR) of a 'clear usurpation of functions' and pleaded to the executive to denounce the American Convention on Human Rights. See Alexandra Huneeus and René Urueña, 'Treaty Exit and Latin America's Constitutional Courts' (2017) 111 AJIL 456, 457. In February 2017, the Argentinian Supreme Court refused to execute the judgment of the IACHR because of the latter's alleged overstepping of its competence. Raffaela Kunz, 'Judging International Judgments Anew? The Human Rights Courts before Domestic Courts' (2019) 30(4) EJIL 1129, 1130–1131. The Italian Constitutional Court in 2015 also made a drastic turn in its jurisprudence by establishing certain criteria to scrutinize the jurisprudence of the ECtHR and decide whether it is 'well established case-law' (ibid 1131).

61 For more on the execution of ECtHR judgments, see George Stafford, 'The Implementation of Judgments of the European Court of Human Rights: Worse Than You Think – Part 1: Grade Inflation' (*EJIL: Talk!*, 7 October 2019) <https://bit.ly/3vemnVX>, and 'Part 2: The Hole in the Roof' (*EJIL: Talk!*, 8 October 2019) <https://bit.ly/3fcsch3> both accessed 30 April 2022.

62 For more details, see Chapters 5, 11 and 12 in this volume.

63 For more details, see Chapter 6 in this volume.

64 See Concha Roldán, 'The Thinning and Deformation of Ethical and Political Concepts in the Era of Globalization' in Concha Roldán, Daniel Brauer, and Johannes Rohbeck (eds), *Philosophy of Globalization* (De Gruyter 2018) 109, 122.

'separating', 'distinguishing'; as a noun, it referred to a 'decision',' judgment', 'choice', or 'election'; in legal discourse, it meant 'judgment of a court', 'result of a trial, condemnation'; and in medicine, 'turning point of a disease, sudden change for better or worse'.[65] Today the term is rather a buzzword. Koselleck, in his study of the term, blames the media for inflating its meaning:[66]

> The concept of 'crisis', which once had the power to pose unavoidable, harsh and non-negotiable alternatives, has been transformed to fit the uncertainties of whatever might be favored at a given moment. Such a tendency towards imprecision and vagueness, however, may itself be viewed as the symptom of a historical crisis that cannot as yet be fully gauged.[67]

The indiscriminate use of the term does not allow for differentiating those phenomena that are crisis-driven from those that are not. Let's take, for example, Brexit – a sensational event in contemporary history. Was it driven by the crisis of trust, or should it be understood as a new form of sovereigntism? In the same way, what is the difference between the scepticism vis-à-vis some international institutions that can be spotted throughout modern history (frames of crisis as described above) and *the* crisis that is capable of undermining the very foundations of world order?

After the 2008 Global Financial Crisis, scholarly literature addressing 'crisis' has abounded. But the majority of crisis-related books and papers proceed on the basic assumption of *a* crisis. As Giblert ironically observes: 'It is through constructing a narrative account of the causes and symptoms of a crisis that scholars generate evidence which points towards solutions, remedies, or lessons.'[68]

Defining a crisis is not as simple as it appears. Despite the abundant use of this term in the scholarship the concept remains elusive and controversial, as scholarly literature often fails to define its meaning. Any concept serves as a point of reference for communicating meaning and interpretation of reality.[69] Hence when speaking of *the* crisis, we need to look at this concept within its 'conceptual paradigm'[70] or 'symbolic generalization',[71] i.e. within

65 'Κρίσις' in Henry G Liddell and others, *A Greek-English Lexicon* (OUP 1940) 997.

66 Reinhart Koselleck and Michaela W Richter, 'Crisis' (2006) 67(2) J Hist Ideas 357.

67 Ibid 399.

68 Andrew S Gilbert, *The Crisis Paradigm: Description and Prescription in Social and Political Theory* (Palgrave Macmillan 2019) 3.

69 See Thomas S Kuhn, *The Structure of Scientific Revolutions* (2nd edn, University of Chicago Press 1970) 94.

70 Gilbert (n 68) 7.

71 Niklas Luhmann, *Social Systems* (Stanford UP 1995) 94.

the range of assumptions and generalities within which the concept is deployed. In this sense, frames of crisis activate specific units of knowledge or ideas in the memory of recipients, who discriminate between moments of crisis and moments of normality.[72]

The conceptual paradigm of 'crisis' entails some pre-existing state of affairs that is assumed to be 'normal', and which is destroyed, discontinued, or torn apart in the moment of crisis. *The* crisis is a divide between perceived normalcy and non-conforming reality. In this sense, the moment of crisis destabilizes and relativizes our knowledge and perception of reality, as it denotes a rupture and discontinuity. This is the moment when our cognitive mapping becomes blurred. This discrepancy or mismatch generates frames of crisis as we attempt to rationalize, conceptualize, articulate, and narrate ruptures in the social order and the historical continuum. Not by chance, the crisis awakens historical criticism and the revision of all dogmatic positions.

4 Understanding the crisis: international order and its cosmology

The international normative order and its components (international law, morals, diplomatic practices, IOs, communications, and scholarship) are grounded on certain generally accepted and shared schemata, vocabulary, and belief systems. This 'cosmology' imposes a specific world-view and the interpretative tools to assess and process social reality. This 'cosmological consensus' rests on the 'great rock of western belief'[73] or, in Berlin's words, on a 'central tradition in Western thought'[74] since Antiquity, which operates via three undisputable underlying assumptions:

1 Every genuine question has one true answer and one only: all others being false. Unless this is so, the question cannot be a real question – there is a confusion in it somewhere.
2 The method which leads to correct solutions to all genuine problems is rational in character; and is, in essence, if not in detailed application, identical in all fields.
3 These solutions, whether or not they are discovered, are true universally, eternally, and immutably: true for all times, places, and men, as in the old definition of natural law, they are *quod semper, quod ubique, quod omnibus.*[75]

72 Robert Holton, 'The Idea of Crisis in Modern Society' (1987) 38(4) Br J Sociol 502, 503.
73 John O Cole, 'Thoughts from the Land of And' (1987) 39 Mercer Law Rev 907, 911.
74 Isaiah Berlin, 'The Divorce between the Sciences, and the Humanities', in Isaiah Berlin, *Against the Current: Essays in the History of Ideas* (The Viking Press 1980) 80, 81.
75 Ibid.

In a practical sense, this cosmological consensus means belief in the possibility of steady progress in human development; in the existence of universal and unamendable core values; confidence in the liberal conception and one-size-fits-all methods to achieve unrestricted growth and to substantiate the core values. Gradually this consensus has brought about a kind of liberal fundamentalism that dogmatizes these beliefs. It postulates that opposing them means opposing progress and may not be explained except by ignorance, prejudice, superstition, and other forms of unreason. This claim of universality empowers the existence of universally-applicable international law as a single integrated set of clear principles and rules which, if correctly applied, make possible unrestricted development and unending progress of the international community.[76] The irony of this universal truth/world-view is that it does not tolerate pluralism, as its ultimate setting is based on a rigid true/false dichotomy and on the assumption that the ultimate truth can be asserted.[77]

To grasp the essence of these phenomena for international law and multilateralism, we need to look at the cosmological consensus in its historical perspective. The idea of international law emerged as part of the Enlightenment project, with its intellectual rationale laid by the Scientific Revolution.[78] The Enlightenment offered new conceptions of political legitimacy, public order, and the legislative State. It marginalized and suppressed the multinormativity of the preceding era[79] and posited one normative order – law as the emanation and embodiment of the sovereign will. International law went through similar transformations – from a purely Christian system that comprised numerous normative orders – Morals, Ethics, Theology, Politics, Law, and Tradition – it was secularized and rationalized into a uninormative set of rules. It still retains extra-legal residues, like the moral reasoning incorporated in international humanitarian law, the *jus cogens* doctrine, and general principles of law, which are neatly built into the legal edifice of the international order and, hence, contest its consensual structure.[80]

The social revolutions of the eighteenth century brought about a society of confinement[81] and the bureaucratic nation-state. Its survival and effectiveness

76 See Homi Kharas and Dennis Snower, 'The Future of Multilateralism. Towards a Responsible Globalization that Empowers Citizens and Leave No One Behind' (2020) 5 Glob Solutions J 78, 80.

77 See Euan MacDonald, *International Law and Ethics after the Critical Challenge. Framing the Legal within the Post-Foundational* (Brill/Nijhoff 2011) 373.

78 Isaiah Berlin comments that, although opinions within this tradition or cosmological consensus differed, all thinkers shared the belief that there is only one true method or combination of methods to find answers. See Isaiah Berlin (n 74) 81.

79 See Thomas Duve, 'European Legal History – Concepts, Methods, Challenges' in Thomas Duve (ed), *Entanglements in Legal History: Conceptual Approaches* (Max Planck Institute for European Legal History 2014) 29, 51.

80 See Nico Kirsch, 'The Decay of Consent: International Law in an Age of Global Public Goods' (2014) 108(1) AJIL 1.

81 See Michel Foucault, *Discipline and Punish: The Birth of the Prison* (Duke UP 2007) 297.

required making society legible to 'arrange the population in ways that simplified the classic State functions of taxation, conscription, and prevention of rebellion'.[82] This legibility paradigm, born in the late Renaissance along with the Scientific Revolution and further matured in the Enlightenment era, was intended to improve the human condition.[83] This ideological edifice required rationalization, normalization, and the unification of the society, social practices, and social authority. Not by coincidence, great modern codifications and constitutions appeared at the same relatively short period of the late eighteenth/early nineteenth centuries.[84] This triumphant moment of Great Revolutions set in motion the suppression and marginalization of the multinormativity of preceding epochs, heralding an uncompromised rupture with the old illegible and 'unreasonable' society.

Transformations in international law followed similar patterns of uniformity: enlarging the society of nations should be legible, predictable, and manageable. The sovereign will of civilized nations should be the ultimate source of its normative order. International law thus became complicit in legitimizing imperialism;[85] it meant to bring non-European polities into the ambit of international law as the 'public law of Europe', i.e. to oust and marginalize indigenous social regulators, in the same way as mono-normativity was pursued earlier in European societies. Colonialism allowed for the imposition of a uniformized set of rules that governed relations between European States globally, as the European law of nations was perceived to be true universally, eternally, and immutably. Other nations needed to accept it to gain subjectivity. However, the Cartesian logic that structured the Western law as a system may have been entirely alien to non-Western societies and their legal cultures, which were premised on different values.[86]

82 James C Scott, *Seeing Like a State: How Certain Schemes to Improve the Human Condition Have Failed* (Yale UP 1998) 2.

83 See Norman Yoffee, *Myths of the Archaic State: Evolution of the Earliest Cities, States, and Civilizations* (CUP 2004) 92.

84 Specifically in this period new legal terminology superseded ancient and open-ended regula (rule, règle, regel, regola, regla). New 'norms' entered the legal discourse to constitute uniformity, to isolate, define, combine, and rearrange societal regulation from a series of distinct patterns into a rationalized and standardized system.

85 See Sundhya Pahuja, 'The Postcoloniality of International Law' (2005) 46(2) Harv Int L J 459, 469; Antony Anghie, 'Towards a Postcolonial International Law' in Prabhakar Singh and Benoît Mayer (eds), *Critical International Law: Postrealism, Postcolonialism and Transnationalism* (OUP 2014) 127.

86 Colonialism thus marked the epoch of the imposed juridicalization of non-western societies and the end of histories of local law. According to Jean-Louis Halpérin, 'Historically, there is no doubt that the scheme of the modem Western State has been extended, by imperialism, to the whole world, and this phenomenon is already a clue to a massive and successful legal transplant from Europe to the other continents' (Jean-Louis Halpérin, 'The Concept of Law: A Western Transplant?' (2009) 10(2) Theor Inq Law 333, 335).

In the first half of the twentieth century, the modern nation-state reached its apex with its totalitarian extremes. The reverse process produced the 'post-modern State', with its reformed cosmological consensus forged around constitutional values, democracy, and human rights, with constitutional courts and tribunals as guardians against majoritarian whims. The Second World War thus marked the collapse of the modern State and its posited societal order. However, the new post-modern concepts of political legitimacy and legal order have become re-conceptualized around the Enlightenment ideal of the legislative state, from which the concept of the rule of law has emerged as the new political theology.

Cold War international organization was characterized by two conflicting concepts: a liberal international order founded on universal liberal values of democracy, the rule of law and market economy, and a conservative international order based on coexistence, promoting policy coordination, and the ability of States to pursue their own national interests.[87] However, this evolution developed along the structures of a cosmological consensus: neither the Soviet bloc nor the democratic countries, nor third world leaders ever questioned the accepted world-view architecture – all of them operated within this Enlightenment tradition of belief in one truth that is immutable and universal. Of course, differences abounded with respect to the methods to find true solutions to all the genuine problems. The collapse of the Soviet system weakened the proponents of the second concept, but did not remove the tension between them in international politics.

The post-Cold War international organization has resulted in the proliferation and further specialization of IOs and international regimes dealing with narrow fields in international trade, climate change, weapons, cyberspace, etc. This process reinvigorated multilateralism and multiplied legalities, but fell short of producing *the* international community. The post-Cold War international order has never evolved into 'World Order 2.0'.[88]

The irony of the current critical condition is that this failure of multilateralism has been programmed in the intellectual development of Western societies. Personalism, which was thought of as a new foundation of an international order based on democracy and human rights, industrialization, and further economic growth, had another powerful collateral effect – fracturing traditional social networks and pushing for the 'atomization' of the individual.[89] Intellectuals, in response to the 'mass man', proposed to emancipate individuals from State-sponsored truth and generated the precursors of a new form of cognitive confinement – 'post-truth'. Lyotard defined post-modernism as incredulity towards metanarratives: 'This incredulity is undoubtedly a product of progress in

87 See Liselotte Odgaard, 'Between Integration and Coexistence: US-Chinese Strategies of International Order' (2013) 7(1) SSQ 15.

88 See Richard N Haass, 'World Order 2.0 – The Case for Sovereign Obligation' (2017) 96(1) For Aff 2.

89 See Dwight Macdonald, 'Masscult and Midcult' in Dwight Macdonald (ed.), *Essays Against the American Grain* (Da Capo Press 1962) 8.

the sciences: but that progress in turn presupposes it'.[90] So in reacting to State-sponsored 'truth', European intellectuals unintendedly attacked the cosmology of the post-modern world and its grand narrative.[91]

The advent of social media – democratic and revolutionary, empowering everyone irrespective of sex, race, social status, residence, age, origin, etc., with the right to speak, to take part in developing the virtual world map – further desacralizes the traditional institutions of power. The post-truth condition that upsets the cosmological consensus – in ever-enlarging narratives and discourses that produce and reproduce information – delegitimizes 'Western humanity' in its self-understanding.[92] What we are witnessing now is the terminal stage of the 'crisis of reason',[93] the critical erosion of the 'cosmological consensus' that underpins our modern world-view and international order. This is *the* crisis, as universal, eternal, and immutable truth is put into question. Its frames – within which meaning is generated – are challenged, causing the entire cosmology of international order, with its unitary and universal validity, to become fragile and crumbling.

It would be an oversimplification to treat the effects of COVID-19 as discrete phenomena or the result of policy choices.[94] It is not the evil mind of a policymaker or a group of politicians that should be blamed for these effects. These are systemic failures, long before anticipated as a gut feeling by many.[95] The pandemic has exposed many tectonic processes in international organization that have been ongoing.[96] It seems that multilateralism's perceived

90 Jean-François Lyotard, *The Postmodern Condition: A Report on Knowledge* (University of Minnesota Press 1984) xxiv.

91 From a historical perspective, this reaction to rationalism and the cosmological consensus tradition is within the range of social and emotional reactions to rational argument (see Berlin (n 74) 82).

92 See Norman K Swazo, *Crisis Theory and World Order. Heideggerian Reflections* (State University of New York Press 2002) 4.

93 Norman Swazo conceptualizes the crisis of reason as a crisis of political understanding due to the decentring of the dominant position of European nation-states (ibid 5).

94 Colleen Flood and others, 'Overview of COVID-19: Old and New Vulnerabilities' in Colleen Flood and others (eds), *Vulnerable: The Law, Policy and Ethics of COVID-19* (University of Ottawa Press 2020) 1, 10.

95 There is an abundance of crisis sentiments expressed in various fora and under various circumstances, including the most telling in this respect the World Economic Forum (WEF) 2020 Annual Meeting held a few weeks prior to the pandemic outbreak. In its 2019 edition of The Global Competitiveness Report series, the WEF made a telling prophecy: 'The world is at a social, environmental and economic tipping point. Subdued growth, rising inequalities and accelerating climate change provide the context for a backlash against capitalism, globalization, technology, and elites' ('Global Competitiveness Report 2019: How to End a Lost Decade of Productivity Growth' (*World Economic Forum*, 8 October 2019)) <https://bit.ly/3wtOqRu> accessed 30 April 2022.

96 Lukasz Gruszczynski, 'The COVID-19 Pandemic and International Trade: Temporary Turbulence or Paradigm Shift?' (2020) 11(2) EJRR 337, 341–342 (noting '[i]t seems that some fundamental reorganization of the global economy and

failure, coupled with the severe consequences of the pandemic for international trade and supply chains, economic growth, public debt, employment, and human well-being, threatens to resurrect the nation-state and reverse the process of globalization, or at least fracture it into multi-layered regionalization.[97] And the irony of the moment is that multilateralism is actually re-emerging as a weapon of the weak, as the challenge to the status quo of the global governance comes from developed economies.[98]

COVID-19 has exposed and created vulnerabilities that follow the fault lines of pre-existing structural inequities.[99] Along with the pandemic, we can witness the expansion of protest movements in many previously stable societies. The police killing of George Floyd has galvanized a wave of anti-racism protests in the US, Canada, the UK, and other countries. The rage and anger that have erupted under the motto of 'Black Lives Matter' transcend 'conventional' protest patterns. The BLM agenda has shifted public discourses. It integrates and incorporates into an augmented network a range of 'subaltern counter-publics' – public spaces for marginalized voices.[100] The BLM resists and rejects the dominant narratives in pursuit of affirmation of the identities of those aligned with it. What we are witnessing is a steady transformation of counter-discourses, previously perceived as too radical, into mainstream narratives and discourses.

Multilateralism's perceived failure during the COVID-19 pandemic contributes to acceleration of the emotionally colouring and changing perceptions of multilateral institutions' legitimacy. Anti-elitist sentiments will likely to be incorporated into the national agendas of many States and will affect the current mode of multilateral institutions. Club model multilateralism – previously animated and invigorated by globalization – has become vulnerable to globalization's backfire. So the years to come will be a period of putting in motion the insertion of marginalizing and exterminating forces into the overall

international order has been going on for some time. In this context, it is worth noting that some multilateral institutions have already been marginalized').

97 Stewart Patrick notes, with respect to multilateral health institutions, that '[t]o the extent that global health governance has failed, it has failed by design, reflecting the ambivalence of states torn between their desire for effective international institutions and their insistence on independent action'. Stewart Patrick, 'When the System Fails: COVID-19 and the Costs of Global Dysfunction' (2020) 99(4) For Aff 40. This diagnosis is by implication relevant to multilateralism generally.

98 See Peter Wittig, 'Hope for the Future of American Leadership Dies Hard. Germany Holds a Special Stake in the U.S. Election' (For Aff, 16 October 2020) <https://fam.ag/3fC9Gh3> accessed 30 April 2022 ('Nothing epitomized the rejection of multilateralism more clearly than Trump's withdrawal from the World Health Organization in the midst of a global pandemic. Instead of demonstrating leadership and using an imperfect WHO to coordinate international efforts, the United States just abandoned ship').

99 Cf. Flood and others (n 94) 13.

100 See Nancy Fraser, 'Rethinking the Public Sphere: A Contribution to the Critique of Actually Existing Democracy' (1990) 25/26 Social Text No. 25/26, 56, 67.

context of the struggle to reform multilateral institutions, or even dismantle some of them.

5 Conclusion

The post-Cold War era celebrated the proliferation of multilateral co-operation and globalization. But as Schechter foresaw in 1999, 'multilateralism is not inevitable. To the degree that it expands, it is likely to address the globe's key social problems only selectively. Moreover, the form that multilateralism takes is likely to be contested.'[101]

The birth of multilateralism was intrinsically related to the proliferation and augmentation of networks in world politics, which ranged from informal intergovernmental arrangements, cross-border advocacy, to transnational crime. The growing numbers of actors on the international plane and 'civil globalization' have driven the dynamics that are thought to enable collective action and co-operation and to evolve into a new mode of international governance. These international networks are heterarchical and represent a set of relationships that form structure.[102] However, these networks developed within the club model; they suffer from the same legitimacy deficit.

Multilateralism, as a systemic quality of international organization, has never been ideologically neutral. It evolved on the solid bedrock of a cosmological consensus that ideologically saturates it. The operation of multilateralism requires trusting relationships that emerge within a historical process and are dependent on timing, sequencing, outcomes (both intended and unintended), shocks, and disruptions. Trust in this sense lies at the conjunction of ignorance and faith that is possible in a community with a history(ies) built up of actors sharing 'practices' that incrementally build upon the experiences of interaction and become part of the 'historical body' of its members, identities, interests, traditions, sentiments, and values. The current crisis of trust in international organization can therefore be conceptualized as multilateralism confronting its own limits.

Multilateralism has, for a long time, been a hostage of the continual debate on the source of legitimate power in world politics. The neoliberal thought that has driven post-Cold War development assumed the existence of *the* international community (or at least its feasibility); as one that integrates all nation-states and is governed by shared rules, principles, and values. Multilateralism was thus conceived as a vehicle to generate common goods and achieve common goals under the post-Cold War development consensus. But the assembly of existing nation-states never evolved into *the* international community.

101 Michael G Schechter, 'International Institutions: Obstacles, Agents, or Conduits of Global Structural Change?' in Michael Schechter (ed), *Innovation in Multilateralism* (UNUP 1999) 1, 3.

102 See Emilie M Hafner-Burton, Miles Kahler, and Alexander H Montgomery, 'Network Analysis for International Relations' (2009) 63(3) Int Organ 559, 560.

A two-pronged question thus arises: Should the crisis of multilateralism we are dealing with here be conceptualized as a natural limit of multilateral interaction, or is this indeed *the* crisis as a *process* within the international organization? My answer to both questions is affirmative. In the international organization, we encounter growing mismatches between perceived normalcy, our conceptualization of multilateralism, and non-conforming reality. Our attempts to rationalize, conceptualize, articulate, and narrate the growing anomalies generate frames of crisis as a self-fulfilling prophecy. Assumed to be purely heterarchical, international organization has been evolving under constant political anxiety about the *locus* of power. Multilateralism is indeed in *the* crisis. And the nature of this crisis lies in the fear that the *locus* of power – the symbolically empty space – among the perceived community of nations may become really empty.

3 Believing Is Seeing

Normative Consensus and the Crisis of Institutional Multilateralism

Sean Butler

1 Introduction: the retreat of the liberal international order

The international system of institutional multilateralism, which had been in a phase of significant expansion since at least the end of the Cold War in 1991, has in recent times witnessed the waning of this expansive momentum and is now facing a period of comparative retreat. While in terms of absolute numbers as regards institutions and State members thereof, this is a relatively small setback for the system as a whole, the scale of this development has been amplified by the high-profile character of a number of the withdrawals, such as the exit of Burundi and the Philippines from the International Criminal Court (and the later rescinded attempts to withdraw by The Gambia and South Africa)[1] and the departure of the United Kingdom from the European Union (EU), as well as the sudden and unexpected nature of this reversal and the concurrence of these developments with wider changes in the global political landscape, such as the ascendancy to the Presidency of Donald Trump, the growth of populist nationalism and the re-emergence of authoritarianism as a significant global force after a period of dormancy.[2]

Indeed, the conjunction of this institutional retreat with wider developments in global politics, and in particular the belief that the tide is turning against the core universalist projects – human rights, democracy, and free trade – championed by the United States (US) and Western interests, and consolidated in the normative priorities of the United Nations (UN) and the Bretton Woods institutions, has been aggregated in the discourse into a claim that the 'liberal international order' is in decline. Under this conception, 'there is a long-term shift in the global system away from open trade, multilateralism and cooperative security [as] [g]lobal order is giving way to various mixtures of nationalism, protectionism, spheres of influence and regional Great Power projects'.[3] This claim characterises the institutional and

1 For a more detailed discussion, see Chapter 6 in this volume.
2 See also Chapters 2 and 5 in this volume.
3 G John Ikenberry, 'The End of the Liberal International Order?' (2018) 94(1) Int Aff 7; see also Edward Luce, *The Retreat of Western Liberalism* (Atlantic Monthly Press 2017).

DOI: 10.4324/9781003312857-4

normative developments as elements of a holistic trend, in which 'the tectonic plates that underpin [the liberal order] are shifting, and little can be done to repair and rescue it',[4] leaving liberal internationalism as 'essentially an artefact of the rapidly receding Anglo-American era'.[5]

This chapter seeks to examine this phenomenon, with a particular focus upon the relationship between the institutional and normative retreats. Using the distinction between the 'operating system' and the 'normative system' of international law, from the work of Paul Diehl and Charlotte Ku, to analyse the symbiotic relationship between the institutional and normative aspects of the aforementioned developments, it argues that the evolution undergone by the principle of State sovereignty in the era of institutional multilateralism must be understood as emerging from distinct (though not wholly unrelated) pressures exerted separately by the operating and normative systems. Furthermore, it contends that the full nature of this process was disguised by the normative hegemony enjoyed by the US (and more generally the West) in the post-Cold War era, presenting the increased conditionality of sovereignty as a function solely of the normative project of liberal internationalism. As Western power has declined in the aftermath of the 2008 financial crisis, this normative hegemony has been shattered, exposing the dissensus over sovereignty at the heart of international society between the actors who have adopted the conditional variant and those who continue to favour the classical Westphalian conception. Moreover, it has brought to the fore the fundamental incompatibility between Westphalian sovereignty and the operational logic of institutional multilateralism, generating resentment at the extent of the restraints imposed upon sovereignty by the current international system and ultimately resulting in a backlash against the system as a whole. In order for the structure of institutional multilateralism to endure and progress, it will be necessary to engage in a meaningful global discourse on the nature of contemporary sovereignty, in pursuit of a new normative consensus on the subject.

This chapter is divided into five sections. After these introductory remarks, Section 2 outlines Diehl and Ku's conception of the operating and normative system of international law, focusing in particular on the symbiotic nature of these two aspects of the international legal systems and how the process of change functions therein. Section 3 considers the operation of the State sovereignty under the structure of institutional multilateralism, examining the separate evolutionary processes at work under the operating and normative systems and the dissensus over sovereignty that is emerging as a result. Section 4 analyses the role of US hegemony in disguising the true nature of this evolutionary process, leading States to focus on 'neo-imperialism' as the primary driver of the changes undergone by sovereignty over the past 25 years.

4 John J Mearsheimer, 'Bound to Fail: The Rise and Fall of the Liberal International Order' (2019) 43(4) Int Sec 7.

5 Ikenberry (n 3) 7.

The final section considers the implications of this dissensus over sovereignty for the maintenance of world order, and briefly discusses the necessary steps forward to overcome this impasse.

2 The operating and normative systems of international law

The primary theoretical lens used in this chapter is the distinction between the operating and normative systems of international law, introduced by Paul Diehl and Charlotte Ku in their 2010 work *The Dynamics of International Law*,[6] established in order to explore what the authors refer to as the 'dual character of international law'.[7] In this taxonomy, the operating system 'provides the platform and structure to govern and to manage international relations' by organising 'the distribution of authority and responsibilities for governance within the system',[8] through the collective decisions of the constituent actors as regards the establishment of fundamental rules, on matters such as sources of law, jurisdiction, and the range of rights and responsibilities of actors, and the creation of formal structures, such as international institutions to coordinate action and courts to ensure compliance.[9] The operating system thus functions as the structural framework that facilitates the role of international law in organising collective decision-making and establishing minimum standards of behaviour.

Conversely, the role of the normative system is to imbue international law with substantive content. Diehl and Ku perceive this as the 'quasi-legislative' aspect of international law, in which 'participants in the international legal process engage in a political and legislative exercise that defines the substance and scope of the law',[10] thereby 'defin[ing] the acceptable standards for behaviour in the international system, [through] issue-specific prescriptions and proscriptions'.[11] Specific examples provided by the authors include the status of women within human rights, the treatment of prisoners of war, and the breadth of territorial waters.[12] The normative system is thus concerned with the goals of the collective decision-making process and the precise content of the minimum standards of behaviour, functioning within the parameters of permissibility established by the operating system. As the authors acknowledge, there is a loose analogy in this taxonomy with the conception of primary and secondary rules elucidated by Hart, though Diehl and Ku differ from Hart as regards the dynamics of engagement between the two aspects of the system and their particular roles in the legal system.[13]

6 Charlotte Ku and Paul F Diehl, *The Dynamics of International Law* (CUP 2010).
7 Ibid 28.
8 Ibid 28–29.
9 Ibid 28–46.
10 Ibid 43.
11 Ibid 44.
12 Ibid.
13 Ibid 44 and 49.

In examining the phenomenon under consideration in this chapter, we can thus see the institutional retreat as a process occurring primarily with regards to the operating system and the normative retreat as being concerned with the normative system. However, what is of particular interest here is the relationship between these two processes, derived from the relationship between the operating and normative systems. As Diehl and Ku argue, the two subsystems can be understood as collectively forming an 'interconnected evolutionary system', existing in a kind of symbiotic relationship where each impacts the other in a mutually reinforcing manner, though this relationship can be subject to misalignments and lags in time.[14] These misalignments occur because changes to each subsystem are not automatic, but instead require deliberate choices by the necessary agents (i.e. usually States) to make such alterations, though there is a pressure exerted over time in favour of re-alignment, as the actors in favour of the change endeavour to bring it about.[15]

What is most crucial to extract from the above analysis for the present discussion is the dynamics of interaction between the operating and normative systems as regards change: while each can spur change in the other through this mutually evolutionary process, this dynamic also means that each subsystem can act as a drag, hampering radical changes in the other system, e.g. if a proposed change to the normative system is too extreme to fit within the parameters of permissibility established by the structure imposed by the operating system. This dynamic feeds into the international system's natural tendency towards stasis and stability, on account of the difficulties associated with treaty negotiations, the inherent 'stickiness' and path dependencies of legal systems in general, and other institutional obstacles, such as bureaucratic inertia,[16] meaning that the international legal system tends to follow a pattern of 'punctuated equilibrium' as regards major change, where long periods of relative calm are interrupted by interstices of dramatic overhaul caused by exogenous shocks, such as wars.[17]

As I have argued elsewhere, this general dynamic is complicated by the particular nature of the contemporary international system, in which a structure of institutional multilateralism of hitherto unseen complexity has emerged, imposing significant restrictions on the type and scale of changes that it will be possible to make to both the operating and normative systems in the future.[18] Short of an unlikely event such as a major global conflict, rising States, such as China, India and Brazil, will need to temper their ambitions as regards any desired alterations to the subsystems because of the

14 Ibid 51–59.
15 Ibid.
16 Ibid 64–67.
17 Ibid 67–70. The creation of the UN in 1945 is a prominent example of this phenomenon.
18 Sean Butler, 'Gemeinschaft as the Lynchpin of Multilateralism: World Order and the Challenge of Multipolarity' (2018) 29 Ir Stud Int Aff 17.

realities imposed by the institutional multilateral structure.[19] This obstacle is manifesting itself in the present travails facing the global political system, as the restrictions imposed by the operating system are causing a significant misalignment with the evolutionary trajectory of the normative system desired by a number of major actors, resulting in the system entering a period of perceived crisis. As will be explored in Section 3, the key issue in this regard is the principle of State sovereignty, as two competing interpretations of this core norm clash for supremacy.

3 Sovereignty under institutional multilateralism

State sovereignty is perhaps the most important norm in the international legal system, creating a clear demarcation between the domestic and international domains of jurisdiction, and allocating rights and obligations therein. In its classical formulation, sovereignty is conceptualised in a 'Westphalian' form, in which the State has unchallenged primacy in the domestic domain and international law may only engage with matters internal to that domain to the extent that the State consents to it. The central principle of Westphalian sovereignty is thus the notion of State freedom of action, in which '[r]estrictions upon the independence of States cannot … be presumed'.[20] As best elucidated in the landmark *Wimbledon* case, States are understood to acquire obligations in international law through using their sovereign freedom to voluntarily bind themselves to agreements (or customary practices),[21] with the principles of *pacta sunt servanda* and *rebus sic stantibus*[22] establishing an asymmetric relationship between entry (i.e. the acquisition of the obligation) and exit (i.e. withdrawal from it).

While this understanding of sovereignty is adequate for conceptualising the international legal system in its classical 'anarchic' form,[23] in which agreements are primarily bilateral in nature and governance of the international space occurs in an *ad hoc* and decentralised manner, it is a woefully inadequate tool for understanding the operation of international law in the contemporary era of enduring and complex multilateral institutions. As Christian Tomuschat argued in his landmark 1993 *Recueil des Cours* course, the modern international legal system is rife with examples 'where legal commitments cannot easily be

19 Ibid.

20 *The Case of S.S. Lotus (France v Turkey)* 1927 PCIJ Ser A No 10, 44.

21 *S.S. Wimbledon (U.K. v Japan)* 1923 PCIJ Ser A No 1, 35.

22 Meaning 'things thus standing', this principle permits a State to withdraw from a treaty due to a 'fundamental change in circumstances'. It was codified in the Vienna Convention on the Law of Treaties (entry into force 27 January 1980) 1155 UNTS 331, in its Article 62 and was interpreted very narrowly by the International Court of Justice in *Fisheries (UK v Iceland)*, in which the change must 'imperil the existence or vital development of one of the parties'. See *Fisheries Jurisdiction (UK v Iceland)* (1973) ICJ Rep 3 [38].

23 Hedley Bull, *The Anarchical Society: A Study of Order in World Politics* (Columbia UP 1977).

explained as validated through the consent given by the States concerned',[24] with the UN the example par excellence in this regard.[25] While there is a sizable constituency in the international system who continue to cling to the myth of Westphalian sovereignty (as discussed further below), 'in reality [States have] renounce[d] the sovereign right to be governed only in accordance with [their] own will'.[26]

This feature of the institutional multilateral structure is not simply a consequence of choices made by States that can easily be reversed, but emerges from the operation of two distinct processes, one concerning the operating system of international law and the other concerning the normative system.

3.1 Operating system: pooled sovereignty and public order norms

As regards the operating system, it is a consequence of the operational logic of the institutional multilateral structure itself, which is inherently parasitic upon the principle of State sovereignty. This occurs through two features of the operating system: (1) the consequences of the pooling of sovereignty; and (2) the evolution of 'public order norms' under institutional multilateralism.

The pooling of sovereignty into enduring institutions, providing that this conveyance of function advances beyond mere agency relationships to what Dan Sarooshi categorises as 'delegations' or 'transfers' of sovereignty,[27] necessitates the ceding of competences to the international domain in order to ensure those institutions can function adequately, a process that over time generates a type of principal-agent problem.[28] The autonomous nature of the organisation can become the engine through which the terms of the agreement are slowly altered in an iterative process, with the State having very limited say over this process and only the extreme option of withdrawal available to it, or in some organisations (such as the UN) no such option at all. As Kratochwil argues, any arrangement based upon 'long-term iterated transactions' requires the use of principles or other higher-order abstractions to compensate for the inability to foresee every possible contingency.[29] As conditions evolve over time and the entity faces situations or decisions not foreseen or accounted for by its creators, the abstract nature of the guiding principles result in a vesting of power into those tasked with interpretation, as the initial agreement becomes 'more and more a framework for continuous

24 Christian Tomuschat, 'Obligations Arising for States Without or Against Their Will' 241 RCADI 195, 248.
25 Ibid 248–257.
26 Ibid 327.
27 Dan Sarooshi, *International Organizations and Their Exercise of Sovereign Powers* (OUP 2005) 29, 33.
28 Friedrich Kratochwil, 'The Limits of Contract' (1994) 5 EJIL 465, 471–472; Tom Ginsburg, 'Bounded Discretion in International Judicial Lawmaking' (2004) 45 Va J Int L 631, 644–647.
29 Kratochwil (n 28) 471.

negotiation rather than a historic document which freezes the "meeting of the wills" of the parties at a given time'.[30] Over time, the autonomous nature of the interpretative act enables the organisation to undertake decisions and actions that, while legitimated in a general sense by the State consent that facilitated its establishment, are increasingly divorced from the specific parameters the framed this consent in the initial agreement.

This loss of State freedom is exacerbated by the necessity for States to take positive actions to uphold a vastly expanded series of public order norms, such as *jus cogens* norms and *erga omnes* obligations, as a consequence of the maintenance of the institutional multilateral structure requiring a vastly expanded 'international public space' to ensure systemic stability. Public order norms are the skeleton upon which the operating system of international law functions: as Schwarzenberger argues, 'they can be eradicated from international law only at the price of destruction of international law itself',[31] and are designed to 'operate a public order protecting the legal system from incompatible laws, acts and transactions'.[32] These norms range from *pacta sunt servanda*, the sovereign State as the base unit, and the rules governing customary international law,[33] to *jus cogens* norms and *erga omnes* obligations.[34]

Unlike under the classical 'anarchic' structure of international law, in which any international order that emerges must do so in an *ad hoc* and bottom-up manner through agreements voluntarily entered into by States and consequently the system requires only a sparse governing architecture and a reasonably small set of structural norms, the system of institutional multilateralism necessitates a greatly increased role for public order norms. This is because the pooling of sovereignty by States into multilateral institutions results in the generation of a vastly expanded international public space as an emergent property. This phenomenon is a consequence of the institutions, and the structures that emerge as a functional necessity from their relationships with each other and with States, becoming a venue for the promotion and pursuit of collective interests and goals, goods which could not manifest in the classical anarchic structure due to their unrealisability. This public space, and the efforts undertaken towards its endurance, are often captured rhetorically by the notion of the 'international community', an entity understood to possess interests that cannot be adequately captured through a simple aggregation of the interests of individual States.[35]

30 Ibid 471, 472.

31 Georg Schwarzenberger, 'The Fundamental Principles of International Law' (1955) 87 RCADI 326.

32 Alexander Orakhelashvili, *Peremptory Norms in International Law* (OUP 2006) 10.

33 Ibid 45.

34 Ibid 44–48.

35 Bruno Simma, 'From Bilateralism to Community Interest in International Law – Bilateralism and Community Confronted' (1994) RCADI 217, 243–249. For a useful overview of the literature concerning the 'international community' as a

The maintenance of this expanded international public space requires a commensurate expansion in governing norms to accommodate the increase in structural complexity and the resulting challenges associated with maintaining systemic stability. In this regard, it is notable that concepts such as *jus cogens* norms and *erga omnes* obligations only emerged as accepted components of the governing architecture of the international legal system in the UN era. The perceived importance of *jus cogens* norms, in 'guarding interests fundamental to international society',[36] and *erga omnes* obligations, as duties owed to the international community taken as a collective whole,[37] lies in the promotion of a collective ethos through the protection of what is considered to be the shared core values of the community.[38] These concepts are thus central to the project of constructing this community in an ideational sense, under the assumption that without this minimum moral content, the system would be at risk of losing social cohesion.[39] As this extensive set of public order norms is necessary for systemic stability, the contemporary international order must thus allow a significantly reduced scope for alterations to the normative system of international law than in the classical model: in particular, amendments to the content of *jus cogens* norms and *erga omnes* obligations must be understood to be severely restricted, if not outright impermissible.

Through pooled sovereignty and the increased scope of public order norms, Westphalian sovereignty under institutional multilateralism is thus transformed by the operational logic of the system into a more conditional form, in which it becomes a system of norms concerned as much with obligations as with rights and in which State freedom of action is no longer paramount.

3.2 Normative system: conditional sovereignty

The process acting upon the normative system concerns the evolutionary pressure to which sovereignty has been subject in the institutional multilateral era, as the classical Westphalian conception has faced contestation from actors advocating for the recognition of a more conditional variant. Under

legal concept, see Gleider I Hernandez, 'A Reluctant Guardian: The International Court of Justice and the Concept of "International Community"' (2013) 83(1) BYIL 13, 19–27.

36 Gordon A Christenson, 'Jus Cogens: Guarding Interests Fundamental to International Society' (1987) 28 Va J Int L 585, 648.

37 *Erga omnes* obligations were first recognised in the *Barcelona Traction* case in 1970. See *Case Concerning Barcelona Traction, Light, and Power Company, Limited* (1970) ICJ Rep 3.

38 William E Conklin, 'The Peremptory Norms of the International Community' (2012) 23(3) EJIL 837, 855–861.

39 It is important to emphasise here the role of evolutionary pressure in the selection of governing norms in the international system, and the absence of conscious choice in this process. The argument here is that *jus cogens* norms and *erga omnes* obligations have persisted in the system because they perform a useful social role, namely the protection of systemic stability.

this conception, sovereignty and its constituent rights ought not to emerge as automatic entitlements accruing from the control of territory and recognition by other States as in the Westphalian model, but as privileges bestowed by the international community in response to the meeting of specific normative criteria, principally concerned with the conduct of the State towards the population within its territory.[40] The most fully elaborated form of this idea is found in the 'sovereignty as responsibility' concept, first advocated by Francis Deng in 1996,[41] which became the conceptual basis for the Responsibility to Protect (R2P) doctrine, a soft law norm endorsed by the UN in the mid-2000s which recognised the right of the international community to intervene in the internal matters of a State in situations of mass atrocity crimes, including a provision for military intervention authorised by the UN Security Council as a last resort.[42]

3.3 Relation between operating and normative system processes

While these two processes, the operational logic of institutional multilateralism and the emergence of the conditional variant of sovereignty, should be understood as two distinct mechanisms, it is important to note that they can act in a mutually reinforcing manner on account of the symbiosis between the two subsystems as identified by Diehl and Ku. During the era of hegemonic dominance by the US (discussed further below), this mutual reinforcement created a kind of virtuous cycle that deepened and legitimised the changes occurring to the international system: the increased interdependence of States, from the sovereignty pooling process, and the rising awareness of a shared normative vision of an 'international community', from the shared expectations regarding the upkeep of the public order norms,[43] provided the conditions in which universalist projects could be fostered and rigorously pursued, and this new universalist ethos in turn justified more expansive changes at the operational level, in a weaker version of the 'spillover'

40 See Louis Henkin, 'That "S" Word: Sovereignty, and Globalization, and Human Rights, et Cetera' (1999) 68 Fordham LR 1; Anne Peters, 'Humanity as the Alpha and Omega of Sovereignty' (2009) 20(3) EJIL 513.

41 Francis M Deng and others, *Sovereignty as Responsibility: Conflict Management in Africa* (Brookings Institution Press 2010). See also Gareth Evans, *The Responsibility to Protect: Ending Mass Atrocity Crimes Once and For All* (Brookings Institution Press 2008) 38 (who discusses the proposed transformation of sovereignty from being rooted in 'control' to being concerned with 'responsibility').

42 International Commission on Intervention and State Sovereignty (ICISS), 'The Responsibility to Protect: Report of the International Commission on Intervention and State Sovereignty' (2001); UN General Assembly (UNGA) Res 60/1 World Summit Outcome Document (24 October 2005) UN Doc A/RES/60/1 [138]-[139]; UN Security Council (UNSC) Res 1674 (2006) on protection of civilians in armed conflict (28 April 2006) UN Doc S/RES/1674.

43 Butler (n 18).

phenomenon that helped drive the integration of the EU.[44] However, this blending of the institutional and normative aspects of the changes undergone by the international system disguised the multifaceted nature of the process, with the normative project of universalism and conditional sovereignty becoming perceived as the sole driver of the evolution. As Section 4 will explore, the decline of US hegemony shattered the consensus that underpinned this normative project, resulting in a resurgence of the Westphalian model of sovereignty and severe tensions between it and the current structure of institutional multilateralism.

4 Hegemony and normative consensus

Hegemony, the situation in which one State has an overwhelming preponderance of power and influence in the international system or a subset thereof, is a well-studied phenomenon in international relations.[45] Hegemony can usually be sourced from a dominant position with regards to military or economic power, and allows the State in question to have a disproportionate influence in political and normative matters, in a configuration analogous to the metropole in an imperial system (indeed, historically most hegemons have used the resources of empire to construct the power base upon which their hegemonic aspirations rely).[46] As Charles Kupchan argues, hegemons generally seek to consolidate their position and the benefits accruing thereof by imposing a distinctive normative order, in which the hegemon's preferences for systemic organisation in geopolitical, socio-economic, cultural, and commercial dimensions, typically sourced from the ideas and rules that govern its domestic space, are projected from the core of the hegemonic system to its periphery.[47]

In a process that began in the aftermath of the Second World War, but was most firmly consolidated after the collapse of the Soviet Union in 1991, the US has operated as a hegemonic power in international relations for much of the recent past.[48] Its strategy in this regard has been largely to eschew formal empire in favour of an approach known as 'liberal hegemony', in which the US has focused on the creation of a multilateral institutional order, through entities such as the UN and the Bretton Woods institutions, and the

44 Ernst B Haas, *The Uniting of Europe: Political, Social, and Economic Forces 1950–1957* (University of Notre Dame Press 2004).

45 See Paul Kennedy, *The Rise and Fall of the Great Powers: Economic Change and Military Conflict from 1500 to 2000* (Vintage 1989); Robert Cox, *Production Power and World Order Social Forces in the Making of History* (Columbia UP 1987); Ian Clark, *Hegemony in International Society* (OUP 2011); Charles A Kupchan, 'The Normative Foundations of Hegemony and the Coming Challenge to Pax Americana' (2014) 23(2) Sec Stud 219, 257.

46 Kupchan (n 45) 224–227.

47 Ibid.

48 Ibid 246–251; G John Ikenberry, *Liberal Leviathan: The Origins, Crisis, and Transformation of the American World Order* (Princeton UP 2012).

promotion of 'universalist' projects, such as human rights, democracy and free trade,[49] so as to enable it to realise its goals without the need for excessive resort to direct coercion.[50] This outcome is achieved by the institutional order significantly reducing the transaction costs of regulation for the hegemon,[51] and the 'socialisation' of foreign elites to the dominant governance values of the system bolstering US control by legitimising hegemonic rule.[52]

The promotion of the conditional variant of sovereignty can be perceived as an important aspect of this strategy of liberal hegemony. Aside from the obvious benefits to the parts of the project that would be hampered by a more protective approach to sovereignty, such as human rights oversight and the globalisation of free trade, Nico Krisch argues that the attack on Westphalian sovereignty is consistent with the common practice of hegemonic powers to shape the existing legal infrastructure into a more hierarchical and flexible form that is 'more amenable to unequal power', a process he refers to as the 'legalization of inequality'.[53] Krisch sees 'the concept of an 'international community' of shared values and a particular emphasis upon human rights' as a vehicle by which the US (and its ideologically-aligned allies in the West) have sought to divide the world into a 'sphere of peace' and an 'area of lawlessness',[54] in a strategy similar to the 'standard of civilisation' metric from the nineteenth century that permitted 'civilised' Western States to dominate the 'non-civilised' world that did not adopt European models of governance.[55]

This linking of conditional sovereignty with the 'standard of civilisation' idea is a common critique in the academic literature,[56] and forms the kernel of a broader attack, prominent among critical scholars as well as developing world elites, that sees Western-supported universalist projects as a whole as little more than camouflage for the advance of imperialist and neo-colonialist aspirations.[57] As regards concrete policies initiated by international institutions, this critique has been most frequently deployed against the Structural

49 Ibid.

50 Nico Krisch, 'International Law in Times of Hegemony: Unequal Power and the Sharing of the International Legal Order' (2005) 16(3) EJIL 369, 373.

51 Ibid.

52 G John Ikenberry and Charles A Kupchan, 'Socialization and Hegemonic Power' (1990) 44(3) Int Organ 283, 315.

53 Krisch (n 50) 389–400.

54 Ibid 393

55 Ibid 386–387.

56 See Antony Anghie, *Imperialism, Sovereignty and the Making of International Law* (CUP 2005); Luke Glanville, *Sovereignty and the Responsibility to Protect: A New History* (University of Chicago Press 2014); Mohammed Ayoob, 'Third World Perspectives on Humanitarian Intervention and International Administration' (2004) 10(1) Glob Gov 99, 118; Andrew Hurrell, *On Global Order: Power, Values, and the Constitution of International* (OUP 2007).

57 See e.g. BS Chimni, *International Law and World Order: A Critique of Contemporary Approaches* (2nd edn, CUP 2017); Anghie (n 56) 245–303; Martti Koskenniemi, *The Gentle Civiliser of Nations: The Rise and Fall of International*

Adjustment Programs (SAPs) administered by the International Monetary Fund (IMF) in the developing world, as well as the 'Washington Consensus' of neoliberal policy prescriptions that formed its ideological core.[58] The general form of this argument was that the focus in the SAPs on trade liberalisation and pro-capitalist governance reforms prioritised the economic interests of Western corporations over the needs of the populations concerned, dismantling the regulatory and welfare-protection powers of the State in favour of a messianic belief in the 'market' to cure all ills.[59]

During the period of US hegemony, such critiques, however, remained on the fringes of the normative discourse of international society. Those who continued to advocate for a more protective approach to sovereignty, such as the Westphalian model, were similarly marginalised, with the two positions often linked through a perception that a robust defence of sovereignty was necessary as a bulwark against the advance of Western imperialism.[60] Over time, the mainstream of the normative discourse became increasingly dominated by the conditional variant of sovereignty, a process facilitated by the use of material incentives, such as improved trade deals and compliance with IMF reform standards, to encourage elite support for the hegemonic normative positions,[61] and the connection of legitimacy vis-à-vis international governance to core universalist ideals, such as human rights protection and the prevention of atrocity crimes.[62] The R2P doctrine was the most elaborate manifestation of the latter, though ideas such as a potential right to democratic government were also raised by prominent scholars.[63]

Law 1870–1960 2 (CUP 2001); Anne Orford, *International Authority and the Responsibility to Protect* (CUP 2011).

58 Dani Rodrik, *The Globalisation Paradox: Why Global Markets, States, and Democracy Can't Coexist* (OUP 2011); Michael Hardt and Antonio Negri, *Empire* (Harvard UP 2001); Ruth Buchanan and Sundhya Pahuja, 'Legal Imperialism: Empire's Invisible Hand?' in Jodi Dean and Paul Andrew Passavant (eds), *Empire's New Clothes: Reading Hardt and Negri* (Routledge 2003).

59 Rodrik (n 58); Hardt and Negri (n 58); Buchanan and Pahuja (n 58).

60 See Frederic Megret, 'The Politics of International Criminal Justice' (2002) 13(5) EJIL 1261, 1284; Christopher Clapham, 'Sovereignty and the Third World State' in Robert Jackson (ed), *Sovereignty at the Millennium* (Blackwell 1999); Andrew Hurrell, 'Order and Justice in International Relations: What Is at Stake?' in Rosemary Foot, John Gaddis, and Andrew Hurrell (eds), *Order and Justice in International Relations* (OUP 2003).

61 Ikenberry and Kupchan (n 52); Christopher Scherrer, 'Double Hegemony? State and Class in American Economic Policymaking' (2001) 46(4) Amerikastudien 573, 591. On co-option in general, see Antonio Gramsci, *Selections from the Prison Notebooks* (Duke UP 2007).

62 See Peters (n 40); Eyal Benvenisti, 'Sovereigns as Trustees of Humanity: On the Accountability of States to Foreign Stakeholders' (2013) 107(2) AJIL 295, 333. See also Thomas M Franck, 'Legitimacy in the International System' (1988) 82 (4) AJIL 705, 759.

63 Thomas M Franck, 'The Emerging Right to Democratic Governance' (1992) 86 (1) AJIL 46, 91; Susan Marks, 'What Has Become of the Emerging Right to Democratic Governance?' (2011) 22(2) EJIL 507, 524.

With the decline of the US and Western hegemony in the aftermath of the 2008 financial crisis, and the concomitant rise in power and influence of the so-called 'New Great Powers',[64] most notably the BRICS States,[65] this dominance of the normative discourse was shattered, and the perceived 'consensus' on the interpretation of sovereignty was exposed as a gross misunderstanding of the situation at hand. The Westphalian conception of the sovereign State, once seemingly in irreversible decline,[66] has returned to a position of prominence in the international system as a consequence of the influence of the rising powers, most notably China, whose foreign policy has been imbued with a deep respect for the value of the principle of non-interference throughout the entirety of the UN era[67] (and is moreover a position with deep historical roots related to China's semi-colonial past).[68] As Section 5 will explore, the consequence of this shift in the normative discourse has been the exposure of a fundamental dissensus over the content of sovereignty in international society, such that when the major powers in the international order speak about 'sovereignty', they are frequently referring to wildly differing conceptions of what this term means in practice. Given the centrality of sovereignty to the structure of international society, and the aforementioned tensions between the Westphalian model and the requirements of institutional multilateralism, this dissensus poses a serious threat to the stability and functioning of the international system.

5 The dissensus over sovereignty

In retrospect, the response of the international community to the crises in Libya and Syria in 2011 can be seen as a watershed moment in the evolution of sovereignty, as it provided the clearest example of the shattering of normative consensus over the principle and the consequences of this for the co-operation of the major powers at the UN level. In March 2011, following the Gaddafi regime's violent response to Arab Spring protests and the imminent threats of atrocities in the city of Benghazi, the UN Security Council adopted Resolution 1973, which authorised NATO to impose a no-fly zone over the Libyan territory and undertake 'all necessary measures' (i.e. military force) to protect the civilian

64 Congyan Cai, 'New Great Powers and International Law in the 21st Century' (2013) 24(3) EJIL 755, 795.
65 Brazil, Russia, India, China, and South Africa.
66 See Anne-Marie Slaughter, 'The Real New World Order' (1997) 76(5) For Aff 183, 197.
67 Butler (n 18).
68 For a polemic that explains the historical roots of the Chinese position vis-à-vis sovereignty and 'hegemonism', see 'Full Text of Chinese FM's Signed Article on Int'l Rule of Law' (*People's Daily*, 24 October 2014) <http://en.people.cn/n/2014/1024/c90883-8799769.html> accessed 30 April 2022. See also Sung Won Kim, 'Human Security with an Asian Face?' (2010) 17(1) Ind J Global Legal Stud 83, 103 for a broader discussion on Asian perceptions of universalist projects.

population from the regime's violent intentions.[69] NATO's interpretation of this Resolution, in which it engaged in offensive operations against the regime's command and control infrastructure, leading eventually to the overthrow of the regime and the death of Gaddafi, was met with strong condemnation from the BRICS States, who saw it as a violation of the agreed mandate and a worrying precedent in the implementation of the R2P doctrine.[70] The backlash against NATO's Libya operation was in part a contributory factor to the Security Council's deadlock over its response to the Syrian civil war, as China and Russia vetoed a series of Resolutions in late 2011 and early 2012 for fear of facilitating another Libyan-style regime change.[71]

At the heart of the dispute over Resolution 1973 was the putative conditionality of sovereignty, specifically whether a government could forfeit the protections deriving from sovereignty through its conduct within its domestic jurisdiction. By staunchly arguing that such an approach unduly stretched the letter and spirit of the UN Charter, the political leadership of the BRICS States affirmed their rejection of conditional sovereignty and thus of their support for a vision of world order that deviated significantly from the universalist projects emerging from US hegemony, towards a more Westphalian and pluralist world.[72] Further evidence for such a position can be discerned from the foreign policy approaches of these States in recent years, most notably the support of China and India for an 'Eastphalian' model of world order[73] and Russia's advocacy of 'sovereign democracy'.[74] In essence, sovereignty has become the primary battleground for the contestation of differing visions of world order among the major powers.[75] While one can criticise misalignment between the pro-sovereignty rhetoric of these States and the reality of their foreign policy, especially with regards to China,[76] the sovereigntist language that is used by these States is notable for its distinctiveness from the traditional Western position, and marks a major divide in the conceptualisation of international order.

69 UNSC Res 1973 (2011) on the situation in the Libyan Arab Jamahiriya (17 March 2011) UN Doc S/RES/1973.
70 Sean Butler, '"To Unite Our Strength to Maintain International Peace and Security": The International Response to the Syrian Civil War & the Global Discourse on State Sovereignty' (2016) 9 Irish Yb Int L 7, 24.
71 Ibid.
72 See UNSC, 'Record of the meeting on protection of civilians in armed conflict' (9 November 2011) UN Doc S/PV.6650; for a debate in which the relevant states' positions in this regard are outlined in further detail, see Butler (n 18).
73 Butler (n 18).
74 Xymena Kurowska, 'Multipolarity as Resistance to Liberal Norms: Russia's Position on Responsibility to Protect' (2014) 14(4) Confl Secur Dev 489, 508.
75 Butler (n 18).
76 See Peter Cai, 'Understanding China's Belt and Road Initiative Analysis' (Lowy Institute for International Policy 2017); Yong Wang, 'Offensive for Defensive: The Belt and Road Initiative and China's New Grand Strategy' (2016) 29(3) Pacific Rev 455, 463.

Concerns over the dilution of sovereignty have also been prominent in the rise of the populist right in the West, as seen in the isolationism-nationalism of Donald Trump (which during his Presidency led to the US withdrawing from the UN Human Rights Council[77] and UNESCO,[78] and to the Trump Administration's attacks on the World Trade Organization[79] and the Paris Climate Agreement system),[80] the 'take back control' rhetoric of the Leave campaign in the Brexit referendum and the worries about the loss of national identity prevalent in the anti-immigration movement.[81] Similarly, the central point of contention in the discourse over the withdrawal of African States from the International Criminal Court concerned the power of the UN Security Council to remove the head of State immunity of former Sudanese President Omar al-Bashir, an issue intimately related to the question of sovereign privileges and the right of the international community to impose conditions upon sovereignty, with the debate featuring the fusion of pro-sovereignty rhetoric with the strand of argumentation concerned with the 'neo-colonialist' nature of Western-backed universalist projects.[82] The current crisis over the direction and purpose of the international order can thus be seen primarily as a crisis over sovereignty, specifically its normative content in the contemporary world.

6 Consequences: adaptation, frustration, or dysfunctional re-ordering?

Implicit in this debate on the content of sovereignty is a disagreement about the kind of world order that is to be sought by the international community. Should universalist projects, such as human rights and democracy promotion, be central to the work of the international community, in which case, conditional sovereignty is a functional necessity in order to allow for robust action in pursuit of these projects to be taken, or should the protection of sovereignty be paramount, in which case, the principle of non-intervention in domestic affairs will be strictly enforced and international action will focus primarily upon the facilitation of agreements of mutual benefit between

77 'US Quits "Biased" UN Human Rights Council' (*BBC World*, 20 June 2018) <https://www.bbc.com/news/44537372> accessed 30 April 2022.

78 'US and Israel Formally Quit UNESCO' (*Al Jazeera*, 1 January 2019) <https://bit.ly/3c5RVWx> accessed 30 April 2022.

79 'Trump Says, "Will Have to Do Something" About WTO After China Ruling' (*Reuters*, 15 September 2020) <https://www.reuters.com/article/us-usa-trade-china-trump-idUKKBN26639D> accessed 30 April 2022. See also Chapters 11 and 12 in this volume.

80 Emily Holden, 'Trump Begins Year-Long Process to Formally Exit Paris Climate Agreement' *The Guardian* (5 November 2019) <https://bit.ly/3c4ZUmx> accessed 30 April 2022.

81 Owen Worth, 'Globalisation and the "Far-Right" Turn in International Affairs' (2017) 28 Ir Stud Int Aff 19, 28.

82 Kurt Mills, '"Bashir Is Dividing Us": Africa and the International Criminal Court' (2012) 34(2) HRQ 404, 447.

States, or (to use the parlance of contemporary Chinese foreign policy rhetoric) a system of 'win-win co-operation'?[83] As I have argued elsewhere, at its core, this is a choice between the establishment of a society of mutual interest, or *Gesellschaft*, and a community of shared normative vision, or *Gemeinschaft*.[84]

If this was a simple question of configuring the normative system of international law with no extraneous effects, the *Gesellschaft/Gemeinschaft* choice would be an unproblematic one. However, as I have discussed above, while the dissensus over sovereignty may be a function of the shattering of the US normative hegemony, the shift towards the conditional variant of sovereignty must be understood to have originated as much in the operational logic of institutional multilateralism as in the universalist projects pursued by the US. Thus, while the waning of US power may have reduced the appeal of the conditional variant of sovereignty, it does little to alter the brute fact that Westphalian sovereignty is a poor fit (one may even go so far as to say it is a maladaptation)[85] to the requirements of the operating system of international law under institutional multilateralism. As the Brexit debacle has demonstrated, a State retrieving its sovereignty from an international institution is a somewhat more convoluted affair than it simply declaring that it wishes to do so.

There is thus a zero-sum tension between sovereignty and the requirements of international public order that will hamper any efforts to impose a revisionist pro-sovereignty blueprint upon the normative system of international law. Three possible scenarios are visible as a consequence of this tension, as pro-sovereignty States seek to 'break the chains' imposed by institutional multilateralism – these possibilities can be labelled the *adaptation, frustration*, and *dysfunctional re-ordering* scenarios. In the *adaptation* scenario, the most promising of the three possibilities, the need to adapt the pro-sovereignty model in light of the constraints imposed by the institutional multilateral structure is recognised, with the States promoting sovereignty compromising in favour of a more limited pursuit of normative re-shaping in the international system. In this scenario, the core universalist projects of the international community will be maintained, but the focus therein may shift to better accommodate the rising States, e.g. the emphasis on human rights in the UN system may shift from its historical focus upon civil and political rights to a greater emphasis upon the protection of economic, social, and cultural rights.[86] As well as aligning closer to the historical cultural emphases of

83 See The Ministry of Foreign Affairs of the People's Republic of China, 'Position Paper of People's Republic of China for the 73rd Session of the United Nations General Assembly' (2018) <https://bit.ly/3p9JZJ1> accessed 30 April 2022.

84 Butler (n 18); Ferdinand Tönnies, *Fundamental Concepts of Sociology (Gemeinschaft und Gesellschaft)* (Charles P Loomis tr, American Book Company 1940).

85 On international law as an evolutionary system, see Anthony D'Amato, 'Groundwork for International Law' (2014) 108 AJIL 650, 679.

86 For discussions on the possible impact of the rise of China on human rights in the international system, see Bentley B Allan, Srdjan Vucetic, and Ted Hopf, 'The Distribution of Identity and Future of International Order: China's

China and other rising powers,[87] oversight of such rights at the international level tends to be perceived as being less antagonistic towards sovereignty due to the preference of international bodies for a more holistic approach to the examination of such rights, focused upon 'achieving progressively the full realization' of said rights within the context of a State's 'available resources',[88] rather than the more binary approach of rights protection in the civil and political rights tradition.[89]

The other two possible outcomes predict a less stable and functional international order. In the *frustration* scenario, the States promoting the pro-sovereignty model do not alter their approach to the normative order as in the adaptation scenario above, but continue to seek, and ultimately fail, to impose their particular normative vision upon the international system. This failure could lead to elites in the States favouring sovereignty to seek an alternative strategy to realise their vision for world order, namely progressing their struggle to the next level by seeking to make substantive alterations to the operating system of international law. This could lead to efforts by these States to withdraw from, or even dismantle, international institutions, in a process echoing the ongoing attacks upon the international order emerging from populist politicians in the Western world.[90] This strategy is likely to lead to an increased instability in the international system, as the interdependence that is central to the maintenance of international peace in the contemporary system is eroded and States find it more difficult to realise their collective interests as a result of the decreased functionality of the international system at the institutional level.

In the *dysfunctional re-ordering* scenario, the pro-sovereignty States succeed in re-shaping the normative system of international law to incorporate the model's core values, with the international system consequently moving towards a *Gesellschaft* framework of social relations. The issue with this scenario is that, short of a similar overhaul of the operating system,[91] the

Hegemonic Prospects' (2018) 72(4) Int Organ 839, 869; Ingrid Wuerth, 'International Law in the Post-Human Rights Era' (2017) 96 Tex L Rev 279, 349.

87 Allan and others (n 86); Wuerth (n 86).

88 Article 2(1) of the International Covenant on Economic, Social and Cultural Rights (entry into force 3 January 1976) 993 UNTS 3 (ICESCR); for a fuller examination of the specificities of States' obligations vis-à-vis rights protection under the ICESCR, see Committee on Economic, Social and Cultural Rights, 'General Comment No 3' (14 December 1990).

89 For the distinction in language deployed in Article 2(1) of the International Covenant on Civil and Political Rights (entry into force 23 March 1976) 999 UNTS 171 versus Article 2(1) ICESCR. This distinction can also be discerned through the competence vested in the European Court of Human Rights to judge potential violations of civil and political rights through legally binding cases, while economic, social, and cultural rights are provided weaker protection in the Council of Europe system through the European Social Charter only.

90 Worth (n 81) 24–27.

91 An outcome that would simply replicate the negative outcomes mentioned in the frustration scenario above.

normative shift would result in a significant misalignment between the two component parts of the international legal system. Given the importance of interdependence and pooled sovereignty to the international system's functionality, the consequence of this misalignment will be an increasingly dysfunctional system, as an operating system requiring a high level of co-operation to function effectively would be undermined by a normative system promoting particularism and shallower relationships between States. In addition to the detrimental effects such a misalignment would have on universalist projects such as human rights and democracy promotion, it would also significantly hamper the generation of political will necessary for humanity to tackle the series of significant collective action problems it is facing.[92]

To reverse course on sovereignty is thus to begin a process that could lead to a dismantling of the international order as a whole. Effective international organisation, particularly in a world bound by an enduring deep interdependence in economics and communications and facing major collective action problems, most notably climate change, will require a complex institutional multilateralism that in turn will need the principle of State sovereignty to be accommodating to such an arrangement. If the conditional variant of sovereignty is now considered an unacceptable relic of a lost era of US dominance, and the Westphalian variant is ultimately incompatible with the kind of international order required for the contemporary world, then a new consensus on sovereignty will need to be constructed, one that is sensitive to the concerns of those opposed to the loss of sovereign freedom while simultaneously allowing for an international order with effective power to emerge. Squaring this particular circle will require a truly global discourse on the desired world order and the role of the State therein, which in this current political climate is easier said than done.

92 Butler (n 18).

4 Revisiting the 'Crisis' of International Law

Maria Varaki

1 Introduction

The fabric of international law has been woven by a series of factual, normative, or even purely hypothetical crises. International law seems to operate in an everlasting aura of crisis, presented either as a force of progress and just rectification, or alternatively as a driver of further inequality and injustice. International law is equally and unquestionably depicted as both a benevolent project and a normative structure that facilitates well-established biases and hegemony. International law is invited to address both internal and external crises, respond with decisiveness (despite its inherent weakness) in times of crisis, and find its path somewhere between complacency and scathing critique. One of the latest *crises* that has raised intense scholarly concern is that of multilateralism, and, in particular, the so-called *backlash* against the post-Second World War liberal multilateral legal order. Several concurring phenomena have challenged the widespread sense of intransigence about the future of liberalism in the context of international practice, questioning simultaneously both facts and myths.

Within this framework, the current contribution initially contextualizes the current 'crisis', questioning the alleged distinctiveness of our era. Is it a moment of crisis-as-usual, or is it an exceptional crisis moment? Several scholars have shed light on the different shades of our era, and in this endeavour I concur that there is an identifiable call for more responsive governance. As a second step, the chapter explores to what extent different international law actors, while exercising their judgement, can operate cathartically to mend normative loopholes and structural biases and thus preserve the 'innocence' of international law, balancing between faith and critique. In this endeavour, the Aristotelian virtue of *phronesis*, or practical wisdom, will shed more light on the importance of human agency for the future of international law, with examples from the areas of international criminal justice and forced displacement/migration.

However, before proceeding further, it should be clarified that the concept of multilateralism is understood here broadly, as embracing elements of the

DOI: 10.4324/9781003312857-5

liberal multilateral legal order, related either to liberal democracy, the international 'rule of law', the praxis of international law, and finally the emerging law of global governance. In this spirit, the current contribution attempts to shed light upon the different shades of 'backlash' towards multilateralism and the way it has been identified by various thinkers and scholars, by exploring its different drives and diverse parameters.

2 The state of the art

Almost 30 years ago, the late Thomas Franck wrote his seminal article on the emerging right to democratic governance.[1] The timing of the article coincided with an overall euphoric feeling triggered by the end of the Cold War, and reflected a sense of faith in a liberal legal order.[2] Three decades later the so-called 'backlash' against liberal ideals and institutions of global governance – whose mission is the further promotion of human rights protection, the strengthening of international criminal justice, and the dissemination of the rule of law framework,[3] – has triggered a vivid discussion among various experts and scholars on populism, its causes, roots, and dynamics,[4] the future

1 Thomas Franck, 'The Emerging Right to Democratic Governance' (1992) 88 AJIL 46; but see also Gregory H Fox and Brad R Roth (eds), *Democratic Governance and International Law* (CUP 2000), with insightful and diverse contributions by Crawford (based on his Inaugural Lecture at the University of Cambridge), Slaughter, Koskenniemi, and others.

2 See e.g. Anne-Marie Slaughter, 'International Law in a World of Liberal States' (1995) 6 EJIL 503 503, and Fernando Teson, 'The Kantian Theory of International Law' (1992) 92(1) Colum L Rev 53; but see the critique by José E Alvarez, 'Do Liberal States Behave Better? A Critique of Slaughter's Liberal Theory' (2001) 12 EJIL 183; Susan Marks, 'The End of History: Reflections on Some International Legal Theses' (1997) 8(3) EJIL 449; Gerry Simpson, 'Two Liberalisms' (2001) 12(3) EJIL 537 and Gerry Simpson, *Great Powers and Outlaw States* (CUP 2004). For a thorough and critical analysis of liberal internationalism, see Daniel Joyce, 'Liberal Internationalism' in Anne Orford and Florian Hofmann (eds), *The Oxford Handbook on the Theory of International Law* (OUP 2016) 472.

3 In this regard, see Mark Mazower, *Governing the World: The History of an Idea, 1815 to the Present* (Penguin Books 2012).

4 See Philip Alston, 'The Populist Challenge to Human Rights' (2017) 9(1) J Hum Rights Pract 1; Erik Posner, 'Liberal Internationalism and Populist Backlash' (2017) 49 Ariz St L J 795; Heike Krieger, 'Populists Governments and International Law' (2019) 30(3) EJIL 971; Karen Alter, 'The Future of International Law' iCourts Working Paper No 101–2017. See also David Caron and Esme Shirlow, 'Dissecting Backlash: The Unarticulated Causes of Backlash and Its Unintended Consequences' in Andreas Follesdal and Geir Ulfstein (eds), *The Judicialization of International Law: A Mixed Blessing?* (OUP 2018); Mikael Madsen, Pola Cebulak, and Micha Wiebusch, 'Backlash Against International Courts: Explaining the Forms and Patterns of Resistance of International Courts' (2018) 14(2) Int J Law Context 197; Leslie Vinjamuri, 'Human Rights Backlash' in Stephen Hopgood, Jack Snyder, and Leslie Vinjamuri (eds), *Human Rights Future* (CUP 2017) 120–121; Joseph Powderly, 'International Criminal Justice in an Age of Perpetual Crisis' (2019) 32 LJIL 1.

(death or survival) of liberal democracy,[5] and the rise or decline of the international rule of law.[6] The 'global liberal' legal order, as we have known it, or as we thought we knew it,[7] together with the admittedly contested 'oceanic feeling'[8] of common shared values, interests, and preferences, appears to be challenged and perhaps is losing ground, even to the surprise of those who repeatedly criticized the liberal project as a hegemonic one.[9]

Especially during the last five years, following the election of President Trump, the Brexit decision, and the rise of authoritarian leaders in various parts of the world who not only opt for politically incorrect language but also adopt policies that threaten domestically civil and political liberties and target multilateral fora of global cooperation and security, the notion of 'backlash' has become the most recurrent research question.

Looking at these developments, Francis Fukuyama expressed his concerns about the future of liberal democracy, 25 years after his famous proclamation of the end of the history.[10] He situated the heart of the problem in the unevenness of globalization, which rendered parts of society to feel isolated and marginalized.[11] According to him, the old 'establishment', in the form of traditional political parties and transnational institutions, had not managed to address the fears of a large portion of the middle class, who looked for alternatives in nationalist/parochialist and populist voices from both the right and left wings of the political spectrum.

The financial crisis of 2008 was important as well, as it highlighted the structural problems of the global financial market. Although it did not trigger a 'revolutionary' moment of reconsideration, it has reinvigorated academic discussion on the risks of 'hyper-globalization' for democracy and sovereignty.[12] Some scholars have attempted to explain, among other things, how

5 See e.g. Edward Luce, *The Retreat of Western Liberalism* (Little, Brown Books 2017), Steven Levitsky and Daniel Ziblatt, *How Democracies Die* (Crown 2018).
6 Heike Krieger, Georg Nolte, and Andreas Zimmermann (eds), *The International Rule of Law: Rise or Decline?* (OUP 2019).
7 See Tom Ginsburg, 'Authoritarian International Law?' (2020) 114 AJIL 2; Stephan Talmon, 'The United States under President Trump: Gravedigger of International Law' (2019) 18 Chin J Int Law 645; Andrea Birdsall and Rebecca Sanders, 'Trumping International Law' (2020) 21 Int Stud Perspect 275.
8 Martti Koskenniemi, 'Projects of World Community' in Antonio Cassese (ed), *Realizing Utopia: The Future of International Law* (OUP 2012) 3.
9 James Crawford, 'The Current Political Discourse Concerning International Law' (2018) 81 MLR 1, where he questions the 'susceptibility' of international law in the current context of defiance by political practice, Alain Pellet, 'Values and Power Relations – The Disillusionment of International Law?' KFG Working Paper No 34.
10 Francis Fukuyama, *The End of History and the Last Man* (Free Press 1992).
11 See Ishaan Tharoor, 'The Man Who Declared the "End of History" Fears for Democracy's Future' *The Washington Post* (9 February 2017) <https://wapo.st/353WMmY> accessed 30 April 2022.
12 See e.g. Dani Rodrik, *The Globalization Paradox: Democracy and the Future of World Economy* (WW Norton 2011).

the international institutions that addressed human rights questions and concerns or promoted international economic policies contributed to the development of this nationalist outburst by ignoring the early signs of dissatisfaction regarding the development of a globalized form of governance – one that privileged particular interests or values – and drifted towards more parochial preferences in decision making.[13] Equally important were the refugee and migration crises of recent years, which fuelled another round of anxiety among nationals and the international polity alike, as traditional platforms of multilateral interaction could not provide adequate answers.

It is therefore not surprising that in these circumstances right-wing xenophobic parties gained power all over Europe, some of them with clear neo-Nazi ideology, while, in the United States (US), the election of President Trump unleashed dangerous extreme forces of white supremacist rhetoric and violence. In countries, such as Turkey and Russia, dissenting voices have been systematically targeted and silenced, whereas, within the heart of the European Union (EU), Hungary and Poland have gradually transformed into archetypes of illiberal democracy, as was prophetically described by Zakaria 20 years ago.[14]

On the legal front, a series of scholars have also tried to 'unveil' the actual or alleged backlash against the liberal legal order of the post-Cold War era, highlighting a wide range of salient elements. Martti Koskenniemi, in a lecture he delivered at the Asser Institute in December 2018, while situating the genesis of the current crisis in the euphoria of the 1990s, with seeds already stretching back to the 1960s, saw it as an expression of cynicism that mirrors both a problem of expert knowledge and a problem of politics.[15] For him, the so-called 'backlash' reflects the anxiety of those people who have lost 'white male privilege' and want to regain control. It is not about 'economic deprivation', but is rather 'a cultural war against the values and priorities associated with the "international" or the "global" order that became dominant in the 1990s'.[16]

Doreen Lustig and Joseph Weiler, when analysing three global waves of judicial review within national constitutional orders, saw the most recent one as a form of 'self-correction' on the side of national counts – a response to the overexpansion of transnationalism, reflecting legitimate concerns about identity and a lack of democratic legitimacy. As the authors noted:

13 See Robert Howse, 'Economics for Progressive International Lawyers: A Review Essay (2017) 5(1) London Rev Int L 187 (reviewing the work of Piketty, Rodrik, and Stiglitz); Dani Rodrik, 'Populism and Economics of Globalization' (2018) 1 JIBP 12.

14 Fareed Zakaria, 'The Rise of Illiberal Democracy' (1997) 76(6) For Aff 22; Bojan Bugaric, 'A Crisis of Constitutional Democracy in Post-Communist Europe: "Lands in Between" Democracy and Authoritarianism' (2015) 13(1) Int J Con L 219.

15 Martti Koskenniemi, *International Law and the Far Right; Reflections on Law and Cynicism* (TMC Asser Press 2019).

16 Ibid.

> The traditional opposition to "internationalism" came from nationalism and was conceptualized as a tension between national sovereignty and international law. The opposition we are alluding to is, instead, not a concern with sovereignty – at least not with the classical sovereignty of the state. It takes the international legal order as an acquis – but it is unwilling to celebrate the benefits of that acquis when gained by a disenfranchisement of people and peoples. There is, thus, in our view a deep paradox in the spread of liberal democracies to an increasing number of states and populations around the world.[17]

Still, for both authors the tragic path of our era continues, since the main focus of judicial review does not expand beyond the strict protection of individuals nor address fundamental concerns of social justice, equality, and distribution.[18]

On a different note, Eyal Benvenisti and Cass Sunstein have meticulously noted how new technologies trigger a number of unprecedented challenges for democracy.[19] Sunstein in particular identifies a series of areas where new technologies are playing a constantly increasing role, such as governance by machines, manipulation of information channels, and the privatization of communication, and highlights that the previous traditional culture of accountability and bi-directional communication is not enough.[20] For Benvenisti, the law of global governance should proactively secure the concept of human dignity and the preservation of the democratic State.[21] From his side, Cass Sunstein sheds more light on the divisive dimension of social media and their impact on democracy while promoting fragmentation, polarization, and extremism.[22] His suggestion is an 'architecture of serendipity' as a counter practice to the 'architecture of control'.[23] His main argument is that for the sake of democracy and liberty, channels of deliberation and inclusiveness

17 Doreen Lustig and Joseph HH Weiler, 'Judicial Review in the Contemporary World – Retrospective and Prospective' (2018) 16(2) Int J Const L 315, 371.

18 Ibid 372. Martha Nussbaum has described the *Cosmopolitan Tradition: A Noble but Flawed Ideal* due to its indifference towards material aid (Belknap Press 2019).

19 Eyal Benvenisti, 'Upholding Democracy Amid the Challenges of New Technology: What Role for the Law of Global Governance?' (2018) 29(2) EJIL 671; Cass Sunstein, *#Republic: Divided Democracy in the Age of Social Media* (Princeton UP 2018).

20 Sunstein (n 19).

21 Benvenisti (n 19). In another text, Benvenisti, while addressing the rise or decline of international rule of law, highlights the role of international law to correct injustices via securing access to information for the non-privileged classes and thus accommodating political deliberation (Eyal Benvenisti, 'Ensuring Access to Information: International Law's Contribution to Global Justice' in Heike Krieger, Georg Nolte, and Andreas Zimmermann (eds), *The International Rule of Law: Rise or Decline?* (OUP 2019) 345).

22 Sunstein (n 19).

23 Ibid.

should replace what he describes as 'echo chambers' where like-minded people interact solely among each other.[24]

This diverse scholarship has shed light on different components of the crisis, or 'backlash' against multilateralism. Whether it is cynicism about the gap between expectations and reality, the 'rehabilitation' of domestic identity concerns together with the utopia of the global demos, or the advancement of technology to the detriment of human dignity, public deliberation, and contestation, scholars appear to echo the prophetic observation of Thomas Franck about the importance of a governance responsive to the concerns and interests of the affected populations as an alternative model of legitimate authority.[25]

I assert that this common call for a more responsive governance – which entails the background for the proposition of this chapter – encompasses the need for critical self-reflection among various actors of international law via the exercise of phronetic judgement. This is of particular importance when both scholars and policy-makers face the dilemma of how to explain the 'obvious' without becoming either apologists for a system that has structural issues, or complicit in the expansion of an isolationist mentality hidden in over-simplistic discourse.

3 Revisiting the crisis of international law in 2021

In a seminal 2002 article, Hillary Charlesworth contested the proposition, supported by some scholars, that international law is a discipline of crisis. Instead, she argued that we should develop an understanding of international law that reflects the 'everyday' life.[26] Jan Klabbers recently argued that international law and crisis seem to develop hand-in-hand, and that international law is in a perennial state of crisis irrespective of its era.[27] For him, the crisis thread is very much related to the presumption that international law is a force for good, and he suggests instead that maybe international lawyers are in a state of crisis due to the unsatisfactory praxis of international law in various promising fields, such as international criminal justice.[28] Since 'crisis' implies a need for radical change, other scholars have highlighted the importance of not diluting the meaning of the word by overstretching it, arguing that it should be preserved for really catastrophic events.[29] Jean d'Aspremont

24 Ibid.

25 Thomas Franck, 'The Centripede and the Centrifuge: Principles for the Centralisation and Decentralisation of Governance' in Tomer Broude and Yuval Shany (eds), *The Shifting Allocation of Authority in International Law: Considering Sovereignty, Supremacy and Subsidiarity* (Hart 2008) 28.

26 Hillary Charlesworth, 'A Discipline of Crisis' (2002) 65 MLR 3.

27 Jan Klabbers, 'The Love of Crisis', in Makane Mbengue and Jean d'Aspremont (eds), *Crisis Narratives in International Law* (Brill 2021).

28 Ibid.

29 Jean d'Aspremont, 'International Law as a Crisis Discourse: The Peril of Wordlessness', in Makane Mbengue and Jean d'Aspremont (eds), *Crisis Narratives in International Law* (Brill 2021).

in particular vividly invites lawyers to think about the perils of transforming international law into wordlessness.[30]

For the purposes of this chapter, I acknowledge the plurality of opinions regarding the genesis or even existence of a 'crisis'. Yet, I endorse what Bobbio once said while writing on the future of democracy: 'I prefer to talk of transformation rather than of crisis, because "crisis" suggests an imminent collapse.'[31] For this reason I distance myself from both calls for a cataclysmic change of the entire legal framework/paradigm, and nihilistic pronouncements that nothing has changed.

In the same mode, I refrain from providing any particular definition of the terms 'crisis' or 'backlash', which I perceive as a highly controversial exercise that can only operate as an academic trap and provide fertile, but ultimately futile, grounds for endless scholarly debates. Instead, I acknowledge the elusive character of these concepts and take note – without any predetermined normative prejudice – of some recurrent but uneven signs of contestation, and subsequently explore how individual actors can, through their resilience or adaptation, preserve the 'innocence of international law'.[32]

On this note, it can be argued that irrespective of how one understands 'crisis' – as a call for a radical change; as a pretext for domination; or as a discourse of existential preservation – it has unequivocally become one of the most used words, especially during the year 2020, and also today in 2022. International law seems to be in the midst of another 'crisis', this time triggered by the pandemic, which has forced the entire world into an absurd 'normality' of repeated lockdowns filled with Zoom meetings and apocalyptic headlines.

Within this framework, one could observe a mixed scholarly reaction about the *demise* or *resilience* of the international legal order, at least as we knew it. A series of special scholarly issues on the impact of the COVID-19 pandemic upon international law demonstrate this nuanced reflection, both through doctrinal and theoretical pieces that highlight scepticism and self-critique, but also hope.[33] From one side, building upon the latest 'backlash' against liberal ideas and institutions of global governance that are supposed to accommodate further cooperation in the promotion of the common good, several

30 Ibid.

31 Norberto Bobbio, *The Future of Democracy* (Wiley 1987) Preface.

32 Krieger and Nolte adopt a similar minimalist attitude, whereas D'Aspremont describes the rise or decline of the international Rule of Law as a manifestation of the liberal legal thought (see Heike Krieger and Georg Nolte, 'The International Rule of Law – Rise or Decline? – Approaching Current Foundational Challenges', and Jean D'Aspremont, 'Do Non-State Actors Strengthen or Weaken International Law?', both in Heike Krieger, Georg Nolte, and Andreas Zimmermann (eds), *The International Rule of Law: Rise or Decline?* (OUP 2019)).

33 'AJIL Agora – The International Legal Order and the Global Pandemic' (2020) 114 AJIL 4.

surveys and commentators have stressed the lack of trust in both domestic and international institutions, and the rise of mistrust between States.[34]

On the other hand, there are propositions for a less dramatic and more nuanced view regarding the *death* of the legal global order *as we knew it*, shedding light on a selective position towards international organizations that can provide an alternative reading of the so-called 'backlash'.[35] Similarly, against the background of a return to nativism, at least from some of the big powers, it should not go unnoticed that other smaller States have expressed their intention to fill the gap in the global arena. This grey dimension of global governance, in contrast to the simplified binary of white and black, reveals a more complex reality that may simultaneously confirm the decline of some elements of the international legal framework and the emergence or strengthening of others. In this spirit, definitive proclamations of 'the end of the world as we knew it' not only do not do justice to the perplexity and complexity of our era, but they may also obscure a better understanding of the deeper structural and ideological misgivings. I argue that these various aspects of greyness should not be perceived solely as a sign of scholarly exaggeration, but additionally as an analytical tool that should properly be assessed and wisely used.

4 Phronetic judgement

Inspired by Charlesworth's famous crisis article, I propose that her encouragement to address the everyday life of international law could also be read as the actual daily performance of the relevant actors of international law. This call for performance could be substantiated in various ways. One possible avenue is confrontation. This argument could unfold along the following lines: Since these are challenging times, a legitimate response would be a similar reaction. Relevant actors should fiercely and forcefully defend the 'fundamentals' of international law via a rigid approach, in a defensive/offensive mode. Another version of reaction could be acceptance of the tragedy of international law and democracy, or else of its 'broken promises' between expectations and reality.[36] This second hypothetical performance could be expressed via cynicism, in a nihilistic mode. Yet one could reasonably observe that both attitudes suffer from self-righteousness and intransigence.

34 See the recent comment by Chesterman (Simon Chesterman, 'COVID-19 and the Global Legal Disorder' (*Simon Chesterman's blog*, undated) <https://bit.ly/3pCf889> accessed 30 April 2022). It was not only in the US, Russia, China, and the UK, but also within the European Union where several States did not show the expected solidarity a pandemic should trigger. See also Chapters 2 and 3 in this volume.

35 See Klabbers and his fine observations about the World Health Organization in the COVID-19 times (Jan Klabbers 'The Second Most Difficult Job in the World: Reflections on Covid-19' (2020) 11(2) J Int Humanit Leg Stud 270).

36 Bobbio (n 31) Preface.

However, beyond those binary behaviours (presented here in an over-simplistic way), the current thesis argues that there are also those who believe in the bright side of international law, while still acknowledging its contradictions, limits, and elements of darkness. These are people who do not abide by strict binaries, but instead struggle with uneasiness before the complexity of an overly aggressive environment. So how can legal actors balance between faith and critique? The suggestion here revolves around the invitation to engage in a self-cathartic critique, accompanied by what I call critical judgement.

The word 'crisis' originates from the Greek word 'κρίσης' which means judgement, and thus discretion.[37] Hannah Arendt believed that every crisis could be a new beginning, but at the same time it requires the exercise of 'κρίσης' or judgement, reflecting an enhanced sense of common responsibility.[38] On this note, I invite the readers to consider the importance of *phronetic* judgement, as conceived by Aristotle in his book VI of *Nichomachean Ethics*, which analyses the intellectual virtues.[39]

The reason for refocusing on the normative theory of virtue ethics[40] lies in the importance it carries for human agency, emphasizing the particular traits that those in positions of power and influence should have.[41] Virtue ethics are distinct from the deontological and consequentialist theories of ethics, as expressed by Kant and others. In this regard, while focusing on ethics we can distance ourselves from the controversy of values and concentrate on virtues. This can be reasonably achieved, since the theory of virtue ethics provides a

37 See Maria Varaki, 'Quest for Phronesis in Holy Land', in Jan Klabbers, Maria Varaki, and Guilherme V Vilaca (eds), *Towards Responsible Global Governance* (University of Helsinki 2018), citing Florian Hoffman, 'Facing the Abyss: International Law before the Political' in Marco Goldoni and Chris McCorkindale (eds), *Hannah Arendt and the Law* (Hart 2012) 175.

38 In this regard, see Jan Klabbers, 'Possible Islands of Predictability: The Legal Thought of Hannah Arendt' (2007) 20 LJIL 1; Jan Klabbers, 'Hannah Arendt and the Languages of Global Governance' in Marco Goldoni and Chris McCorkindale (eds), *Hannah Arendt and the Law* (Hart 2012) 246.

39 Aristotle, *Nicomachean Ethics* (James Thomson tr, Penguin 1976). See also Aristotle, *The Eudemian Ethics* (Anthony Kenny tr, OUP 2011); Daniel Russell, 'Phronesis and the Virtues' in Ronald Polansky (ed), *The Cambridge Companion to Aristotle's Nicomachean Ethics* (CUP 2014) 203; Amalia Amaya, 'The Role of Virtue in Legal Justification' in Amalia Amaya and Hock Lai Ho (eds), *Law, Virtue and Justice* (Hart 2013) and Jamie Gaskarth, 'The Virtues of International Society' (2012) 18 EJIR 431.

40 For a comprehensive theoretical analysis and case-specific application of virtue ethics in international practice, see Guilherme V Vilaca and Maria Varaki (eds), *Ethical Leadership in International Organizations: Concepts, Narratives, Judgment and Assessment* (CUP 2021).

41 Since the mid-1950s there has been a revival of interest in virtue ethics; GEM Anscombe, 'Modern Moral Philosophy' (1958) 33 Philosophy 1; Alasdair MacIntyre, *After Virtue: A Study in Moral Theory* (University of Notre Dame Press 1981), Rosalind Hursthouse, *On Virtue Ethics* (OUP 1999).

more modest and less polarized platform of cognition, moving the discourse from a universal project to one more oriented on human agency.[42]

In particular, the Aristotelian theory of *phronesis* does not condone the 'middle way' but requires choices and judgement in hard cases of indeterminacy and discretion.[43] My own proposition of *phronesis*, as I have developed elsewhere, is very much based on the notion of common sense,[44] and in particular on a dialectic format based on the interpretation Outi Korhonen has described.[45] *Phronesis* is that kind of intellectual wisdom which operates in a strictly contextual way, oscillating between the general and the particular; in that sense, *phronesis* is 'dialogic', whereas *tekhne* is 'dogmatic knowledge'.[46] *Phronesis* understood in this way provides simultaneously the means for deliberation and liberation, while strengthening the capacity of the decision-maker to accommodate the wisest way for the particular *topo* and *kairo* before making a choice.[47] The essence of *phronesis* also rests with its lack of predetermined criteria that can secure a phronetic judgement.[48] Instead, the exercise of *phronesis* reveals the 'mean' or else 'μέτρο', and this fine balance becomes the substance of *phronetic judgement*.[49] In this sense, the trait of *phronesis* entails elements of both moderation and imagination; elements that function simultaneously in a self-limiting, but also accelerating, sensibility and thus materialize the art of the possible, beyond excess and dogmatisms.

This particular shade of judgement is of paramount importance for addressing some of the 'dark' sides of the phenomenon I described at the beginning of this chapter. Irrespective of whether we call it 'crisis' or 'backlash', 'business as usual' or 'hypocritical exaggeration', arguably several structural elements of the liberal legal order appear to accommodate and even enhance discrimination, inequality, anger, and reaction. Reconceiving the word 'crisis' as κρίσης and wise judgement for action or inaction might provide a more nuanced and less polarized response,

42 Michael Slote, 'Agent-Based Virtue Ethics' (1995) 20 Midwest Stud Philos 83.

43 Rachana Kamtekar, 'Ancient Virtue Ethics: An Overview with an Emphasis on Practical Wisdom' in Daniel Russell (ed), *The Cambridge Companion to Virtue Ethics* (CUP 2013) 34–35, citing *Nichomachean Ethics*.

44 See Maria Varaki, 'Quest for Phronesis in Holy Land' in Jan Klabbers, Maria Varaki, and Guilherme V Vilaca (eds), *Towards Responsible Global Governance* (University of Helsinki 2018). For Arendt as well, the exercise of judging was developed around the notion of common sense, see Jonathan P Schwartz, *Arendt's Judgment* (University of Pennsylvania Press 2016) 151.

45 See the seminal work of Outi Korhonen, 'New International Law: Silence, Defense or Deliverance?' (1996) 7 EJIL 1, on situationality.

46 Ibid.

47 Rosalind Hursthouse, 'Practical Wisdom: A Mundane Account' (2006) 106 Proceedings of the Aristotelian Society 1; Daniel Russell, *Practical Intelligence and the Virtues* (OUP 2009), Bronwyn Finnigan, 'Phronesis in Aristotle: Reconciling Deliberation with Spontaneity' (2015) 91(3) PPR 674.

48 As Macintyre argues, 'the exercise of such judgment is not a routinizable application of rules' (Alasdair MacIntyre, *After Virtue: A Study in Moral Theory* (Bloomsbury 2013) 176), whereas later he attributes the lack of criteria to the interrelationship of virtues (182).

49 Ibid 180–181.

one that can build bridges instead of walls. For this reason, Section 5 will focus on two areas of international law and multilateralism that have provided some of the most heated debates about the future of legal liberalism and multilateralism. The invitation to use critical judgement will be substantiated through the scholarly and institutional role of two prominent actors, i.e. on the future of the International Criminal Court (ICC) and the adoption of the Global Compact on Migration.

5 International law and critical judgement

Two areas within the framework of international legal practice reflect the importance of phronetic judgement in the most characteristic way. The choice to focus on these areas stems from the fact that they appear to exist within a permanent actual or fictional crisis discourse. The first field which is 'infected' by the crisis virus is that of international criminal justice. To be clear, for quite some time now the 'project' of international criminal justice has been both praised and attacked severely at the same time.[50] The initial euphoria of the post-Cold War period, after the foundation of the ad hoc tribunals and the establishment of the International Criminal Court (ICC), gave way to new challenges and critiques,[51] and the particularities or 'anxieties' of the international criminal justice 'crisis' have triggered a very rich scholarship on questions of legitimacy, credibility, and the effectiveness of the entire project of 'global justice'.[52]

Whether it was a matter of ideology, a question of religion, or simply faith,[53] the initial narrow pursuit of global justice via the ICC advocated for a particular understanding of moral cosmopolitanism.[54] This attitude was

50 Darryl Robinson, 'The Identity Crisis of International Criminal Law' (2008) 21 LJIL 925; Darryl Robinson, 'Inescapable Dyads: Why the International Criminal Court Cannot Win' (2016) 29 LJIL 323.

51 David Bosco, *Rough Justice: The International Criminal Court in a World of Power Politics* (OUP 2014); Christine Schwobel (ed), *Critical Approaches to International Criminal Law* (Routledge 2014); Christian De Vos, Sara Kendall, and Carsten Stahn (eds), *Contested Justice: The Politics and Practice of International Criminal Court Interventions* (CUP 2015).

52 See Frederic Mégret, 'The Anxieties of International Criminal Justice' 29 LJIL (2016).

53 Frederic Mégret, 'Three Dangers for the International Criminal Court: A Critical Look at a Consensual Project' (2002) 12 Finnish Yb Int L 193; Immi Tallgren, 'The Sensibility and Sense of International Criminal Law' (2002) 13(3) EJIL 561; David Koller, 'The Faith of the International Criminal Lawyer' (2008) 40 NY Univ J Int Law Politics 1019.

54 See Sarah Nouwen and Wouter Werner, 'Monopolizing Global Justice: International Criminal Law as a Challenge to Human Diversity' (2015) 13 JICJ 157; Immi Tallgren, 'The Voice of the International: Who Is Speaking?' (2015) 13 JICJ 135; Frederic Mégret, 'What Sort of Global Justice Is "International Criminal Justice"?' (2015) 13 JICJ 77; Luigi DA Corrias and Geoffrey M Gordon, 'Judging in the Name of Humanity: International Criminal Tribunals and the Representation of a Global Public' (2015) 13 JICJ 97; Tor Krever, 'International Criminal Law: An Ideology Critique' (2013) 26 LJIL 701.

heavily criticized for monopolizing the normative discourse on justice, hiding structural biases that trigger collective violence, excluding alternative forms of justice, and dogmatically representing the international community as a whole.[55]

On a different critical mode, there were several propositions for addressing the shortcomings and deficiencies of international criminal justice by focusing on methods of improving the effectiveness, legitimacy, and credibility of the courts.[56] This latter critique did not give rise to existential dilemmas but acted as a post-ontological functional narrative that accepts some role(s) of international criminal justice but strives to correct its flaws and fill its gaps.[57]

Yet, nowadays, contrary to the previous predominantly defensive attitude towards the 'project', a more robust wave of new critique is emerging which reflects the worries of a broader segment of the supporters of international criminal justice. This latest critique differs from the previous ones, which were founded either on allegations of neo-colonialism and hegemony or advocated for a less decisive corrective intervention. A series of controversial judicial decisions, such as the rejection of the Office of the Prosecutor's (OTP) application to open an investigation in Afghanistan,[58] exacerbated the tone of critical voices that actually talk about 'fixing', reform, and the need to remain

55 Ileana M Porras, 'Liberal Cosmopolitanism or Cosmopolitan Liberalism', in Mortimer Sellers (ed), *Parochialism, Cosmopolitanism and the Foundations of International Law* (CUP 2012) 118–148; and more characteristically Ruti G Teitel, *Humanity's Law* (OUP 2011) and Darryl Robinson 'A Cosmopolitan Liberal Account of International Criminal Law' (2013) 26 LJIL 127.

56 In 2013, the Journal of International Criminal Justice published a special volume 11(3) devoted to the performance of international criminal justice from a critical perspective. See especially William A Schabas, 'The Banality of International Justice'; Mireille Delmas-Marty, 'Ambiguities and Lacunae: The International Criminal Court Ten Years'; Payam Akhavan, 'The Rise, and Fall, and Rise, of International Criminal Justice'; David Luban, 'After the Honeymoon: Reflections on the Current State of International Criminal Justice'. Similarly, LJIL published a series of articles that drew attention to the *problématique*, e.g. Carsten Stahn, 'Between "Faith" and "Facts": By What Standards Should We Assess International Criminal Justice?' (2012) 25 LJIL 251; Dov Jacobs, 'Sitting on the Wall, Looking In: Some Reflections on the Critique of International Criminal Law' (2015) 28 LJIL 1; Sergey Vasiliev, 'On Trajectories and Destinations of International Criminal Law Scholarship' (2015) 28 LJIL 701; Elies van Sliedregt, 'International Criminal Law: Over-Studied and Underachieving?' (2016) 29 LJIL 1.

57 See e.g. Yuval Shany, *Assessing the Effectiveness of International Courts* (OUP 2014), and more specifically Nobuo Hayashi and Cecilia Bailliet (eds), *The Legitimacy of International Criminal Tribunals* (CUP 2017).

58 Dapo Akande, 'ICC Appeals Chamber Holds that Heads of State Have No Immunity Under Customary International Law Before International Tribunals' (*EJIL: Talk!*, 6 May 2019) <https://bit.ly/3gqz0am>; Ben Batros, 'A Confusing ICC Appeals Judgment on Head of State Immunity' (*Just Security*, 7 May 2019) <https://bit.ly/3g2Z4t1> both accessed 30 April 2022.

both aspirational and practical.[59] The Court appears to be either too utopian or too much of an apologist. No one is happy and Koskenniemi's theory once more proves the limits and inherent contradictions of the international legal framework.

Among the various aspects of the international criminal justice project, the exercise of prosecutorial discretion by the OTP of the ICC has generated a particularly intense controversy. The choice of situations and the subsequent focus on some debatable cases, but mainly the wooden reaction on behalf of the Court officials that they simply apply the law irrespective of other considerations, reflect a deeply problematic sensibility and praxis that do not do justice to the complex reality that necessitates nuanced responses. Interestingly enough, in one of the first pieces that attempted to understand populism and its effect on the global rule of law, Philip Alston touched upon the fragility of the ICC and highlighted the importance of persuasion in an era of great challenges, where absolutism and self-righteousness cannot provide an adequate answer.[60] In his article, while exploring tenable strategies to deal with populist manifestations against international institutions, he recommends a 'calibrated approach' that takes into consideration the context and particularities of the relevant time in order to achieve the 'art of the possible'.[61] In particular, he uses the example of the controversy raised by head of State immunity questions vis-à-vis the cooperation obligations for other States to execute the arrest warrant against the now former President Bashir. While he talks about moving beyond righteousness, he does not hesitate to speak of concessions in order to respond to the challenges the ICC project faces. In this sense he reiterates his faith and commitment to the ideals of multilateralism, but at the same time provides a cathartic critique of its complacency.

Alston's observations reflect the kind of *critical* judgement I argue is capable of providing an exodus from the never-ending crisis discourse, if only the relevant practitioners of international criminal justice showed the virtue of *phronesis* in their interventions, or their silence. His recommendations concerning the ICC can be translated into a phronetic exercise of judgement about the complexities of the issues that surround the project of international criminal justice. He does not advocate an unconditional surrender; instead he proposes a responsible tactical choice that might appease the overall polarized, divisive, and hostile environment of either support for or resistance to the function of the Court. Equally, he does not put an intermediate solution

59 See Zeid Raad Al Hussein and others, 'The International Criminal Court Needs Fixing' (*Atlantic Council*, 24 April 2019) <https://bit.ly/3x6KdDy>; the Independent Expert Review of the International Criminal Court and the Rome Statute System, 'Final Report' 30 September 2020 <https://bit.ly/3g6tiLA> both accessed 30 April 2022.

60 Philip Alston, 'The Populist Challenge to Human Rights' (2017) 9 J Hum Rights Pract 1.

61 Ibid.

on the table. He calls for a clear position and he justifies this position as the wisest choice, with a vision of the future. *Phronesis* does not condone the middle way but accommodates the wisest way for the particular *topo* and *kairo*. This is why it is the epitome of a situational approach to sophisticated dilemmas of a legal and moral nature.

Alston's suggestion about the ICC is also an example of imaginative scholarship, because it encourages us to place ourselves in the shoes of the 'other side' and thus consider the unthinkable. In that sense, imagination can be seen as the complementary side of *phronesis*, where the latter is the initial step in the exercise of judgement, and the former completes this intellectual exercise with a meta step. Put differently, phronetic judgement operates as either a restraining or accelerating exercise of discretion, but imaginary judgement completes the picture while creating the foundation for something other than what might be expected. In that sense, imaginary judgement provides not only wisdom but also inspiration, and thus becomes a paradigm of exemplarism.[62]

The second area that deserves enhanced attention evolves around the *crisis* in the forced displacement or mixed migration movements, which reached its peak during 2015–2016 and paved the way for the adoption of the UN New York Declaration for Refugees and Migrants.[63] The NY Declaration facilitated the production of two Compacts, one for refugees and the other one for migrants, whereas the International Office for Migration (IOM) has been elevated to a *related agency* within the UN system.[64]

The UN Global Compact for Migration (GCM) was negotiated for years, after several rounds of consultations among several stakeholders, and it was scheduled for adoption at a major intergovernmental conference in Morocco.[65] The GCM is founded upon a set of guiding principles and a vision of collective commitment to enhance further cooperation.[66] Yet, the GCM is not

62 Amalia Amaya, 'Exemplarism and Legal Virtue' (2013) 25 Law Lit 428.

63 New York Declaration for Refugees and Migrants (13 September 2016) A/71/L.1*. For a thorough analysis of this area of international legal practice, see Maria Varaki, 'Imaginary Leadership and Displacement, A Laboratory of Dilemmas' in Guilherme V Vilaca and Maria Varaki (eds), *Ethical Leadership in International Organizations: Concepts, Narratives, Judgment and Assessment* (CUP 2021).

64 For an initial critical comment on the nature of the IOM as a 'non-normative' organization, see Elspeth Guild, Stefani Grant, and Kees Groenendijk, 'IOM and the UN: Unfinished Business' Queen Mary School of Law Legal Studies Research Paper No 255/2017.

65 UN General Assembly, Res 73/195 Global Compact for Safe, Orderly and Regular Migration (11 January 2019) UN Doc A/Res/73/195.

66 For an initial introductory analysis on the genesis and final shape of the GCM, see Michele Solomon and Suzanne Sheldon, 'The Global Compact for Migration: From the Sustainable Development Goals to a Comprehensive Agreement on Safe, Orderly and Regular Migration' (2018) 30 Int J Refug L 584; Kathleen Newland, 'The Global Compact for Safe, Orderly and Regular Migration: An Unlikely Achievement' (2018) 30 Int J Refug L 657; Elspeth Guild, 'The UN Global Compact for Safe, Orderly and Regular Migration: What Place for

a legally binding document and does not create new legal obligations for the State Parties, as is repeatedly highlighted in its text.

However, despite all these assurances that the Compact reflects solely a political commitment, a series of countries decided not to sign the UN Global Compact for Migration just before its adoption in Marrakesh on 10–11 December 2018.[67] The US opened the Pandora's box already in 2017, when President Trump stated that the Global Compact would 'undermine the sovereign right of the United States to enforce our immigration laws and secure our borders'.[68] Other countries, such as Australia, Israel, and Brazil followed this path, including a considerable number of EU Members,[69] where the Compact triggered political crises.[70] This provoked a bitter comment from the UN Special Representative for International Migration, Louise Arbour, who noted that these 'U-turns on the Global Compact reflect poorly on countries concerned'.[71] Images of mixed migratory movements in countries already susceptible to populist rhetoric, nationalist hysteria, and xenophobic sentiment[72] triggered daunting dilemmas for political leaders, diplomats, and the civil society. The perceived danger of migration for state sovereignty, together with some admittedly anaemic references to human rights law, generated hostility regarding an emerging 'human right to immigration'. At the end, the Compact was adopted: 152 States voted in favour, 5 cast a negative vote (i.e. Czech Republic, Hungary, Israel, Poland and the US), and 12 abstained.

Human Rights?' (2018) 30 Int J Refug L 661; Elspeth Guild, 'The UN's Search for a Global Compact on Safe, Orderly and Regular Migration' (2018) 30(4) GLJ 661.

67 'Intergovernmental Conference on the Global Compact for Migration, 10–11 December 2018 Marrakech, Morocco' <http://www.un.org/en/conf/migration/index.shtml> accessed 30 April 2022.

68 Rick Gladstone, 'U.S. Quits Migration Pact, Saying It Infringes on Sovereignty' *The New York Times* (3 December 2017) <https://nyti.ms/3ivDNtr> accessed 30 April 2022.

69 See e.g. Amy Remeikis and Ben Doherty 'Dutton says Australia won't "surrender our sovereignty" by signing UN migration deal' *The Guardian* (25 July 2018) <https://bit.ly/3zj11Jc>; Francois Murphy, 'Austria to Shun Global Migration Pact, Fearing Creep in Human Rights' (*Reuters*, 31 October 2018) <https://reut.rs/357AelA> both accessed 30 April 2022.

70 Most characteristically in Belgium, 'Theo Francken sur le pacte migratoire de l'ONU: «C'est au chef du gouvernement de trouver une solution»' *Le Soir* (20 November 2018) <https://bit.ly/3g7CFuq> accessed 30 April 2022.

71 'U-turns on Global Compact "Reflect Poorly" On Countries Concerned: Senior UN Migration Official' (*UN News*, 27 November 2018) <https://news.un.org/en/story/2018/11/1026791> accessed 30 April 2022.

72 In this regard, see the Venice Commission and OSCE/ODIHR, 'Hungary: Joint Opinion on the Provisions of the So-Called "Stop Soros" Draft Legislative Package Which Directly Affect NGOs' (25 June 2018) <https://www.osce.org/odihr/385932?download=true> accessed 30 April 2022; Report of the UN Special Rapporteur on contemporary forms of racism, racial discrimination, xenophobia, and related intolerance (6 August 2018) UN Doc A/73/305.

Despite the lack of strong legal normativity,[73] the Compact is considered to be the very first global response to the phenomenon of mixed forced displacement,[74] responding to Aleinikoff's description of the legal fragmentation of migration, as *substance without architecture*.[75] This is of no small importance, especially in an era where the fundamental conceptions of the international legal order are severely challenged. When leaders adhere to the normative framework of the Compact, they express their commitment to keep open the modes of communication that can trigger action and thus further normative developments. Additionally, in an era of de-formalization and managerialism, the Compact operates as an alternative platform for policy-making and norm creation. In this sense the Global Compact is a major achievement that can be further developed, functioning as a platform of common action, shared perceptions, and normative crystallization.[76]

Throughout the whole period of negotiations and until the final adoption of the GCM, the UN Secretary-General António Guterres played a very important and active role. For years he had acted as the UN High Commissioner for Refugees and his later interventions mirror his enhanced interest in this area. In December 2017, Guterres provided his input to the ongoing negotiations regarding the Global Compact for safe, orderly, and regular migration. Already the title of the report 'Making Migration Work for All', was indicative of his vision, which was further substantiated with strong and clear suggestions to the participants in the consultation and negotiation process. In particular, the Secretary-General, after framing his intervention around four 'fundamental considerations' that should guide joint State action (maximize the benefits of migration for everyone instead of minimizing risks; strengthen the rule of law by committing to international law and human rights; promote a vision of security that reflects both state and human components; and transform migration from an act of desperation to a workable

73 For an overview of the legal normativity of the Compact, see Thomas Gammeltoft-Hansen and others (eds), *What Is a Compact?* (Raoul Wallenberg Institute 2017).

74 In this regard, a series of scholars from various disciplines have highlighted the importance of the GCM as a centralized and multilevel attempt to understand migration, Colleen Thouez, 'Strengthening Migration Governance: The UN as 'Wingman'' (2019) 45 J Eth Migr Stud 1242.

75 Alexander Aleinikoff, 'International Legal Norms on Migration: Substance Without Architecture' in Ryszard Cholewinski, Richard Perruchoud, and Euan MacDonald (eds), *International Migration Law: Developing Paradigms and Key Challenges* (TMC Asser Press 2007) 467-479; Alexander Betts (ed), *Global Migration Governance* (OUP 2011).

76 Vincent Chetail, *International Migration Law* (OUP 2019), speaking of the perils and promises of soft law in the migration front; Anne Peters, 'The Global Compact for Migration: To Sign Or Not to Sign?' (*EJIL: Talk!*, 21 November 2018) <https://www.ejiltalk.org/the-global-compact-for-migration-to-sign-or-not-to-sign/> accessed 30 April 2022.

choice for everyone),[77] encouraged participants to facilitate 'a respectful and realistic debate about migration'. António Gutteres stressed that:

> [W]e must sadly acknowledge that xenophobic political narratives about migration are all too widespread today … [P]olitical leaders must take responsibility for reframing national discourses on the issue, as well as for policy reforms.
>
> [W]e must also show respect for communities that fear they are "losing out" because of migration … Communities blighted by inequality and economic deprivation frequently blame migration for their troubles. While it is necessary to explain why such views are mistaken, it is essential to address the underlying vulnerabilities and fears of all citizens so that we can make migration work.
>
> [W]e should reinforce more realistic policy debates with better data about migration.
>
> [A] final way to promote more respectful discussions regarding migration is to avoid dehumanizing language. Pejorative talk of "illegal immigrants" blocks reasoned discussions about the motives and needs of individuals … We should aim to discuss migrants in terms that respect their dignity and rights, just as we must respect the needs and views of communities affected by migration.[78]

This call for a respectful and realistic debate, apart from the symbolic validation that it conferred upon the entire negotiation process of the GCM, can also be perceived as a phronetic exercise. The Secretary-General denounces in the strongest terms xenophobia and dehumanizing language; urging instead the use of data and evidence. At the same time, he acknowledges the concerns of the receiving communities; inviting the relevant stakeholders to operate beyond complacency and intransigence.

In this sense it can be claimed that Guterres' intervention is also a reflection of critical judgement that assesses both the general and the specific;

77 'Making Migration Work for All: Report of the Secretary-General' (12 December 2017) UN Doc A/72/643 [5]:

> In the light of these four considerations, Member States must act together to protect the human rights of migrants and expand pathways for safe, orderly and regular migration, while safeguarding their borders, laws and the interests of their societies. National authorities are responsible for defining effective responses to migration, but no State can address the issue alone. Individual Governments can set the terms for access to their territory and the treatment of migrants within their borders – subject to international legal obligations – but they cannot unilaterally override the economic, demographic, environmental and other factors that shape migration and will continue to do so, including in ways we do not yet fully anticipate. Migration, as noted in the New York Declaration for Refugees and Migrants (see resolution 71/1), demands global approaches and solutions).

78 Ibid [18].

promotes a progressive agenda but at the same acknowledges its limits; and highlights the need for contextualization, creativity, and responsibility. Similarly to Alston's position, Guterres' language also reflects an imagination that complements his initial phronetic judgement. The invitation to consider the other side can be translated into a responsible warning for both action and constraint. It is a cautious call from an actor who understands what is at stake and tries to provide an umbrella of protection from both hostile conservatives and overzealous activists. It is a call for responsible and phronetic action.

6 Conclusion

The two areas of international criminal justice and forced displacement have triggered a proliferation of excellent scholarship that focuses on their survival or rescue. Yet what is of interest is that the majority of the suggestions operate on an abstract level, i.e. that 'The "Court" should behave differently' or 'States should adopt particular policies'. In contrast, the current contribution adopts a human agency approach and focuses on the importance of phronetic judgement by relevant actors in international legal praxis.[79]

This is not a blueprint exercise, but nevertheless it is becoming more and more obvious that different actors can dramatically change the way legal projects are tested in practice. A phronetic judicial actor might decide to abstain from a particular intervention, while assessing the general and the particular. A phronetic leader may resist a toxic anti-migration climate and justify his/her actions while reiterating his/her commitment to the rule of law and fundamental principles. A phronetic legal adviser may insist on the importance of including a reference to international law, even when the political context shows elements of hostility. A phronetic scholar of international law can make a difference by communicating to the public, using convincing and simple arguments, concepts which are elusive and result into normative misunderstandings.

All of these actors, when they exemplify and practise the art of *phronesis*, must constantly doubt themselves, but at the same time they must know when and how to exercise constructive and not destructive critique. The privilege of ethical critique implies a responsibility not to produce harm or unintended consequences that may jeopardize the entire foundation of those norms we used to consider robust.[80]

In other words, this is not only a question about different judicial or immigration policies. The proposition for critical judgement can instead be translated into a sensibility of resistance or adaptability, that entails both

79 Klabbers (n 27) and his reference to the concept of praxis, citing further Friedrich Kratochwil, *Praxis: On Acting and Knowing* (CUP 2018).

80 In this regard, see Jeremy Waldron, 'Deep Morality and the Laws of War', in Seth Lazar and Helen Frowe (eds), *The Oxford Handbook on Ethics of War* (OUP 2015).

order and change. If one understands international law as a force of both order and change, then this call for phronetic engagement may transform the *crisis* of the field into a critical moment of reassessment – beyond complacency and intransigence and away from dogmatism and cynicism, open to acknowledge its limits and recognize its potential. Speaking of κρίσης rather than crisis might provide another way, less explosive and more modest, for a cathartic change, while oscillating between faith and critique. This other κρίσης of international law might preserve the elements of its innocence, partly as a project of goodness, but it can also facilitate an honest discourse about its weaknesses and darkness, beyond perpetual debates about the existence, or not, of a new crisis. The history of international law and multilateralism is not of a linear nature. Bumpy episodes have defined their development. It is a story of backtracking, resilience, and adaptation. Exercising phronetic judgement is a valuable tool for comprehending the notoriously multifaceted reality, the way it is constructed by different actors in different areas and times in international practice. A finely-tuned, balanced judgement can assess critical episodes and transform them into critical contemplations about the kind of international law we want to have.

5 The Multilateral International Order – Reports of Its Death Are Greatly Exaggerated

Mary E. Footer

1 Introduction

The multilateral international order is in crisis but it is not necessarily in terminal decline. During a visit to London in 1897, the American author, Mark Twain, heard a rumour that he was seriously ill. One American newspaper even went so far as to print prematurely his obituary, leading Twain to state that, 'The report of my death was an exaggeration.'[1] And so it is with the multilateral international order. While it may be in crisis, rumours of its death have similarly been 'exaggerated'. Even if those rumours turn out to be true, in whole or in part, there is still good reason to expect that the multilateral international order may re-assert itself, potentially embracing a new hierarchy and structure that differ from any of its previous or current manifestations.

This contribution reflects on some of the reasons for the decline of multilateralism over the past decade. They range from the retreat from globalisation, following the financial crisis, to the tectonic economic and security shifts between East and West, caused by the rise of China and the demise of the West. Whereas the decline of multilateralism began to materialise in such diverse fields as international criminal law, arms control, and to some extent multilateral trade, we are witnessing the demise of multilateralism in the fields of climate change, cyber security, and more recently, global health in the context of the COVID-19 pandemic.

Contrary to those who are sceptical of the continuance of the multilateral international order, this contribution argues that there are reasons to be optimistic when one considers how things might be done differently. One development is the growing trend towards so-called 'multistakeholderism', which embodies a multi-faceted, transnational and international actor-orientated approach that is capable of dealing pragmatically with problems and crises in the multilateral international order. By harnessing multistakeholder initiative (MSI) processes that are beginning to merge, within and outside the State-centric system of international law, multistakeholderism offers an opportunity for us to re-imagine the multilateral international order for the

1 Cable from Europe to the Associated Press in *The Oxford Dictionary of Quotations* (3rd edn, OUP 1983) 554, no 22.

DOI: 10.4324/9781003312857-7

twenty-first century and to address some of the most urgent problems in the contemporary world.

On the one hand, I analyse what I believe to be the main causes of the crisis in the multilateral international order. One is the process of tectonic economic and security shifts between East and West. Another is the rise of authoritarianism, indifference to, or even disregard for, multilateralism in the international order, and the growing trend towards algorithmic governance, which can lead to forms of totalitarianism. Yet another is the challenge that regionalism poses for multilateral economic cooperation. And, finally, there is the failure of the State-based international community to cooperate effectively on climate change and governance of the oceans.

On the other hand, I argue that governments and intergovernmental institutions should consider how things could be done differently. One avenue could be to examine the rise and role of non-stakeholders in the multilateral international order by means of MSI processes which originate from the sustainable development movement,[2] and other forms of transnational governance. Arguably, the COVID-19 pandemic has paused momentarily the course of global society. The extent to which the international community can deliver COVID vaccines globally, rather than resorting to vaccine nationalism, may demonstrate the usefulness of multistakeholder governance, an issue that lies at the heart of the GAVI COVAX initiative.[3]

A multistakeholder approach, which embraces cooperation between the State, corporations, social and environmental NGOs, and other civil society actors,[4] could be applied more holistically to address equally significant crises, such as climate change. Consequently, the multilateral international order may find itself undergoing change and needing to adapt to new and potentially unfamiliar ways of doing things, with transnational actors working alongside governments and intergovernmental institutions in developing new forms of governance of the rules-based multilateral order.

2 Causes of the crisis in the multilateral international order

Since the Millennium, the neo-liberal economic order,[5] which manifested itself in free trade, the deregulation of financial markets and the retreat from

2 Nancy Vallejo and Pierre Hauselmann, 'Governance and Multi-stakeholder Processes' (International Institute for Sustainable Development 2004) <https://www.iisd.org/system/files/publications/sci_governance.pdf> accessed 30 April 2022 at 3.

3 The Gates Foundation-supported Alliance for Vaccines and Immunisations (GAVI) COVAX is the vaccines pillar of the Access to COVID-19 Tools (ACT) Accelerator. GAVI, together with the Coalition for Epidemic Preparedness Innovations (CEPI) and the World Health Organization (WHO), is leading the COVAX facility, see <www.gavi.org/covax-facility> accessed 30 April 2022.

4 Vallejo and Hauselmann (n 2). See also Chapter 14 in this volume.

5 The neo-liberal economic order of the 1990s encapsulated five notions: privatisation; deregulation; depoliticalisation of economic reform; liberalisation of the

State-centred welfare provision, has begun to unravel. The multilateral international order is best known for the rise of international organisations, which have worked alongside, and together with, States since 1945. More recently, there has been a growing decline in the idea of an international order built on multilateralism, seen by some as 'an architectural form' of organising State relations 'on the basis of generalized principles of conduct'.[6] Some of the reasons for this are as follows.

2.1 Tectonic economic and security shifts between East and West

Undoubtedly the most significant trend in international relations for the past three decades has been the rise of China and the accelerating shift of economic power and strategic defence from the West to the Asia-Pacific region.[7] It means that the Washington-designed post-1945 multilateral international order created by, and mainly for the benefit of, the United States (US), Europe, Japan and their allies, is drawing to a close.[8] Not only has the Bretton Woods[9] model of multilateralism and the World Trade Organization (WTO) multilateral trading system,[10] combined with lending for development and the 'Washington Consensus'[11] come under increasing strain,[12] so too have former alliances for security and defence.

market; and monetarism. See Stephanie L Mudge, 'The State of the Art: What Is Neo-liberalism?' (2008) 6 Socio-Econ Rev 703, 706–7 and 718–19.

6 G John Ikenberry, *A World Safe for Democracy: Liberal Internationalism and the Crises of Global Order* (Yale UP 2020) 35, citing John G Ruggie, 'Multilateralism: The Anatomy of an Institution' in John G Ruggie (ed), *Multilateralism Matters: The Theory and Praxis of an Institutional Form* (Columbia UP 1993) 11.

7 Daniela Schwarzer, 'Europe, the End of the West and Global Power Shifts' (2017) 8:4 Glob Policy 18; John J Mearsheimer, 'Bound to Fail: The Rise and Fall of the Liberal International Order' (2019) 43(4) Int Secur 7; by contrast, see Amitav Acharya, 'Power Shift or Paradigm Shift? China's Rise and Asia's Emerging Security Order' (2014) 58(1) Int Stud Q 158.

8 See Doug Stokes, 'Trump, American Hegemony and the Future of the Liberal International Order' (2018) 94(1) Int Aff 133. For a more nuanced view, see Branko Milanovic, 'The Clash of Capitalisms: The Real Fight for the Global Economy's Future' (2020) 99 For Aff 10, 13.

9 'Proceedings and Documents of the United Nations Monetary and Financial Conference' Bretton Woods, New Hampshire 1–22 July 1944, Vol 1 (1947) at 941.

10 See Peter Van den Bossche and Werner Zdouc, *The Law and Policy of the World Trade Organization: Text, Cases and Materials* (4th edn, CUP 2017) 81–85.

11 For the 'Washington Consensus' in terms of 10 specific policy reforms, including rule of law and good governance prescriptions, for developing countries, see John Williamson (ed), *Latin American Adjustment: How Much Has Happened* (Institute of International Economics 1990) at 5–20.

12 See Kevin Gallagher and Richard Kozul-Wright, 'Crocodile Capitalism and the Multilateral System Crisis' *Financial Times* (10 April 2019) <https://on.ft.com/3vKfPhh> accessed 30 April 2022.

The United Nation (UN) system, with its dysfunctional Security Council, arising from the schism among its five permanent members (P5), has stumbled from one crisis to another. Divergent P5 members' views have obstructed and hindered a robust response to the Libyan and Syrian conflicts, as well as the ethnic cleansing of Myanmar's Rohingya minority.[13] More recently, great power tensions between the US and China have arisen over the status of Hong Kong and China's potential use of military force against Taiwan.[14] Additionally, the US continues to pressure China over its maritime territorial claims in the South China Sea[15] and has stepped up deployment of missile defence systems in East Asia.[16]

China's more muscular approach spells the end of the West's global supremacy in the multilateral international order since the Second World War.[17] The post-1945 rules-based, liberal international order is being eroded and may never return; if it does, it may well take on new and very different dimensions.

2.2 *Authoritarianism and indifference to multilateralism*

The emergence of autocratic leaders, such as Donald Trump, Xi Jinping, Vladimir Putin, or even Boris Johnson, with their insistence on sovereignty and a nationalist view of the world, has been coupled with derision over the usefulness of international organisations, irrespective of the fact that they represent four of the P5 Members of the UN Security Council.[18] Their often undemocratic view of the world polity is unhelpful in seeking a multilateral approach to problem-solving both nationally and internationally.

A blatant disregard for institutional frameworks and the rule of law, particularly when rooted in multilateral treaties, as in the case of the environment

13 Richard Gowan, 'The Price of Order? Multilateralism and the Rule of Law' (*UNU Centre for Policy Research*, 23 September 2018) <https://cpr.unu.edu/publications/articles/the-price-of-order.html> accessed 30 April 2022.

14 Nick Wadhams 'U.S. Eases Limits on Taiwan Contacts as China Tensions Climb' (*Bloomberg*, 9 April 2021) <https://bloom.bg/34a7VCl> accessed 30 April 2022.

15 See 'Territorial Disputes in the South China Sea' (*Council on Foreign Relations, Global Conflict Tracker* as of 30 April 2021) <https://microsites-live-backend.cfr.org/global-conflict-tracker/conflict/territorial-disputes-south-china-sea> accessed 30 April 2022.

16 Christian Alwardt, 'US Missile Defence Efforts and Chinese Reservations in East Asia' (2020) 51(3) Asian Aff 605.

17 Schwarzer (n 7) 19–22. See also Y-H Chu and Y Zheng (eds), *The Decline of the Western-Centric World and the Emerging New Global Order: Contending Views* (Routledge 2021).

18 In the case of the United Kingdom, questions have been raised concerning the country's future as a P5 Member after Brexit, including its pursuit of a 'Global Britain' policy; see Jess Gifkins, Jason Ralph, and Samuel Jarvis, 'Diplomats Reveal Concerns over UK's Waning Influence on UN Security Council' *The Conversation* (26 September 2018) <https://bit.ly/3qcas9i> accessed 30 April 2022.

or human rights, is beginning to have longer-term ripple-down effects in the search for equality among, and within, nation-states. This has even occurred within regional institutional frameworks, such as the European Union (EU). In late 2020, the leaders of Hungary and Poland blocked approval of the EU's Multi-annual Financial Framework, worth just under €1.1 trillion, and the €750 billion COVID-19 recovery fund, known as 'Next Generation EU'. They did so over a clause tying access to those funds to adherence with the rule of law, for which a compromise by EU leaders was subsequently reached.[19]

The stance of some world leaders is beginning to harm the operation of the rules-based, multilateral order, as, for example, with the paralysis of the WTO dispute settlement system due to the dysfunctionality of the Appellate Body.[20] In the case of the recent COVID-19 pandemic, the world has witnessed a decisive lack of collective action in addressing it, particularly on the effective roll-out of a vaccine to address the spread of the pandemic.

More specifically, the leaders of the US, Russia, and China have engaged in acts of harm to the multilateral international order, as described hereinafter. For example, there have been blatant acts of renewed nationalism (in some instances spurred on by populism) and isolationism. Former US President, Donald Trump, in pursuing his America First Policy,[21] demonstrated an abrupt retreat from multilateralism over climate change[22] and human rights,[23] which is being reversed under his successor, President Joe Biden. Following Trump's earlier withdrawal of the US from the Iran nuclear accord,[24] there may be hopes for renewed multilateral cooperation in the future on nuclear disarmament under Joe Biden.

President Vladimir Putin of Russia has repeatedly shown disdain for a rules-based international order, with his annexation of Crimea in 2014[25] and

19 See further European Council meeting (10 and 11 December 2020), Conclusions, Brussels, 11 December 2020 (Council Conclusions, 11/12/20) [2], especially sub-para (c).

20 See WTO, *Annual Report for 2019–2020 Appellate Body* (July 2020) 7–8.

21 Klaus W Larres, 'Trump's Foreign Policy Is Still "America First" – What Does That Mean, Exactly?' *The Conversation* (27 August 2020) <https://bit.ly/3xO6AOD> accessed 30 April 2022.

22 For example, the US withdrawal from the Paris Agreement (entry into force 4 November 2016) 55 ILM 740, which was reversed by President Joe Biden by means of an executive order on his first day in office.

23 Following US withdrawal from the UN Human Rights Council under Donald Trump, the Biden Administration is committed to 'a foreign policy centered on democracy, human rights, and equality' and has signalled that it will re-join the UN Human Rights Council as an observer; see 'US moves to Re-Engage with UN Human Rights Council in Reversal of Trump' *The Guardian* (8 February 2021) <https://bit.ly/3gGSN5m> accessed 30 April 2022.

24 Mark Landler, 'Trump Abandons Iran Nuclear Deal He Long Scorned' *The New York Times* (8 May 2018) <https://nyti.ms/3xxyhuM> accessed 30 April 2022.

25 Steven Pifer, 'Crimea: Six Years After Illegal Annexation' (*Brookings Institution*, 17 March 2020) <https://brook.gs/33D4Qur> accessed 30 April 2022.

the Russian incursions into Eastern Ukraine,[26] both of which arguably have done much to damage Europe's post-Cold War security order,[27] and threaten global security. Various studies on the effect of economic sanctions by the European Union (EU) and the US against Russia, significantly those that seek to target specific individuals and corporate entities (otherwise known as 'smart' sanctions[28]) demonstrate that such sanctions have only been moderately effective[29] or not effective at all.[30] The problem is compounded by the extent to which Heads of State, like Putin, use offshore financial centres and complex corporate structures to evade tax, launder money, and flout the binding force of the sanctions regime,[31] and the paltry attempts undertaken to address such perverse forms of transnational legal ordering.[32]

China under President Xi Jiping presents something of an enigma in the international community. Seeking to position itself as a champion of globalisation and international law, China has been a staunch supporter of the WTO, which it joined in 2001, and it supports action on climate change. And yet it has not been afraid to enter a trade war with the US, by engaging in tit-for-tat tariff escalation, which threatens to undermine the very multilateral trading system it supports.

At the same time, President Xi Jinping has shown a blatant disregard for freedom of expression. Initially restricted to the mainland, the Chinese authorities with reliance on censorship laws have shut down bookstores selling material that is critical of the Chinese Communist Party (CCP). Similarly, the CCP has maintained its censorship of the Internet[33] and its stranglehold on social media in China,[34] which goes beyond the Google debacle of a

26 Taras Kuzio, 'Vladimir Putin's Forever War against Ukraine Continues' (*Atlantic Council*, 20 August 2020) <https://bit.ly/3hjM9nz> accessed 30 April 2022.
27 Pifer (n 25).
28 See David Cortright, George A Lopez, and Elizabeth S Rogers, 'Targeted Financial Sanctions: Smart Sanctions That Do Work' in David Cortright and George A Lopez (eds), *Smart Sanctions: Targeting Economic Statecraft* (Rowman & Littlefield Publishers 2002) 23–40.
29 On the 'mixed record' of economic sanctions by the EU and the US against Russia, see Nigel Gould-Davies, 'Russia, the West and Sanctions' (2020) 62(1) Survival: Global Politics and Strategy 7.
30 L Jan Reid, 'The Effect of American and European Sanctions on Russia' (*SSRN*, 14 May 2019) <https://ssrn.com/abstract=3439207> accessed 30 April 2022.
31 Mary E Footer, 'The Panama Papers, Corporate Transnationalism and the Public International Order' (2017) 6(1) ESIL Reflections 1, especially at 5 and note 14.
32 Terence C Halliday and Gregory Shaffer, 'Transnational Legal Orders' in Terence C Halliday and Gregory Shaffer (eds), *Transnational Legal Orders* (CUP 2015) 11.
33 Milanovic (n 8) at 19; see also Gary King, Jennifer Pan, and Margaret E Roberts, 'How Censorship in China Allows Government Criticism but Silences Collective Expression' (2013) 107(2) Am Political Sci Rev 326.
34 Beina Xu and Eleanora Albert, 'Media Censorship in China' (*Council on Foreign Relations*, 17 February 2017) <www.cfr.org/backgrounder/media-censorship-china> accessed 30 April 2022.

decade ago.[35] More recently, in the name of national security, China has taken the fight against freedom of expression to Hong Kong with its far-reaching and ongoing crackdown against pro-democracy supporters.[36]

2.3 The rise of algorithmic governance

The story of authoritarianism would not be complete without considering the rise of 'algorithmic governance'. A relatively new term, it can be defined as 'a form of social ordering that relies on coordination between actors, is based on rules and incorporates particularly complex computer-based epistemic procedures'.[37] In the evolving digital society an algorithm has the power 'to influence, shape and guide our behaviour and the governance of our societies'.[38]

Algorithmic governance has become particularly common in the automation of social services, regulatory oversight, policing, the justice system, and the military in many countries globally. The COVID-19 pandemic has simply 'supercharged' this trend whereby national authorities have turned to experimental systems for collecting a host of data on individuals' movements and behaviour,[39] such as contact tracing systems or facial recognition technology, claiming they will improve the efficiency of government operations,[40] such as the monitoring of quarantine measures or the issuance of digital vaccination passports by means of a mandatory app.[41]

What has perhaps not been so widely appreciated is the extent to which such automated decision-making (ADM), through the extensive use of algorithms, has the power to exercise a degree of centralised authority over our lives by way of a creeping authoritarianism. It could even lead to totalitarianism if more aspects of ADM are made available to data harvesting,

35 See further Mary E Footer and Andrew R Forbes, 'Changing Ideologies in Trade, Technology and Development: The Challenge of China for International Trade Law' in Sam Muller and others (eds), *The Law of the Future and the Future of Law*. Vol II (Torkel Opsahl Academic EPublisher 2012) 313.

36 Kenneth Roth, 'China Is Desperate to Stop Hong Kong's Pro-Democracy Movement' *Los Angeles Times* (19 August 2020) <https://bit.ly/3hRkPNE> 30 April 2022.

37 Christian Katzenbach and Lena Ulbricht, 'Algorithmic Governance' (2019) 8(4) Internet Pol Rev 1, 2.

38 John Danaher and others, 'Algorithmic Governance: Developing a Research Agenda Through the Power of Collective Intelligence' (2017) 4(2) Big Data and Society 1, 1.

39 Siddharth Venkataramakrishnan, 'Algorithms and the Coronavirus Pandemic' *The Financial Times* (10 January 2021) <https://on.ft.com/3gTwHwK> accessed 30 April 2022.

40 Ibid.

41 An example of such AI surveillance can be found in Poland, see Fabio Chiusi and others (eds), *Automated Decision-Making Systems in the COVID-19 Pandemic: A European Perspective*, Special Issue of the Automating Society Report 2020 (1 September 2020) <https://algorithmwatch.org/automating-society-2020-covid19> accessed 30 April 2022, 26–27.

potentially leading States and/or corporations to control and change human relations and interactions – two key prerequisites for a totalitarian transition.[42]

Not surprisingly, EU institutions and the World Health Organization (WHO),[43] among others, have called on States in the first instance to ensure that surveillance technologies do not violate human rights. They have even gone so far as to issue guidelines that include criteria for surveillance technologies, such as voluntary participation, non-discrimination, and compliance with data protection requirements.[44] If such guidelines are not respected, then many States in the international order may find themselves operating closer to the China model, which makes 'full use of the digital surveillance infrastructure … to deliver ADM solutions that strongly prioritise public health and safety concerns over individual rights'.[45]

2.4 Regional challenges to multilateral economic cooperation

Lately the multilateral economic order has come under strain in terms of cooperation, or the lack of it, due in part to the rise of regionalism. Over a 25-year period from 1990–2015, the number of regional trade agreements has roughly quadrupled from 70 to 270.[46] Significant too, is the increase in so-called 'megaregional' trade agreements that span clusters of countries in one or more geographic regions.

One example is the Japanese and western countries-backed Comprehensive and Progressive Agreement for a Trans-Pacific Partnership (CPTPP).[47] This ambitious megaregional trade agreement covers nearly 500 million people and about 13.3 per cent of global GDP. Another is the Chinese-supported Regional Comprehensive Economic Partnership (RCEP).[48] It forms the world's largest

42 H Akın Ünver, 'Artificial Intelligence, Authoritarianism and the Future of Political Systems' Centre for Economics and Foreign Policy Studies 2018 at 6.
43 Constitution of World Health Organization (entry into force 7 April 1948) 14 UNTS 185.
44 Chiusi and others (n 41) 7–9.
45 Ibid 5.
46 'Why Everyone Is So Keen to Agree New Trade Deals' *The Economist* (6 October 2015) <https://econ.st/3xCAtkS> accessed 30 April 2022.
47 Comprehensive and Progressive Agreement for the Trans-Pacific Partnership between Australia, Brunei Darussalam, Canada, Chile, Japan, Malaysia, Mexico, Peru, New Zealand, Singapore, and Vietnam, 8 March 2018, in force for Australia, Canada, Japan, Mexico, New Zealand, Singapore on 30 December 2018, and between Canada and Vietnam on 14 January 2019. For the text, see <https://bit.ly/3i0XVUn> accessed 30 April 2022.
48 The RCEP was signed in Hanoi on 15 November 2020 by Australia, China, Japan, New Zealand and South Korea, and the 10 members of the Association of South East Asian Nations (ASEAN) – Brunei Darussalam, Cambodia, Indonesia, Laos PDR, Malaysia, Myanmar (Burma), the Philippines, Singapore, Thailand, and Viet Nam. It will come into force when at least six ASEAN and three non-ASEAN signatories have ratified it. For the text, see <https://bit.ly/3zSlyVA> accessed 30 April 2022.

regional trading bloc, covering some 2.2 billion people, and approximately 30 per cent of global GDP. Seen by some as a 'shallow agreement' in terms of tariff reductions, and lacking strong rules to cover State-owned enterprises (SOEs), labour rights, and environmental protection,[49] the RCEP could reduce Western influence in Asia. In particular, if it were to succeed in become a platform for developing trade rules in the absence of a reformed multilateral trading system.[50]

The China-EU Comprehensive Agreement on Investment (CAI)[51] is another geopolitically significant but hotly contested agreement that is intended to address bilaterally major asymmetries over the past 20 years in flows of East-West foreign direct investment (FDI).[52] The CAI is intended to lay down clear level-playing field obligations for Chinese State-owned enterprises investing in Europe in exchange for fairer treatment and more sectoral access for EU companies in the Chinese market. The proposed CAI also includes important commitments on implementation of the Paris Agreement, and labour standards, to be evidenced by China's adherence to a series of International Labour Organization (ILO) conventions.[53]

Even so, when it comes to the CAI, the tide may be turning away from regionalism, given EU concerns about China's human rights abuses, especially its incarceration and forced labour among millions of Uighurs in the north-west province of Xingjing,[54] and its increasing suppression of the pro-democracy movement in Hong Kong.[55] On 4 May 2021, European Commission Vice-President, Valdis Dombrovskis, announced that current relations between Brussels and Beijing, following EU sanctions over China's treatment of its Uighur population, were not conducive to ratification of the CAI.[56]

49 Tobias Sytsma, 'RCEP Forms the World's Largest Trading Bloc. What Does This Mean for Global Trade?' (*The Rand Blog*, 9 December 2020) <www.rand.org/blog/2020/rcep-forms-the-worlds-largest-tradomng-bloc-what-does.html> accessed 30 April 2022.

50 Ibid.

51 Agreement on the China-EU Comprehensive Agreement on Investment was reached 30 December 2020 but has yet to be signed, ratified, and concluded.

52 'Press Release: Key Elements of the EU-China Comprehensive Agreement on Investment' (European Commission, 30 December 2020) <https://bit.ly/3zKagSY> accessed 30 April 2022.

53 Constitution of the International Labour Organization (entry into force 28 June 1919). For the eight key conventions and the ILO Declaration on Fundamental Principles and Rights at Work and its Follow-up of 1998, see *The International Organization's Fundamental Conventions* (Geneva 2003).

54 See Zsuzsa Ferenczy, 'Will the EU-China Investment Agreement Survive Parliament's Scrutiny?' *The Diplomat* (27 January 2021) <https://bit.ly/3iWed1g> accessed 30 April 2022.

55 Austin Ramzy, 'How the Dream of Hong Kong Democracy Was Dimmed' *The New York Times* (11 November 2020) <https://nyti.ms/3gLzo35> accessed 30 April 2022.

56 Vincent Ni, 'EU Efforts to Ratify China Investment Deal "Suspended" After Sanctions' *The Guardian* (4 May 2021) <https://bit.ly/3iVfSDX> accessed 30 April 2022.

The CAI follows China's earlier foray into the financing of infrastructure development projects through its ambitious Belt and Road Initiative (BRI),[57] which aims at revitalising the old Silk Road, territorial and maritime routes of extra-territorial sovereignty, and which Japan has subsequently agreed to help finance.[58] A final example of a mega-regional is the Japan-EU Partnership Agreement (JEEPA)[59] that represents the 'world's largest open economic zone'.[60] It covers some 600 million people and roughly 20% of global GDP.

As a result, there is growing pressure on the WTO multilateral trading system to accommodate a broader range of regional arrangements, including megaregionals. There are also growing calls for WTO reform.[61] The reasons are not hard to discern. The WTO, despite being the supreme body to oversee the multilateral trading system, including enforcing WTO disciplines through a mandatory dispute settlement process, has shown itself to be increasingly ineffective.

First, it has become less successful in dealing with tit-for-tat trade disputes, many of which are centred on rules designed to ensure fair trade, i.e. subsidies, antidumping, and safeguards.[62] It has also not been especially adept at dealing with doubtful invocations of Article XXI of the General Agreement on Tariffs and Trade[63] for non-essential security interests.[64]

57 China's BRI, previously known as 'One Belt, One Road', is a vast infrastructure development project that seeks to connect Asia with Africa and Europe via land and maritime networks. See OECD, 'OECD Business and Finance Outlook 2018: China's Belt and Road Initiative in the Global Trade, Investment and Finance Landscape' 2018 <https://bit.ly/3KYEUwu> accessed 30 April 2022.

58 In June 2017, Japan reversed its previous policy on the BRI when it announced that it would 'provide cooperation and financial backing', see Shutaro Sano, 'Japan Buckles Up to join China's Belt and Road' (*Australian Institute for International Affairs*, 23 February 2018) <https://bit.ly/3w47rK8> accessed 30 April 2022.

59 Agreement between Japan and the European Union for an Economic Partnership (JEEPA) [2018] OJ L 330/3.

60 Emil Kirchner, 'EU-Japan Trade Deal Comes into Force to Create World's Biggest Trade Zone' *The Conversation* (30 December 2019) <https://bit.ly/3vS8w7n> accessed 30 April 2022.

61 A proposal for five principles for a new multilateralism, which could form the basis for WTO reform, can be found in Kevin P Gallagher and Richard Kozul-Wright, *A New Multilateralism for Shared Prosperity: Geneva Principles for a New Green Deal* Boston University Global Development Policy Center/UNCTAD 2019 2.

62 See Chad P Brown and Melina Kolb, 'Trump's Trade War Timeline: An Up-to-Date Guide' (*Peterson Institute for International Economics*, 30 April 2021) <www.piie.com/sites/default/files/documents/trump-trade-war-timeline.pdf> accessed 30 April 2022.

63 General Agreement on Tariffs and Trade 1994, Annex 1 of the WTO Agreement (entry into force 1 January 1995) 1867 UNTS 190.

64 Mona Pinchis-Paulsen, 'Trade Multilateralism and U.S. National Security: The Making of the GATT Security Exception' (2020) 41(1) Mich J Intl Law 109.

Second, the WTO Members collectively have been unable to face up to the bullying tactics of the US which, in accordance with the consensus principle, has consistently failed to approve the nomination of new members to the Appellate Body. In particular, the US has been allowed to get away with its criticism of the work and the working procedures of the Appellate Body.[65]

In a different and equally concerning move, South Africa and India have led a number of WTO developing countries and least-developed countries in seeking a temporary waiver on intellectual property rights on COVID-19-related medicines and technologies.[66] The US, supported by the UK, the EU, Canada, Australia, Japan, Switzerland, Norway, and Brazil – all WTO Members with corporate interests in the pharmaceutical industry – finally joined the consensus to approve the aforementioned waiver for an initial five-year period.[67] At the WTO 12th Ministerial Conference (MC12) in June, 2022, a temporary time-bound waiver was reached.

2.5 Climate change

Some of the most significant challenges for the multilateral international order lie in the realms of climate change and governance of the oceans. Global warming is an apocalyptic crisis in the making. In particular, human-driven or anthropogenic climate change is the most significant issue of our generation. And yet at the beginning of the third decade of the twenty-first century there is significantly less enthusiasm for acting on climate change when compared to dealing with the COVID-19 pandemic. Why is this so?

While invisible, COVID-19 is seen by most people as presenting a 'clear and present danger' to their lives and livelihoods. The basic human instinct of survival calls for individual and collective measures to protect ourselves.[68] Governments across the globe have acted, often under emergency powers, in taking scientific-led decisions to contain the spread of the virus. National lockdowns necessarily entail personal sacrifices and limit individual freedoms until the take-up of vaccination against COVID-19 and its variants has been widely distributed among the general population. Just like the COVID-19

65 Working Procedures for Appellate Review (16 August 2010) WT/AB/WP/6, Rule 15. For an overview of the US position and its ramifications, see Geraldo Vidigal, 'Living Without the Appellate Body: Multilateral, Bilateral and Plurilateral Solutions to the WTO Dispute Settlement Crisis' (2019) 20 JWIT 862, 864.

66 On 20 November 2020, the WTO TRIPS Council was convened in an informal, virtual meeting to discuss a proposal (IP/C/W/669), co-sponsored by Eswatini, India, Kenya, and South Africa, for a waiver from certain provisions of the TRIPS Agreement for the prevention, containment, and treatment of COVID-19.

67 See Gallagher and Kozul-Wright (n 12) for the predatory form of rent-seeking behaviour by corporate actors, supported by State-backed treaty systems, which they describe as 'crocodile capitalism'.

68 Robert Hamwey and Tim Sullivan, 'Coronavirus Vaccine Won't Protect Us Against Climate Change' (*UNCTAD*, 5 June 2020) <https://bit.ly/3wIw7bJ> accessed 30 April 2022.

pandemic, the climate crisis is also an existential threat. Greenhouse gases are invisible, but they remain ever present in our natural surroundings. However, unlike the COVID-19 pandemic, there is no quick fix for climate change,[69] nor seemingly is there an overriding desire for collective action.

The pandemic has demonstrated that international cooperation is possible. Teams of scientists, supported by global leaders, have worked across national and regional boundaries in an accelerated time frame to develop the Pfizer-BioNTech, Oxford Astra Zeneca, and Moderna vaccines[70] to address the threat that COVID-19 poses to our collective well-being. And yet, those same global leaders appear less determined in fighting climate change. The same lack of urgency does not exist in the case of climate change; instead, essential action needed to curb it, is being postponed.[71] Even so, climate change, like COVID-19, will lead to extensive loss of life, unemployment, and substantial decline in GDP across the globe. Whereas vaccines against COVID-19 will eventually build (herd) immunity, possibly leading to it becoming another form of 'seasonal flu', the impacts of climate change will persist and last longer unless there is national and global solidarity to tackle it.

There are several factors to consider when looking at the crisis that climate change has engendered in the multilateral international order. One is the failure of the international community to treat climate change as a public good and to act collectively to regulate the reduction of CO_2 emissions. Even so, there has been a rise in public interest litigation nationally, beginning with the crowdfunded *Urgenda Foundation* case[72] in the Netherlands. In 2019, the Dutch Supreme Court held that 'the State [was] acting unlawfully … by failing to pursue a more ambitious reduction as of end-2020 and that [it] should reduce emissions by at least 25% by end-2020'. Effectively, the Court determined that a State has a positive responsibility to prevent climate change even if 'it is caused by a multiplicity of other actors who share responsibility for its harmful effects'.[73]

While a step in the right direction, public interest litigation is not enough. There needs to be a collective response from governments to act multilaterally to '[avert] the risk of global climate change' as a global public good,[74] i.e. as something that is available to all members of society.

69 Ibid.

70 There have been parallel COVID-19 vaccines developed and deployed by Russia (Sputnik V) and China (SinoVac) during 2020 and 2021.

71 The Conference of the Parties 26 of the UN Climate Change Conference took place 18 months later than originally scheduled, in Glasgow, from 1 to 12 November 2021.

72 *State of the Netherlands v Urgenda Foundation* ECLI:NL:HR:2019:2007, Judgment, Sup Ct Neth 20 December 2019; see further Maiko Meguro, 'State of the Netherlands v Urgenda Foundation' (2020) 114(4) AJIL 729.

73 Andre Nolkaemper and Laura Burgers, 'A New Classic in Climate Change Litigation: The Dutch Supreme Court Decision in the Urgenda Case' (*EJIL: Talk!*, 6 January 2020) <https://bit.ly/3hnpEOH> accessed 30 April 2022.

74 Inge Kaul and others, 'Why Do Global Public Goods Matter Today?' in Inge Kaul (ed), *Providing Global Public Goods* (OUP 2003) 2.

Second, consequential changes in weather patterns and sea level rise mean that a major aim of the Paris Agreement to '[H]old the increase in global average temperature to well below 2°C above pre-industrial levels and to pursue efforts to limit the temperature increase to 1.5°C above pre-industrial levels',[75] is already looking increasingly unrealistic. Many countries are not evenly sensitised or capable of responding to the emerging crisis of climate change in the multilateral international order.

Third, there is the realisation that climate change is re-shaping geopolitics,[76] which could lead to wider political instability. Some States stand to lose hugely from the anticipated shift away from global oil and gas consumption, such as Russia, Saudi Arabia, and Qatar.[77] Others stand to gain from speed and efficiency in moving to sources of renewable energy (chiefly solar and wind power), such as Chile, India, and the US.[78]

2.6 Governance of the oceans

Another area of environmental concern in the multilateral international order is the complex issue of the conservation and sustainable use of the oceans' resources. Despite the UN Convention on the Law of the Sea (UNCLOS),[79] the ocean governance regime is highly fragmented, mainly because it is organised by sector, e.g. shipping, fishing, and marine pollution. Admittedly, UNCLOS and other specific, multilateral conventions call upon States to safeguard fish stocks and to limit marine pollution.

Meanwhile, the International Seabed Authority (ISA)[80] is working multilaterally to draft a workable deep seabed mining code. Currently, the ISA has issued 30 commercial licences to prospect for – but not exploit – seabed minerals. On exploitation, the draft ISA Mining Code,[81] which will belatedly set rules for deep-sea resources by private companies, is still under negotiation. Even so, deep seabed mining is already considered to have caused irrevocable damage to marine ecosystems and a loss of unique species.[82]

75 See Paris Agreement, Article 2(a).

76 Global Commission on the Geopolitics of Energy Transformation, *A New World: The Geopolitics of the Energy Transformation* (International Renewable Energy Agency 2019) <https://bit.ly/3w49wWs> accessed 30 April 2022.

77 Ibid 29–30.

78 Ibid 18.

79 United Nations Convention on the Law of the Sea (entry into force 16 November 1984) 1833 UNTS 397.

80 Ibid, Article 156 – for the establishment of the ISA. In accordance with paragraph (2) of Article 15 UNCLOS, all States Parties to UNCLOS are *ipso facto* members of the ISA.

81 The 'Mining Code', which is only partially complete, refers to the comprehensive set of rules, regulations, and procedures issued by the ISA to regulate prospecting, exploration, and exploitation of marine minerals in the international seabed area.

82 Luc Cuyvers and others, *Deep Seabed Mining: A Rising Environmental Challenge* (IUCN and Gallifrey Foundation 2018) 88.

In terms of marine biodiversity, States are presently negotiating a UN treaty to ensure 'conservation and sustainable use of marine biodiversity in areas beyond national jurisdiction' (ABNJ).[83] Once concluded, a regime for conservation and sustainable use of marine diversity convention would potentially fill the regulatory gap that currently exists whereby, under the UNCLOS, coastal States have exclusive rights over the exclusive economic zone (EEZ) up to 200 nautical miles from their coasts. Beyond the EEZ, the situation is unclear. Early in 2021, government representatives were due to meet, under the auspices of the UN Convention on Biological Diversity (CBD)[84] to set new, voluntary goals for marine protected areas in accordance with the Aichi Biodiversity Targets.[85]

Will these twin measures under two separate but related multilateral regimes be enough to redress the imbalances in ocean governance? Both anticipate extensive cooperation between States parties to the underlying multilateral conventions when participation in multilateral fora, especially multilateral treaty making, is waning. A possible answer may lie in using multistakeholderism to address complex resource management and conservation issues under such multilateral regimes, as explained in Section 3.

3 Doing things differently: the turn to multistakeholderism

There is a growing trend towards doing things differently in the multilateral international order. It could mean multilateralism is turned on its head, rendered obsolete, or even transformed. One reason why reports of the death of the multilateral international order may be exaggerated is that States and non-state actors alike are beginning more widely to embrace 'multistakeholderism', which holds out the possibility for multilateralism to adapt to new forms of governance.

Multistakeholderism – often referred to as multistakeholder initiatives or MSIs – denotes a governance structure that seeks to bring so-called 'stakeholders' together to participate in dialogue, decision-making, and the implementation of solutions to common problems or goals. MSIs represent a multifaceted, transnational and international actor-orientated, collective approach to governance, which has its origins in the domain of transnational private

83 Negotiations have commenced, based on UN General Assembly (UNGA) Res 72/249 International legally binding instrument under the United Nations Convention on the Law of the Sea on the conservation and sustainable use of marine biological diversity of areas beyond national jurisdiction (24 December 2017) UN Doc A/RES/72/249.

84 Convention on Biological Diversity (entry into force 29 December 1993) 1760 UNTS 69.

85 In 2010, the Parties to the CBD adopted the Strategic Plan for Biodiversity 2011–2020, which included the 20 Aichi Biodiversity Targets (Aichi Targets). Target 11 aimed broadly for at least 17 per cent of terrestrial and inland water, and 10 per cent of coastal and marine areas, to be more effectively conserved and protected.

governance.[86] Multistakeholderism also provides an opportunity for a 'networked multilateralism that links global and regional institutions' and delivers a more inclusive multilateralism that 'engages businesses, cities, universities and movements'.[87]

The rise of multistakeholderism can be traced back to the 1970s when the number of multinational corporations (MNCs) on the world stage grew exponentially but so too did their power to influence events. And yet, attempts to regulate the activities of MNCs and to make them more responsible for *inter alia* sustainable development and human rights have remained slow and painful.[88] Concurrently with the expansion of MNC activity across the globe, civil society organisations (CSOs) have gained political strength and pushed for increased participation in global governance. In particular, CSO input into key UN summits[89] such as the 1992 Rio Earth Summit[90] and the Fourth World Conference on Women in Beijing in 2000[91] saw the consolidation of CSOs, as stakeholders, in multilateral fora.

The spread of corporatism both nationally and globally combined with the emergence of CSOs, keen to curtail the harmful impacts of globalisation, has set the stage for multistakeholderism. As MNCs have increasingly wielded their power and consistently sought to block regulation and advance their influence within national global governance forums, MSI governance, which combines some form of legitimation with a vague undefined form of accountability, has served their interests.[92]

Similarly, there have been various attempts to expand the scope and reach of global civil society to tackle global problems through multilateral

86 Philip Schleifer, 'Varieties of Multi-Stakeholder Governance: Selecting Legitimation Strategies in Transnational Sustainability Politics' (2019) 16(1) Globalizations 50, 52 *et seq.*

87 UN Secretary-General António Guterres, cited in Anne-Marie Slaughter and Gordon LaForge, 'Opening Up the Order: A More Inclusive International System' (2021) 100(2) For Aff 154, 155.

88 Examples of the regulation of MNCs in the international order include: the OECD Guidelines for Multinational Enterprises, adopted 21 June 1976, updated on 27 June 2000 and 25 May 2011 <http://mneguidelines.oecd.org/text/>; the UN Global Compact, established by former UN Secretary-General, Kofi Annan in 1999 <www.unglobalcompact.org/> both accessed 30 April 2022; Human Rights Council, 'UN Guiding Principles on Business & Human Rights: Implementing the Protect, Respect and Remedy Framework' (21 March 2011) UN Doc A/HRC/17/31.

89 Nick Buxton, *Multistakeholderism: A Critical Look* Workshop Report (Transnational Institute, October 2019) <https://bit.ly/2Ryrthi> accessed 30 April 2022 at 4.

90 UN Conference on Environment and Development 1992 (Rio Conference UN Doc A/CONF.151/26 (vol I)) 31 ILM 874.

91 Fourth World Conference on Women, Beijing Declaration and Platform of Action (15 September 1995) UN Doc A/CONF.177/20 (1995) and A/CONF.177/20/Add.1 (1995).

92 Buxton (n 89) 5.

solutions. One example is the UN-sponsored 'People-Centred Multilateralism: Call to Action in 2018',[93] which was in part driven by the 2030 Agenda for Sustainable Development and its elaboration of 17 Sustainable Development Goals (SDGs).[94] Two goals under SDG17 recognise multistakeholder partnerships, with SDG17.17 going as far as to state the importance of civil society in promoting effective MSIs.[95] On the same theme, the Call to Action 2018 envisages the expanded role of civil society partnerships, alongside MNCs and UN Members in order to address transnational problems such as climate change.[96] Significantly, it aims to do so by developing a form of multilateralism that shares responsibility and accountability among all stakeholders, hence the move to an MSI model.[97]

It is important to note that where multistakeholderism differs from multilateralism is that 'multistakeholder global governance is based on a different allocation of power and a different conception of democracy'.[98] As Harris Gleckman explains:

> [I]n multilateralism, governments, as representative of their citizens, take the final decisions on global issues and direct international organizations to implement these decisions. This is in sharp contrast to multistakeholderism, where "stakeholders" become the central actors. Decision-making and the implementation of these global decisions are often disconnected from the inter-governmental sphere.[99]

Even so, the idea of multistakeholderism is not new in the multilateral international order, especially for some intergovernmental organisations like the UN Food and Agricultural Organization (FAO).[100] Since 2009, the reformed FAO Committee on Food Security (CFS)[101] has expanded its scope and outreach by adopting an MSI model. Thus, the CFS includes *inter alia*

93 'People-Centred Multilateralism: Call to Action – We the Peoples … Together Finding Global Solutions for Global Problems', 67th UN Department of Public Information (DPI) NGO Conference (22–23 August 2018).

94 UNGA Res 70/01 'Transforming Our World: the 2030 Agenda for Sustainable Development' (25 September 2015) UN Doc A/RES/70/1, which includes the 17 Sustainable Development Goals.

95 Ibid, SDG 17.17 seeks to '[E]ncourage and promote effective public, public-private and civil society partnerships, building on the experience and resourcing strategies of partnerships.'

96 DPI/NGO (n 93), opening paragraph.

97 Ibid (under the heading 'A Time to Join with Civil Society').

98 Harris Gleckman, *Multistakeholder Governance and Democracy: A Global Challenge* (Routledge 2018) xiii.

99 Ibid.

100 Constitution of the United Nations Food and Agriculture Organisation (entry into force 4 January 1949) 120 UNTS 13.

101 The Committee on World Food Security was established on 26 November 1975 at the 18th Session of the FAO Conference, Res 21/75, under Article III, para 9 of the FAO Constitution, as a committee of the FAO Council.

participants from the FAO, the World Food Programme[102] and the International Fund for Agricultural Development,[103] as well as other international representatives, all of whom, individually or through their institutions, have a link to the human right to food, e.g. the Special Rapporteur on the Right to Food,[104] the Office of the UNHCR,[105] WHO, UNICEF,[106] and UNDP.[107]

As an MSI, the CFS reaches out to other intergovernmental organisations that do not have a specific link to human rights or food security, such as the IMF, the World Bank, and the WTO. The CFS also embraces civil society and NGOs, private sector associations and private philanthropic foundations.[108] The broadening of the CFS' participatory base means that it has become 'the foremost inclusive international and intergovernmental platform for stakeholders'[109] to address a wider range of subject matter, including food security, nutrition, food sovereignty, and the right to food more holistically.[110] Multistakeholderism in international governance has broadened to encompass a whole range of issues from ocean governance,[111] to governance of the global Internet.[112]

Governance of the maritime commons, which lies at the heart of the proposed multilateral convention on the conservation and sustainable use of marine biological diversity of ABNJ, could benefit from an MSI model for implementation. The International Union for Conservation of Nature (IUCN), which provides advice to environmental conventions, such as the CBD, has proposed a strong institutional structure for the ABNJ that encompasses a multistakeholder approach. The ABNJ should have a global decision-making body that is participatory, in the broader MSI sense of the

102 World Food Programme, permanent establishment pursuant to UNGA Res 1714 (XVI) (19 December 1961).

103 Agreement establishing the International Fund for Agricultural Development (entry into force 30 November 1977) 1059 UNTS 191.

104 The mandate of the Special Rapporteur on the right to food was established by the former UN Commission on Human Rights, Res 2000/10 The right to food (17 April 2000) E/CN.4/RES/2000/10.

105 The United Nations High Commissioner for Refugees was founded on 14 December 1950 as the UN agency to lead and coordinate international action to protect refugees and resolve refugee problems worldwide. Its work extends to supporting the link between health and nutrition and food security.

106 The United Nations Children's Fund (UNICEF) was established by UNGA Res A/RES/57(I) (11 December 1946).

107 The United Nations Development Programme (UNDP) was established by UNGA Res A/RES/2029(XX) (22 November 1965).

108 Hand Page, *Global Governance and Food Security as Global Public Good* (Center on International Cooperation, New York University, August 2013) 12.

109 Gleckman (n 98) 13.

110 Mary E Footer, 'Trade-Related Aspects of International Food Security and the Developing World' (2014) 6(2) TL&D 288, 328.

111 L B Crowder and others, 'Resolving Mismatches in U.S. Ocean Governance' (2006) 313(4) Science 617.

112 Slavka Antonova, '"Capacity-Building" in Global Internet Governance: The Long-Term Outcomes of "Multistakeholderism"' (2011) 5 Regul Gov 425.

word, with meetings open to non-Parties, relevant inter-governmental organisations, NGOs, and other stakeholders in an observer capacity. Likewise, existing regional and sectoral organisations, and civil society, should be allowed to provide input in the decision-making process.[113]

MSIs have already entered the realm of global public health with the establishment in April, 2020 of the Covid Vaccine Access (COVAX) Facility,[114] which is one of three pillars of the Access to COVID-19 Tools (ACT) Accelerator, launched by the WHO, the European Commission, and France in response to the Corona virus pandemic. The COVAX Facility is led by the Gates Foundation-supported GAVI, which oversees an MSI that counts donor governments, pharmaceutical companies, CSOs and the Coalition for Epidemic Preparedness Innovations (CEPI),[115] together with the WHO, UNICEF, and the World Bank, among its stakeholders. Its overarching aim is to support the research, development, and manufacture of a wide range of COVID-19 vaccine candidates, to negotiate their pricing and to support their global supply through global participation and pooled demand, especially to developing countries.

Aside from being a global risk-sharing mechanism for pooled procurement and equitable distribution of COVID-19 vaccines within the COVAX Facility, there is an entirely separate funding mechanism. This is the COVAX Advance Market Commitment, which is designed to support access to COVID-19 vaccines for developing country economies and is funded mainly through Official Development Assistance (ODA),[116] together with contributions from the private sector and philanthropy.

Unlike some other MSIs that are designed to address ongoing problems in the international order relating to food security or the allocation of natural resources, the COVAX Facility has been initiated to address a clear and present danger of the Corona virus to people's lives and livelihoods. Ann-Marie Slaughter and Gordon LaForge argue that the COVAX Facility could serve as a prototype of an issue-specific international organisation that is a problem-solving, networked 'hub' in the global order.[117] But could an MSI approach be used to tackle climate change, which presents a more diffuse and future danger to international society? Before answering the question, it is worth reflecting on some of the advantages and disadvantages of

113 See 'Suggestion 5: Operation of a Global Decision-Making Body', on the IUCN website <https://bit.ly/3gNNKjJ> accessed 30 April 2022.

114 See for further details, COVAX Facility (n 3).

115 CEPI is an Oslo-headquartered global partnership, which was launched in 2017, to develop vaccines to stop future epidemics <https://cepi.net/> accessed 30 April 2022.

116 For the most recent list of the official Donor Assistance Countries and territories that are eligible to receive official development assistance, see ODA webpage <https://bit.ly/3yByUEP> accessed 30 April 2022.

117 Slaughter and LaForge (n 87) consider the COVAX Facility to be a prototype for an issue-specific type of organisation, which they characterise as a problem-solving, networked 'hub' in the global order.

multistakeholderism. In terms of advantages, MSI's can deal with the multi-faceted, cross-cutting issues that engage a variety of State and non-state actors, sometimes at different governance levels, i.e. international, national/regional, and local. Where the latter applies, then the MSI is potentially organised as a multi-level governance structure.[118] Multistakeholderism can allow a problem to be thrashed out and for solutions to be proposed from a variety of different stakeholders, acting both jointly and severally. It can be particularly useful in large-scale policy and programmatic exercises, especially in the equitable sharing of resources.

Climate change could be a candidate for an MSI approach, as the International Climate Governance Coalition (ICGC)[119] believes. In a 2018 communiqué, the ICGC stressed the importance of both a multi-level and a multistakeholder approach to address climate change adaptation and mitigation.[120] It anticipates that at the macro-level 'the Parties' current pledges will not be sufficient to achieve the agreed goals'. Instead, at the micro-level, transformative action is needed by 'civil society and social movements, business and trade unions … in coordination with subnational governments, cities and municipalities', particularly in helping governments to reach their targets under their respective nationally determined contributions (NDCs).[121]

However, there are also disadvantages to multistakeholderism. The use of an MSI does not necessarily imply that decisions will be reached faster. If anything, they may be slower and may prove more difficult to implement in the long run, if at all. MSIs are often highly technocratic but that does not necessarily mean that the technical knowledge is sufficient, as was proven in the case of the CFS when it was discovered that it lacked the relevant technical knowledge about food security in the reformed Committee.[122] A further disadvantage can be that the MSI is grappling with a problem in the multilateral international order, the sheer enormity of which overwhelms it.

This could be the fate of multistakeholderism in dealing with climate change. While calling on 'the UNFCCC regulatory framework [to] acknowledge this form of bottom-up governance by formally recognising its role in

118 For a typology of multi-level governance, see Gary Marks and Liesbet Hooghe 'Contrasting Visions of Multi-level Governance' in Ian Bache and Matthew Flinders (eds), *Multi-level Governance* (OUP 2004) 15–30.

119 The International Coalition on Multi-level and Multi-stakeholder Climate Governance for the Paris Agreement (International Climate Governance Coalition) is co-managed by the European Economic and Social Committee, the European Committee of the Regions, Comité 21, OECD, European Network for Community-Led Initiatives on Climate Change and Sustainability (ECOLISE) and International Council for Local Environmental Initiatives (ICLEIs).

120 ICGC, 'Key Arguments Supporting a Multi-Level and Multi-Stakeholder Approach to Climate Change Adaptation and Mitigation' (*ICGC Communiqué* 2018) <https://www.climate-chance.org/wp-content/uploads/2018/11/why-is-a-multi-stakeholder-approach-to-climate-change-more-relevant.pdf> accessed 30 April 2022.

121 Ibid.

122 See Footer (n 110) 328.

the decision-making process regarding climate change',[123] it is unclear how such a horizontally and vertically integrated MSI can be achieved.

There may also be significant difficulties in holding MSIs to account. All too often, the participation of different stakeholders in a dialogue, a decision-making process or the implementation of an MSI initiative is considered sufficient evidence of its accountability.[124] Even so, as the case of the reformed CFS shows, the MSI model may still face challenges especially when it comes to the implementation and monitoring of the Committee's decisions, which have been faulted by CSOs for failing to provide greater policy coherence around food security.[125] The same could hold true in the field of climate change unless there is universal acceptance of the Paris Agreement targets and bolder action taken to meet them under the individual country NDCs.

The structure and composition of any MSI also beg the question as to the power of the different stakeholders, particularly concerning the participation of corporate actors, such as pharmaceutical companies in the COVAX Facility. The same charge could be levelled at the private sector when implementing the Paris Agreement, especially given the surge of business interest in the green economy. And yet China's reaction should not be dismissed lightly. Multistakeholderism in the multinational international order is driven by transnational private actors but 'China puts more emphasis on State-owned companies and consider the State as the only legitimate stakeholder'.[126]

Finally, CSOs' involvement in a particular MSI may not fully reflect the constituencies it represents (see the Civil Society and Indigenous Peoples' Mechanism or CSM, which has re-grouped and reformed to address participation in the CFS at the FAO). Often the case of civil society representation in an MSI is limited in weight and involvement.[127] And there is no reason to assume that it would be any different when it comes to climate change under the UNFCC, given the range and diversity of CSOs at the local, national, regional, and international level.

4 Conclusion

There are some conclusions to be drawn from the foregoing analysis of the potential demise of the multilateral international order. One is that there continues to be a decline in multilateralism in the international order for a number of reasons, which range from the retreat by States from globalisation,

123 *ICGC Communiqué* 2018 (n 120) 2.

124 For an analysis of the legitimation strategies employed by three MSIs in the field of agricultural commodity roundtables, see Schleifer (n 86) 55–57.

125 Secretariat of the Civil Society and Indigenous Peoples' Mechanism for relations with the UN Committee on World Food Security, Annual Report, August 2014–August 2015 <http://www.csm4cfs.org/wp-content/uploads/2016/04/En-CSM_Annual-BR.pdf> accessed 30 April 2022 at 7–8; Footer (n 110) 355.

126 Buxton and others (n 89) 13 (under the heading 'Future of Multistakeholderism').

127 Ibid 7 *et seq* (under the heading 'Accountable to Whom?').

the rise of authoritarianism coupled with indifference of some major powers towards, or neglect of, multilateralism, as well as the rise of algorithmic governance that can itself lead to forms of authoritarianism. Furthermore, what were once seen as established regimes for the governance of multilateral trade, climate change or marine resources in areas beyond national jurisdiction have been challenged respectively by the turn to growing forms of regional economic cooperation, a lack of collective action globally or gaps in reaching satisfactory solutions to natural resource allocation and management.

Another conclusion is that a greater degree of 'actorness' in multilateral governance processes has emerged, within and outside the State-centric system of international law, most commonly in the form of MSIs which may offer us the opportunity to re-imagine the multilateral international order for the twenty-first century. While multistakeholderism may not be a panacea for crisis problem-solving in the international order, it would be worth considering its expansion to other areas of multilateral activity. This could even include the multilateral regime governing climate change, which is rooted in a State-centric system of treaty making and performance. At the same time, any attempts to broaden the range and scope of MSI activity in the multilateral international order need to come with a greater degree of accountability, which from the outset should be built into the institutional design of the MSI. Otherwise such MSI processes will not achieve the degree of legitimacy that is required in order for them to be effective.

Part II

Dynamics and implications of the crisis

6 State Withdrawals of Jurisdiction from an International Adjudicative Body

Christopher Lentz[1]

1 Introduction

International courts and tribunals play a crucial role in upholding the multilateral order, a fact that has been recognised at the highest levels of government.[2] Yet despite this recognition, or perhaps precisely because of it, State support for international adjudication seems to have become increasingly malleable in recent years.

States can calibrate a reduction in support for international adjudicative bodies through a variety of means, such as lowering financial contributions, refusing to cooperate, or invoking outright criticism. Stronger measures are available as well, including a State's complete withdrawal from the jurisdictional basis upon which an international adjudicative body operates. While such revocations are not a new phenomenon, they are gaining in frequency, thereby demanding increased attention to withdrawals as a stand-alone issue that could impact the very framework of the multilateral legal order.

To this end, Section 2 addresses State conferrals of jurisdiction upon an adjudicative body and sets out the legal framework that governs a subsequent withdrawal from an international agreement conferring such jurisdiction. Sections 3–6 turn to identifying the extent to which this has manifested in different areas of international law. In this regard, a comprehensive review has uncovered 16 such examples in fields as diverse as inter-State disputes, international human rights law, international investment law, and international criminal law.[3] Following these discussions of each individual termination,

1 This chapter was prepared in my personal capacity, and the views reflected herein do not necessarily represent those of any organisation with which I am or have been affiliated.
2 See United Nations Security Council, 8262nd meeting (17 May 2018) UN Doc S/PV.8262, 11.
3 This was done largely through the United Nations Treaty Collection (UNTC) website, which lists the multilateral treaties deposited with the Secretary-General of the United Nations (UN) along with notes about State activity in relation to each treaty. See 'Multilateral Treaties Deposited with the Secretary-General' (*UNTC*, undated) <https://treaties.un.org/Pages/ParticipationStatus.aspx> accessed 30 April 2022. In addition to a State's withdrawal from an agreement

DOI: 10.4324/9781003312857-8

Section 7 evaluates them holistically and assesses their causes, consequences, and dynamics. It posits that the three main reasons for a State's withdrawal of jurisdiction have been: (1) in response to an adverse case outcome; (2) in anticipation of impending litigation; or (3) due to systemic concerns about the international adjudicative body itself. Such withdrawals have become markedly more frequent in recent years, suggesting that they are symptoms of a broader contemporary malaise in multilateral affairs. While a possible 'cascade' of additional withdrawals can prompt existential concerns for the adjudicative body in question, thus far each withdrawal has been self-contained or followed, at most, by two additional States. Moreover, notwithstanding these withdrawals, the number of States conferring jurisdiction on the international adjudicative body in question has continued to grow over time.

While the impact of withdrawals to date must be kept in perspective, the risk they pose to international courts and tribunals can be alleviated if the relevant agreements mandate an appropriate period between notification and the time that the withdrawal of jurisdiction takes effect. This is discussed, along with concluding remarks, in Section 8.

2 Legal framework governing a State's conferral and withdrawal of jurisdiction

It is a 'well-established principle of international law' that a court 'can only exercise jurisdiction over a State with its consent'.[4] While States may grant such consent on an *ad hoc* basis in order to resolve a particular issue,[5] jurisdictional consent is more commonly conferred as part of a broader agreement with other States. It can take many forms, which include a State's recognition of compulsory jurisdiction before the International Court of Justice (ICJ) with respect to legal disputes with other States,[6] as well as a treaty-specific designation of a forum, frequently the ICJ, to resolve disputes arising out of the interpretation or application of that treaty.[7] In addition, States

conferring jurisdiction, a State could partially withdraw jurisdiction, such as by denouncing an international treaty and re-acceding with a new reservation excluding a specific area from jurisdiction. A State could also withdraw its jurisdiction conferred through a treaty that is more regional, supranational, or bilateral in nature. Although these possibilities are outside the scope of this chapter, examples of each are noted below when they arise in relation to a State's complete withdrawal of jurisdiction from an international agreement.

4 *Case of the Monetary Gold Removed from Rome in 1943 (Italy v. France, United Kingdom, and United States)* Preliminary Question, Judgment (1954) ICJ Rep 19, 32.

5 See Statute of the International Court of Justice (entry into force 24 October 1945), Article 36(1).

6 Ibid, Articles 36(2)–36(5).

7 See Optional Protocol to the Vienna Convention on Consular Relations concerning the Compulsory Settlement of Disputes (entry into force 19 March 1967) 596 UNTS 487 (VCCR Optional Protocol), Article 1; Optional Protocol to the

agree among themselves to confer jurisdiction upon an international body to receive and adjudicate complaints against them by individual persons on specific grounds, such as those pertaining to human rights or financial investments.[8] They also agree to share their jurisdiction with an international court or tribunal, including the criminal jurisdiction they wield over their nationals or with respect to specific crimes committed on their territories.[9]

Conferrals of jurisdiction are not inherently permanent, as States are permitted to withdraw from a treaty under various circumstances.[10] Many treaties expressly provide for this possibility, some of which both require the State to give a certain amount of notice before the withdrawal takes effect and delineate whether the adjudicative body may consider new matters arising after this notification but prior to the withdrawal.[11] Where the latter provision exists, it prevents a State from withdrawing solely in order to avoid an imminent claim involving the jurisdiction conferred by that State. For treaties that are silent on withdrawal, this is nevertheless permissible so long as it is established that the States parties intended for that to be possible, or otherwise if a right of withdrawal may be implied by the nature of the treaty, with either situation requiring 12 months' notice.[12]

A notification of withdrawal may be revoked at any time before it takes effect.[13] As will be seen below, where such a period exists, it permits time for a State to reconsider its notification of withdrawal for any number of reasons,

Vienna Convention on Diplomatic Relations, concerning the Compulsory Settlement of Disputes (entry into force 24 April 1964) 500 UNTS 241 (VCDR Optional Protocol), Article 1; Optional Protocol of Signature concerning the Compulsory Settlement of Disputes (entry into force 30 September 1962) 450 UNTS 169 (UNCLOS Optional Protocol), Article 1.

8 See Optional Protocol to the International Covenant on Civil and Political Rights (entry into force 23 March 1976) 999 UNTS 302 (ICCPR Optional Protocol), Article 1; Convention on the Settlement of Investment Disputes between States and Nationals of Other States (entry into force 14 October 1966) 575 UNTS 159 (ICSID Convention), Article 25.

9 See Rome Statute of the International Criminal Court (entry into force 1 July 2002) 2187 UNTS 3 (ICC Rome Statute), Articles 1, 5, 12.

10 See Vienna Convention on the Law of Treaties (entry into force 27 January 1980) 1155 UNTS 331 (VCLT), Articles 42(2), 54, 56, 61–62. The VCLT applies to treaties concluded by States after the Convention entered into force with regard to those States (Article 4).

11 See Article 127(1) ICC Rome Statute (withdrawal takes effect one year from the receipt of a notification, unless the notification specifies a later date), and Article 127(2) (this does not impact a State's duty to cooperate with criminal investigations and proceedings commenced prior to the date on which the withdrawal becomes effective); Article 12(1) ICCPR Optional Protocol (notice period of three months), and Article 12(2) (this is without prejudice to any communication submitted before the effective date of the denunciation); Article 71 ICSID Convention (six months' notice), and Article 72 (does not affect cases initiated before the notice was received).

12 See Article 56 VCLT.

13 Ibid, Article 68.

while also allowing other States and stakeholders to galvanise support against the anticipated withdrawal or otherwise seek to stave off further withdrawals.

3 Inter-State disputes: the ICJ

3.1 Declarations accepting compulsory jurisdiction

Only six times in the ICJ's 75-year history has a State withdrawn its declaration recognising the Court's compulsory jurisdiction: Iran in 1951, South Africa in 1967, France in 1974, the United States (US) in 1985, Israel in 1985, and Colombia in 2001.[14] The reasons have not always been explicit – only Iran and the US appear to have unambiguously explained their withdrawals – but each denunciation closely followed or preceded case activity involving the withdrawing State or, in Israel's case, came shortly after the denunciation by another State.

The first such occasion arose in 1951 in relation to Iran's nationalisation of the oil industry, prompting the United Kingdom to initiate proceedings before the ICJ.[15] Only days after the Court ordered provisional measures,[16] Iran withdrew its declaration.[17] In its communication, Iran largely disagreed with the ICJ's conclusion that it had jurisdiction in the case, took issue with the short notice received for oral hearings on the matter, and stated that the order infringed upon its sovereignty so as to benefit nationals of a more powerful State, thereby shaking its confidence in the Court's role.[18] Iran left no doubt that its withdrawal was a direct result of the ICJ's provisional measures order a few days before.

Conversely, it is more difficult to discern the reason for South Africa's withdrawal in 1967.[19] The previous year, the ICJ had denied the efforts of Ethiopia and Liberia to bring a claim against South Africa for its policies in administering South West Africa (today Namibia).[20] The judgment was close

14 This does not include declarations recognising the ICJ's compulsory jurisdiction for a specific period of time that were not renewed, or instances where a declaration was replaced by one with new reservations. The years above pertain to the dates of notification.
15 *Anglo-Iranian Oil Co. Case (United Kingdom v Iran)* Application Instituting Proceedings (26 May 1951) [4]–[8] <https://www.icj-cij.org/public/files/case-related/16/016-19510526-APP-1-00-EN.pdf> accessed 30 April 2022.
16 *Anglo-Iranian Oil Co. Case (United Kingdom v Iran)* Order on Interim Protection (1951) ICJ Rep 89, 93–94.
17 Telegram from the Iranian Minister for Foreign Affairs to the UN Secretary-General, dated 9 July 1951 (translation), in *Anglo-Iranian Oil Co. Case (United Kingdom v Iran)* Memorial Submitted by the Government of the United Kingdom of Great Britain and Northern Ireland (10 October 1951) 130, 134 <https://www.icj-cij.org/public/files/case-related/16/8981.pdf> accessed 30 April 2022.
18 See ibid 132, 134.
19 See 595 UNTS 363. South Africa notified its withdrawal on 12 April 1967.
20 *South West Africa Cases (Ethiopia v South Africa; Liberia v South Africa)* Second Phase, Judgment (1966) ICJ Rep 6 [1], [99]–[100].

and controversial, with the judges being equally divided,[21] and international opprobrium was intensifying against South Africa.[22] It may be that South Africa notified its termination in order to forestall another case before the ICJ, or that it wanted to express frustration with the international community coalescing against it, but the true motivation remains unidentified.

France's withdrawal from compulsory ICJ jurisdiction came in 1974, a few months after the ICJ's provisional measures orders to France to avoid nuclear tests causing radioactive fallout on Australian and New Zealand territory, notwithstanding France's submission that the ICJ manifestly lacked jurisdiction over the case.[23] The notification letter referred obliquely to the French Government's views about the proper scope of ICJ jurisdiction,[24] and *Le Monde* reported that the termination was 'visibly in retaliation against the attitude of the Court in this case'.[25]

More than a decade passed before the next such notification, from the US in 1985 following the ICJ's determination that the *Case Concerning Military and Paramilitary Activities in and against Nicaragua* was admissible before it.[26] Explaining the withdrawal in a press statement, the US Department of State referred to this case and alleged that Nicaragua 'and its Cuban and Soviet sponsors' were using the Court 'as a political weapon'.[27] The press statement also noted that a majority of States did not accept the ICJ's compulsory jurisdiction over disputes, and that the US 'would endanger [its] vital national interests' if it continued to do so under those circumstances.[28]

21 Ibid [100].

22 See UN General Assembly (UNGA) 1431st Plenary meeting (5 October 1966) [4]-[306]; UNGA Res 2145 (XXI) (27 October 1966) UN Doc A/RES/2145(XXI) (terminating South Africa's administration of South West Africa, resolving that the UN would discharge these responsibilities instead, and establishing a committee to make recommendations to the General Assembly no later than April 1967); UNGA Res 2248 (S-V) (19 May 1967) UN Doc A/RES/2248(S-V).

23 *Nuclear Tests Case (New Zealand v France)* Order on Interim Protection (1973) ICJ Rep 135, 136, 142; *Nuclear Tests Case (Australia v France)* Order on Interim Protection (1973) ICJ Rep 99, 100, 106.

24 See 'Notification de la France' C.N.3.1974.TREATIES-1 (6 February 1974) <https://treaties.un.org/doc/Publication/CN/1974/CN.3.1974-Frn.pdf> accessed 30 April 2022. France's notification was received on 10 January 1974.

25 'La France ne reconnaît plus la juridiction obligatoire de la Cour internationale de justice' *Le Monde* (21 January 1974) <https://bit.ly/34HynDT> accessed 30 April 2022 (author's translation into English).

26 *Case Concerning Military and Paramilitary Activities in and against Nicaragua (Nicaragua v United States)* Jurisdiction and Admissibility, Judgement (1984) ICJ Rep 392 [113].

27 'United States: Department of State Letter and Statement Concerning Termination of Acceptance of I.C.J. Compulsory Jurisdiction' (1985) 24(6) ILM 1742, 1744. The US's notification was dated 7 October 1985 and indicated that it would take effect six months later.

28 Ibid 1743–1744.

Another denunciation followed shortly thereafter, with Israel notifying its withdrawal later the same year.[29] No explanatory statement was released, but commentators have posited that the withdrawal was prompted by the manner in which the ICJ handled the case,[30] which is further supported by the fact that Israel and the US were the only two States to vote against multiple General Assembly resolutions calling for compliance with the ICJ's eventual merits judgment.[31] Yet although other States expressed some reservations with the possibility of the ICJ being used in a political manner,[32] none of them withdrew their declarations recognising its compulsory jurisdiction over disputes.

In fact, it was not until some 16 years later that the ICJ experienced its next – and the most recent – withdrawal from its compulsory jurisdiction. On 5 December 2001, Colombia submitted its notification seeking to terminate immediately its recognition of the ICJ's compulsory jurisdiction.[33] No reason was given, but Nicaragua had made it known for some time that it was preparing to initiate a case against Colombia before the ICJ.[34] And indeed, Colombia's withdrawal came on the very eve of Nicaragua filing that application,[35] permitting Colombia to subsequently argue that the ICJ had no jurisdiction over that case because it had withdrawn its declaration before Nicaragua's application.[36]

29 Israel informed the UN Secretary-General on 21 November 1985 that it was withdrawing its declaration. See 'Report of the International Court of Justice: 1 August 1985-31 July 1986' (1 August 1986) UN Doc A/41/4(Supp) [8].

30 Lori Fisler Damrosch, 'The Impact of the *Nicaragua* Case on the Court and Its Role: Harmful, Helpful, or In Between?' (2012) 25(1) LJIL 135, 138; Renata Szafarz, *The Compulsory Jurisdiction of the International Court of Justice* (Martinus Nijhoff 1993) 75.

31 See UNGA meeting (3 November 1986) UN Doc A/41/PV.53, 92 (voting on what would become UNGA resolution 41/31); UNGA meeting (12 November 1987) UN Doc A/42/PV.68, 21 (voting on UNGA resolution 42/18); UNGA meeting (25 October 1988) UN Doc A/43/PV.36, 36 (voting on UNGA resolution 43/11); UNGA meeting (7 December 1989) UN Doc A/44/PV.77, 27 (voting on UNGA resolution 44/43).

32 See UNGA meeting (3 November 1986) (n 31) 96–97; UNGA meeting (12 November 1987) (n 31) 17, 27; UNGA meeting (25 October 1988) (n 31) 37.

33 'Multilateral Treaties Deposited with the Secretary-General: Status as at 31 December 2002' (*UN*, 2003) ST/LEG/SER.E/21 Vol I 14 <https://treaties.un.org/doc/source/publications/MTDSG/2002-vol.1-english.pdf> accessed 30 April 2022.

34 See *Territorial and Maritime Dispute (Nicaragua v Colombia)* Written Statement of the Government of Nicaragua (26 January 2004) [3.102] <https://www.icj-cij.org/public/files/case-related/124/13872.pdf> accessed 30 April 2022.

35 *Territorial and Maritime Dispute (Nicaragua v Colombia)* Application Instituting Proceedings (6 December 2001) <https://www.icj-cij.org/public/files/case-related/124/7079.pdf> accessed 30 April 2022.

36 *Territorial and Maritime Dispute (Nicaragua v Colombia)* Preliminary Objections, Judgment (2007) ICJ Rep 832 [127]. The ICJ considered that because there was a separate basis for jurisdiction, it need not examine the issue of whether the denunciation would have deprived it of jurisdiction for the application filed the next day (see [132]).

While none of the six States to have withdrawn their recognition of the ICJ's compulsory jurisdiction have since changed course, the number of States accepting this jurisdiction continues to rise. After the US and Israel submitted their notifications in 1985, there were 46 States willing to accept the ICJ's compulsory jurisdiction. That number had grown to 64 by the time Colombia sought to withdraw in 2001, and it has since increased further to include 74 States today.[37]

3.2 Treaties conferring jurisdiction

There are more than 100 international treaties containing clauses providing jurisdiction to the ICJ, typically to resolve any dispute over the treaty's interpretation or application.[38] Despite this number, only three instances have been identified when a State withdrew from such a treaty: the US in 2005 from the VCCR Optional Protocol (the Optional Protocol to the Vienna Convention on Consular Relations concerning the Compulsory Settlement of Disputes), Colombia in 2017 from the UNCLOS Optional Protocol (the Optional Protocol of Signature concerning the Compulsory Settlement of Disputes), and the US in 2018 from the VCDR Optional Protocol (the Optional Protocol to the Vienna Convention on Diplomatic Relations, concerning the Compulsory Settlement of Disputes).

The first instance grew out of the US's displeasure with an ICJ judgment in 2004 which rejected the US's objections to jurisdiction based on the VCCR Optional Protocol, found that the US breached its obligations in capital punishment cases involving Mexican nationals, and required the US to review and reconsider their convictions and sentences.[39] A year later, the US withdrew from the VCCR Optional Protocol, confirming that 'the United States will no longer recognize the jurisdiction of the International Court of Justice reflected in that Protocol'.[40] When asked to discuss the rationale behind the denunciation, a US official brought up the recent judgment and explained that 'the decision the ICJ handed down is a decision, frankly, that we don't agree with' and that 'it's not appropriate that there be some international court that comes in and can reverse decisions of our national courts'.[41] The

37 See ICJ Report 1985–1986 (n 29) [8]–[9]; 'Report of the International Court of Justice: 1 August 2001–31 July 2002' (5 August 2002) UN Doc A/57/4(Supp) [53]–[54]; 'Report of the International Court of Justice: 1 August 2019–31 July 2020' (1 August 2020) UN Doc A/75/4 [51].

38 See 'Treaties' (*ICJ*, undated) <https://www.icj-cij.org/en/treaties> accessed 30 April 2022.

39 *Case Concerning Avena and Other Mexican Nationals (Mexico v United States)* Judgment (2004) ICJ Rep 12 [15], [26], [153].

40 UNTC (n 3) Chapter III.8, fn 1. This notification was received on 7 March 2005.

41 US Department of State, 'Daily Press Briefing' (10 March 2005) <https://2001-2009.state.gov/r/pa/prs/dpb/2005/43225.htm> accessed 30 April 2022.

US Secretary of State elaborated that the ICJ's 'interpretation there is a problem for our federal system'.[42]

The US has not re-acceded to the VCCR Optional Protocol, but no State followed it in withdrawing, either in 2005 or at any time since. To the contrary, the VCCR Optional Protocol boasts six new parties since then,[43] bringing the number of parties from 46 after the US's withdrawal to a current total of 52.

It was not until 12 years later that another State withdrew from a treaty whose purpose is to confer jurisdiction on the ICJ, when Colombia withdrew in 2017 from the UNCLOS Optional Protocol. This too was in reaction to adverse findings by the ICJ, which handed down two judgments on the same day in March 2016 rejecting Colombia's preliminary objections to jurisdiction based on a different treaty from which it had since withdrawn.[44] Almost immediately after the judgments, the President of Colombia declared that his country 'will not continue appearing before the ICJ in this matter',[45] and he later elaborated that the ICJ judgments 'were a confirmation that that Court is not what is convenient for Colombia' as it was not impartial and had made decisions that were prejudicial to the country's interests.[46]

Even though the UNCLOS Optional Protocol had not conferred jurisdiction on the ICJ over these cases, Colombia still withdrew from it the following year,[47] perhaps to avoid its being used in the future as a basis for jurisdiction. This did not precipitate any further withdrawals, and at the time of writing, the number of parties to the UNCLOS Optional Protocol remains unchanged.

Most recently, the US announced in October 2018 that it would withdraw from the VCDR Optional Protocol, which it directly linked to Palestine's

42 US Department of State, 'Remarks with Mexican Foreign Secretary Ernesto Derbez' (10 March 2005) <https://2001-2009.state.gov/secretary/rm/2005/43229.htm> accessed 30 April 2022.

43 UNTC (n 3) Chapter III.8, 1–2.

44 See *Alleged Violations of Sovereign Rights and Maritime Spaces in the Caribbean Sea (Nicaragua v Colombia)* Preliminary Objections, Judgment (2016) ICJ Rep 3 [15]–[17], [22]–[23], [111]; *Question of the Delimitation of the Continental Shelf Between Nicaragua and Colombia Beyond 200 Nautical Miles from the Nicaraguan Coast (Nicaragua v Colombia)* Preliminary Objections, Judgment (2016) ICJ Rep 100 [13]–[15], [20]–[21], [126]. Because this treaty was regional in nature, it is not set out in more detail in this chapter.

45 Juan Manual Santos (*Twitter*, 17 March 2016) <https://twitter.com/JuanManSantos/status/710510811215765505> accessed 30 April 2022 (author's translation into English).

46 Colombia Presidency, 'Seguiremos defendiendo los derechos de los raizales de San Andrés mediante negociaciones bilaterales, anunció el Presidente Santos' (18 March 2016) <https://bit.ly/3fwoZZO> accessed 30 April 2022 (author's translation into English).

47 UNTC (n 3) Chapter XXI.5, fn 4. Colombia's notification of withdrawal was received on 15 September 2017.

initiation of ICJ proceedings – grounded in the VCDR Optional Protocol[48] – against it concerning the relocation of its embassy to Jerusalem.[49] Shortly thereafter, the US formalised its withdrawal.[50] No further withdrawals have been submitted as of the time of writing, and the number of parties to this protocol remains steadfast at 70.

4 International human rights: the CCPR

Of the 22 international human rights treaties deposited with the UN,[51] only one has experienced any withdrawals: the ICCPR Optional Protocol (the Optional Protocol to the International Covenant on Civil and Political Rights), whose parties recognise the competence of the Human Rights Committee (CCPR) to receive and consider communications from individuals.[52] Despite the number of individual complaints received by the CCPR (more than 3,600) and the number adjudicated that find a violation by a State party (in excess of 1,200),[53] it is perhaps remarkable that there have been only two withdrawals and that none has taken place since 2000.

Jamaica was the first to submit its withdrawal notification, in 1997.[54] Following the Privy Council's imposition of a five-year limit for capital punishment cases, including the resolution of any petitions to the CCPR,[55] Jamaica reduced the number of persons sentenced to death, streamlined its appellate process, and liaised with the CCPR in an effort to shorten the latter's

48 See *Relocation of the United States Embassy to Jerusalem (Palestine v United States)* Application Instituting Proceedings (28 September 2018) [25]–[35] <https://www.icj-cij.org/public/files/case-related/176/176-20180928-APP-01-00-EN.pdf> accessed 30 April 2022.

49 See US White House, 'Press Briefing by Press Secretary Sarah Sanders, Small Business Administrator Linda McMahon, and National Security Advisor' (3 October 2018) <https://bit.ly/3pdDjtD> accessed 30 April 2022. Earlier that day, the ICJ had granted provisional measures to Iran with respect to sanctions imposed by the US, prompting the US to also denounce a bilateral treaty with Iran. See *Alleged Violations of the 1955 Treaty of Amity, Economic Relations, and Consular Rights (Iran v United States)* Order on Provisional Measures (2018) ICJ Rep 623 [19]–[22], [102]; US Department of State, 'Remarks to the Media' (3 October 2018) <https://2017-2021.state.gov/remarks-to-the-media-3> accessed 30 April 2022.

50 UNTC (n 3) Chapter III.5 fn 10. The notification was received on 12 October 2018.

51 Ibid Chapter IV.

52 Article 1 ICCPR Optional Protocol.

53 'Report of the Human Rights Committee: 126th session (1 26 July 2019), 127th session (14 October–8 November 2019), 128th session (2–27 March 2020)' (2020) UN Doc A/75/40 [24].

54 Jamaica notified the UN Secretary-General of its denunciation on 23 October 1997, which took effect three months later on 23 January 1998. See UNTC (n 3) Chapter IV.5, fn 3; *Forbes v Jamaica* (Views of 20 October 1998) UN Doc CCPR/C/64/D/649/1995 [10].

55 See *Pratt v Attorney-General for Jamaica* (1994) 2 A.C. 1, 34–35.

procedure as well.[56] In the meantime, Jamaica had practically stopped applying the death penalty, leading its people to roundly criticise the Government for 'its incompetence, in other words, its inability to enforce Jamaican law as it existed'.[57] Jamaica's efforts to shorten the CCPR timelines appear to have been unsuccessful, and after Jamaica concluded that it was impossible to simultaneously retain capital punishment, comply with the Privy Council time limits, and also confer jurisdiction on the CCPR for individual complaints, it notified its withdrawal from the ICCPR Optional Protocol.[58]

The following year, and also prompted by the timelines enunciated by the Privy Council, Trinidad and Tobago withdrew from the ICCPR Optional Protocol and immediately re-acceded with a reservation indicating that the CCPR could not exercise jurisdiction over capital punishment cases.[59] But in 1999, the CCPR decided that Trinidad and Tobago's reservation was incompatible with the object and purpose of the ICCPR Optional Protocol, and accordingly accepted an individual communication from a citizen of Trinidad and Tobago who was sentenced to death.[60] Shortly thereafter, Trinidad and Tobago submitted its withdrawal from the ICCPR Optional Protocol,[61] linking this revocation to the CCPR's decision while adding that the Government needed to fulfil its obligations to its people and 'avoid anarchy'.[62] Although Trinidad and Tobago warned the CCPR that other Caribbean States were 'also considering adopting the practical solution' of withdrawal,[63] this never materialised.

In fact, neither Jamaica's nor Trinidad and Tobago's withdrawal prompted any other State to revoke jurisdiction from the CCPR. To the contrary, after Jamaica's withdrawal became effective in 1998, four States became parties to the ICCPR Optional Protocol before Trinidad and Tobago could withdraw in 2000. Since then, the ICCPR Optional Protocol can boast 21 further

56 'Summary record of the 1622nd meeting' (23 October 1997) UN Doc CCPR/C/SR.1622 [34]–[37], [41]; 'Concluding observations of the Human Rights Committee: Jamaica' (19 November 1997) UN Doc CCPR/C/79/Add.83 [6]–[7], [11].

57 CCPR 1622nd meeting (n 56) [38], [40].

58 See ibid [37], [41]; 'Summary record of the second part (public) of the 1623rd meeting' (23 October 1997) UN Doc CCPR/C/SR.1623/Add.1 [48].

59 See 'Third and Fourth periodic reports of States parties due in 1990 and 1995 respectively: Addendum: Trinidad and Tobago' (15 September 1999) UN Doc CCPR/C/TTO/99/3 [102]; UNTC (n 3) Chapter IV.5, fn 1.

60 *Rawle Kennedy v Trinidad and Tobago* (Decision of 2 November 1999) UN Doc CCPR/C/67/D/845/1999 [1], [6.7]–[6.8].

61 See UNTC (n 3) Chapter IV.5, fn 1. Trinidad and Tobago notified its denunciation of the ICCPR Optional Protocol on 27 March 2000, with effect from 27 June 2000.

62 'Compte rendu analytique de la 1871ème séance' (17 October 2000) UN Doc CCPR/C/SR.1871 [3] <https://bit.ly/3wEjUVq> accessed 30 April 2022 (author's translation into English). See 'Summary record of the 1870th meeting' (17 October 2000) UN Doc CCPR/C/SR.1870 [14], [84].

63 CCPR 1871st meeting (n 62) [3] (author's translation into English).

parties, raising its total from 95 to 116.[64] Like other States that have withdrawn jurisdiction from an international adjudicative mechanism, however, neither Jamaica nor Trinidad and Tobago have re-acceded to the ICCPR Optional Protocol.

5 International investment law: ICSID

Investment law, too, has seen a limited procession of States withdrawing their jurisdiction from an international treaty, only to have their withdrawals counteracted by multiple new members. This has been the experience of the International Centre for Settlement of Investment Disputes (ICSID), whose Convention provides for jurisdiction over legal disputes arising directly out of an investment between a Contracting State and a national of another Contracting State, where both parties consent to submitting the dispute to ICSID.[65]

In 2007, Bolivia became the first Contracting State to withdraw.[66] When explaining the reasons behind it, the Bolivian Ministry of Foreign Affairs referred to ICSID's alleged conflict of interest as part of the World Bank, bias towards corporations, partiality of some of its arbitrators, lack of an appeals mechanism, lack of investment jurisprudence, and confidentiality of arbitration proceedings concerning matters of public interest.[67] More broadly, this denunciation took place shortly after other Latin American States expressed their intention to withdraw from ICSID as well, and while Bolivia was embarking on efforts to nationalise certain industries.[68] It also followed the initiation of arbitration by three claimants and Bolivia over a mining concession, which would lead to the constitution of an arbitral tribunal under ICSID later in 2007.[69]

Yet it would be more than two years before another State would withdraw from the ICSID Convention.[70] In that instance, while Ecuador's reasons may

64 See UNTC (n 3) Chapter IV.5.
65 Article 25 ICSID Convention.
66 'List of Contracting States and Other Signatories of the Convention (as of June 9, 2020)', ICSID/3 5 <https://icsid.worldbank.org/sites/default/files/ICSID-3.pdf> accessed 30 April 2022. Bolivia deposited its notice on 2 May 2007, and formally withdrew on 3 November 2007.
67 Marco Tulio Montañes, 'Introductory Note to Bolivia's Denunciation of the Convention on the Settlement of Investment Disputes Between States and Nationals of Other States' (2007) 46(5) ILM 969, 970, citing Bolivia Ministry of Foreign Affairs, Press Release (3 May 2007).
68 See ibid 970–971. See also Bolivia, 'Decreto Supremo N° 29117 de 1 de mayo de 2007' (1 May 2007) <http://www.mineria.gob.bo/juridica/20070501-15-52-5.pdf> accessed 30 April 2022.
69 See *Quiborax S.A. et al. v Bolivia* (Decision on Jurisdiction) Case No. ARB/06/2 [17], [20]. The claimants appointed their arbitrator in November 2006, while Bolivia appointed its arbitrator in April 2007, less than a month before it denounced the ICSID Convention. The third arbitrator was appointed in December 2007, and the arbitral tribunal was constituted that same month.
70 See ICSID/3 (n 66) 5. Ecuador's notification was received on 6 July 2009, and it withdrew on 7 January 2010.

not have been explicit, its denunciation followed its accession to ALBA-TCP, an organisation aimed at integrating Latin American and Caribbean States.[71] Notably, participants at an ALBA-TCP Extraordinary Summit two weeks earlier – when Ecuador joined the organisation – issued a declaration that formally 'welcomed the decision of Bolivia and Ecuador to denounce [ICSID]',[72] portraying this as a regional effort to withdraw in light of shared concerns about the role played by ICSID.

Venezuela became the third State to notify its withdrawal from ICSID, in 2012.[73] By that time, Venezuela had faced the highest number of cases registered before ICSID for three consecutive years (a total of 16), far outpacing other States in this respect (the next highest total was 7).[74] Venezuela also claimed that by the time of its denunciation, ICSID had 'ruled 232 times in favour of transnational interests' out of 234 cases, amply justifying Venezuela's decision to withdraw its jurisdiction from this body.[75]

Yet not only did these withdrawals fail to presage an exodus from ICSID, they heralded new members submitting themselves to the jurisdiction foreseen in the Convention. Only a week after Bolivia's notification of withdrawal in 2007, Serbia signed the Convention. Within a few months of Ecuador's notification in 2009, Haiti deposited its ratification and became a Contracting State, followed by three other States in subsequent years. Since Venezuela's denunciation took effect in 2012, ICSID has gained eight new Contracting States. While Bolivia, Ecuador, and Venezuela remain outside the jurisdiction provided through the ICSID Convention, they have been replaced by 15 new Contracting States, raising the number from 143 to 155 since Bolivia first notified its withdrawal in 2007.[76]

6 International criminal law: the ICC

International criminal law has also faced its own cascade of withdrawals from the Rome Statute of the International Criminal Court (ICC). In the span of a

71 See Alianza Bolivariana para los Pueblos de Nuestra América – Tratado de Comercio de los Pueblos (ALBA-TCP), 'Accession of Ecuador to ALBA' (24 June 2009) <https://bit.ly/3wjGPW2>; 'ALBA-TCP' (undated) <https://bit.ly/3p3xAXd> both accessed 30 April 2022.

72 ALBA-TCP, 'Joint Declaration' (24 June 2009) <https://bit.ly/34xm3Wq> accessed 30 April 2022.

73 See ICSID/3 (n 66) 5. Venezuela notified its denunciation on 24 January 2012, and it took effect on 25 July 2012.

74 See ICSID, '2012 Annual Report' (6 September 2012) 28 <https://bit.ly/34u4A1b>; ICSID, '2011 Annual Report' (9 September 2011) 28 <https://bit.ly/3yNxxDm>; ICSID, '2010 Annual Report' (8 September 2010) 24 <https://bit.ly/3wFkZMg> all accessed 30 April 2022.

75 See Venezuela Ministry of Popular Power for Foreign Affairs, 'Comunicado' (25 January 2012) <https://bit.ly/2ROnywW> accessed 30 April 2022 (author's translation into English).

76 See ICSID/3 (n 66).

month in 2016, South Africa, Burundi, and The Gambia all notified their decisions to withdraw from the Rome Statute after the statutory one-year period had expired, though only Burundi would eventually withdraw in 2017. The Philippines submitted its own notification in 2018 and withdrew the following year.

The abbreviated backstory to this initial cascade was that, by 2013, the African Union (AU) had become concerned that the ICC was 'no longer a Court for all but only to deal with Africans in the most rigid way',[77] while expressing its view that Heads of State should be immune from legal proceedings while in office.[78] This latter position prompted consternation when, in 2015, South Africa welcomed the Sudanese President for an AU Assembly session, notwithstanding two ICC warrants for his arrest.[79] By 2016, South Africa, Burundi, and The Gambia had all signalled their intention to withdraw from the Rome Statute,[80] with their respective notifications coming in rapid succession in October and November 2016.[81] They were to take effect a year later, pursuant to Article 127(1) of the Rome Statute.

This cascade of notifications prompted numerous African States and international organisations to coalesce against State withdrawal from the ICC and renew their commitment to the Court.[82] As this was taking place, domestic

77 'Statement by the Hon. Frederick Ruhindi, Deputy Attorney General/Minister of State for Justice and Constitutional Affairs of the Republic of Uganda on Behalf of the African Union at the 12th Assembly of States Parties to the Rome Statute of the International Criminal Court (ICC) The Hague, Netherlands 21 November 2013' 3 <https://bit.ly/34rTqKb> accessed 30 April 2022.

78 See 'Decision on Africa's Relationship with the International Criminal Court (ICC)' (12 October 2013) Ext/Assembly/AU/Dec.1(Oct.2013) [10(i)] <https://bit.ly/2SVuicM> accessed 30 April 2022.

79 See *The Minister of Justice and Constitutional Development et al. v The Southern African Litigation Centre* (Judgment) [2016] ZASCA 17 [3]–[7].

80 See Reuters Staff, 'South Africa plans to leave International Criminal Court' (*Reuters*, 11 October 2015) <https://reut.rs/3c5yHQH> (reporting a statement by a deputy minister in the South African Presidency); Burundi, 'Loi N°1/14 du 18 octobre 2016 portant retrait de la République du Burundi du Statut de Rome de la Cour pénale internationale adopté à Rome le 17 juillet 1998' (18 October 2016) <https://bit.ly/3yM2TKu>; Reuters Staff, 'Gambia announces withdrawal from International Criminal Court' (*Reuters*, 26 October 2016) <https://reut.rs/3pJGUjc> (reporting a statement by the Gambian Information Minister) all accessed 30 April 2022.

81 UNTC, C.N.786.2016.TREATIES-XVIII.10 (Depositary Notification) (25 October 2016) <http://treaties.un.org/doc/Publication/CN/2016/CN.786.2016-Eng.pdf> (South Africa's withdrawal notification was received on 19 October 2016); UNTC, C.N.805.2016.TREATIES-XVIII.10 (Depositary Notification) (28 October 2016) <http://treaties.un.org/doc/Publication/CN/2016/CN.805.2016-Eng.pdf> (Burundi's notification was received on 27 October 2016); UNTC, C.N.826.2016.TREATIES-XVIII.10 (Depositary Notification) (11 November 2016) <http://treaties.un.org/doc/Publication/CN/2016/CN.862.2016-Eng.pdf> (The Gambia's notification was received on 10 November 2016) all accessed 30 April 2022.

82 See 'General Debate - 15th session (16-17 November 2016)' (*Assembly of States Parties to the Rome Statute*, undated) <https://bit.ly/3p2RX6z> (statements of

developments in The Gambia as well as South Africa would lead both States to withdraw their notifications before they could take effect: following an election in The Gambia, the new Government reconsidered the matter,[83] while a South African court found the notification unconstitutional because it lacked parliamentary approval.[84]

Burundi, however, went through with its notification and withdrew at the conclusion of the one-year period.[85] It was not lost on anyone that shortly before Burundi notified its withdrawal, a UN report described 'abundant evidence of gross human rights violations' by the Government of Burundi,[86] and that the ICC Prosecutor had recently announced the opening of a preliminary examination into the situation there as well.[87]

A similar pattern emerged the following year, when the ICC Prosecutor announced her decision to open a preliminary examination into the situation in two States,[88] prompting one to withdraw from the Rome Statute. With respect to the Philippines, the Prosecutor referred to allegations of killings 'since 1 July 2016',[89] the day after the new President assumed his role. Shortly afterwards, the Philippine President released a statement denouncing 'the baseless, unprecedented and outrageous attacks on my person as well as against my administration' and the ICC Prosecutor's attempt 'to place my person within the jurisdiction' of the Court, which prompted the President to declare that the Philippines was immediately withdrawing its ratification of the Rome Statute.[90] Days later, the Philippines announced its withdrawal, which it described as being a 'principled stand against those who politicize

83 See UNTC, C.N.62.2017.TREATIES-XVIII.10 (Depositary Notification) (16 February 2017) <http://treaties.un.org/doc/Publication/CN/2017/CN.62.2017-Eng.pdf> accessed 30 April 2022 (The Gambia's 'withdrawal of notification of withdrawal' of 10 February 2017).

84 See UNTC, C.N.121.2017.TREATIES-XVIII.10 (Depositary Notification) (7 March 2017) <http://treaties.un.org/doc/Publication/CN/2017/CN.121.2017-Eng.pdf> accessed 30 April 2022 (South Africa's 'withdrawal of notification of withdrawal' of 7 March 2017).

85 See UNTC (n 3), Chapter XVIII.10, fn 2. Following its notification on 27 October 2016, Burundi's withdrawal took effect on 27 October 2017.

86 'Report on the independent investigation on Burundi carried out pursuant to Human Rights Council resolution S-24/1' (25 October 2016) UN Doc A/HRC/33/37 [125].

87 'Statement of the Prosecutor of the International Criminal Court, Fatou Bensouda, on opening a Preliminary Examination into the situation in Burundi' (25 April 2016) <https://www.icc-cpi.int/Pages/item.aspx?name=otp-stat-25-04-2016> accessed 30 April 2022.

88 'Statement of the Prosecutor of the International Criminal Court, Fatou Bensouda, on opening Preliminary Examinations into the situations in the Philippines and in Venezuela' (8 February 2018) <https://www.icc-cpi.int/Pages/item.aspx?name=180208-otp-stat> accessed 30 April 2022.

89 Ibid.

90 Azer Parrocha, 'Duterte: PH to withdraw from ICC' (*Philippine News Agency*, 14 March 2018) <https://www.pna.gov.ph/articles/1028667> accessed 30 April 2022.

and weaponize human rights, even as its independent and well-functioning organs and agencies continue to exercise jurisdiction over complaints, issues, problems and concerns arising from its efforts to protect its people'.[91]

The two States that have ultimately withdrawn – Burundi and the Philippines – remain outside the Rome Statute. Their withdrawals, however, have not sparked others to follow suit. To the contrary, Kiribati subsequently acceded to the Rome Statute, thereby stabilising the number of States Parties to the Rome Statute at 123.[92]

7 Causes, consequences, and dynamics

7.1 Causes

The instances detailed above show that a State has been most likely to withdraw jurisdiction from an international adjudicative body after suffering an adverse case outcome. This is hardly surprising, and it appears to be a relatively constant feature of international law in the past 75 years rather than one brought about by the current crisis in multilateralism. Examples include the termination of ICJ compulsory jurisdiction by Iran in 1951, France in 1974, and the US in 1985; Trinidad and Tobago's withdrawal of jurisdiction from CCPR individual complaints in 2000; and the denunciations of ICJ jurisdiction arising out of optional protocols by the US in 2005 and Colombia in 2017. It must be remembered, however, that there have been thousands of case determinations against a State that have not prompted any revocation at all. Even if an adverse judgment is the most common circumstance leading to withdrawal, this result has nevertheless been exceedingly rare.

Another frequent reason underlying a State's withdrawal appears to be concern about a case that is expected to be initiated soon. Naturally, this is rarely identified as the reason for the withdrawal, leaving it to observers to assess whether this is the unspoken motivating factor. While some commentary has been circumspect in concluding that Colombia's 2001 withdrawal from the ICJ was motivated by anticipated litigation,[93] there is no shortage of affirmation that Burundi in 2016 and the Philippines in 2018 notified their withdrawals from the ICC because the Prosecutor had opened a preliminary examination in those States earlier that year.[94] The US, by contrast, withdrew

91 UNTC, C.N.138.2018.TREATIES-XVIII.10 (Depositary Notification) (19 March 2018) 2 <http://treaties.un.org/doc/Publication/CN/2018/CN.138.2018-Eng.pdf> accessed 30 April 2022. This notice of withdrawal was received on 17 March 2018, and it took effect on 17 March 2019. See UNTC (n 3), Chapter XVIII.10, fn 2.

92 See UNTC (n 3), Chapter XVIII.10.

93 See Vanda Lamm, *Compulsory Jurisdiction in International Law* (Edward Elgar 2014) 231.

94 See Hannah Woolaver, 'Withdrawal from the International Criminal Court: International and Domestic Implications' in Gerhard Werle and Andreas Zimmermann (eds), *The International Criminal Court in Turbulent Times* (TMC Asser Press/Springer 2019) 25–26; Manisuli Ssenyonjo, 'State Withdrawal Notifications from the Rome Statute of the International Criminal Court: South Africa,

from an optional protocol only after Palestine had already initiated ICJ proceedings in 2018, and so it was unconstrained in making clear that its withdrawal was directly linked to the new case.[95]

Finally, States withdraw jurisdiction because of concerns about systemic issues in the adjudicative institution that could negatively impact State sovereignty. While many denunciations feature rhetoric concerning sovereignty, and may indeed be motivated in part by this and related issues, only a few withdrawals portray this as the primary or sole concern. This rationale can be seen in the ICSID denunciations lodged by Bolivia in 2007, Ecuador in 2009, and Venezuela in 2012. It may also be discerned in Israel's withdrawal from the ICJ in 1985, whose only case activity was decades old[96] and which was said to be concerned about the 'politicization' of the ICJ.[97] Jamaica, too, ultimately denounced an optional protocol in 1997 because of concerns that the CCPR was taking too long to determine individual complaints, thereby frustrating Jamaica's desire to impose capital punishment.[98]

Complaints about systemic issues can play another role beyond merely motivating a State to withdraw its jurisdiction: they can also portend a series of terminations from aligned or similarly affected States. The largest cascade seen thus far took place in ICSID with the staggered denunciations of Bolivia, Ecuador, and Venezuela. Israel's withdrawal notification from the ICJ followed closely on the heels of the US and was said to be based on the same concerns. Jamaica's preference to withdraw jurisdiction from CCPR individual complaints in order to maintain the death penalty was shared by Trinidad and Tobago, which itself withdrew a few years later. Most recently, the ICC faced a series of notifications that raised systemic concerns, though the only two States to actually withdraw are said to have been motivated by preliminary examinations against high-ranking officials of their respective Governments.

7.2 *Consequences*

At its most basic level, a State's withdrawal of jurisdiction not only changes its relationship vis-à-vis the adjudicative body, it also deprives other actors of the ability to lodge a case before the relevant court or tribunal. Given the nature of the institution, a withdrawal will negatively impact other States, individual persons, investors, or victims of alleged crimes that might seek resolution of their various claims. In addition, a State's withdrawal negatively impacts the institution itself as well as the purpose it is meant to serve.[99] This

Burundi and The Gambia' (2018) 29 CrimLF 63, 68–69; Karen Lema and Neil Jerome Morales, 'Duterte to withdraw Philippines from ICC after "outrageous attacks"' (*Reuters*, 14 March 2018) <https://reut.rs/3uH2sOt> accessed 30 April 2022.

95 US White House (n 49).

96 *Case Concerning the Aerial Incident of July 27th, 1955 (Israel v Bulgaria)* Preliminary Objections, Judgment (1959) ICJ Rep 127.

97 Szafarz (n 30) 75.

98 CCPR 1622nd meeting (n 56) [37]–[41].

loss seems enduring, too, given that there is not yet any example where a withdrawing State later chooses to confer jurisdiction anew.

The harm caused by a single State's withdrawal of jurisdiction cannot be quantified. We will never know the cases that would have been brought and adjudicated, but for the revocation. It stands to reason, however, that the withdrawing State was relatively likely to have been the subject of future additional claims, some of which might have been deemed meritorious. This seems even more probable if the State's denunciation was motivated by the imminent prospect of facing a claimant or the recent outcome of a case against it, thereby increasing the expected impact of that particular State's withdrawal from the international adjudicative body.

Of course, not all States are perceived equally, and the lack of jurisdiction over some States is generally seen to be more problematic than for others. There is '[n]o question that one of the weakest points' of the ICJ's compulsory jurisdiction is that, owing to France's withdrawal in 1974 and that of the US the following decade, it covers only one of the five permanent members of the Security Council;[100] indeed, the US referred to a similar concern when justifying its own withdrawal.[101] Likewise, a common critique of the ICC is that it has no jurisdiction over a number of permanent Security Council members, a fact referenced by South Africa when announcing its initial intention to withdraw from the ICC.[102] Aside from perceived power, a State's jurisdiction might be deemed more or less crucial depending on other factors specific to the disputes that come before the adjudicative body in question – for instance, Venezuela's departure from ICSID presumably had an outsized consequence, given that it faced the greatest number of cases prior to withdrawal. While these issues must be acknowledged, they do not lend themselves well to objective analysis, not least because assessing the impact of a specific State's withdrawal of jurisdiction requires engaging with an alternate universe.

A more ascertainable way to assess the consequences of a State's withdrawal of jurisdiction is to see how other States respond with regard to their own jurisdiction: do they also terminate their provision of jurisdiction or, conversely, do more States opt to bestow it upon the international adjudicative body? This inquiry is especially pertinent, for regardless of the harm caused by an individual State's withdrawal, a greater risk to an adjudicative body – as well as its purpose and the interests of other participants – is that

99 See Sub-Commission on the Promotion and Protection of Human Rights, Resolution 2000/27 (18 August 2000) in 'Report of the Sub-Commission on the Promotion and Protection of Human Rights on its fifty-second session' (23 November 2000) UN Doc E/CN.4/2001/2, 74–75 (noting that even when a State may lawfully withdraw from a human rights mechanism, attempts to do so 'seriously weaken the international effort towards the promotion and protection of human rights in all parts of the world').

100 Lamm (n 93) 261.

101 US Department of State (n 27) 1743–1744.

102 South Africa notification (n 81) 1.

the single departure could trigger further withdrawals. Such a cascade would, at minimum, compound the loss felt by a withdrawal, and it could also increase the risk of even more terminations, raising the spectre of a downward spiral of departures.

Roughly half of withdrawals have been part of a cascade, including all revocations outside of the inter-State dispute context. But they have nevertheless been limited. Three times they involved only one additional State,[103] with the most intensive involving a total of three States over a five-year period.[104]

Importantly, all but the most recent withdrawals have been offset by the willingness of other States to accept the jurisdiction of the international body. States parties to the ICCPR Optional Protocol have increased from 95 to 116 since the last withdrawal in 2000; the ICJ's compulsory jurisdiction was accepted by 64 States in 2001 and by 74 today; and the number of parties to the VCCR Optional Protocol has risen from 46 in 2005 to 52 at present. ICSID, which experienced the most extensive cascade, has received 15 new Contracting States since the first withdrawal was notified in 2007, with eight of them joining since the cascade ended in 2012. Looked at in this light, withdrawals have not weakened the multilateral system, but rather have correlated with an increase in States' conferral of jurisdiction to the relevant adjudicative body.

7.3 Dynamics

Withdrawals are becoming more frequent. Of the 16 instances identified above, seven took place in the 50 years from 1951–2000 and nine occurred in the 20 years since, with a quarter of all examples being seen in the past few years. This not only impacts the role and perceived legitimacy of the international adjudicative body at issue, it also raises the likelihood of a wholesale withdrawal of jurisdiction by States. Even if this latter outcome has been avoided so far, it remains a possible existential threat to an international court, as the ICC's recent experience and the reaction to it have illustrated. Left unchecked, withdrawals could also prompt systemic concerns about international dispute resolution, either in specific fields or more broadly.

These concerns are real, but they should also be kept in perspective. Although withdrawals are taking place with greater frequency, this has occurred alongside an increasing number of international courts and tribunals, an increasing number of State conferrals of jurisdiction to these bodies, and an increased role that international adjudication is expected or asked to

103 The US and Israel in 1985 before the ICJ; Jamaica and Trinidad and Tobago before the CCPR in 1997 and 2000, respectively; and Burundi and the Philippines from the ICC, respectively, in 2016 and 2018.

104 In ICSID, Bolivia in 2007, Ecuador in 2009, and Venezuela in 2012. For ease of comparison, the years in this note and the preceding one refer to the notifications of withdrawal.

play. Even if withdrawals are becoming more prevalent in absolute terms, this does not lead to the conclusion that States are moving towards a reduction of the jurisdiction they entrust to international adjudicative bodies. Yet this will be cold comfort to the aggrieved State, individual, or investor who can no longer initiate an international case concerning the State that has withdrawn jurisdiction.

In this respect, it is worth observing that withdrawals might be more common were it not for the inclusion in many international treaties of a mandatory notice period before a revocation can take effect. Having such a period reduces the likelihood that a State will notify its withdrawal just to avoid an upcoming claim, because it would not preclude the case being initiated in the intervening period. Moreover, a notice period of appropriate duration permits an opportunity for domestic developments – such as an upcoming presidential election or the resolution of a challenge before the judiciary, as in The Gambia and South Africa, respectively – that could lead to a reversal of the impending withdrawal. Finally, as seen recently with the ICC, having a sufficient notice period allows an opportunity for the existence of a cascade to emerge, thereby ensuring that all actors can consider the holistic impact of multiple withdrawals, while permitting States and other interested parties to seek dialogue as to the merits or otherwise of a mass withdrawal of jurisdiction.

8 Conclusion

It should not be inherently concerning that States on occasion have exercised their ability to withdraw from international treaties conferring jurisdiction, particularly given the rarity of this occurrence and that many agreements contain clauses specifically providing for such a course of action. For supporters of multilateralism, it will be reassuring that a State's withdrawal generally does not precipitate further revocations among States with similar interests, and that in no instance has an overwhelming cascade of States denounced jurisdictional conferrals. Along with the fact that instances of withdrawal have been followed by a greater number of States conferring jurisdiction, these demonstrate a resiliency among international adjudicative bodies and the multilateral order which they help to uphold.

Although past instances have been relatively limited, withdrawals are increasing in frequency alongside other facets of the current crisis in the multilateral legal order. While this should not provoke alarmism, the existential risk to an international court or tribunal should not be ignored, and indeed it appears that States have been alert to such a risk when faced with a critical mass of possible withdrawals. Moreover, regardless of whether a State's denunciation prompts others to follow suit, a withdrawal of jurisdiction brings about its own negative impact both on those who can no longer initiate a claim involving the departed State and on the adjudicative body itself.

States can avoid this issue entirely if relevant treaties or protocols specify that an acceding State will not be permitted to withdraw,[105] but the prevalence of withdrawal clauses is an indication that States consider it necessary or otherwise preferable for this possibility to persist. In light of that, one way to minimise any undue impact, while also containing the danger of an impulsive stampede of withdrawals, is for agreements conferring jurisdiction to include an appropriate time period between notification and the withdrawal of jurisdiction taking effect. This would not prevent a State from withdrawing because of an adverse case outcome or systemic concerns, but it would preclude a State from acting strategically to dodge the imminent initiation of proceedings, while also providing adequate opportunity for any domestic or international challenges to the withdrawal to be resolved.

105 See Articles 42(2), 54, 56(1) VCLT.

7 Multilateralism, Community of Interests, and Environmental Law

Malgosia Fitzmaurice

1 Preliminary considerations

The contemporary and fashionable approach to multilateralism is based on the premise that it is 'facing its final day[s]'.[1] There are numerous examples illustrating such a view, quite a few of them in the area of international environmental law, such as the United States (US) withdrawal from the Paris Agreement. Indeed, the denial that global climate change has an effect on all of the Earth's ecosystems and human beings does not instil optimism in terms of environmental multilateralism. At the same time, however, it is already becoming obvious that the next US administration will not follow Trump's policies. Therefore, drawing general, final, and fatalistic conclusions based on the current situation should be done with a certain degree of restraint. As correctly noted by Maulaya:

> The gloomy picture of multilateralism has been painted. Nevertheless, there is no ground for us to perceive the future of multilateralism in a pessimistic manner. Multilateralism is indeed going through a decline. Yet, the phase will not last forever. The potency of multilateralism is observable by looking through its prolificacy in other parts of the world [such as G20 meetings, BRICS, etc.].[2]

The legal question of multilateralism and the community of interests in international environmental law is not monolithic. There are several different aspects to it, i.e. procedural and substantive. The fundamental principles underlying international environmental law can be analysed from these points of view. As an example, one may refer to the legally-mandated principle of environmental impact assessments, which have both substantive and procedural content (duty to inform and cooperate) elements. This principle can, similar to the precautionary principle, be assessed from the points of view of either their unifying or fragmenting aspects. Obviously, within the confines of

1 Mahbi Maulaya, 'Cynicism and the Collapse of Multilateralism' (2020) 4 Aegis 89.
2 Ibid 103. See on the ICJ: Priya Urs, 'Obligations erga omnes and the question of standing before the International Court of Justice', Leiden Journal of International Law (2021), 34, 505–525.

DOI: 10.4324/9781003312857-9

one chapter limited in scope, it is impossible to analyse all the various aspects which international environmental law possibly fulfils in multilateralism. Thus, this chapter is focused on one particular theme of multilateralism in international environmental law, i.e. the recent phenomenon of communitarian protection of the environment, which has been evolving despite the classical bilateralism of international law. However, it is not the intention of this chapter to analyse general legal questions concerning the character of the community of interests and the related concepts of *erga omnes* and *erga omnes partes* obligations.[3] This chapter will focus on the issue of *locus standi* in the protection of the community of interests, including its historical development. Therefore, the chapter is devoted to the implementation and evolution of a procedural right of standing in the context of international adjudication to protect the community of interests in environmental matters. The *locus standi* of States in relation to the protection of the environment before international courts and tribunals, such as the International Court of Justice (ICJ or Court) and the International Tribunal for the Law of the Sea (ITLOS), and human rights courts such as the European Court of Human Rights (ECtHR) and the Inter-American Court of Human Rights (IACtHR), is also scrutinised. It is suggested in this chapter that the recent developments in environmental multilateralism are firmly entrenched in human rights law, as has been evidenced by the case law of human rights courts, national courts, and the jurisprudence of the Human Rights Committee (HRC). The Institut de Droit International has confirmed that States have communitarian obligations relating to the environment of common spaces, based on their common values and concern for compliance in order to take action in the event of a breach of that obligation.[4]

Considering that there are various definitions of multilateralism,[5] in this chapter multilateralism is understood as a concept closely linked to, if not

3 There are a multitude of publications on this subject matter; to mention but a few: Christian Tams, *Enforcing Obligations Erga Omnes in International Law* (CUP 2005); Giorgio Gaja, 'The Protection of General Interests in the International Community General Course on Public International Law' (2011) 364 RCADI; Bruno Simma, 'From Bilateralism to Community Interest in International Law' (1994) 250 RCADI. See also an interesting dissertation, Tuomas Palosaari, 'More than Just Wishful Thinking? Existence and Identification of Environmental Obligations *Erga Omnes*' (Master's thesis, University of Eastern Finland 2018) <https://erepo.uef.fi/handle/123456789/19351> accessed 30 April 2022.

4 The Institut de Droit International, 'Resolution on Obligations *Erga Omnes* in International Law' (2005), Article 1.

5 For example, in a recent article by Criddle and Fox-Decent, the concept of multilateralism is understood as 'the coordination of national policies and practices among multiple states in a manner that reflects due regard for the participant states' respective legal rights and authority to represent their people internationally'. They also note that '[m]ultilateralism, under this definition, has both a nominal dimension and a qualitative dimension' (Evan J Criddle and Evan Fox-Decent, 'Mandatory Multilateralism' (2019) 113 AJIL 271, 274).

coterminous with, community of interests. This definition of multilateralism is in line with that of Julio Barboza, who describes multilateralism as a system which has developed 'from a bilateralism which had sought to provide reparation for the injured party only to a system of multilateralism in which a community response to the violation of community values was possible'.[6] Crawford has defined communitarian norms as multilateral rights and obligations established in the interest of and owed to the international community as a whole, entailing a recognised legal interest of each of its members to invoke compliance with it.[7]

The *locus standi* in relation to *erga omnes* obligations means that

> [it] may function to allow enforcement of obligations in case of a grave breach, by conferring standing on a State even if it did not suffer injury to its national territory. Some treaties specifically provide for enforcement by any party, even if it has not itself been directly harmed.[8]

This general principle also encompasses standing in environmental matters.

Multilateralism is not a recent concept and can be traced to a little-known 1934 case, *Oscar Chin*, of the Permanent Court of International Justice (PCIJ).[9] In particular, the concept of multilateralism is reflected in the Separate Opinions of Judges van Eysinga and Schückling.

Judge van Eysinga commented on the legal character of the 1885 General Act of Berlin, which he describes as follows:

> It will be seen from this survey that the Berlin Act presents a case in which a large number of States, which were territorially or otherwise interested in a vast region, endowed it with a highly internationalized statute, or rather a constitution established by treaty, by means of which the interests of peace, those of 'all nations' as well as those of the natives, appeared to be most satisfactorily guaranteed … The General Act of Berlin does not create a number of contractual relations between a number of States, relations which may be replaced as regards some of these States by other contractual relations; it does not constitute a *jus dispositivum*, but it provides the Congo Basin with a régime, a statute, a constitution. This régime, which forms an indivisible whole, may be modified, but for this the agreement of all contracting Powers is required.

6 Julio Barboza, 'International Criminal Law' (1999) 278 RCADI 109.

7 James Crawford, 'Multilateral Rights and Obligations in International Law' (2006) 319 RCADI 325, 344.

8 Cymie R Payne, 'Collective Responsibility for Sound Marine Resource Management: *Erga Omnes* Obligations and Deep Seabed Mining' in *Environmental Rule of Law: Trends from America* (OAS 2015) 313.

9 *The Oscar Chin Case (United Kingdom v Belgium)* 1934 PCIJ Ser A/B No 63, 65. See also *Case of SS Wimbledon (Great Britain and Others v Germany)* 1923 PCIJ Ser A No 1, 15.

> An inextricable legal tangle would result if, for instance, it was held that the régime of neutralization provided for in Article II of the General Act of Berlin might be in force for some contracting Powers while it had ceased to operate for certain others.[10]

Judge Schückling agreed with the aforementioned opinion of Judge van Eysinga. He added that:

> It is beyond doubt that the signatory States of the Congo Act desired to make it absolutely impossible, in the future, for some of their number only to amend the Congo Act, seeing that any modifications thus introduced would have been a danger to their vested rights in that vast region.[11]

Arguably, the most significant impact on the modern development of the law of community of interests was exercised by Gerald Fitzmaurice, who during his period of serving as a Special Rapporteur of the International Law Commission (ILC) on the law of treaties, classified international obligations of States into the following categories: reciprocal, interdependent, and integral. His classification found a partial reflection in the 1969 Vienna Convention on the law of treaties (mostly in the structure of Article 60 on material breach). According to Fitzmaurice, human rights treaties embody 'integral obligations' (that is, they have to be performed as such and in their entirety) and establish a regime 'towards all the world rather than towards particular parties', as contrasted with contractual treaties, which are based on reciprocity of the parties to the treaty. The treaties characterized by interdependent obligations are of such a nature as to make the performance of one party dependent on that of all the other parties (such as a disarmament treaty).[12]

Since then, international law has evolved towards the conceptualisation of what has been defined by many scholars, such as Bruno Simma, as an 'international community', progressing from bilateral relations towards a more 'socially conscious order', which is an amalgamate of the interests of the international community as well as those of States.[13] These developments have been reflected on a practical level by the 2001 Responsibility of States for Internationally Wrongful Acts (ARSIWA), i.e. in Article 48, which allows for the invocation of State responsibility by a State other than a directly affected State,[14] for the

10 *The Oscar Chin Case (United Kingdom v Belgium)*, Individual Opinion of Judge van Eysinga 133–134.

11 Ibid. See also Separate Opinion of Judge Schückling 18–49.

12 Gerald Fitzmaurice, 'Second Report on the Law of Treaties' (1957) 2 UN Yb ILC 18, 54, UN Doc A/CN.4/107.

13 Bruno Simma, 'From Bilateralism to Community Interest in International Law' (1994) 250 RCADI 233.

14 Article 48 states:

> Invocation of responsibility by a State other than an injured State: 1. Any State other than an injured State is entitled to invoke the responsibility of another State in accordance with paragraph 2 if: (*a*) the obligation breached is

protection of the collective interest, deriving from the obligations *erga omnes* and *erga omnes partes.*[15] Article 48 is a departure from the classical international law based on bilateral relations between States, which allows standing only to a State which is directly injured, as envisaged in Article 42 ARSIWA.

2 The general international jurisprudence

The Advisory Opinion on the reservations to the Genocide Convention[16] can be said to be the first harbinger of the later jurisprudence of the ICJ with respect to collective interests (*erga omnes* and *erga omnes partes* obligations). The Court stated as follows:

> In such a Convention [as the Genocide Convention] the contracting states do not have any interests of their own; they merely have, one and all, a common interest, namely, the accomplishment of those high purposes which are the *raison d'être* of the convention. Consequently, in a convention of this type one cannot speak of individual advantages to states, or of the maintenance of a perfect contractual balance between rights and duties. The high ideals which inspired the Convention provide, by virtue of the common will of the parties, the foundation and measure of all its provisions.[17]

In the same vein, it is worth noting the Dissenting Opinion of Judge Alvarez, who classified the Genocide Convention as having a universal character:

> owed to a group of States including that State, and is established for the protection of a collective interest of the group; or (*b*) the obligation breached is owed to the international community as a whole. 2. Any State entitled to invoke responsibility under paragraph 1 may claim from the responsible State: *(a)* cessation of the internationally wrongful act, and assurances and guarantees of non-repetition in accordance with article 30; and *(b)* performance of the obligation of reparation in accordance with the preceding articles, in the interest of the injured State or of the beneficiaries of the obligation breached … 3. The requirements for the invocation of responsibility by an injured State under articles 43, 44 and 45 apply to an invocation of responsibility by a State entitled to do so under paragraph 1.

See also James Crawford, Jacqueline Peel, and Simon Olleson, 'The ILC's Articles on State Responsibility Adopted for Internationally Wrongful Acts: Completion of the Second Reading' (2001) 12 EJIL 963; James Crawford, 'Responsibility for Breaches of Communitarian Norms: An Appraisal of Article 48 of the ILC Articles on State Responsibility of States for Internationally Wrongful Acts', in Ulrich Fastenrath and others (eds), *From Bilateralism to Community Interest: Essays in Honour of Bruno Simma* (OUP 2011) 224–240.

15 Crawford, Peel, and Olleson (n 14) 976.

16 *Reservations to the Convention on the Prevention and Punishment of the Crime of Genocide*, Advisory Opinion, (1951) ICJ Rep 15.

17 Ibid 32.

'They are, in a sense, the Constitution of international society, the new international constitutional law. They are not established for the benefit of private interests but for that of the general interest'.[18]

In the *Barcelona Traction*[19] case *erga omnes* obligations were verbalised for the first time, as

> an essential distinction should be drawn between the obligations of a State towards the international community as whole, and those arising vis-à-vis another State in the field of diplomatic protection. By their very nature the former are the concern of all States. In view of the importance of the rights involved, all States can he held to have a legal interest in their protection: they are obligations *erga omens.*[20]

The Court gave examples of such obligations (prohibition of aggression, genocide, basic human rights, outlawing of slavery and racial discrimination).[21] The rights to self-determination were confirmed as an obligation *erga omnes* in the *East Timor*[22] case and also in the *Wall* Advisory Opinion. In the *Wall* Advisory Opinion,[23] the Court referred to applicable norms of humanitarian law as obligations *erga omnes partes.* It may be added that in the *Nuclear Testing* cases, claimants invoked *erga omnes* obligations, but the Court limited itself to dealing with the legal effect of unilateral declarations made *erga omnes*, which in fact is a substantively different issue than communitarian *erga omnes* obligations.[24]

The next question which arises is the procedural aspect of the substantive communitarian obligations in the Court's practice, i.e. who has standing regarding such obligations, as the substantive and procedural aspects are not coterminous. The issue of standing before Court has been the subject of quite a radical evolution from the *South West Africa* cases to *Belgium v Senegal.*[25]

In the *East Timor* case, where the Court attributed an *erga omnes* character to self-determination, it nonetheless upheld the indispensable third-party rule and declined the jurisdiction.[26] The Court stated as follows:

18 Ibid, Dissenting Opinion of Judge Alvarez 51.
19 *Barcelona Traction Light and Power Company Limited (Belgium v Spain)*, Second Phase Judgment (1970) ICJ Rep 3.
20 Ibid 33. The Court here reversed its judgment handed down in *Case Concerning South West Africa, Second Phase (Ethiopia v South Africa and Liberia v South Africa)*, Judgment (1966) ICJ Rep 6.
21 *Barcelona Traction Light and Power Company Limited (Belgium v Spain)* 34.
22 *Case Concerning East Timor (Portugal v Australia)*, Judgement (1995) ICJ Rep 96.
23 *Legal Consequences of the Construction of a Wall in the Occupied Palestinian Territory*, Advisory Opinion (1996) ICJ Rep 136. See Crawford (n 14) 235.
24 *Case Concerning Nuclear Testing (Australia v France; New Zealand v France)*, Judgment (1974) ICJ Rep 457, 474.
25 The *locus standi* in environmental cases based on communitarian norms will be discussed in the second part of this chapter.
26 Crawford (n 14) 232.

> Whatever the nature of the obligation involved, the Court could not rule on lawfulness of the conduct of the State when its judgment would imply an evaluation of the lawfulness of the conduct of another State, which is not a party to the case. When this is so, the Court cannot act, even if the right in question is a right *erga omnes*.[27]

A diametrically-opposed approach was adopted by the Court in the *Belgium v Senegal* case. In this case the Court had to assess the standing of Belgium on claims that Hissène Habré should be either prosecuted or extradited by Senegal for acts deemed criminal according to the Convention against Torture. The ICJ, in the following statement, explained the standing of Belgium (which was not a directly injured State in this case):

> The States parties to the Convention have a common interest to ensure, in view of their shared values, that acts of torture are prevented and that, if they occur, their authors do not enjoy impunity. All the other States parties have a common interest in compliance with these obligations by the State in whose territory the alleged offender is present. That common interest implies that the obligations in question are owed by any State party to all the other States parties to the Convention. All the States parties 'have a legal interest' in the protection of the rights involved (Barcelona Traction, Light and Power Company, Limited, Judgment, I.C.J. Reports 1970, p. 32, para. 33). These obligations may be defined as 'obligations *erga omnes partes*' in the sense that each State party has an interest in compliance with them in any given case.[28]

The Court used the construct of Article 48 on State responsibility, which at the time of the adoption of 2001 ARSIWA was considered to be a progressive development. It should be noted that the Court relied on the *Barcelona Traction* case, which referred to obligations *erga omnes*, not *erga omnes partes* (as the type of obligations in this case), which accords to a party of a multilateral treaty the right of *locus standi*.[29] Obligations *erga omnes* derive from customary international law and give *locus standi* to the entire international community of States. The approach of the ICJ is thus lacking clarity in this respect.

3 The protection of communitarian interests in environmental law

The main focus of this section is on the changes in exercising the right of standing before national and international courts and tribunals in order to protect the interest of the community.

27 *Case Concerning East Timor (Portugal v Australia)* 102 [29].

28 *Questions Relating to the Obligation to Prosecute or Extradite (Belgium v Senegal)*, Judgment (2012) ICJ Rep 422, 449–450 [68]–[69].

29 Inna Uchkunova, '*Belgium v. Senegal*: Did the Court End the Dispute between the Parties?' (*EJIL: Talk!*, 23 July 2012) <https://bit.ly/3bZLMLy> accessed 30 April 2022.

The idea that environmental protection is in the interest of the whole community of States is not new. In 1975, it was already suggested that the classical rules on standing do not sufficiently protect the global environment for the benefit of humankind. It was stated that: 'a critical evaluation [was needed] of how the existing legal rules concerning *locus standi* should be adopted in order to cope more adequately with the interests of society in general and of each member of society in particular'.[30]

3.1 Historical context of community interest

The history of *locus standi* in order to protect the community of interest can be traced back to the *Nuclear Tests* cases. In these cases, both Australia and New Zealand relied on obligations *erga omnes.*[31] Australia asserted that the prohibition of nuclear testing and the duty to observe the prohibition existed in customary international law and that it involved the same kind of legal obligations as existed in relation to the law concerning the basic rights of a human person, as listed in paragraph 34 of the Judgment in the *Barcelona Traction* case, i.e. obligations *erga omnes.* The Applicant (New Zealand) further argued that in consequence the right of States in relation to observance of the prohibition of nuclear testing corresponds with the duty of each State not to breach the prohibition. The duty is owed by each State to all other States. New Zealand pleaded that it follows from the character of obligations *erga omnes* that its claim against France relates to a right of all States – of the whole of the international community – and that such a right is not owed to each member of that community on a bilateral basis.[32] The individual opinions of the judges in this case were very different in relation to the issue of *locus standi* before the Court. For example, Judge de Castro was in general very sceptical regarding obligations *erga omnes* and standing before the Court in the case of such obligations. He was of the view that obligations *erga omnes* should treated *cum grano salis.*[33]

30 Barend van Niekerk, 'The Ecological Norms in Law or the Jurisprudence in the Right against Pollution' (1975) SALJ 92, 78, cited in: Thomas A Mensah, 'Using Judicial Bodies for the Implementation and Enforcement of International Environmental Law', in Isabelle Buffard and Gerhard Hafner (eds), *International Law between Universalism and Fragmentation: Festschrift in Honour of Gerhard Hanber* (Martinus Nijhoff 2008) 797, 809. Mensah states that Nieker's opinion was support by Judge Pickering in the case *Wildlife Society of Southern Africa and Others v Minister of Environmental Affairs and Tourism & Others*, Supreme Court, Case No 1672/95, 21 June 1996.

31 Memorial of Australia in *Case Concerning Nuclear Testing (Australia v France)* [431] and [448].

32 Memorial of New Zealand in *Case Concerning Nuclear Testing (New Zealand v France)* [207].

33 *Case Concerning Nuclear Testing (New Zealand v France)*, Judge de Castro Dissenting Opinion [253], [287].

A different view was expressed by Judge Berwick. He supported the view of the Applicant Australia that the prohibition of nuclear testing and the corresponding duty of observance of this prohibition extended to the whole community of States and constitutes an obligation *erga omnes.* He further explained that as to the question of *locus standi*, France's duty towards Australia 'to refrain from the atmospheric testing of nuclear weapons, would be an obligation. The parties would be in dispute as to their respective rights'.[34] The joint Dissenting Opinion of Judges Onyeama, Dillard, de Arechaga, and Waldock adopted a very cautious and measured approach to obligations *erga omnes* and the issue of standing before the Court. In principle, they were of the view that there is a possibility of standing for other States before the Court in a case of such obligations, provided the evidence of a substantive rule of customary international law has been persuasively evidenced, stating that:

> Although we recognise that the existence of so-called *actio popularis* in international law is a matter of controversy, the observation of the Court in the *Barcelona Traction, Light and Power Company, Limited* case suffice to show that the question is one that may be considered as capable of rational legal argument and a proper subject of litigation before the Court.[35]

In the 1994 case *Nuclear Testing II*, the question of obligations *erga omnes* also arose.[36] Australia in its pleadings to intervene argued that: 'The legal interests of every member of the international community, even those States not bound by the judgment are thus "affected" or *en cause* within the meaning of Article 62 of the Statute'.[37]

The aforementioned cases evidence the cautious approach of the Court in relation to *locus standi* in communitarian matters. The Court has not addressed the issues raised by parties in their pleadings in this respect. The legal questions in the area of the interests of the community were only raised by Judges in their individual judgments This indicates the awareness of the members of the Court regarding these issues, on one hand, and the conservative approach expressed by the majority of the Court, on the other.

34 Ibid, Judge Berwick Dissenting Opinion [253], [157].

35 Joint Dissenting Opinion of Judges Onyeama, Dillard, de Arechaga, and Waldock [117]–[118].

36 *Request for Examination of the Situation in Accordance with Paragraph of the Court's Judgment of 20 December 1974 in the Nuclear Tests (New Zealand v France) case* (1998) ICJ Rep 286.

37 Application for the Permission to Intervene under Article 62 of the Statute submitted by the Government of Australia [20].

3.2 Communitarian interests in the contemporary jurisprudence of international courts and tribunals

The judicial practice with respect to the protection of communitarian environmental interests is rather limited and modest. There is only one contentious case – 2014 *Whaling in the Antarctic* (ICJ)[38] – and one Advisory Opinion – *Responsibilities and Obligations of States Sponsoring Persons and Entities with Respect to Activities in the Area* (Seabed Disputes Chamber of ITLOS).[39]

3.2.1 Whaling in the Antarctic *case*

In this case, Australia (the applicant) and New Zealand (intervening) were not States directly injured by Japan's scientific whaling. As was stated: 'This case was driven by conflicting attitudes towards whaling, and also towards global common spaces'.[40] In its Judgment, the ICJ decided that Japan must halt its current whaling programme in the Southern Ocean. The decision did not apply directly to Japan's whale hunt in the northern Pacific, and it did not foreclose Japan from all whaling.[41]

The issue of the community of interest was not elaborated on in the Judgment. However, in its pleadings Australia claimed to be acting on behalf of such community, for which it was credited. According to Crawford, Australia had invoked Japan's responsibility *erga omnes partes.*[42] During the proceedings, Australia claimed to be presenting the case before the ICJ exclusively in the general interest. It argued that notwithstanding the fact that some of Japanese hunting activities had taken place in its territorial waters, it was a directly injured State. It argued that every party has some interest in ensuring compliance by every other party with its obligations under the 1946 Whaling Convention. Accordingly, it claimed to be seeking to uphold the collective interest under the Convention. Tams expressed the view that perhaps the *Whaling* case is a logical follow-up to the 2011 Judgment in *Belgium v. Senegal* (see above). In that latter case, the Court surprised commentators by going out of its way to accept the applicant's standing to endorse a multilateral treaty protecting collective interests.[43] In relation to this case, views were expressed that the current ecosystem approach and the notion of the

38 *Whaling in the Antarctic (Australia v Japan: New Zealand intervening)*, Judgment (2014) ICJ Rep 226.

39 *Responsibilities and Obligations of States Sponsoring Persons and Entities with Respect to Activities in the Area*, Advisory Opinion, ITLOS Reports 2011 at 10; Cymie Payne, 'ICJ Halts Antarctic Whaling – Japan Starts Again' (2015) 4(1) TEL 181.

40 Payne (n 39).

41 Ibid.

42 Crawford (n 14) 236. James Crawford, *State Responsibility* (CUP 2011) 62–94, 325.

43 Christian Tams, 'Roads Not Taken, Opportunities Missed. Procedural and Jurisdictional Questions Sidestepped in the *Whaling* Judgment', in Malgosia

common heritage of humankind may be considered by States as matters that give rise to obligations *erga omnes* and *erga omnes partes*, and thus can result in redress pursuant to Article 48 ARSIWA.[44] It was thus argued that the case illustrates that multilateral environmental agreements (MEAs) – such as the Whaling Convention in the case at hand – are not a simple sum of bilateral relationships. Their multilateral effect is reflected by the interest of Australia and New Zealand in mutual compliance, irrespective of whether they could claim any specific injury arising out of Japan's violations.[45]

However, a different view was expressed on the attempt (on the part of both Australia and New Zealand) to use Article 48 ARSIWA (obligations *erga omnes partes*) to establish their *locus standi* in the *Whaling* case. It was argued that use of Article 48 as the basis of their standing before the ICJ might be justified in cases such as the Genocide Convention or the Convention against Torture, however, in the view of certain authors in cases of a lesser importance – such as the *Whaling in the Antarctic* case, which related to the protection of whales – in attempting to derive a *locus standi* from the obligations of States based on the International Convention for the Regulation of Whaling there is no *raison d'être* for an action based on obligations *erga omnes partes*, even taking into account the 'special character' of whales.[46]

3.2.2 The Advisory Opinion of the ITLOS

The Advisory Opinion of the ITLOS concerned mining activities in the Area defined in Article 1(1) of the United Nations Convention on the Law of the Sea (LOSC) as 'the seabed and ocean floor and subsoil thereof, beyond the limits of national jurisdiction'. Article 136 of the Convention states that '[t]he Area and its resources are the common heritage of mankind'. The International Seabed Authority (ISA) has established an administrative regime to manage the exploration of the Area in conformity with the LOSC. The legal status of the Area is also defined in Article 137, which states that '[a]ll rights in the resources of the Area are vested in mankind as a whole, on whose behalf the Authority shall act'. The Advisory Opinion defined sponsoring State obligations as *erga omnes*. The rights to compensation for

Fitzmaurice and Dai Tamada (eds), *Whaling in the Antarctic: Significance and Implications of the ICJ Judgment* (Brill/Nijhoff 2015) 193, 201–207.

44 Simone Borg, 'The Influence of International Case Law on Aspects of International Law Relating to Conservation of Living Marine Resources beyond National Jurisdiction' (2017) YIEL 23, 44–79, 57–71.

45 Priya Urs, 'Are States Injured by Whaling in Antarctic?' (*Opinio Juris*, 14 August 2014) <http://opiniojuris.org/2014/08/14/guest-post-states-injured-whaling-antarctic/> accessed 30 April 2022.

46 Hironobu Sakai, 'After the *Whaling* Case: Its Lessons from a Japanese Perspective', in Malgosia Fitzmaurice and Dai Tamada (eds), *Whaling in the Antarctic: Significance and Implications of the ICJ Judgment* (Brill/Nijhoff 2015) 10–11.

damage to the Area and its resources for potential Claimants are based on their common interest in the marine environment. *Locus standi* was based on Article 48 of the ILC Articles. In this connection it was observed that:

> The Chamber's statement may be read as treating all states – whether parties to the LOSC or not – as rights holders under a customary law theory that the marine environment and the Area are the heritage of all humankind … [however], … some consider both the common heritage element of the Law of the Sea Convention and the ILC Draft Articles' article 48 to be progressive rather than customary law.[47]

3.2.3 National cases

There are very few cases reflecting communitarian interests in national law. There are, however, a few, which can be said to represent communitarian litigation, the most important being the *Minor Oposa*[48] and the *Faroogue* cases.[49] Both cases are also connected to the idea of international equity, which was first conceptualised by Edith Brown-Weiss.[50] According to her, this concept encompasses all generations because 'we, the human species, hold the natural environment of our planet in common with all members of our species: past generations, the present generation, and future generations'.[51] Accordingly, each generation is both a trustee for the planet with duties to care for it, and a beneficiary with rights to use it.[52]

In the *Minor Oposa* case, a group of children, including those of environmental activist Antonio Oposa, brought a lawsuit in conjunction with the Philippine Ecological Network, Inc (a non-profit organisation) to stop the destruction of the rapidly-disappearing rainforests in their country. The minors claimed that they were 'entitled to the full benefit, use and enjoyment of t.he natural resource treasures that is the country's virgin tropical rainforests'.

The children claimed that they represented themselves and generations yet unborn, thereby incorporating intergenerational equity into their suit. Standing was permitted insofar as it accommodated the right to a healthful ecology as embodied in Sections 15 and 16 of Article II of the Philippine Constitution.

47 Payne (n 8).
48 *Minors Oposa v Secretary of The Department of Environment and Natural Resources (DENR)*, Supreme Court of the Philippines, 30 July 1993, (1994) 33 ILM 173 <https://bit.ly/3lgHHnS> accessed 30 April 2022.
49 *M. Faroogue v Bangladesh*. This case was rejected by the majority. 1 BLC, Opinion of Mustafa Kamal J (analysed in Mensah).
50 Edith Brown-Weiss, 'Our Rights and Obligations to Future Generations for the Environment' (1990) 84 AJIL 198, 198–199. On new developments, please see, 'Intergenerational Equity', Oxford Publlic International Law, https://opil.ouplaw.com/view/10.1093/law:epil/9780199231690/law-9780199231690-e1421?print=pdf.
51 Ibid.
52 Ibid 203.

The Court held that:[53]

> Needless to say, every generation has a responsibility to the next to preserve that rhythm and harmony for the full enjoyment of a balanced and healthful ecology. Put a little differently, the minors' assertion of their right to a sound environment constitutes, at the same time, the performance of their obligation to ensure the protection of that right for the generations to come.
>
> (…)
>
> While the right to a balanced and healthful ecology is to be found under the Declaration of Principles and State Policies and not under the Bill of Rights, it does not follow that it is less important than any of the civil and political rights enumerated in the latter. Such a right belongs to a different category of rights altogether for it concerns nothing less than self-preservation and self-perpetuation – aptly and fittingly stressed by the petitioners – the advancement of which may even be said to predate all governments and constitutions. As a matter of fact, these basic rights need not even be written in the Constitution for they are assumed to exist from the inception of humankind. If they are now explicitly mentioned in the fundamental charter, it is because of the well-founded fear of its framers that unless the rights to a balanced and healthful ecology and to health are mandated as state policies by the Constitution itself, thereby highlighting their continuing importance and imposing upon the state a solemn obligation to preserve the first and protect and advance the second, the day would not be too far away when all else would be lost not only for the present generation, but also for those to come – generations which stand to inherit nothing but parched earth incapable of sustaining life.

This case, however, also illustrates the legal difficulties in the position of future generations in issues such as standing before the Court, relating to a very broad concept of the *locus standi*, which is at odds with national laws. These considerations were very aptly expressed by Judge Feliciano in his Separate Opinion.[54]

Similar considerations were expressed by Gatmaytan, who was of the opinion that 'Oposa is overrated', and that the praise and acclamation it has received in recent years are misdirected.[55] He stated, *inter alia*, that the decision did not affect the government's conduct towards Timber Licensing Agreements, which were not cancelled. Thus the Judgment of the Court had

53 Ibid.

54 *Minors Oposa v Secretary of The Department of Environment and Natural Resources (DENR)*, Judge Feliciano Separate Opinion.

55 Dante B Gatmaytan, 'The Illusion of Intergenerational Equity: *Oposa v. Factoran* as Pyrrhic Victory' (2003) 15 Geo Envtl L Rev 459.

no practical effect on future generations. He also opined that the granting of standing to sue on behalf of future generations was only *obiter dictum*, thereby not affecting the value of intergenerational equity as a binding legal right or obligation. Similarly to Judge Feliciano, Gatmaytan observed that in this case the issue of standing in the Philippines is approached very widely and loosely. Overall, Gatmaytan has admitted that the *Oposa* case was a valuable decision, but only as it recognised the constitutional right to a healthful ecology as justiciable, in contrast to issues regarding intergenerational equity in this case, which he did not consider as meaningful or adding any new legal dimension.

Lowe has also expressed a negative evaluation of the *Oposa* case. He stated that: 'it is not the right of a future generation, but the duty of some members of the *present* generation that is being enforced at the instance of other members of the *present* generation'.[56] According to him, future generations cannot possess rights of enjoyment or exercise their duty even to mitigate logging, because they do not exist. Lowe argued that the invocation of future generations in this case only served as a rhetorical device.[57]

In the *Farooq* case, the legal question was whether a non-governmental organisation could bring a case to challenge actions which allegedly violated the provisions on environmental protection. One of the Judges was of the view that although a personal injury is a requisite condition for bringing the case before the Court, such a principle should not be reasonably applied to the situation where public injuries were present. He stated as follows:

> The traditional view remains true, valid and effective till today in so far as individual rights and individual infractions thereof are concerned. But when a public injury or public wrong or information of a fundamental right affecting an indeterminate number of people is involved, it is necessary, in the scheme of our Constitution, that the multitude of individuals who have been collectively wronged or injured or whose collective fundamental rights have been invaded are to invoke the jurisdiction [under the Constitution] in a multitude of individual writ petitions, each representing each own portion of concern. In so far as it concerns public wrong or public injury or invasion of fundamental rights of an indeterminate number of people, any member of the public, being a citizen, suffering the common injury or common invasion in common with other or any citizen or an indigenous association, as distinguished from a local component of a foreign association, espousing that particular cause is a person aggrieved and has the right to invoke the jurisdiction [under the Constitution].[58]

56 Vaughan Lowe, 'Sustainable Development and Unsustainable Arguments' in Alan Boyle and David Freestone (eds), *International Law and Sustainable Development: Past Achievements and Future Challenges* (OUP 1999) 27.

57 Ibid.

58 WP 998 of 1994, 17 BLD (AD) 1997, Vol XVII, 1–33.

In India, in the case of *People United for Better Living Calcutta v State of West Bengal* (1992)[59] – which concerned water pollution and the maintenance of wetlands in Calcutta – the Court held that 'there shall be a proper balance between the development and the environment' thereby invoking sustainable development whilst claiming that '[t]he present day society has a responsibility towards the posterity… to breathe normally and live in a cleaner environment …',[60] thereby creating an ethos of intergenerational duty. In *S. Jagannath v Union of India*,[61] the petitioners filed a claim against intensified shrimp farming, which posed a serious threat to the environment and ecology. The Court held that:

> [it had] no hesitation in holding that Sustainable Development … has been accepted as a part of the customary international law, thereby recognising the rights of future generations … some of the salient principles of Sustainable Development … are Inter-Generational Equity.[62]

In recognising sustainable development as primary international law, the Court recognised and identified intergenerational equity as such, and required that it be an element to be taken into account in any environmental impact assessment.

In the High Court of Delhi, in the case of *Vedanta Alumina Ltd. v Prafulla Samantra & Ors*,[63] the petitioner filed a complaint against the construction of an aluminium smelter plant. Reference was made to *N.D. Jayal v Union of India*,[64] which stated that '[w]eighty concepts like inter-generational equity … public trust doctrine … could only be nurtured by ensuring sustainable development'.[65]

As some of aforementioned cases indicate, at a national level, the protection of the communitarian interest is closely linked to the concept of intergenerational equity. However, this concept has been subjected to severe critical comments, focusing on its lack of legal substance and its broadening of the scope of *locus standi*, thus highlighting the difficulty of its general application. The nebulous character of this concept has led to its characterisation as a 'rhetorical device'.

Thus, due to the inherent problems relating to the concept of intergenerational equity, the protection of the interests of the community at a national level is very patchy and there is not a consistent pattern of its redress nor of *locus standi* in cases of such a character.

59 AIR 1993 Cal 215, 97 CWN 142.
60 Ibid.
61 *S. Jagannath v Union of India* AIR 1997 SC 811 (1996).
62 Ibid.
63 *Vedanta Alumina Ltd. v Prafulla Samantra & Ors* LQ 2009 HC 8828 (2009).
64 *N.D. Jayal v Union of India* 9 SCC 36 (2004).
65 Ibid.

4 Human rights courts: an emerging regime for the protection of environmental communitarian interests

As was established already with regard to the Genocide Convention Advisory Opinion (see above), the protection of human rights is the classic example of the communitarian character of obligations. Human rights treaties, despite being concluded between States, are much more than 'reciprocal engagements between contracting States. They create, over and above a network of mutual, bilateral undertakings, objective obligations which, in the words of the Preamble, benefit from "collective enforcement".'[66]

This statement of the ECtHR, however, has not opened the door for *locus standi* to other than directly injured persons, a rule which has been until recently rigidly observed by the ECtHR. This is not to say that there are no changes in the Court's approach. The recent jurisprudence of the Court indicates that there is a certain degree of flexibility in its approach. In some (a few) cases, applications by persons not directly injured were admitted.[67] In one such case, the Court stated that:

> [A]lthough the primary purpose of the Convention system is to provide individual relief, its mission is also to determine issues on public-policy grounds in the common interest, thereby raising the general standards of protection of human rights and extending human rights jurisprudence throughout the community of Contracting States.[68]

Recent developments indicate a certain degree a synergy between human rights and the environment, which may result in more advanced and effective protection of the community of interests in relation to the protection of the common environment.

On 15 November 2018, the IACtHR rendered a landmark Advisory Opinion on the Environment and Human Rights.[69] The IACtHR has defined the

66 *Ireland v UK* App no 5310/71 (ECtHR, 18 January 1978) [239]. See Farid Ahmadov, *The Right of Actio Popularis before International Courts and Tribunals* (Nijhoff/Brill 2018) 53.

67 The author of this study is aware of many cases before the ECtHR which concerned the environment, such as the *López Ostra* case (*López Ostra v Spain* App no 16798/90), *Hatton* cases (*Hatton and Others v the United Kingdom* App no 36022/97; *Hatton and Others v the United Kingdom* App no 36022/97), *Fadeyeva* case (*Fadeyeva v Russia* App no 55723/00) and many others. The practice of the ECtHR has attracted a great number of contributions of books and articles. However, all these cases were based on a bilateral basis, vis-à-vis a directly injured person. Therefore, there were no *locus standi* questions of a communitarian nature.

68 Ibid.

69 *Requested by the Republic of Colombia: The Environment and Human Rights* (IACtHR Advisory Opinion, 15 November 2017) OC-23/17. See Giovanny Vega-Barbosa, 'Human Rights and the Protection of the Environment: The Advisory Opinion of the Inter-American Court of Human Rights' (*EJIL: Talk!*, 26 February 2018) <https://bit.ly/3vKbv1V>; Maria L Banda, 'Inter-American Court of

role of environmental protection. It has not only found that there is an autonomous right to a healthy environment, but also stated that any human right can be affected by environmental harm.[70] Most importantly, the Court has recognised the existence of an 'autonomous' right to a healthy environment under the Inter-American Convention. The Court has found that the right to a healthy environment is encompassed by Article 26 of the Convention (Progressive Development) and is further reflected in member States' constitutions and some international instruments.[71] The Court also accorded an exterritorial effect to the breach of a human right to a clean environment in the case of transboundary pollution.[72] However, such jurisdiction is 'exceptional' and must be interpreted on a case-by-case basis.[73] The Court also fleshed out the content of such an environmental right vis-à-vis States' duties, such as the duty to prevent transboundary harm and the general duty of prevention of significant harm; the precautionary principle; the duty to cooperate; and procedural environmental rights.

General Comment 36 on the Right to Life of the Human Rights Committee is also a notable example of the synergy between human rights and the environment. According to the General Comment, the protection of the right to life (Article 6) encompasses the duty of States to protect the environment.[74]

National developments in relation to standing in environmental matters, which can to some extent support the communitarian interest, are very encouraging. For example, in 2018, the Supreme Court of Colombia issued a decision favourable for environmental law, human rights, and the rights of nature. In the case, the plaintiffs (between 7–25 years) alleged that the government violated their rights to life, to health, and to enjoy a healthy environment. It was alleged that it failed to control deforestation in the Amazon region, which contributes to environmental degradation and climate change. The Court recognised legal rights of the Amazon River ecosystem.

Human Rights Advisory Opinion on the Environment and Human Rights' (2018) 22(6) ASIL Insights <https://bit.ly/2QRCPfX>; Monica Feria-Tinta and Simon Milne 'The Rise of Environment Law in International Dispute Resolution: Inter-American Court of Human Rights Issues Landmark Advisory Opinion on Environment and Human Rights' (*EJIL: Talk!*, 26 February 2018) <https://bit.ly/3epvz3z> all accessed 30 April 2022.

70 Banda (n 69) 1.

71 Ibid 2.

72 Ibid 3.

73 Ibid 4.

74 According to the Human Rights Committee:

> The duty to protect life also implies that States parties should take appropriate measures to address the general conditions in society that may give rise to direct threats to life or prevent individuals from enjoying their right to life with dignity. These general conditions may include … degradation of the environment …

Human Rights Committee, 'General comment No 36 (2018) on article 6 of the International Covenant on Civil and Political Rights, on the right to life' (30 October 2018) CCPR/C/GC/36 [26].

The Court's opinion ordered the creation of an 'Intergenerational Pact for the Life of the Colombian Amazon', with the participation of the plaintiffs, affected communities, scientific groups, and others.

In its decision, the Supreme Court relied on some of the key principles of environmental law and environmental ethics, including intergenerational equity and the precautionary principle, within the context of both Colombia's constitution as well as international law.[75] *Locus standi* in such cases recognises the communitarian interest.

Finally, the landmark 2019 Judgment of the Dutch Supreme Court (following a lengthy previous litigation) in *State of the Netherlands v Urgenda* needs to be mentioned.[76] The Supreme Court held that on the basis of the European Convention on Human Rights the Netherlands has a positive obligation to take measures for the prevention of climate change and that it has to reduce its greenhouse gas emissions by at least 25 per cent (compared to 1990 levels) by the end of 2020. However, the importance of this case is of a limited value from the point of view of global, communitarian interests. As Nollkaemper and Burgers explain:

> In the Urgenda case, the Supreme Court appeared to be only concerned with the protection of interests of inhabitants in the Netherlands, due to the fact that Urgenda relied on art. 3:305a DCC, and that the State had not disputed standing in so far as the claim concerned the protection of the interests of the inhabitants of the Netherlands from dangerous climate change … In first instance, the District Court had accepted Urgenda's standing on behalf of people outside the Netherlands and on behalf of future generations, to which the State objected. The Court of Appeal did not assess whether Urgenda could have standing in this latter respect, noting that anyway, Urgenda's standing on behalf of current Dutch nationals was undisputed between the parties (and thus had to be accepted as a matter of civil procedure). The Supreme Court, therefore, did not discuss whether the jurisdictional scope of the ECHR would have allowed it to consider also interests outside the Netherlands, but limited itself to the Netherlands' inhabitants. It was perhaps for this reason that the court

75 Nicholas Bryner, 'Colombian Supreme Court Recognizes Rights of the Amazon River Ecosystem' (*IUCN*, 20 April 2018) <https://bit.ly/3xDZ5tq>. The legal personality of rivers has been considered in several jurisdictions. In India, the High Court recognised the legal personality of the Ganges and Yamuna rivers in March 2017; however, this decision was overturned in July 2017. In contrast, the Whanganui river was recognised as a living entity in New Zealand in March 2017 by way of legislation. Bronagh Kieran, 'The Legal Personality of Rivers' (*EMA Human Rights Blog*, 16 January 2019) <http://www.emahumanrights.org/2019/01/16/the-legal-personality-of-rivers/> both accessed 30 April 2022.

76 André Nollkaemper and Laura Burgers, 'A New Classic in Climate Change Litigation: The Dutch Supreme Court Decision in the Urgenda Case' (*EJIL: Talk!*, 6 January 2020) <https://bit.ly/3gPJCj5> accessed 30 April 2022.

specifically singled out the risk of a sharp rise in the sea level, which may make the low-lying Netherlands partly uninhabitable.[77]

5 Conclusion

This chapter has endeavoured to analyse the issue of *locus standi* with respect to the protection of communitarian interests relating to protection of the environment at the international and national levels. There is no doubt that many scholars have expressed an opinion that such a community interest exists vis-à-vis the environment. For example, Judge Gaja opined that the protection of natural resources could fall within the realm of interests of the international community and that the community interest can be expressed through the imposition of certain restrictions on their exploitation. He also was of the view that the concept of the common heritage of humankind belongs to the category of concepts which engage the public interest. Article 48 ARSIWA can be relied on in cases of breaches involving the community of interests.[78] By the same token, Shotaro Hamamoto was of the view that MEAs are a source of collective interests; therefore Japan, in principle (even before the *Belgium v. Senegal* Judgment), would have been in a difficult position to assert the inadmissibility of the claim of Australia on the basis of the lack of a legal interest. According to Hamamoto, a non-admissibility plea on the part of Japan would have been – after the *Belgium v Senegal* case – in the case against Australia 'virtually hopeless'.[79] Kolb was of the view that the *Whaling* case is an example of the exercise of discretionary powers in relation to the protection of the common good (in this instance, whaling).[80]

Thus the question may be asked whether multilateralism regarding *locus standi*, insofar as concerns international environmental law, is declining or thriving.

Despite the scholarly views, at a practical level, international and national jurisprudence in relation to cases involving the protection of the communitarian interest has not flourished as much as was expected. The Judgment of the Court in the *Whaling* case was symptomatic of the trend towards a more cautious approach to the issue of *locus standi* in matters involving the communitarian interest. Although there is no doubt that this case is an example of granting standing with respect to *erga omnes partes* obligations, the Court refrained from mentioning this expressly in its Judgment. This omission was a

77 Ibid.

78 Giorgio Gaja, 'The Protection of General Interests in the International Community' (2011) 364 RCADI 171–80.

79 Shotaro Hamamoto, 'Procedural Questions in the *Whaling* Judgment: Admissibility, Intervention and the Use of Experts', Japanese Society of International Law, The Honourable Shigeru Oda Commemorative Lectures 1, 6.

80 Robert Kolb, 'Short Reflections on the ICJ's *Whaling* Case and the Review by International Courts and Tribunals of "Discretionary Powers"' (2014) 32 Aust Yb Int L 135.

major departure from the Advisory Opinion of the ITLOS, where the issues of obligations *erga omnes* and *erga omnes partes* were analysed in detail by the Tribunal.

There may be various reasons for such (unwelcome) developments. One is probably the inherent vagueness of international environmental norms. As Payne correctly states, '[t]he general principle that obligations are owed to the international community is only useful when the content of those obligations is defined'.[81] Therefore, international environmental law norms which have a well-defined content should be considered as a basis for *locus standi* in the event of a communitarian obligation. It is suggested that an Environmental Impact Assessment (EIA) may be considered as the best-defined principle of international environmental law, as evidenced by the Judgment in the *Pulp Mill* case, although the precise scope of application and content of the EIA obligation are still not firmly established.[82]

Obviously, the lack of a clearly defined content with respect to principles of international environmental law affects the lodging of an effective communitarian claim. It may be said that in MEAs which contain a requirement of conducting an EIA, the content of States' obligations is defined in a more detailed and precise manner, thus constituting a possible ground for the protection of environmental communitarian interests of an *erga omnes partes* character and granting *locus standi* to all parties to the MEA. An example of such an MEA is the 1991 Espoo Convention, which is a global treaty.[83]

In general, the views which are expressed in the literature and by some of the Judges of the ICJ are that the Court is ill-equipped to accommodate multilateral disputes involving interrelated (interdependent) obligations, such as disarmament.[84] The inherent formalism of the ICJ procedures (especially concerning jurisdictional issues and the indispensable third-party rule), has proved at times to be an obstacle to the redress of communitarian interests.[85]

81 Payne (n 8) 116.

82 *Pulp Mills on the River Uruguay (Argentina v Uruguay)*, Judgment (2010) ICJ Rep 14 [204]. See also *Certain Activities Carried out by Nicaragua in the Border Area (Costa Rica v Nicaragua) and Construction of a Road in Costa Rica along the San Juan River (Nicaragua v Costa Rica) (Joined Cases)*, Judgment (2015) ICJ Rep 665.

83 Convention on Environmental Impact Assessment in a Transboundary Context (the Espoo Convention), 1989 UNTS 309.

84 Vincent-Joël Proulx, 'The World Court's Jurisdictional Formalism and Its Lost Market Share: The Marshall Islands Decisions and the Quest for a Suitable Dispute Settlement Forum for Multilateral Disputes' (2017) 30 LJIL 925, 944. The author specifically refers to the Marshall Islands cases – *Obligations concerning Negotiations relating to Cessation of the Nuclear Arms Race and to Nuclear Disarmament (Marshall Islands v India; Marshall Islands v Pakistan; Marshall Islands v UK)* Judgment (Jurisdiction and Admissibility, Preliminary Objections) (2016) ICJ Rep 255, 552, 833.

85 *Obligations concerning Negotiations relating to Cessation of the Nuclear Arms Race and to Nuclear Disarmament (Marshall Islands v India, Pakistan, UK) (Jurisdiction and Admissibility)*, Judge Tomka Separate Opinion [1].

These considerations also apply to community interests in environmental matters. The existing, very limited and patchy, judicial practice in this respect does not give sufficient grounds for drawing any general conclusions regarding the issue of *locus standi* in the protection of environmental communitarian interests. Since 2014 (the *Whaling* case), there has not been any contentious case or an Advisory Opinion in international jurisprudence regarding obligations *erga omnes* and *erga omnes partes* in environmental matters on behalf of the community of States, which indicates a certain stagnation in this respect. In the opinion of this author, a revival of judicial practice in relation to the redress of these obligations is doubtful. This is due to the above-mentioned procedural obstacles and the lack of judicial consistency in matters of standing. It is also possible that the controversial judgment in the *Whaling* case, which was subject to certain criticism, has had an adverse effect on States and discouraged them from initiating proceedings on behalf of the international community in environmental matters. This situation is compounded by the fact that many environmental obligations are characterised by a woolly and imprecise content.

In this author's view, the more promising way of protecting communitarian environmental interests is based on a human rights approach. The new developments in this area are very encouraging. The Supreme Court of Columbia accorded an extraterritorial application to the protection of environmental human rights. *Locus standi* in relation to communitarian environmental interests is growing in importance as the obligation to protect the environment is considered by some scholars as an emerging obligation *erga omnes*.[86]

The synergy with human rights norms gives the ill-defined environmental principles more substance and fleshes them out in terms of content. In linking environmental protection with human rights, the IACtHR has accorded it justifiability. This appears to be the best way forward towards the use of a more liberal *locus standi* for the protection of communitarian environmental interests.

86 Nicholas A Robinson, 'Environmental Law: Is an Obligation *Erga Omnes* Emerging?' Panel Discussion at the United Nations, New York, 4 June 2018.

8 The Advent and Fall of Trust as a Cornerstone of Judicial Cooperation in Multilateral Regimes in Europe: A Cautionary Tale

Vassilis Pergantis

1 Introduction: trust as a cornerstone of judicial cooperation in Europe

The multi-layered supranational governance regimes established in Europe in the aftermath of the Second World War, such as the Council of Europe (CoE) and the European Economic Communities (EEC), hinged on the idea that Member States (MSs) shared a set of common values that would allow for the development of multilateral cooperation in their respective fields of activity. This is squarely reflected in their principal instruments. For instance, Article 3 of the CoE Statute provides that each MS 'must accept the principles of the rule of law and of the enjoyment by all persons within its jurisdiction of human rights and fundamental freedoms'.[1] In the same vein, the Treaty on European Union (TEU) stipulates in Article 2 that '[t]he Union is founded on the values of respect for human dignity, freedom, democracy, equality, the rule of law and respect for human rights … These values are common to the Member States.'[2]

This commitment to a heritage of common values in the European continent is evidenced by the design and evolution of the respective systems of judicial review in the CoE[3] and the European Union (EU). As regards the former, the European Court of Human Rights (ECtHR) is not directly embedded in the national judicial systems of the contracting parties to the European Convention on Human Rights (ECHR),[4] meaning it does not serve as a 'fourth instance' Court reviewing the application of domestic law by

1 Statute of Council of Europe (entry into force 3 August 1949) 87 UNTS 103. See also the Preamble of the Convention on Human Rights and Fundamental Freedoms (entry into force 3 September 1953) 213 UNTS 221.

2 See also the Charter of Fundamental Rights of the European Union [2007] OJ C303/2; Tampere European Council, 'Presidency Conclusions' 16 October 1999 <https://bit.ly/3vPnxH0> accessed 30 April 2022 [1].

3 Steven Greer, *The European Convention on Human Rights: Achievements, Problems and Prospects* (CUP 2006) 15, 16.

4 Laurence Helfer, 'Redesigning the European Court of Human Rights: Embeddedness as a Deep Structural Principle of the European Court of Human Rights Regimes' (2008) 19 EJIL 125, 135, 150.

DOI: 10.4324/9781003312857-10

national courts.[5] And even in relation to the application and interpretation of Convention rights, until recently the ECtHR did not enjoy a direct mechanism of dialogue with national courts in the mould of the preliminary ruling mechanism of the Court of Justice of the European Union (CJEU).[6] Its role in ensuring the effective protection of Convention rights is thus subsidiary to that of national authorities.[7] This is exemplified primarily by the admissibility requirement that the applicant exhaust local remedies before using the ECtHR.[8] As the Court has explained, this requirement is premised on the presumption 'that there is an effective remedy available in respect of the alleged breach in the domestic system'.[9]

Furthermore, in providing for the collective guarantee of human rights,[10] the ECHR establishes a set of minimum, but not rigidly uniform, human rights protection standards.[11] On that basis, the ECtHR recognizes that the contracting parties enjoy a margin of appreciation in their application of the ECHR.[12] The requirement to exhaust local remedies and the margin of appreciation doctrine encourage national judges 'to appropriate the Convention and make it their own',[13] thus ensuring their increased involvement in the filtering and diffusion of Convention standards at the domestic level.[14] The safety net of common values has allowed the ECtHR to entrust domestic judiciaries with the aforementioned tasks and the constant, albeit indirect, socialization between the Court and national judges has further enabled the former to enhance its trust towards the latter with respect to the effective application of Convention standards.[15]

The judicial system of the EU (initially the EEC) is, for its part, structured differently, in the sense that it provides for the preliminary ruling mechanism, thus effectively establishing a direct line of communication between the CJEU

5 Steven Greer, Janneke Gerards, and Rose Slowe, *Human Rights in the Council of Europe and the European Union: Achievements, Trends and Challenges* (CUP 2018) 133.
6 Laurence Helfer and Anne-Marie Slaughter, 'Toward a Theory of Effective Supranational Adjudication' (2017) 107 Yale L J 273, 297. Cf Protocol No 16 to the Convention on the Protection of Human Rights and Fundamental Freedoms (entry into force 1 August 2018) CETS No 214.
7 See Protocol No 15 to the Convention on the Protection of Human Rights and Fundamental Freedoms (entry into force 1 August 2021) CETS No 213, Article 1.
8 ECHR, Article 35(1).
9 *Anchugov and Gladkov v Russia* App no 21893/93 (ECtHR, 16 September 1996) [65].
10 *Soering v UK* App no 14038/88 (ECtHR, 7 July 1989) [87].
11 *Sunday Times v UK* App no 6538/74 (ECtHR, 26 April 1979) [61].
12 Robert Spano, 'Universality or Diversity of Human Rights? Strasbourg in the Age of Subsidiarity' (2014) 14 HR L Rev 487, 492–494.
13 Paolo G Carozza, 'Subsidiarity as a Structural Principle of International Human Rights Law' (2003) 97 AJIL 38, 75.
14 David Kosař and Jan Petrov, 'The Architecture of the Strasbourg System of Human Rights: The Crucial Role of the Domestic Level and the Constitutional Courts in Particular' (2017) 77 ZaöRV 585, 595.
15 Eyal Benvenisti, 'Margin of Appreciation, Consensus, and Universal Standards' (1999) 31 NYU J Int L & Pol 843, 853, 854.

and national courts. This latter mechanism was, indeed, a game-changer: it inaugurated a scheme of collaborative justice,[16] whereby the CJEU and the national courts play complementary roles in the application and interpretation of EU law.[17] Forging such a close cooperation depended both on the creation of a relationship of trust between the national courts and their supranational counterpart, i.e. that the former would implement their mandate of ensuring the effectiveness of EU law,[18] as well as gradually leading to its furtherance through the integrative pull of the preliminary ruling mechanism.[19]

Trust is not only vertically present in the relations between the CJEU and national judges, but also embedded horizontally among national courts. Specifically, enhanced cooperation of the MSs in the Area of Freedom, Security and Justice (AFSJ) is predicated on the principle of mutual trust, namely that each MS shows trust in the respective legal systems of its peers and that, owing to their common commitment to the aforementioned values, the latter will comply in an equivalent way with minimum normative standards, effectively creating a level playing field for all MSs.[20] This presumption of equivalent compliance translates into a duty on the part of each MS to recognize and enforce in a quasi-automatic way the judgments and administrative decisions of other MSs, without having the right to review them, save in exceptional cases.[21]

Such presumptions of compliance or equivalence, which are omnipresent in transnational judicial networks, constitute the tangible legal expression of the bonds of trust forged between judicial actors, while also generating further trust between them.[22] This has been eloquently articulated by the CJEU in the *Achmea* judgment, where it singled out intra-EU Member States' relations as being premised on mutual trust so as to exclude external judicial review therein.[23] Yet, this complex network of trust-based and trust-enhancing

16 Joseph HH Weiler, 'The European Court, National Courts and References for Preliminary Rulings: The Paradox of Success – A Revisionist View of Article 177 EEC' (1985) EUI Working Paper no 203.

17 Opinion 1/09 [2011] ECLI:EU:C:2011:123 [68]–[69], [83]–[84].

18 Joseph HH Weiler, 'The Transformation of Europe' (1991) 100 Yale L J 2403, 2451.

19 Juan Mayoral, 'Impact through Trust: The CJEU as a Trust-enhancing Institution' in Marlene Wind (ed), *International Courts and Domestic Politics* (CUP 2018) 160.

20 Directive 2010/64/EU on the right to interpretation and translation in criminal proceedings [2010] OJ L 280/1, Recital 3; Directive 2012/13/EU on the right to information in criminal proceedings [2012] OJ L 142/1.

21 Opinion 2/13 [2014] ECLI:EU:C:2014:2454 [191]–[194].

22 Cf Brunessen Bertrand, 'La systématique des présomptions' (2016) 32 RFDA 331, 332; Armin von Bogdandy and Michael Ioannidis, 'Systemic Deficiency in the Rule of Law: What It Is, What Has Been Done, What Can Be Done' (2014) 51 CMLR 59, 60.

23 C-284/16 *Slowakische Republik v Achmea BV* [2018] ECLI:EU:C:2018:158 [31]–[37].

mechanisms is nowadays confronted with the advent of illiberal democracies in Europe, resulting in human rights and/or rule of law backsliding.[24] In the remainder of this chapter, first the notion of trust is fleshed out in order to better comprehend its multifaceted nature (Section 2). Then, after analysing the notion of human rights/rule of law backsliding, the chapter examines the way multilateral judicial cooperation networks in Europe attempt to adjust to the above phenomenon, turning first to the ECtHR (Section 3.1) and second to the EU's judicial system (Section 3.2), before offering some tentative conclusions (Section 4).

2 Trust as a multi-dimensional phenomenon

The concept of trust has a rich sociological and philosophical content, although it remains rather understudied in the legal field. It is thus necessary to highlight its main features before examining the relations of trust within multilateral judicial cooperation networks in Europe. First, trust evokes human relationships and a specific mental state. At the same time, it has also been invoked within the framework of institutional relationships, in the sense that trust can be placed in an abstract system, such as the banking sector or the judiciary.[25] Moreover, trust flourishes beyond relations of familiarity between the trustor and the trustee; it intervenes in situations where there is a lack of full knowledge with regard to the expected relationship and its outcomes. In such cases, there is an element of risk in the purported transaction, increasing its costs.[26] Nevertheless, there must be a common language/set of values between the two sides of the relationship of trust (trustor-trustee) and, inescapably, if this cooperation is fruitful and becomes embedded (or institutionalized), familiarity increases too.[27] Additionally, trust is usually distinguished from reliance, which denotes the act but not the motives and the complex calculations and factors that shape the notion of trust,[28] as well as from confidence, the latter implying a lack of alternatives while trust is characterized by the existence of options.[29]

Regarding the subject of this study, the options available to supranational judiciaries were between isolation and cooperation. Such cooperation

24 See Nancy Bermeo, 'On Democratic Backsliding' (2016) 27 J Democr 5.

25 Michael Schwarz, 'Let's Talk about Trust, Baby! Theorizing Trust and Mutual Recognition in the EU's Area of Freedom, Security and Justice' (2018) 24 ELJ 124, 132.

26 Niklas Luhmann, 'Familiarity, Confidence, Trust: Problems and Alternatives' in Diego Gambetta (ed), *Trust: Making and Breaking Cooperative Relations* (OUP 2000) 94, 95.

27 For more on the way socialization between courts in the context of the preliminary reference mechanism impacts on trust, see Mayoral (n 19) 170–171.

28 Karen Jones, 'Trust: Philosophical Aspects' in James D Wright (ed), *International Encyclopedia of the Social and Behavioral Sciences* (2nd edn, Elsevier Science & Technology 2015) 668, 669.

29 Luhmann (n 26) 97.

manifestly involved the risk of trusting a judiciary which might undermine rather than further the common project, thus weakening the role and authority of the respective supranational courts. In other words, trust is a means to cope with the inherent uncertainty[30] of the aforementioned cooperation mechanisms, i.e. of granting discretion to the trustee without having sufficient guarantees that the latter will fulfil the trustor's expectations. In that sense, trust intertwines with vulnerability, as the trustor depends on the trustee's *good will* and cooperative attitude.[31] This is a crucial element in judicial multilateral cooperation regimes, where the trust shown by supranational courts towards national judiciaries – that they will fulfil their role as enforcers of the values and legal norms decreed at the supranational level – is frequently presented as deference towards them.[32] In reality, deference is part of trust, if one takes into account the vulnerability involved therein, although blind trust or absolute deference imposed by law cannot be associated with trust and might lead to an opposite result, generating distrust.[33]

Trust is equally a calculated, rational choice by the parties involved. Supranational courts entrust national judiciaries with important responsibilities because they correctly understand that the latter have a series of motives to redeem the former's trust, particularly in order to maintain the applicable cooperative scheme, which is based on shared values and a concomitant shared responsibility for their advancement.[34] These overlapping interests of the trustor and the trustee are furthered by the fact that in the said judicial multilateral cooperation systems this trust is reciprocal, from the supranational to the national level and vice versa, as well as between national judiciaries in the AFSJ.[35]

This brings us to the last element of this theoretical take on trust: what makes a trustee trustworthy? Some elements have already been highlighted, such as the existence of shared values, juridically conveyed, for instance, through a presumption of procedural and substantive equivalence,[36] or the trustee's competence and willingness to meet the trustor's expectations so as to preserve its reputation as a reliable collaborator. The more an authority (or

30 M. Levi, 'Trust, Sociology of' in James D Wright (ed), *International Encyclopedia of the Social and Behavioral Sciences* (Elsevier Science & Technology 2015) 664.

31 For more on the element of vulnerability, see Annette Baier, 'Trust and Antitrust' (1996) 96 Ethics 231, 235.

32 Ed Bates, 'Activism and Self-Restraint: The Margin of Appreciation's Strasbourg Career and Its "Coming of Age"?' (2016) 36 HRLJ 261.

33 Juan Mayoral, 'In the CJEU Judges Trust: A New Approach in the Judicial Construction of Europe' (2017) 55 JCMS 551, 554.

34 See Russel Hardin, *Trust and Trustworthiness* (Sage 2002) 3, who speaks about 'encapsulated interest'.

35 Rob van Gestel and Jurgen de Poorter, *In the Court We Trust: Cooperation, Coordination and Collaboration between the ECJ and Supreme Administrative Courts* (CUP 2019) 185. My analysis of trust in vertical relations will be, however, unidirectional, from the supranational to the national level and not vice versa.

36 *Bosphorus v Ireland* App no 45036/98 (ECtHR, 30 June 2005) [155].

effectively a State) builds its reputation as a human rights-compliant actor, the stronger the trust shown will be. In contrast, trustworthiness cannot be enhanced by a strict system of monitoring, since this would showcase an element of distrust and might undermine trustworthiness by creating resentment on the part of the monitored party.[37] This may explain the exhaustion of local remedies rule, or the CJEU's 'light touch' approach in mutual trust cases.

Consequently, trust is the belief, under conditions of uncertainty, that someone will show good faith and follow an expected course of action. On that conceptual basis, the current crisis of democratic backsliding challenges two of the main traits of trust: the extent of certainty and the requirement of good faith.

3 Rule of law/human rights backsliding and the fate of trust-based multilateral cooperation regimes

In recent years, rule of law guarantees have come under attack in various European States. According to a comprehensive definition, the term 'rule of law backsliding' describes 'the process through which elected public authorities deliberately implement governmental blueprints which aim to systematically weaken, annihilate, or capture internal checks on power with the view of dismantling the liberal democratic state and entrenching the long-term rule of the dominant party'.[38] Such backsliding can take various forms, such as, *inter alia*, capture of the courts through the dismissal or retirement of judges and their packing with new judges who are loyal to the regime; attacks on freedom of expression, and particularly on freedom of the press; hostility towards NGOs and the civil society in general; use of emergency powers to detain people and quash dissent; suppression of media pluralism; discrimination against vulnerable groups.[39]

In this framework, the question of the fate of trust within multilateral judicial regimes is raised. Can the 'ethical decentralization'[40] of judicial review to national peers survive in cases of gross, bad faith, human rights abuses?[41] Can a common core of shared values persist in an era of diverging

37 Roderick M Kramer, 'Trust and Distrust in Organizations: Emerging Perspectives, Enduring Questions' (1999) 50 Annu Rev Psychol 569, 591.

38 Laurent Pech and Kim L Scheppele, 'Illiberalism Within: Rule of Law Backsliding in the EU' (2017) 9 CYELS 3, 10.

39 For the link between the rule of law, democracy, and human rights, see Venice Commission, 'Rule of Law Checklist' CDL-AD (2016)007 [18]; European Commission, 'A New EU Framework to Strengthen the Rule of Law' [2014] COM 158 final, 4.

40 For more on this term, see Camille Dautricourt, 'A Strasbourg Perspective on the Autonomous Development of Fundamental Rights in EU Law: Trends and Implications' (2010) Jean Monnet Working Paper no 10/10, 42.

41 James A Sweeney, 'Margins of Appreciation: Cultural Relativity and the European Court of Human Rights in the Post-Cold War Era' (2005) 54 ICLQ 459, 472.

tendencies with regard to national policies on human rights protection? And more importantly, are supranational courts endowed with mechanisms which enable them to confront generalized practices of governmental defiance and systemic deficiencies towards rule of law guarantees? The recent jurisprudence of the CJEU and the ECtHR showcases how they have made inroads – but also faced backlash – in their fight against rule of law and human rights backsliding. Their varied judicial strategies notwithstanding, the parameter of trust remains central in their responses.

3.1 The ECtHR and human rights backsliding

Two notable developments related to the phenomenon of human rights and rule of law backsliding can be discerned in the ECtHR's case law: a continuing deference vis-à-vis rule-of-law-defiant regimes by enhancing the grip of the subsidiarity principle in its case law (Section 3.1.1); and an attempt to put pressure on illiberal regimes by activating Article 18 ECHR (Section 3.1.2).

3.1.1 Trust expanded: the ECtHR in the 'Age of Subsidiarity'[42]

From the period of the Brighton Declaration[43] onwards, a new trend in the ECtHR's case law can be observed, whereby the Court grants a wider margin of appreciation to national authorities, when restrictions on human rights have been subject to an extensive parliamentary debate before their enactment, and effective legal remedies are provided for the redress of relevant human rights violations.[44] For instance, in the *JB and others v Hungary* case the ECtHR stressed repeatedly that the early retirement measure that had allowed the Hungarian government to change the composition of courts was the outcome of dialogue between the Hungarian Parliament, the Constitutional Court, the European Court of Justice, the European Commission and the Venice Commission.[45] Consequently, and taking into account also other parameters, it found the complaint manifestly ill-founded because the applicants had not established the seriousness of the measures' impact on their private lives.[46] Despite the fact that the applicants had equally argued that the early retirement measure constituted 'a serious attack against the independence of the Hungarian judiciary as a whole',[47] the Court chose to disregard

42 See Spano (n 12) 487.
43 High-Level Conference on the Future of the European Court of Human Rights, 'Brighton Declaration' (19 April 2012) <https://bit.ly/2SikzfV> accessed 30 April 2022.
44 Oddny M Arnadóttir, 'The Brighton Aftermath and the Changing Role of the European Court of Human Rights' (2018) 9 JIDS 223, 228–232. See *SAS v France* App no. 43835/11 (ECtHR (GC), 1 July 2014) [153].
45 *JB and Others v Hungary* App no 45434/12 (ECtHR, 20 December 2018) [92].
46 Ibid [132]–[137].
47 Ibid [113].

the broader picture, i.e. the rule of law backsliding through the creeping capture of Hungarian courts by the government.[48] Instead it stressed the dialogue between national and supranational institutions.[49] Thus, the ECtHR's judgment evidenced the limitations of the individual application mechanism and legitimized a national process that was seriously flawed, as it is known that supermajorities frequently proceed to parliamentary discussions only as a pretext in order to be able to argue for a wider margin of appreciation.[50] Under these circumstances, a deferential attitude vis-à-vis bad faith national authorities, which are structurally unwilling and incapable of enforcing the Convention standards, undermines the ECHR's collective human rights guarantee.[51]

The same observations can be made with regard to the ECtHR's insistence that applicants exhaust domestic remedies before using it, despite the fact that a general defiance of rule of law guarantees frequently taints the effectiveness of such remedies. For example, a series of cases against Turkey after the 2016 *coup d'état* were declared inadmissible because of the failure of the applicants to exhaust domestic remedies enacted post-*coup* via emergency decrees. Yet these remedies did not allow the applicants to challenge the decrees before the Turkish Constitutional Court,[52] and it became rapidly apparent by the high number of applications declared inadmissible or ill-founded that they did not necessarily satisfy the requirement of effectiveness. Moreover, serious doubts were expressed over the impartiality of the bodies having the competence to examine these remedies.[53] As the ECtHR noted, however, doubts about the prospects of success or fears about courts' impartiality did not suffice to justify the non-exhaustion of an available remedy.[54]

48 David Kosař and Katarina Šipulova, 'The Strasbourg Court Meets Abusive Constitutionalism: Baka v. Hungary and the Rule of Law' (2018) 10 Hague J Rule L 83, 95.

49 *JB and Others v Hungary* [81], [92], [101]. See Renata Uitz, 'Guest Editorial: The Perils of Defending the Rule of Law through Dialogue' (2019) 15 EuConst 1, 6, 7.

50 See Andras Sajó and Sergio Giuliano, 'The Perils of Complacency: The European Human Rights Backlash' in Jan Klabbers and Gianluigi Palombella (eds), *The Challenge of Inter-legality* (CUP 2019) 230, 243; *Baka v Hungary* App no 20261/12 (ECtHR (GC), 23 June 2016) [161].

51 Robert Spano, 'The Future of the European Court of Human Rights – Subsidiarity, Process-Based Review and the Rule of Law' (2018) 18 HRLR 473, 477, 492, 493.

52 See *Mercan v Turkey* App no. 56511/16 (ECtHR, 8 November 2016); *Zihni v Turkey* App no 59061/16 (ECtHR, 8 December 2016); *Çatal v Turkey* App no 2873/17 (ECtHR, 10 March 2017); *Köksal v Turkey* App no 70478/16 (ECtHR, 6 June 2017).

53 *Zihni v Turkey* [20]; Bill Bowring, 'The Crisis of the European Court of Human Rights in the Face of Authoritarian and Populist Regimes', in Avidan Kent, Nicos Skoutaris, and Jamie Trinidad (eds), *The Future of International Courts: Regional, Institutional and Procedural Challenges* (Routledge 2019) 76, 80, 81.

54 *Zihni v Turkey* [29]; *Köksal v Turkey* [23]. The ECtHR should have pressed Turkey on the new remedies' effectiveness and impartiality, since these should be assessed more strictly thereon; see *Burden v UK* App no 13378/05 (ECtHR (GC), 29 April 2008) [41].

Nevertheless, the applicants did not exclusively rely on the above objections, equally making allegations, corroborated by data, about an administrative practice of futility and non-satisfaction of claims stemming from gross violations of human rights caused by the repressive measures of the Turkish State in the aftermath of the *coup*. Such practices – noted by the ECtHR, among others, in the *Alpay* case when it spoke about a general problem in the way anti-terrorist legislation is interpreted by prosecutors and competent courts[55] –were in the past found by Strasbourg organs to be sufficient to permit the applicants to dispense with the admissibility requirement to exhaust local remedies.[56] More particularly, in *The Greek Case* it was argued that when there is a general practice of non-observance of the Convention, local remedies 'will of necessity be side-stepped or rendered inadequate … [and] ineffective by the difficulty of securing probative evidence, and administrative enquiries would either be not instituted or, if they were, would be likely to be half-hearted and incomplete'.[57] Yet this case law was not followed by the Court in its reasoning. Instead, the ECtHR merely warned that its finding of inadmissibility[58] 'in no way prejudices any subsequent review of the question of the effectiveness of the remedy concerned, and in particular of the domestic courts' ability to develop a uniform, Convention-compliant approach to the application [of that remedy]',[59] highlighting that the Turkish government might be asked in the future to prove that the respective remedy is effective.

In the same vein, the Court also declared a series of cases against Hungary inadmissible for lack of exhaustion of local remedies,[60] despite serious doubts concerning the effectiveness of the constitutional complaint mechanism in two respects: first, in relation to the mechanism's inadequacy in remedying the situation of the applicants;[61] and second, with regard to the remedy's patent

55 *Şahin Alpay v Turkey* App no 16538/17 (ECtHR, 20 March 2018) [179].

56 Kevin Boyle and Hurst Hannum, 'Individual Applications under the European Convention on Human Rights and the Concept of Administrative Practice: The Donnelly Case' (1974) 68 AJIL 440, 452.

57 *The Greek Case* App nos 3321–3/67, 3344/67 (ECmHR, 31 May 1968). See Tim Eicke, 'The Court's Approach to Exhaustion of Domestic Remedies in the Age of Subsidiarity' in Linos-Alexandre Sicilianos and others (eds), *Regards croisés sur la protection nationale et internationale des droits de l'homme: Liber Amicorum Guido Raimondi* (Wolf 2019) 231, 232.

58 See *Alparslan Altan v Turkey* App no 12778/17 (ECtHR, 16 April 2019) [80]; *Kavala v Turkey* App no 28749/18 (ECtHR, 10 December 2019) [100]–[101].

59 *Selahattin Demirtaş v Turkey (No 2)* App no 14305/17 (ECtHR, 20 November 2018) [131].

60 *Mendrei v Hungary* App no 54927/15 (ECtHR, 5 July 2018); *Szalontay v Hungary* App no 71327/13 (ECtHR, 12 March 2019); *Karsai v Hungary* App no 22172/14 (ECtHR, 4 June 2019).

61 See Peter Paczolay, 'The Constitutional Complaint in Hungary and the Exhaustion of Domestic Remedies' in Linos-Alexandre Sicilianos and others (eds), *Regards croisés sur la protection nationale et internationale des droits de l'homme: Liber Amicorum Guido Raimondi* (Wolf 2019) 687, 693: 'had the applicant availed

ineffectiveness before the captured Constitutional Court.[62] Consequently, in those cases too, the ECtHR ignored the structural problems of Hungary's judicial system,[63] instead insisting upon trusting national authorities' good faith credentials when enforcing the Convention rights. However, if such trust is misplaced, it risks undermining multilateral cooperation altogether and transforms supranational courts into apologists of national abuses.

3.1.2 Trust withdrawn: the ECtHR dealing with States' bad faith in the application of the ECHR

As the Strasbourg Court is increasingly confronted with the spectre of authoritarianism, it has recently employed another tool to revamp its trust towards national authorities.[64] Specifically, in order to deal with bad faith regimes that try to defy the Convention's collective guarantees, the Court has activated the previously dormant provision of Article 18 ECHR, which prohibits the application of restrictions to Convention rights for ulterior purposes.[65] In other words, Article 18 recognizes that a State might misuse such restrictions to further a hidden agenda,[66] and empowers the Court to rebut the presumption that said State acted *bona fides* when it invoked them.

Article 18 is nowadays crucial to the Court's increasingly vocal denunciation of the hunting down of (political and other) opposition voices by the State machinery.[67] The Court's invocation of Article 18 has, however, raised a series of questions concerning the threshold for finding such a violation, as well as the requisite burden and standard of proof, and the evidence required as such proof. The ECtHR's ambivalence regarding the utility of this proviso in instances of rule of law backsliding is amply reflected in the *Merabishvili* case. There, the ECtHR devised a predominance test, according to which, in case of a plurality of purposes, where some are legitimate *per* the ECHR,

himself of a constitutional complaint *shortly after* the enactment of the law, a positive outcome *may* have secured him redress of an *essentially* preventive nature, rendering a compensatory remedy unwarranted' (emphasis added).

62 Andras Kadar, 'Another Turn of the Screw – Further Restrictions for Hungarian Applications to the ECtHR' (*Strasbourg Observers*, 24 September 2019) <https://bit.ly/3vgfV0u> accessed 30 April 2022.

63 Gabor Halmai, 'The Possibility and Desirability of Rule of Law Conditionality' (2019) 11 Hague J Rule L 171, 173–176.

64 Laurence Helfer, 'Populism and International Human Rights Law Institutions: A Survival Guide' in Gerald L Neuman (ed), *Human Rights in a Time of Populism: Challenges and Responses* (CUP 2020) 218, 228.

65 The terms 'ulterior purposes' and 'ulterior motives' are used interchangeably in this section.

66 See *Khodorkovskyi v Russia* App no 5829/04 (ECtHR, 31 May 2011) [255]; *Selahattin Demirtaş v Turkey (No 2)* [259].

67 Aikaterini Tsampi, 'The New Doctrine on Misuse of Power Under Article 18 ECHR: Is It About the System of *contre-pouvoirs* within the State After All?' (2020) 38 NQHR 134, 146–148.

Article 18 will be violated only if the ulterior motive is predominant.[68] This test, which is linked to the degree of reprehensibility of ulterior motives,[69] has been criticized as utterly vague and leading to their banalization, as the element of bad faith is in a way sidelined and such motives are normalized and tolerated if they are not found to have been predominant.[70] At the same time, the ECtHR abandoned the previously-applicable standard of proof that required the applicant to substantiate *beyond reasonable doubt* the bad faith and hidden agenda of State authorities.[71] Instead it adhered to the idea that circumstantial evidence linked to primary facts could serve as inferences for the State's ulterior motives and shifted some of the burden of proof to the State seeking to disprove the existence of a hidden agenda.[72] Yet the Court curiously failed to apply aggravated consequences to such a violation in the sense of ordering the adoption of specific measures.[73]

The Court has subsequently streamlined its jurisprudence on Article 18. For instance, it has at times avoided the 'predominance test' by focusing only on those instances of State practice where no legitimate aim could be discerned.[74] More importantly, the subsequent case law is much more clearly focused on the systemic aspects of the respondent State's policies. Whereas the ECtHR does not go as far as to accept that a systemic pattern of dysfunction of the State machinery automatically renders the ulterior motive predominant, it employs this fact to establish beyond doubt the reprehensibility of such ulterior purposes, which is crucial for ascertaining a violation of Article 18.[75]

The Court equally examines the effects of the State's behaviour on the applicant regarding not only her/his individual capacity, but equally her/his

68 *Merabishvili v Georgia* App no 72508/13 (ECtHR (GC), 28 November 2017) [305]; *Selahattin Demirtaş v Turkey (No 2)* [268].

69 *Merabishvili v Georgia* [307].

70 Corina Heri, 'Loyalty, Subsidiarity, and Article 18 ECHR: How the ECtHR Deals with *Mala Fide* Limitations of Rights' (2020) 1 ECHR L Rev 25, 36.

71 *Khodorkovskyi v Russia* [256]–[257], [260]. See also Helmut Satzger, Frank Zimmermann, and Martin Eibach, 'Does Art. 18 ECHR Grant Protection against Politically Motivated Criminal Proceedings? (Part 2) – Prerequisites, Questions of Evidence and Scope of Application' (2014) 4 EuCrim 248, 252; Floris Tan, 'The Dawn of Article 18 ECHR: A Safeguard against European Rule of Law Backsliding?' (2018) 9 GoJIL 109, 125–132.

72 *Merabishvili v Georgia* [311]–[317]; Jean-Pierre Marguénaud, 'Une nouvelle approche européenne en demi-teinte du détournement de pouvoir' (2018) 79 RSC 183, 188–190.

73 Başak Çali, 'Coping with Crisis: Whither the Variable Geometry in the Jurisprudence of the European Court of Human Rights' (2018) 35 Wis Int L J 237, 268.

74 *Navalnyy v Russia* App no 29580/12 (ECtHR (GC), 15 November 2018) [164]–[166]; *Navalnyy v Russia (No 2)* App no 43734/14 (ECtHR, 9 April 2019) [93]; *Kavala v Turkey* [218].

75 *Aliyev v Azerbaijan* App nos 68762/14 and 71200/14 (ECtHR, 20 September 2018) [223]–[224].

public one as an opponent of the regime, and reflectively highlights the chilling effect that the alleged State abuses might have on checks and balances (political opposition or civil society), and hence on the essence of democracy and the rule of law in that State.[76] Moreover, it uses the above generalized contextual elements, as well as State attitudes towards other persons, as proof of a reprehensible pattern,[77] and on the basis of such admissions it has sometimes ordered the respondent State to adopt general remedial measures.[78] In this sense, the Court, albeit timidly, underlines the aggravated consequences stemming from the systemic nature of bad faith administrative practices.[79]

Lastly, the Court has by now found violations of Article 18 in conjunction with other Articles, beyond Article 5,[80] though a bolder attitude would be welcomed with regard to ECHR provisions forming the core of rule of law guarantees (Articles 6, 13, and 10), even if some of them do not include a list of aims justifying restrictions.[81] For instance, some lingering questions remain whether the Court will accept that in case of an Article 18 violation in conjunction with Article 6, the burden of proof for the effectiveness of any domestic remedies should be fully borne by the respondent State or, generally, whether any margin of appreciation granted to the latter should be construed restrictively when breaches of Article 18 are in play.

Ultimately, the ECtHR's insistence on generalized patterns against the core of democratic principles and the rule of law while examining individual applications allows it to better highlight the systemic nature of a State's ulterior motives and legitimizes the rebuttal of any presumption of good faith enforcement of the Convention's multilateral standards by those contracting parties. This was clearly the case in the 2020 *Demirtaş* judgment, where the Court adopted a holistic approach and amply substantiated the Turkish State's pattern of undermining the foundations of democracy – even if it could not ascertain (yet) a systematic misuse of the judiciary.[82] The increasing assertion of Article 18 ECHR exemplifies the serious challenges posed by bad faith actors regarding the effective enforcement of multilateral guarantees, and thus the crucial role played by supranational courts.

76 *Selahattin Demirtaş v Turkey (No 2)* App no 14305/17 (ECtHR (GC), 22 December 2020) [437] (pluralism and freedom of political debate); *Aliyev v Azerbaijan* [213] (chilling effect on civil society); *Navalnyy v Russia* [173]–[175] (pluralism, tolerance, and broadmindedness); *Kavala v Turkey* [231]–[232] (dissuasive effect on NGOs).

77 See e.g. *Selahattin Demirtaş v Turkey (No. 2)* [264]; *Selahattin Demirtaş v Turkey (No 2)* (GC) [427]–[428] (pattern … to silence dissenting voices).

78 *Aliyev v Azerbaijan* [216]; *Navalnyy v Russia* [185]–[186].

79 Tsampi (n 66) 151–154.

80 *Navalnyy v Russia* [176] (Article 11).

81 Heri (n 69) 41; Helen Keller and Corina Heri, 'Selective Criminal Proceedings and Article 18 ECHR: the European Court of Human Rights' Untapped Potential to Protect Democracy' (2016) 37 HRLJ 1.

82 *Selahattin Demirtaş v Turkey (No. 2)* (GC) [430], [434].

3.2 The CJEU and rule of law backsliding in EU MSs

During the last decade, a vivid discussion on the mechanisms drafted by the EU to counter instances of rule of law backsliding concerning, among other MSs, Poland and Hungary has flourished in the academic sphere.[83] As EU institutions have become increasingly aware of the looming rule of law crisis,[84] various options for responding to it have been put forward. First and foremost, rule of law is, as we have seen, one of the Union's core values *per* Article 2 TEU, serious violations of which can, according to Article 7 TEU, be subjected to sanctions by the EU Council upon the initiative of the Commission or Parliament.[85] Yet the judicial monitoring and enforcement of those values – irrespective of or parallel to Article 7 TEU proceedings[86] – have been contested.[87] First, it was suggested that Article 2 TEU values lacked justiciability due to their vague and hortatory formulation.[88] Second, and more importantly, many aspects of the rule of law backsliding, and especially the undermining of judicial independence through a new disciplinary system, did not apparently relate to EU law, thus raising the question whether the CJEU's interference into Poland's or Hungary's judicial system impinged upon their exclusive competence therein.[89]

The CJEU dealt with these obstacles by having recourse to a line of reasoning that relied heavily on trust as a cornerstone of the preliminary ruling mechanism (Section 3.2.1). Moreover, it recognized that national courts too enjoy a competence to review the rule of law compliance of other MSs in the AFSJ by virtue of the principle of mutual trust (Section 3.2.2).

83 See Andras Jakab and Dimitry Kochenov (eds), *The Enforcement of EU Law and Values: Ensuring Member States' Compliance* (OUP 2017).
84 See Viviane Reding, 'The EU and the Rule of Law – What Next?' (*European Commission*, 4 September 2013) <https://bit.ly/3u5zvv2> 30 April 2022.
85 These two institutions have recently initiated Article 7 proceedings against Poland and Hungary; see, respectively, European Commission, 'Proposal for a Council Decision on the determination of a clear risk of a serious breach by the Republic of Poland of the rule of law' COM(2017)835 final; European Parliament, Resolution of 12 September 2018 on a proposal calling on the Council to determine, pursuant to Art. 7(1) of the Treaty on European Union, the existence of a clear risk of a serious breach by Hungary of the values on which the Union is founded' (2017/2131(INL)).
86 Parallel Article 7 TEU and infringement proceedings are admissible. See C-619/18 *Commission v Poland (Independence of the Supreme Court)* [2019] ECLI:EU:C:2019:325, Opinion of AG Tanchev [48]–[51].
87 See Carlos Closa and Dimitry Kochenov, 'Reinforcement of the Rule of Law Oversight in the European Union: Key Options' in Werner Schroeder (ed), *Strengthening the Rule of Law in Europe* (Hart Publishing 2016) 173.
88 Jan-Werner Müller, 'Should the EU Protect Democracy and the Rule of Law inside Member States?' (2015) 21 ELJ 141, 146. Cf Christophe Hillion, 'Overseeing the Rule of Law in the EU: Legal Mandate and Means' in Carlos Closa and Dimitry Kochenov (eds), *Reinforcing Rule of Law Oversight in the European Union* (CUP 2016) 59, 66.
89 *Commission v Poland (Independence of the Supreme Court)* [38].

3.2.1 Trust instrumentalized: extending EU rule of law standards to internal situations

The CJEU's competence to review national measures infringing upon judicial independence could be most plausibly based on Article 47(2) of the Charter of Fundamental Rights of the European Union (CFR) establishing the right to a fair trial.[90] Yet, since States are bound by the Charter *per* its Article 51(1) only when a legal situation comes within the scope of EU law,[91] and additionally the CFR is invoked in concrete instances of subjective rights' violations, it would have been challenging to place the Polish or Hungarian laws within the ambit of EU law,[92] and even if that was successful, it would have been ineffective to deal with structural deficiencies regarding rule of law guarantees by tackling individual, concrete violations of the CFR.[93]

This is why the CJEU turned to Article 19(1) TEU enshrining the obligation of MSs to 'provide remedies sufficient to ensure effective legal protection in the fields covered by Union law', which, according to the Court, constitutes a concretization of the rule of law value stipulated in Article 2 TEU.[94] But what this obligation – stemming from the idea that the EU as a Union of law encompasses both the supranational and national levels of governance[95] – entailed and what was the scope of the phrase 'fields covered by Union law' had to be determined by the CJEU. In doing that, the Court appealed to trust as reflected in the functioning of the preliminary ruling mechanism. It invoked that mechanism, calling it the cornerstone of the Union's judicial system,[96] in three crucial steps: (1) in order to corroborate the idea that national judiciaries constitute Union courts[97] and thus must implement the obligations stemming from Article 19(1) TEU; (2) so as to ensure the widest possible scope of application for the MSs' rule of law obligations emanating from Union law; and (3) with the aim of further legitimizing and clarifying

90 Laurent Pech, 'Article 47' in Tamara K Hervey and others (eds), *The EU Charter of Fundamental Rights: A Commentary* (Hart Publishing 2014) 1197, 1255–1258.

91 C-617/10 *Åkerberg Fransson* [2013] ECLI:EU:C:2013:105 [19]–[22]. For such a case, see C-585/18 *A.K. and Others v Sąd Najwyższy* [2019] ECLI:EU:C:2019:982 [114] and [169] (concerning non-discrimination).

92 Francesca Ippolito, 'Quel contrôle du respect de l'Etat de droit? It takes two to tango!' (2019) 55 RTDE 273, 280.

93 Cecilia Rizcallah and Victor Davio, 'L'article 19 du Traité sur l'Union européenne: sésame de l'Union du droit' (2020) 122 RTDH 155, 180.

94 C-64/16 *Associação Sindical dos Juízes Portugueses v Tribunal de Contas* [2019] ECLI:EU:C:2018:117 [32].

95 Case 294/83 *Parti écologiste "Les Verts" v European Parliament* [1986] ECLI:EU:C:1986:166 [23].

96 *Slowakische Republik v Achmea BV* [37]; see Opinion 2/13 [176]; *Associação Sindical dos Juízes Portugueses v Tribunal de Contas* [32].

97 Case 106/77 *Amministrazione delle Finanze dello Stato v Simmenthal SpA* [1978] ECLI:EU:C:1978:49; *Commission v Poland (Independence of the Supreme Court)* [45]–[46].

the contours of the MSs' obligation to ensure the independence and impartiality of national judiciaries.

The last two steps merit further analysis. The Court interprets the caveat 'fields covered by Union law' delineating the ambit of Article 19(1)(2) as comprising a MS's obligation to ensure the judicial independence of any national judicial authority that may rule 'on questions concerning the application or interpretation of EU law'.[98] In essence, this is precisely what virtually all national courts and tribunals are empowered to potentially do, since they are all Union courts via the preliminary ruling mechanism.[99] In other words, the CJEU succeeds in expanding in a bold way the scope of application of Article 19 by exploiting the cooperative scheme of this trust-based mechanism established at the heart of the Union's judicial system.[100]

But what the Court achieves with this move is endangered by the last step in its judicial syllogism, according to which the preliminary ruling mechanism can constitute the *passerelle* allowing national judiciaries to be brought within Article 19's realm only if the national authority is eligible to make such a request, that is, only if it is already independent and impartial;[101] otherwise, the trust laid upon national courts that they will loyally apply EU law is irreparably eroded and the preliminary ruling mechanism cannot be activated.[102] This second link between Article 19 and the preliminary ruling mechanism feels like a *petitio principii*, since the Court proclaims that the Union will review the independence of national courts via Article 19 TEU only if they qualify as courts or tribunals within Article 267 of the Treaty on the Functioning of the European Union (TFEU), namely, if they are independent![103] More worryingly, the Court's stance can be interpreted as suggesting that the right to request preliminary rulings should be suspended for (about-to-be-) captured national judiciaries in countries tainted by systemic rule of law problems.[104] Such proposals might be doubly damaging for the

98 *Associação Sindical dos Juízes Portugueses v Tribunal de Contas* [40]; *Commission v Poland (Independence of the Supreme Court)* [51] and [56].

99 Luke D Spieker, 'Breathing Life into the Union's Common Values: On the Judicial Application of Article 2 TEU in the EU Value Crisis' (2019) 20 GLJ 1182, 1203; Laurent Pech and Sebastien Platon, 'Judicial Independence under Threat: The Court of Justice to the Rescue in the *ASJP* Case' (2018) 55 CMLR 1827, 1840.

100 See Koen Lenaerts, 'Upholding the Rule of Law through Judicial Dialogue' (2019) 38 YEL 3, 5–6.

101 *Associação Sindical dos Juízes Portugueses v Tribunal de Contas* [43].

102 Koen Lenaerts, 'On Judicial Independence and the Quest for National, Supranational and Transnational Justice' in Gunnar Selvik and others (eds), *The Art of Judicial Reasoning: Festschrift in Honour of Carl Baudenbacher* (Springer 2019) 155, 158.

103 Ibid 163–164; Peter van Elsuwege and Femke Gremmelprez, 'Protecting the Rule of Law in the EU Legal Order: A Constitutional Role for the Court of Justice' (2020) 16 EuConst 8, 24–25.

104 Pech and Scheppele (n 38) 42; Matteo Bonelli and Monica Claes, 'Judicial Serendipity: How Portuguese Judges came to the Rescue of the Polish Judiciary'

Court's construction: not only would a national court be unable to use the preliminary ruling mechanism as a means of resistance, but the CJEU itself would be prevented from using this mechanism as a 'bridge' for reviewing national measures against the threshold of EU rule of law values.

The CJEU's subsequent case law has not fully resolved the above paradox. On the one hand, in the aforementioned *Poland v Commission* case, the Luxemburg Court avoided any linkage between Article 267 TFEU and Article 19 TEU regarding the substantive guarantee of judicial independence, focusing instead on Articles 47 CFR and 6/13 ECHR as sources of MSs' obligations to ensure such independence.[105] Yet some months afterwards the CJEU relied on its case law on Article 19(1) TEU in order to assess the notion of independence in the context of the Article 267 TFEU admissibility criteria, thus giving the impression that the two provisions are like revolving doors in that respect.[106] Consequently, further clarification by the CJEU is required on the way trust will be employed through the preliminary ruling mechanism so as to allow the review of otherwise internal affairs. The CJEU's tergiversation on how to instrumentalize trust in such instances showcases its difficult balancing act between policing and facilitating multilateral cooperation.

3.2.2 Trust confirmed: mutual trust as a means for the horizontal review of rule of law deficiencies

As we have analysed above, the fundamental[107] principle of mutual trust within the AFSJ, stemming from the fact that MSs share common values as well as, partly, common standards and equivalent procedures, entails two main consequences: first, it establishes a presumption of conformity of MS measures with EU law and particularly the CFR; and, second, it imposes on other MSs an obligation of non-review of those measures.[108] These consequences are overridden only in exceptional circumstances determined through a two-prong test requiring, cumulatively: (1) the demonstration of systemic or generalized deficiencies in the protection of fundamental rights in a State; and (2) resulting in substantial grounds for believing that the person

(2018) 14 EuConst 622, 637; cf Armin von Bogdandy, 'Principles of a Systemic Deficiencies Doctrine: How to Protect Checks and Balances in the Member States' (2020) 57 CMLR 705, 731, who argues for a duty to refer in case of systemic rule of law deficiencies.

105 *Commission v Poland (Independence of the Supreme Court)* [49]; *A.K. and Others v Sąd Najwyższy* [111].

106 C-274/14 *Banco de Santander* [2019] ECLI:EU:C:2020:17 [56]–[59]. The same is true regarding C-354/20, *L. & P.* [2020] ECLI:EU:C:2020:1033 [44]. See Mathieu Leloup, 'An Uncertain First Step in the Field of Judicial Self-government' (2020) 16 EuConst 145, 167.

107 C-411/10 and C-493/10 *N.S./M.E. and Others* [2011] ECLI:EU:C:2011:865 [83]; Opinion 2/13 [191].

108 Opinion 2/13 [191], [192], [194].

concerned would face a real risk of violation of the essence of his or her fundamental rights.[109]

The rule of law crisis that has embroiled Poland and Hungary has seriously strained this logic, recently forcing the CJEU to confront the question whether this crisis has impacted the functioning of mutual trust. It has been argued, for instance, that EU cooperation based on mutual trust should be fully suspended, since a systemic violation of basic EU values creates an irrebuttable presumption that exceptional circumstances exist.[110] Yet whether this determination, and the subsequent suspension, should be effectuated automatically after either an Article 7(1) TEU Reasoned Proposal by the Commission[111] or a centralized pronouncement by the CJEU,[112] which plausibly took place in the *N.S.* case,[113] or whether it should be applied by national judges as reviewing/executing authorities within the AFSJ,[114] remains a bone of contention. It has been equally stressed that even if no generalized suspension can ensue after the ascertainment of systemic deficiencies, such a determination should shift the burden of proof to the issuing State, which will need to substantiate that no individualized risk of serious violation to the person's fundamental rights can be corroborated under the specific circumstances of the case at hand.[115]

The CJEU has followed a third way, clearly entrenched in the logic of trust. In the context of preliminary rulings and absent any mention of systemic deficiencies, the Court has given specific instructions to executing courts on the judicial independence guarantees that issuing entities should satisfy in order for the latter's decisions to be recognized and enforced within mutual trust regimes.[116] Here, mutual trust is used in order to both substantiate the

109 C-404/15 and 659/15 PPU *Aranyosi and Căldăraru* [2016] ECLI:EU:C:2016:198 [92]; C-216/18 PPU, *Minister for Justice and Equality (Deficiencies in the system of justice) (LM)* [2018] ECLI:EU:C:2018:586 [59].

110 J.-P. Jacqué, 'Etat de droit et confiance mutuelle' (2018) 54 RTDE 239, 240.

111 Petra Bárd and Wouter van Ballegooij, 'Judicial Independence as a Precondition for Mutual Trust? The CJEU in *Minister for Justice and Equality v. LM*' (2018) 9 NJECL 353, 360.

112 Mattias Wendel, 'Mutual Trust, Essence and Federalism – Between Consolidating and Fragmenting the Area of Freedom, Security and Justice after *LM*' (2019) 15 EuConst 17.

113 *N.S./M.E. and Others* [89].

114 Armin von Bognandy and others, 'A Potential Constitutional Moment for the European Rule of Law – The Importance of Red Lines' (2018) 55 CMLR 983, 994.

115 Petra Bárd and Wouter van Ballegooij, 'The Effect of the CJEU Case Law Concerning the Rule of Law and Mutual Trust on National Systems' in Valsamis Mitsilegas, Alberto de Martino, and Leandro Mancano (eds), *The Court of Justice and European Criminal Law: Leading Cases in a Contextual Analysis* (Hart Publishing 2019) 455, 460.

116 See C-551/15 *Pula Parking d.o.o. v Sven Klaus Tederahn* [2017], EU:C:2017:193 [54]; C-508/18 and 82/19 PPU, *Minister for Justice and Equality v OG and PI* [2019] ECLI:EU:C:2019:456 [74].

independence guarantees and empower executing States to review the presence of such guarantees.[117]

Insofar as claims of systemic deficiencies are concerned, the *LM* case constitutes a breakthrough in the CJEU's approach thereto.[118] In that case the Irish High Court, alarmed by the rule of law backsliding in Poland and on the basis of the aforementioned Commission's Reasoned Proposal, submitted a request for a preliminary ruling in relation to the execution of a Polish European Arrest Warrant (EAW). Two points set out in the CJEU's ruling are pertinent for the present analysis. First of all, the Court summarily rejected the view that a systemic deficiency in the rule of law guarantees, such as the lack of independence of the judiciary, constitutes by itself a sufficient reason for the evisceration of mutual trust and the subsequent general suspension of cooperation with the defiant State.[119] In a subsequent ruling, the CJEU explained that a different interpretation would have overridden the 'exceptional circumstances' threshold for the rebuttal of mutual trust, leading to the general exclusion of its application.[120] In addition, the Court stressed that only the European Council and then the Council could, *per* Recital 10 of the EAW Framework Decision, enact the automatic suspension of the EAW regime following an assessment under Article 7(2)-(3) TEU, and that the CJEU or the executing national authority did not have the power to do so.[121]

What is more problematic is the CJEU's insistence that the executing State always proceed to an individualized assessment, despite the presence of systemic deficiencies.[122] The Court seems to suggest that such deficiencies might not necessarily taint the essence of the person's right to a fair trial.[123] In a way, the CJEU underplays the spill-over effect that such a deficiency can have on the entire judicial system of the defiant State, desperately holding on to mutual trust even when it has become an untenable fiction.[124] Consequently, each executing court is in the unenviable position of having to judge for itself whether a rule of law crisis might impact upon the individual fate of the

117 Lenaerts (n 101) 167–173.

118 Mattias Wendel, 'Indépendance judiciaire et confiance mutuelle: A propos de l'arrêt *LM*' (2019) 55 CDE 189.

119 *Minister for Justice and Equality (Deficiencies in the system of justice) (LM)* [70]–[71].

120 *L. & P.* [43].

121 Ibid [57]–[59]; Markus Krajewski, 'Who is Afraid of the European Council? The Court of Justice's Cautious Approach to the Independence of Domestic Judges' (2018) 14 EuConst 792, 810–811.

122 *Minister for Justice and Equality (Deficiencies in the system of justice) (LM)* [60]; *L. & P.* [53]–[56].

123 See Theodore Konstadinides, 'Judicial Independence and the Rule of Law in the Context of Non-execution of a European Arrest Warrant: *LM*' (2019) 56 CMLR 743, 751.

124 Dimitry Kochenov and Petra Bárd, 'The Last Soldier Standing? Courts versus Politicians and the Rule of Law Crisis in the New Member States of the EU' (2019) 1 EYCL 243, 272.

person concerned.[125] This might easily wreak havoc on the regime, since different national courts may well reach divergent conclusions regarding the existence of systemic deficiencies and the individualized risk, thus causing the collapse of this mutual trust regime.[126]

Furthermore, the Court gives a series of guidelines on how to proceed to an individualized review, among which one finds the CJEU's instruction that the executing authority seek from the issuing authority both any information that is pertinent in order to assess the risk as well as assurances enabling the former to reach the conclusion that a risk with regard to the essence of the fundamental right to a fair trial can be ruled out.[127] In other words, the CJEU calls upon the executing authority to trust the issuing authority to engage in a sincere dialogue about the latter's independence![128] And even if the issuing authority refuses to respond to the executing authorities' inquiries, the latter should exercise vigilance but still proceed to the individualized assessment.[129] In this way, the CJEU is demonstrating that trust must be preserved at any cost, even in cases of non-cooperation by the issuing authority.

Ultimately, the CJEU's position provides that elements of horizontal, as well as vertical, mutual trust be applied even in cases of rule of law backsliding.[130] On the one hand, it insists on horizontal trust, keeping in mind that the suspension of multilateral cooperation might not work as an incentive for the defiant State.[131] On the other hand, the CJEU's stance of leaving referring courts to determine whether the two limbs of the *Aranyosi* test have been fulfilled showcases its persistent trust towards national courts – rather than towards the limitations of the preliminary ruling mechanism[132] – and this is a huge gamble. While the direct dialogue between national courts highlights their common responsibility in making integration work,[133] recent

125 Florence Benoît-Rohmer, 'La Pologne, la Cour de Justice et l'Etat de droit: une histoire sans fin?' (2020) 1 Europe des Droits et Libertés 136, 141, 142.

126 Kim L Scheppele and Daniel Kelemen, 'Defending Democracy in EU Member States. Beyond Article 7 TEU' in Francesca Bignami (ed), *EU Law in Populist Times: Crises and Prospects* (CUP 2020) 413, 449, 450.

127 *Minister for Justice and Equality (Deficiencies in the system of justice) (LM)* [76]–[77].

128 See, indicatively, the critique by Kochenov and Bárd (n 124) 274.

129 *L. & P.* [60].

130 Armin von Bogdandy and L. Spieker, 'Countering Judicial Silencing of Critics: Article 2 TEU, Reverse Solange, and the Responsibilities of National Judges' (2019) 15 EuConst 391, 424–425.

131 von Bogdandy and Ioannidis (n 21) 84.

132 See the similar attitude in *Commission v Poland (Independence of the Supreme Court)* [132] and [140]. Cf Benoît-Rohmer (n 124) 149; Leloup (n 105) 152–157, on the CJEU's margin of discretion left to national courts.

133 Erst Hirsch Ballin, 'Mutual Trust. The Virtue of Reciprocity – Strengthening the Acceptance of the Rule of Law through Peer Review' in Carlos Closa and Dimitry Kochenov (eds), *Reinforcing Rule of Law Oversight in the European Union* (CUP 2016) 133.

contradictory decisions of national courts, and protracted procedures where dialogue between national courts has impeded instead of facilitating cooperation within the AFSJ, are an ominous sign that the CJEU's balancing act in the *LM* and *L. & P.* rulings might not be working effectively.

4 Conclusion

It is by now evident that the element of trust as a cornerstone of multilateral cooperation in Europe is facing serious challenges in cases of human rights/rule of law backsliding. The COVID-19 health crisis has put further pressure on the rule of law in Europe, since various governments have sought to further curb fundamental rights and tighten their grip on the state apparatus through controversial constitutional reforms.[134] These measures heavily impact on trust and render even more apparent the dilemmas facing supranational courts that monitor multilateral guarantees.

Under these circumstances, the ECtHR must rethink the way it employs trust if it wants to fully defend the Convention standards against authoritarian tendencies. In such instances, it has been shown that trust may become an impediment to the Court's proper functioning as a defender of multilateral collective guarantees. In contrast, the CJEU's use of trust within the EU's strain of multilateralism is more multi-layered. On the one hand, mutual trust hinders national authorities' attempts to better defend the rule of law against defiant States by prioritizing the survival of multilateral cooperation, even if compromised. On the other hand, trust – as a cornerstone of the preliminary ruling mechanism and an expression of the principle of loyal cooperation – might be crucial to extending the legal bite of Article 2 TEU values, which might in turn allow the CJEU to hold backsliding States accountable for measures intended to undermine the rule of law and, consequently, the process of integration.

While one must never lose sight of the inherent limitations of judicial safeguards vis-à-vis rule of law backsliding and the ensuing distrust among MSs and between States and supranational judiciaries,[135] this actually does not mean that political processes fare better in a context of generalized mistrust. For example, new legislative initiatives from political organs, such as the EU Regulation on a General Regime of Conditionality of the Union Budget,[136] have

134 See Venice Commission, 'Interim Report on the Measures Taken in the EU Member States as a Result of the COVID-19 Crisis and their Impact on Democracy, the Rule of Law and Fundamental Rights' CDL-AD (2020)018 (2020) [47]–[48] (concerning Hungary); United Nations Human Rights, 'Poland Has Slammed Door Shut on Legal and Safe Abortions' (*UN Expert's Statement*, 27 October 2020) <https://bit.ly/3oI5h0g> accessed 30 April 2022.

135 Michael Blauberger and Daniel Kelemen, 'Can Courts Rescue National Democracy? Judicial Safeguards against Democratic Backsliding in the EU' (2017) 24 J Eur Pub Poly 321, 322.

136 Regulation (EU, Euratom) 2020/2092 of 16 December 2020 on a general regime of conditionality for the protection of the Union budget [2020] L 433 I/2; see also European Commission, '2020 Rule of Law Report' COM/2020/580 final.

already been severely compromised during inter-state negotiations.[137] Other tools, such as attempts to expel bad faith States with authoritarian tendencies from the CoE or the EU, have not materialized or remain in the sphere of *lex ferenda*, with the notable recent exception of the Russian Federation, which was first suspended and then expelled from the CoE after its aggression against Ukraine.[138] In the end, as has been pertinently observed, legal tools cannot resolve a crisis in trust; they can only mitigate it and help avoid 'an escalation of distrust', thus enabling 'continued cooperation which implicitly nurtures trust'.[139] Thus, while trust remains a useful tool, under the current circumstances, it is time to turn a more critical eye on it and reappraise its role regarding judicial cooperation within the framework of multilateral institutionalized cooperation.

Acknowledgements

I would like to acknowledge the editorial assistance of Christos Zois. This text was finalized in June 2020 and only a few subsequent developments were taken into consideration.

137 European Council Conclusions, 11 December 2020, EUCO 22/20, 1–2.

138 Kanstantsin Dzehtsiarou and Vassilis P. Tzevelekos, 'The Aggression against Ukraine and the Effectiveness of Inter-state Cases in Case of War' (2022) 3 ECHR L Rev 165; Bartłomiej Krzan, '"PLEXIT"? – Poland, the Rule of Law and the (pre-)Article 7 Procedure' in Hannes Hofmeister (ed), *The End of the Ever Closer Union* (Nomos 2018) 143.

139 Armin von Bogdandy, 'Ways to Frame the European Rule of Law: *Rechtsgemeinschaft*, Trust, Revolution, and Kantian Peace' (2018) 14 EuConst 675, 690.

9 The Nuclear Non-Proliferation Regime at 50

A Midlife Crisis and its Consequences

Agnieszka Nimark

1 Introduction

The 5th of March 2020 marked the 50th Anniversary of the entry into force of the Non-Proliferation of Nuclear Weapons Treaty (NPT). Despite some notable successes and the nearly universal recognition of the NPT as 'the cornerstone of the global non-proliferation regime, the foundation for the pursuit of nuclear disarmament and an important element facilitating the benefits of the peaceful uses of nuclear energy',[1] the treaty's credibility at age 50 has come under severe scrutiny.[2] As this chapter aims to explore, the crisis surrounding the NPT is not new.[3] The frustration among the non-nuclear-weapon States (NNWS) parties to the treaty at the lack of progress in nuclear disarmament has been simmering since at least the mid-1990s. In 1995, the State parties reached a consensus to extend the NPT's life indefinitely based on a negotiated 'package deal'. The subsequent failures to implement the 1995 commitments, along with related pledges agreed to at the 2000 and 2010 NPT Review Conferences, led to a gradual erosion of the nuclear non-proliferation regime's authority. The growing frustration over the impasse surrounding nuclear disarmament led to the negotiation in 2017 of the Treaty on the Prohibition of Nuclear Weapons (TPNW). This so-called 'ban treaty' was adopted by 122 NNWS representing almost two-thirds of the NPT State

1 Preparatory Committee, '2020 Review Conference of the Parties to the Treaty on the Non-Proliferation of Nuclear Weapons' (Second Session, Geneva, 3 May 2018) NPT/CONF.2020/PC. II/CRP.3, 23 April–4 May 2018.

2 Joelien Pretorius and Tom Sauer, 'Is It Time to Ditch the NPT?' (*Bulletin of the Atomic Scientists*, 6 September 2019) <https://thebulletin.org/2019/09/is-it-time-to-ditch-the-npt/#> accessed 30 April 2022; Henry Sokolski, 'The NPT Turns 50: Will it Get to 60?' (2020) 76(2) Bull At Sci 63, 67; Paul Meyer, 'The Nuclear Nonproliferation Treaty: Fin du Regime?' (2017) 47(3) Arms Control Today 16, 22.

3 For a detailed account of the pessimistic assessments over the future of the NPT as well as counter arguments to negative expectations, see Liviu Horovitz, 'Beyond Pessimism: Why the Treaty on the Non-Proliferation of Nuclear Weapons Will Not Collapse' (2015) 38 J Strateg Stud 126, 158.

DOI: 10.4324/9781003312857-11

parties. By the end of 2020, 50 of the signatory States had ratified the Treaty, paving the way for its entry into force on 22 January 2021.[4]

The entry into force of the TPNW requires the elaboration of a new *modus vivendi* between supporters and opponents of the ban treaty within the NPT's community of States. As a new pillar of disarmament, the TPNW will need to be integrated into the non-proliferation regime. The current regime is also widely viewed to be in jeopardy due to the deterioration of the arms control agreements between the US and Russia, the near collapse of the Iran nuclear deal[5] after the US withdrawal from the agreement, and unresolved issues concerning the North Korean nuclear weapons programme. The tenth quinquennial NPT Review Conference, initially planned for 27 April–22 May 2020, was expected to provide a vital opportunity for all States parties to the treaty, and in particular nuclear-weapon States (NWS), to demonstrate their commitment to the full implementation of the treaty and help to explore the regime's shortcomings. Yet, in the current highly polarized environment the postponement of the gathering caused by the COVID-19 pandemic might provide much-needed time for a deeper reflection on the overall condition of the global nuclear regime.[6] This will hopefully take place in the context of other international security challenges, such as global pandemics and climate change, which also require a multilateral response.[7] The latest developments demand thorough analyses not only of the nature of the NPT crisis and its dynamics, but also a search for unconventional ideas on how to address the gradual erosion of the existing non-proliferation regime. This chapter's aim is to contribute to the reflection process on what needs to be done to restore the credibility of the NPT as a core component of this specialized regime.

The chapter consists of six sections. After this introduction, Section 2 discusses the root causes of the NPT crisis lying in the origins of the treaty and

4 The TPNW was opened for signature at the United Nations General Assembly (UNGA) on 20 September 2017. On 24 October 2020, Honduras became the 50th signatory State to ratify the Treaty. As of 16 May 2022, the TPNW has been signed by 86 States and acceded by 60 State parties.

5 The Joint Comprehensive Plan of Action (JCPOA), known commonly as the Iran nuclear deal or Iran deal, is an agreement concerning the Iranian nuclear programme reached in Vienna on 14 July 2015 between Iran and the P5+1 (the five permanent members of the United Nations Security Council plus Germany) together with the European Union.

6 Due to travel restrictions related to COVID-19, the 2020 NPT Review Conference was initially postponed until January 2021, but in October 2020 and in January 2021 the Conference had to be further postponed and is now scheduled to take place on 1–26 August 2022. See United Nations, 'Tenth Review Conference of the Parties to the Treaty on the Non-Proliferation of Nuclear Weapons' (11 March 2022) <https://www.un.org/sites/un2.un.org/files/letter_to_all_sp_11_march_2022.pdf> accessed 16 May 2022.

7 Pugwash Conference on Science and World Affairs, 'The Postponement of the NPT Review Conference. Antagonisms, Conflicts and Nuclear Risks After the Pandemic' (Bulletin of Atomic Scientists, 12 May 2020) <https://bit.ly/3f8rTUg> accessed 30 April 2022.

in its formulation. Section 3 explores the vague language of Article VI of the treaty and disagreements among the NPT State parties regarding the obligation to disarm. Section 4 explains how the transformation of the discourse about nuclear weapons led to the adoption of the nuclear ban treaty (i.e. the TPNW). Section 5 indicates some additional elements of the nuclear regime crisis, such as the near collapse of the arms control architecture, and discusses their consequences. Finally, Section 6 discusses the need to reinvent the nuclear disarmament process in the context of a broader post-pandemic discussion on major threats and a reassessment of what constitutes State security.

2 The origins of the NPT and inherent problems related to the treaty's formulation

The development, possession, and proliferation of nuclear weapons represent some of the greatest threats to international peace and security. Nine States (China, France, India, Israel, North Korea, Pakistan, Russia, the UK, and the US) are known or believed to possess nuclear weapons.[8] More than 30 other States have the technological capability to acquire them. Despite a growing global consensus regarding the need for substantial nuclear arms reductions,[9] if not complete nuclear disarmament, NWS continue to invest billions of dollars in the maintenance and modernization of their nuclear arsenals.[10]

The existing nuclear non-proliferation and disarmament regime, based on the NPT as its core component, is a complex and specialized legal system. The regime encompasses several treaties (e.g. the Comprehensive Nuclear Test Ban Treaty), extensive multilateral agreements (e.g. the Comprehensive Safeguards Agreements and Additional Protocols) and bilateral agreements (e.g. the Intermediate-Range Nuclear Forces (INF) Treaty), as well as multilateral agencies (e.g. the International Atomic Energy Agency), and the domestic laws of participating States (e.g. Section 123 of the US Atomic Energy Act).[11] Yet, despite the NPT's nearly universal membership (191 member States), the current legal framework has failed to prevent States such

8 The estimated worldwide total inventory of nuclear warheads in early-2020 stands at 13,410. See Hans M Kristensen and Matt Korda, 'Status of World Nuclear Forces' (*Federation of American Scientists*, undated) <https://fas.org/issues/nuclear-weapons/status-world-nuclear-forces/> accessed 30 April 2022.

9 UN Security Council, Resolution 1887(2009) 24 September 2009, S/RES/1887 (2009).

10 International Campaign to Abolish Nuclear Weapons, 'Complicit: 2020 Global Nuclear Weapons Spending' (ICAN 2021) <https://www.icanw.org/complicit_nuclear_weapons_spending_increased_by_1_4_billion_in_2020> accessed 30 April 2022.

11 Daniel H Joyner and Marco Roscini, *Non-proliferation Law as a Special Regime: A Contribution to Fragmentation Theory in International Law* (CUP 2012); Gro Nystuen and Torbjorn Graff Hugo, 'The Nuclear Non-Proliferation Treaty' in Gro Nystuen, Stuart Casey-Maslen, and Annie Bersagel (eds), *Nuclear Weapons under International Law* 374 (CUP 2014) 396.

as India, Israel, Pakistan, and more recently North Korea from 'going nuclear'.[12] Not only do four out of the nine nuclear-armed States remain outside the NPT, but also NWS parties to the NPT are failing to make any substantial progress towards nuclear disarmament. The adoption of the TPNW in 2017 exposed, on the one hand, a high level of polarization among the international community with regard to the legal status of nuclear weapons, and, on the other, confirmed the urgent need for reinforcement of the key norms and institutions on which the nuclear non-proliferation and disarmament regimes are based.[13]

The adoption of the NPT in 1968 laid the groundwork for the international nuclear order of today. The treaty was negotiated out of a fear of the uncontrolled spread of nuclear weapons and the potential consequences that entailed. In the words of William Walker:

> An immense international ordering problem had to be addressed after Hiroshima and Nagasaki, after nuclear weapons had entered the bloodstream of international politics with the onset of the East-West conflict, and after the engines of technological development and weapon production had been fired up.[14]

Similarly to other multilateral treaties adopted during the Cold War, such as the Outer Space Treaty of 1967, which constituted a bargain between the superpowers on the usage and demilitarization of outer space, 'the avoidance of nuclear war' was 'a goal of overriding importance' at the time of the NPT's adoption.[15]

The negotiations leading to the treaty began in 1965. By then, four States (the US, the Soviet Union, the UK, and France) had already deployed and tested nuclear weapons. But it was China's entry into the nuclear club in 1964 that provided the push needed to start the negotiations. The new normative order agreed upon three years later clearly reflected the interests and the technological and structural features of the time. Since the use of military measures could not halt or even slow down nuclear proliferation, the adoption of a multilateral instrument designed to impede the expansion of nuclear arms appeared to be the only effective means of reaching the desired result.[16] However, the final outcome of the negotiations was and remains

12 India and Pakistan are being recognized as nuclear weapon States and Israel is believed to possess nuclear weapons. The DPRK, which had acceded to the treaty in 1985, announced its withdrawal from the NPT in 2003 in a controversial manner and believes that it is not bound by the Treaty.

13 Kjolv Egeland and others, 'The Nuclear Weapons Ban Treaty and the Non-Proliferation Regime' (2018) 34(2) Medicine, Conflict and Survival 74, 94; John Carlson, 'Is the NPT Still Relevant? How to Progress the NPT's Disarmament Provisions' (2019) 2(1) J-PAND 97, 113.

14 William Walker, 'Nuclear Order and Disorder' (2000) 76(4) Int Aff 703.

15 Mason Willrich, 'The Treaty on Non-Proliferation of Nuclear Weapons: Nuclear Technology Confronts World Politics' (1968) 77(8) Yale L J 1449.

16 Morton A Kaplan, 'The Nuclear Non-Proliferation Treaty: Its Rationale, Prospects and Possible Impact on International Law' (1969) 18(1) J Pub L 1, 20.

controversial, because it establishes a two-tiered community of States. The 'nuclear-weapon-States' are defined as those which had manufactured and exploded a nuclear weapon or other nuclear explosive device prior to 1 January 1967. This definition encompasses the five veto-powers of the United Nations Security Council: China, France, Russia (at that time the Soviet Union), the UK, and the US. All other States were classified by the treaty as 'non-nuclear-weapon States' (NNWS). The three purposes of the treaty – non-proliferation, disarmament, and the peaceful use of nuclear technology – are often referred to as the NPT's three pillars. The NWS pledged never to transfer nuclear weapons to non-nuclear States (Article I) and the NNWS committed to never acquire them (Articles II and III). The NPT also proclaimed the 'inalienable right' of all parties to use nuclear technology for civilian purposes (Articles IV and V) and committed all parties to pursue negotiations concerning 'effective measures' for disarmament (Article VI).[17]

Since its adoption, the NPT has been referred to as a 'grand bargain' between the nuclear and non-nuclear-weapon States. From the legal point of view, however, there is an ongoing debate about the nature of the obligations contained in the NPT. Regarding the content of the treaties, a distinction is sometimes made between so-called 'law-making' (or 'normative') treaties and 'contract' (or 'reciprocal') treaties. The difference between the classification of the NPT as a 'law-making/normative' treaty or a 'contract' treaty is important for understanding the NPT's credibility crisis. Normative treaties are considered to further community interests by setting up international standards which are best achieved by universal participation and are not based on the principle of reciprocity.[18] Contractual treaties, on the other hand, are seen to further the individual interests of the participating States, aiming at their mutual benefit, which is considered to be best achieved through reciprocal obligations.[19]

Some legal scholars writing about the NPT, such as Daniel H Joyner, argue that the non-proliferation treaty should be interpreted as 'a contract treaty essentially codifying a quid pro quo bargain between two categories of States parties, resulting in differential and reciprocal obligations between the two

17 Egeland and others (n 13).

18 As explained by Malgosia Fitzmaurice: 'These standards have been described by ILC Rapporteur Pellet as being created, above all, to institute common international regulation on the basis of shared values.' Malgosia Fitzmaurice, 'Treaties' in *Max Planck Encyclopedia of Public International Law* (OUP 2010).

19 The International Law Commission (ILC) observed:

> treaties are rarely entirely normative or entirely reciprocal. In most cases, including human rights treaties, they contain both contractual clauses providing rights and obligations as well as "normative" clauses. The term "normative treaty" is therefore generally used to refer to one in which the provisions of a normative character dominate.

(UN ILC 'Report of International Law Commission Covering the Work of its Forty-Eight Session (6 May–26 July 1996)' UN Doc A/51/10)

categories of parties'.[20] As further explained by Joyner, States possessing nuclear weapons took upon themselves the obligation to not proliferate nuclear weapons or related technologies to States that did not possess them. And the States not possessing nuclear weapons took upon themselves the obligation to neither acquire such weapons from nuclear-weapon States, nor to manufacture such weapons domestically. In exchange for their commitments to forego the possession of nuclear weapons, NNWS demanded two additional concessions from the NWS. First, they demanded that the treaty provide not only a recognition of their right to use nuclear technologies for purposes of civilian power generation, but also a further reciprocal obligation on the part of the NWS and other supplier States[21] to provide positive assistance to NNWS in the development of their civilian nuclear programmes. Second, they further demanded that NWS undertake an obligation to move towards nuclear disarmament in good faith, as part of concurrent efforts toward general and complete disarmament.[22]

Some authors disagree with Joyner's interpretation of the NPT. Tom Coppen argues that:

> while a compromise was reached between different groups of States, balancing non-proliferation, disarmament, rights to use nuclear energy for peaceful purposes and nuclear cooperation, which was at the heart of the conclusion of the NPT … such a bargain does not necessarily mean the treaty is a contract.[23]

Coppen believes that there is nothing in the negotiating history of the NPT that indicates that the balance of obligations in the treaty was intended to be a contract involving an element of conditionality.[24] Similarly, while Nigel D White recognizes that there is a fundamental bargain underlying the treaty, he puts this bargain in a constitutional perspective. He argues that certain contracts represent an agreement upon which a society is built; and that these 'social contracts' are socially much more profound than a contractual transaction. At the international level, White mentions the Charter of the United

20 Daniel H Joyner, *Interpreting the Nuclear Non-Proliferation Treaty* (OUP 2011) 27; see generally Richard K Gardiner, *Treaty Interpretation* (OUP 2008) 177, 185.

21 The Nuclear Suppliers Group (NSG) is an informal, multilateral export control group established in 1975. As of 2020, the group was comprised of 48 States that have voluntarily agreed to coordinate their export controls to non-nuclear-weapon States. The NSG governs the transfers of civilian nuclear materials and nuclear-related equipment and technology. For more on the origins and effectiveness of the NSG in the context of the non-proliferation regime, see Jinwon Lee, 'Evaluating the Effectiveness of the Nuclear Suppliers Group: A Functionalist Perspective on the Regime' (2018) 16(2) KJIS 169, 202.

22 Joyner (n 20).

23 Tom Coppen, *The Law of Arms Control and the International Non-Proliferation Regime: Preventing the Spread of Nuclear Weapons* (Brill/Nijhoff 2016) 78, 94.

24 Ibid 90.

Nations and the five Great Powers acting as the world's police force in exchange for voting rights that no other members of the UN would possess. He argues that the NPT is a constitutional Treaty: 'since it develops the grand bargain found in the UN Charter by extending the inequality between the P5 and other members of the UN to the possession of nuclear weapons'.[25]

The basic distinction between a contract treaty and law-making treaty matters greatly in this case because different types of treaties might have different implications when it comes to a material breach of a treaty by a category of States parties. In Joyner's view, the fact that the NPT is the codification of a *quid pro quo* relationship between two classes of State parties, with each class having different rights and obligations accorded them under the treaty, serves to differentiate the NPT from most other large multilateral treaties. He argues that:

> When considering a multilateral lawmaking treaty, a material breach by one party or a group of parties may or may not serve to significantly affect the interests of the other parties to the treaty … However, in the case of a contract treaty, because of the quid pro quo reciprocal structure of the treaty's commitments, a material breach by one or a group of parties will almost certainly strike at the heart of the treaty's object and purpose.[26]

Joyner therefore argues that, in the case of a contract treaty, the aggrieved category of States could opt more easily to individually or collectively suspend the operation of the Treaty between themselves and the breaching States. Considering that the NWS have wasted a number of opportunities to fulfil their end of the bargain and seem to have no intention to give up their nuclear weapons, some of the NNWS might therefore consider withdrawing from the NPT entirely. On the other hand, according to Coppen, the classification of the NPT as a law-making treaty helps to avoid a collapse of the regime in case of a serious breach of the treaty. The interpretation of the NPT as a normative treaty makes it possible to develop the non-proliferation regime despite the lack of progress on the disarmament obligation. It is against this backdrop of existing different treaty interpretations that we can now explain why the vague formulation of Article VI on the obligation and pace of disarmament remains at the heart of the controversy regarding the treaty's implementation.

3 The nuclear disarmament impasse

The NPT established a relatively strong legal norm against the international spread of nuclear weapons. In the half-century of its existence, the State

25 Nigel D White, 'Interpretation of Non-Proliferation Treaties' in Daniel H Joyner and Marco Roscini (eds), *Non-proliferation Law as a Special Regime: A Contribution to Fragmentation Theory in International Law* (CUP 2012) 106, 108.

26 Joyner (n 20) 29.

parties to the treaty have reaffirmed on multiple occasions their commitment to the non-proliferation pillar of the treaty.[27] Despite the fact that four nuclear States currently remain outside of the non-proliferation regime, the nearly universal adherence to the NPT has been credited with slowing proliferation. Before the NPT was adopted, the prediction was that 25–30 States might acquire nuclear weapons relatively quickly. The political commitment to honour the non-proliferation obligations and the verification of treaty observance through the International Atomic Energy Agency (IAEA) constitute safeguards which have been the main factor contributing to the treaty's success in this regard.

Over the last few years, however, the deadlock regarding the disarmament aspects of the NPT has raised the question of the treaty's relevance. As pointed out by Pretorius and Sauer:

> [T]he broader objective of the NPT – to restrict the spread of nuclear weapons – has been corrupted. Instead, states possessing nuclear weapons have used the NPT to legalize their own nuclear weapons and criminalize everyone else's. The result is a one-sided and duplicitous nuclear order that is unstable, dangerous, and contrary to the expectations on which non-nuclear weapon states joined the NPT.[28]

Other scholars, such as Carlson, underline that while frustration at the lack of progress in disarmament is understandable:

> it makes no sense to attack the NPT over the inactions of some treaty parties, especially since it was not possible to reach agreement on specific disarmament provisions when the NPT was concluded, and the treaty defers the details of disarmament to further negotiations.[29]

The history of the negotiations shows that the relationship between the NPT's non-proliferation and disarmament provisions was contentious from the start. While a clear expectation from a majority of NNWS was that the NPT should take the world closer to disarmament, as well as codify the norm of non-proliferation, the Soviet Union and the US were reluctant to include language on disarmament in the NPT. Article VI of the treaty was adopted as a result of the strong push for balanced, mutual responsibilities and obligations between the nuclear and non-nuclear weapon States.[30] The final outcome was a difficult-to-achieve compromise that included provisions on disarmament. These aspects of the NPT remain until today the most

27 Preparatory Committee (n 1).
28 Pretorius and Sauer (n 2).
29 Carlson (n 13).
30 Egeland and others (n 13) 77.

contested of all the provisions of the treaty with respect to their interpretation and application.[31]

Article VI states, in its entirety:

> Each of the Parties to the Treaty undertakes to pursue negotiations in good faith on effective measures relating to cessation of the nuclear arms race at an early date and to nuclear disarmament, and on the treaty on general and complete disarmament under strict effective international control.

The NWS recognized by the NPT argue that this is an open-ended commitment to agree upon nuclear disarmament when they feel the conditions are right. Most recently, at the 2019 Preparatory Committee for the 10th NPT Review Conference, the US introduced a new initiative entitled 'Creating an Environment for Nuclear Disarmament' (CEND).[32] The US initiative is based on the view that the international security environment is not conducive to further progress on disarmament and that a number of conditions would need to be met to facilitate the pursuit of a world free of nuclear weapons.[33] Some of the NPT's non-nuclear weapon States strongly reject the notion that nuclear disarmament is preconditioned on a certain set of circumstances. As argued by the Philippines: '[t]his endeavour is a matter of collective responsibility, particularly between and among the nuclear-weapon states, and it must not be made conditional on the interests of a few.'[34]

In contrast to the 'open-ended' interpretation of the disarmament provisions, the majority of the State parties of the NPT believe that Article VI is a binding obligation upon all states, including nuclear States, to both negotiate and conclude an agreement on comprehensive nuclear disarmament. This

31 Daniel Rietiker, 'The Meaning of Article VI of the Treaty on the Non-Proliferation of Nuclear Weapons: Analysis Under the Rules of Treaty Interpretation', in Jonathan L Black-Branch and Dieter Flick (eds), *Nuclear Non-Proliferation in International Law* Vol 1 (Springer 2014) 47, 84; Daniel H Joyner, 'The Legal Meaning and Implications of Article VI of the Non-Proliferation Treaty' in Gro Nystuen, Stuart Casey-Maslen, and Annie Golden Bersagel (eds), *Nuclear Weapons under International Law* (CUP 2014) 397, 417.

32 The US proposal was first introduced as 'Creating the Conditions for Nuclear Disarmament' in a Working Paper to the 2018 Preparatory Committee. See Shannon Bugos, 'CEND Establishes Two-Year Program' (*Arms Control Today*, January/February 2020) <https://bit.ly/2SjbQKB>; Paul Meyer, 'Creating an Environment for Nuclear Disarmament: Striding Forward or Stepping Back?' (*Arms Control Today*, April 2019) < https://bit.ly/3bNW4OB> both accessed 30 April 2022.

33 Christopher A Ford, 'Lessons from Disarmament History for the CEND Initiative' (*New Paradigm Forum*, 30 April 2019) <https://bit.ly/3yvmcaO> accessed 30 April 2022.

34 Alicia Sanders-Zakre, 'Reporting on the 2019 NPT PrepCom' (*Arms Control Today*, 10 May 2019) <https://www.armscontrol.org/blog/2019-05-10/reporting-2019-npt-prepcom> accessed 30 April 2022.

position has been reinforced by the Advisory Opinion of the International Court of Justice on the *Threat or Use of Nuclear Weapons* (1996). The Court reaffirmed the obligation to disarm, stating that: 'There exists an obligation to pursue in good faith and bring to a conclusion negotiations leading to nuclear disarmament in all its aspects under strict and effective international control'.[35] Unfortunately, the Court's opinion has been openly challenged by some of the NWS.[36]

The NWS have also argued that they *have* honoured the Article VI commitment through various unilateral actions or bilateral arms reduction agreements. Russia and the US point to the major reductions of nuclear weapon stockpiles since the Cold War. However, as clearly differentiated by experts, the Cold War efforts on the part of the superpowers – particularly to forbid among themselves the possession of certain nuclear weapons delivery technologies (e.g. through the Anti-Ballistic Missile Treaty) and to limit and eventually reduce nuclear weapons stockpiles (e.g. the Intermediate-Range Nuclear Forces (INF) Treaty) – should properly be understood as efforts at arms control, and not nuclear weapons disarmament. These two terms are often used interchangeably in discourse concerning nuclear weapons, but they are in fact quite different concepts.[37] According to the Federation of American Scientists, the number of nuclear weapons has declined significantly since the Cold War; down from a peak of approximately 70,300 in 1986 to an estimated 13,410 in early-2020. While government officials often portray that accomplishment as the result of a current or recent arms control agreement, the overwhelming proportion of the reduction happened in the 1990s.[38]

The NWS have not only consistently marginalized the importance of the disarmament pillar of the NPT, they have also failed to implement the various pledges and commitments agreed upon since the indefinite extension of the treaty in 1995. The year 2020 marked not only the 50th Anniversary of the entry into force of the NPT, but also the 25th Anniversary of the extraordinary meeting of the NPT States Parties in 1995.[39] The fifth NPT review conference resulted in a 'package deal' which included the indefinite extension of the Treaty alongside decisions on 'Principles and Objectives'; a strengthened review process; and a resolution calling for the establishment of a

35 *Legality of the Threat and Use of Nuclear Weapons*, Advisory Opinion (1996) ICJ Rep 66.

36 Christopher A Ford, 'Debating Disarmament: Interpreting Article VI of the Treaty on the Non-Proliferation of Nuclear Weapons' (2007) 14(3) Non-proliferation Rev 401. For a legal analysis of NWS' interpretation of Article VI, see Joyner (n 20) 95, 104.

37 Ibid 104.

38 Kristensen and Korda (n 8).

39 Randy Rydell, 'Looking Back: The 1995 Nuclear Nonproliferation Treaty Review and Extension Conference' (*Arms Control Today*, undated) <https://bit.ly/3hK4uKy> accessed 30 April 2022; Jayantha Dhanapala and Randy Rydell, *Multilateral Diplomacy and the NPT: An Insider's Account* (SIPRI and UNIDIR 2005) 3.

weapons of mass destruction-free (WMD) zone in the Middle East.[40] The failure to implement this package over the subsequent 25 years is a primary driver of the current crisis of confidence in the NPT regime.[41] In the eyes of the non-nuclear-weapon States, progress on nuclear disarmament has been woefully inadequate and has essentially ground to a halt in the current period. Efforts by successive NPT review conferences to provide objective benchmarks to measure progress on nuclear disarmament, notably the '13 Practical Steps' endorsed in 2000[42] or the '22 Action Items' agreed upon in 2010,[43] have not resulted in greater results or transparency by the nuclear weapon States. The accumulated frustration over the failure of the designated multilateral body, the Conference on Disarmament, to produce any progress over the last 20 years has led to a deep crisis of confidence in the NPT regime and a concerted pushback by the majority of NNWS.[44]

4 Fundamental change in the discourse about nuclear weapons and the normative impact of the nuclear ban treaty

The final document of the 2010 NPT Review Conference (adopted by consensus) referred for the first time in NPT history to the 'catastrophic humanitarian consequences of any use of nuclear weapons' and reaffirmed the need 'for all States at all times to comply with applicable international law, including humanitarian law'.[45] This call for a new approach was further developed by a series of diplomatic conferences organized in 2013 and 2014 and hosted by Norway, Mexico, and Austria, respectively. The conferences focused on the devastating threat represented by existing nuclear arsenals and on the complete unavailability of an adequate humanitarian response to any detonation of a nuclear weapon.[46] By introducing a new discourse, the gatherings were successful in increasing multilateral diplomatic efforts and in involving ever-greater numbers of States as well as civil society groups.[47] In

40 United Nations Office of Disarmament Affairs, 'Review and Extension Conference of the Parties to the Treaty on the Non-Proliferation of Nuclear Weapons', 17 April–12 May 1995 <https://www.un.org/disarmament/wmd/nuclear/npt1995/> accessed 30 April 2022.

41 Tariq Rauf, 'Is Past Prologue? Examining NPT Review Conference Commitments' (*UNIDIR*, undated) <https://bit.ly/3oK7LuT> accessed 30 April 2022.

42 Review Conference of the Parties to the Treaty on the Non-Proliferation of Nuclear Weapons, 'Final Document' (2000) NPT/CONF.2000/28.

43 Review Conference of the Parties to the Treaty on the Non-Proliferation of Nuclear Weapons, 'Final Document' (2010) NPT/CONF.2010/50.

44 Meyer (n 2).

45 NPT Review Conference (n 43).

46 Gro Nystuen and Kjolv Egeland, 'A "Legal Gap"? Nuclear Weapons Under International Law' (*Arms Control Today*, March 2016) <https://bit.ly/3vcK6Wx> accessed 30 April 2022.

47 Ramesh Thakur, 'The Nuclear Ban Treaty: Recasting a Normative Framework for Disarmament' (2017) 40(4) Wash Q 79; Tom Sauer, 'It's Time to Outlaw Nuclear Weapons. A Treaty Banning the Bomb Could Lead to Real Progress'

contrast to the dominating Cold War narrative of nuclear deterrence and the post-Cold War period's emphasis on nuclear non-proliferation and nuclear security, the humanitarian initiative focused on the necessity of nuclear elimination.[48]

At the conclusion of the last conference in Vienna on 9 December 2014, the Austrian hosts submitted a document calling on States and other stakeholders to 'fill the legal gap for the prohibition and elimination of nuclear weapons'.[49] A few months later, the Austrian government announced that this 'Austrian Pledge' would be called the 'Humanitarian Pledge', thus implying a broader ownership of the document (108 States formally endorsed this initiative). In December 2015, the humanitarian initiative conferences were given diplomatic expression by the adoption of a resolution of the United Nations General Assembly calling for States to work 'to fill the legal gap for the prohibition and elimination of nuclear weapons'.[50] The resolution focused on a long-standing contradiction in the international security framework, namely that the NPT had not subjected nuclear weapons to a comprehensive prohibition similar to that applied to other weapons of mass destruction, i.e. biological and chemical. The Resolution implied that this de facto exemption for nuclear weapons was invalid and should be terminated. This was reinforced with a humanitarian pledge resolution adopted on the same day, which established an Open-ended Working Group. The group decided to operate under General Assembly rules that permit decisions by vote, instead of the decision-blocking consensus rule of the Conference on Disarmament.[51] The working group report of August 2016 asked the General Assembly to convene a conference in 2017, open to all States and with the participation of international organizations and civil society, 'to negotiate a legally binding instrument to prohibit nuclear weapons, leading towards their total elimination'.[52] In response to that request, a resolution deciding to convene a conference in 2017 was adopted by the General Assembly on 23 December 2016.[53] After four weeks of negotiations at the UN headquarters in New York, the United Nations-mandated conference adopted the TPNW.[54]

(*National Interest*, 18 April 2016) <https://nationalinterest.org/feature/its-time-outlaw-nuclear-weapons-15814> accessed 30 April 2022.

48 Rebecca Davis Gibbons, 'The Humanitarian Turn in Nuclear Disarmament and the Treaty on the Prohibition of Nuclear Weapons' (2018) 25(1–2) The Non-proliferation Rev 11, 36.

49 Pledge presented at the Vienna Conference on the Humanitarian Impact of Nuclear Weapons by Austrian Deputy Foreign Minister Michael Linhart (8–9 December 2014) <https://bit.ly/3yujh1X> accessed 30 April 2022.

50 UNGA, Resolution 70/48 (7 December 2015) UN Doc A/RES.70/48.

51 UNGA, Res 70/33 (7 December 2015) UN Doc A/RES/70/33.

52 UNGA, 'Report of the Open-ended Working Group Taking Forward Multilateral Nuclear Disarmament Negotiations' (1 September 2016) UN Doc A/71/371.

53 UNGA, Res 71/258 (11 January 2017) UN Doc A/RES/71/258.

54 Treaty on the Prohibition of Nuclear Weapons (entry into force 22 January 2021).

The adoption of the TPNW has been met with mixed reactions. While supporters have described the Treaty as historic in the struggle for disarmament, others have expressed strong opposition. The nuclear-weapon States and their allies (with the sole exception of the Netherlands[55]) boycotted the negotiations and by doing so denied themselves a voice in the proceedings.[56] Out of a total of 129 States registered to participate in the Conference, 122 voted in favour of the treaty's adoption, Singapore abstained and the Netherlands voted against.[57] For the first time ever, and despite strong pressure from the nuclear powers, the non-nuclear-weapon States and their civil society allies held the steering wheel of nuclear 'governance'.[58]

The adoption of the TPNW by almost two-thirds of the NPT State parties has delegitimized the NPT as the dominant normative framework for nuclear disarmament. The initiatives leading to the adoption of the nuclear ban treaty established a new understanding of nuclear weapons as inherently inhumane, rather than as providers of stability and security. The emphasis on the catastrophic humanitarian consequences of the use of nuclear weapons constituted the basis for anti-weapons activism. The Campaign to Abolish Nuclear Weapons – a co-organizer of the humanitarian conferences – constantly highlighted the questions regarding the morality of both the possession and use of nuclear weapons, asserting their illegitimacy. The supporters of the ban treaty believe that the creation of an international prohibition places political pressure on nuclear-armed States and their allies and stigmatizes the possession of nuclear weapons by creating an anti-nuclear norm that will grow over time.[59] As

55 The Netherlands decided to participate in the TPNW negotiations despite direct pressure from the US urging all NATO allies to vote against the draft resolution to convene ban treaty negotiations and to take part in any negotiations if they should begin. As regards the various factors that influenced the Dutch position on nuclear disarmament and the country's participation in the ban negotiations, see Ekaterina Shirobokova, 'The Netherlands and the Prohibition of Nuclear Weapons' (2018) 25(1–2) The Non-proliferation Rev 37, 49.

56 Anne Gearan, 'U.S. Leads Major Powers in Protesting U.N. Effort to Ban Nuclear Weapons' *Washington Post* (27 March 2017) <https://wapo.st/3hK8zyz> accessed 30 April 2022.

57 The United Nations Conference to Negotiate a Legally-binding Instrument to Prohibit Nuclear Weapons, Leading Towards Their Total Elimination, 'Draft Treaty on the Prohibition of Nuclear Weapons' (7 July 2017) <https://bit.ly/3bJHgRe> accessed 30 April 2022.

58 For more on the process preceding the adoption of the TPNW and the complexity regarding the involvement of various actors, see John Borrie, Michael Spies, and Wilfred Wan, 'Obstacles to Understanding the Emergence and Significance of the Treaty on the Prohibition of Nuclear Weapons' (2018) 30(2) Glob Change Peace & Sec 95, 119.

59 Laura Considine, 'The Treaty on the Prohibition of Nuclear Weapons and the Question of Nuclear Meaning' (2019) 7(1) Critical Studies Secur 87, 90; Beatrice Fihn, 'The Logic of Banning Nuclear Weapons' (2017) 59(1) Survival 43, 50; Matthew Bolton and Elizabeth Minor, 'The Discursive Turn Arrives in Turtle Bay: The International Campaign to Abolish Nuclear Weapons' Operationalization of Critical IR Theories' (2016) 7(3) Glob Policy 385, 395; Elizabeth Minor,

observed by Zia Mian, the real significance of the TPNW might lie in its potential to serve as an alternative framework for mobilizing States to join the cause of nuclear disarmament.[60]

While the emphasis on the humanitarian consequences of any use of nuclear weapons gained the support of 122 States, the NWS have argued that the adoption of the nuclear ban treaty weakens the existing non-proliferation and disarmament regime. Thakur challenges this argument and blames the NWS' non-participation in the negotiations for weakening the NPT:

> [t]he non-participation of the nuclear state parties to the NPT and their allies in a duly established, multilateral negotiation process, placed them in non-compliance with the Article VI obligation to pursue and conclude disarmament negotiations and therefore further weakens the NPT.[61]

Following the adoption of the nuclear ban treaty, France, the UK, and the US issued a statement noting that they had not taken part in the negotiations of the Treaty and that they do not intend to sign, ratify, or ever become party to the TPNW. The three States stated as well that there will be no change in their legal obligations with respect to nuclear weapons and that they will not accept any claim that the TPNW reflects or in any way contributes to the development of customary international law.[62] According to the author of a legal commentary on the TPNW, the statement regarding the TPNW and international customary law is at the very least unfortunate, and potentially misplaced. Casey-Maslen argues that:

> The adoption of the Treaty itself reflects the state practice, and widespread adherence to it and respect of its provisions will confirm this. The Treaty, for example, prohibits all transfer of nuclear weapons by any state party. This may be reflective of a customary prohibition on all transfer of nuclear weapons either *lex lata* (settled law) or at least *lex ferenda* (law in the making).[63]

'Changing the Discourse on Nuclear Weapons: The Humanitarian Initiative' (2015) 97 IRRC 711, 730; Tom Sauer and Mathias Reveraert, 'The Potential Stigmatizing Effect of the Treaty on the Prohibition of Nuclear Weapons' (2018) 25(5–6) The Non-proliferation Rev 437, 455.

60 Zia Mian, 'Taking the Nuclear Ban Treaty Forward' (*Bulletin of the Atomic Scientists*, 30 October 2020) <https://thebulletin.org/2020/10/taking-the-nuclear-ban-treaty-forward/> accessed 30 April 2022.

61 Thakur (n 47).

62 Joint press statement from the Permanent Representatives to the United Nations of the United States, the United Kingdom, and France following the adoption of the TPNW (*United States Mission to the United Nations*, 7 July 2017) <https://bit.ly/3fB9MWd> accessed 30 April 2022.

63 The statement from the UK, the US, and France on the ban treaty, 7 July 2017 and a legal analysis of the 2017 Treaty and Customary International Law. See Nystuen and others (n 11) 52, 58.

One of the most serious criticisms levelled at the TPNW is that it will undermine the long-standing NPT regime. Russian diplomatic representatives stated that the provisions of the new treaty create serious risks for the existing system of nuclear non-proliferation and provoke growing estrangement among members of the international community. Other critics have contended that the new agreement risks eroding the system of safeguards designed to prevent the spread of nuclear weapons, derailing disarmament efforts within the NPT framework and aggravating the political division between nuclear and non-nuclear powers.

Scholars investigating the strength of these contentions argue that not only may the TPNW be reconciled with existing legal instruments, but the new treaty also supports and reinforces key norms and institutions on which the nuclear non-proliferation and disarmament regime is based.[64]

First of all, Article 1(1) TPNW, entitled 'Prohibitions', encompasses general obligations that are more comprehensive than those of any previous disarmament treaty. The article contains a set of undertakings by each State party to 'never under any circumstances' perform certain acts. Accordingly, each State party shall never 'develop; manufacture, produce, or otherwise acquire; possess or stockpile; transfer; test; use; or threaten to use nuclear weapons or other nuclear explosive devices'. Each State party shall also never allow the stationing, installation or deployment of any such weapons or devices within its territory or at any other place under its jurisdiction or control. Furthermore, each State party shall never assist, encourage, or induce, in any way, anyone to engage in any prohibited activity, nor shall it seek or receive any assistance to so engage.[65] The 2017 Treaty does not, however, in its first article on 'prohibitions', require the destruction of any nuclear weapons or other explosive device stockpiles. The obligation to destroy such weapons or devices is set out in a single paragraph of Article 4(2). Thus Article 4 of the ban treaty addresses the key disarmament obligations of nuclear-armed States parties and of States parties hosting third State's nuclear weapons and other nuclear explosive devices.[66]

In the context of its obligations, the TPNW has been criticized by nuclear-armed governments and experts for being divisive and ineffective. Valentino and Scott, for example, have argued that with not a single NWS signing up as a member, even the treaty's strongest proponents acknowledge that it is largely an aspirational document designed to promote disarmament by delegitimizing nuclear weapons. Their main argument for the ineffectiveness of the treaty is that the TPNW does not really 'outlaw' or make nuclear weapons 'illegal' under international law, because any State that is not a member of the

64 Egeland and others (n 13).

65 'Commentary on the Article 1: Prohibitions' in Nystuen and others (n 11) 131, 173.

66 'Commentary on the Article 4: Toward the Total Elimination of Nuclear Weapons' in Nystuen and others (n 11) 189, 201.

treaty is not bound by its terms.[67] Proponents of the ban treaty nevertheless argue that by cementing the prohibition of nuclear weapons in international law they will intensify the stigma against nuclear weapons, discouraging the States from building them and eventually pressuring the nuclear powers to disarm. The TPNW's legal effect lies in strengthening the disarmament norm under Article VI NPT and asserting the illegitimacy of their continued possession and deployment.[68]

Unlike the NPT, which reflects the geopolitical and normative balance of power of the negotiations conducted 50 years ago, the prohibition treaty reflects the voice of the majority of States. In this sense, the TPNW has a symbolic function – a rejection of the nuclear *status quo* established in 1968. As summarized by Thakur:

> The nuclear discourse of the NWS "moves easily from" the position that the NPT permits them to possess and deploy nuclear weapons "to the language of entitlement, legal rights and enduring legitimacy" … But non-nuclear weapon states are the majority shareholders in the NPT society of states and by acting together; they have taken back that legitimacy.[69]

By changing the prevailing normative structure, the TPNW shifts the balance of the costs and benefits of possession and deployment practices, and in the long term might create a deepening crisis of legitimacy.

5 Near collapse of the arms control architecture

In the 50 years since the NPT's entry into force, not a single nuclear warhead has been eliminated through a multilateral agreement. Apart from reductions in nuclear warheads obtained through the bilateral arms control agreements, no multilateral negotiation on nuclear weapons has ever been held under the NPT's provisions. The nuclear weapon States have wasted a number of opportunities to fulfil their end of the bargain embedded in the Non-proliferation Treaty. These include failures to implement the commitments given at the 1995 Review and Extension Conference, the 2000 and 2010 Review Conference conclusions, and boycotting the UN-mandated multilateral negotiations on a legal prohibition of nuclear weapons. In addition to the steady erosion of the NPT's normative authority, the recent near collapse of the arms control architecture provides a clear indication that nuclear-armed States have no intention of giving up their nuclear weapons.

67 Benjamin A Valentino and Scott D Sagan, 'The Nuclear Weapons Ban Treaty: Opportunities Lost' (*Bulletin of the Atomic Scientists*, 16 July 2017) <https://bit.ly/3yySVMv> accessed 30 April 2022.

68 John Krzyzaniak, 'The Nuclear Ban Treaty Is Set to Enter Force. Experts Explain What Comes Next' (*Bulletin of the Atomic Scientists*, 30 October 2020) <https://bit.ly/3bHInAP> accessed 30 April 2022.

69 Thakur (n 47).

The US withdrawal from the landmark INF Treaty, announced in August 2019, is arguably one of the most worrying recent developments related to arms control. The 1987 INF Treaty, negotiated and signed by US President Ronald Reagan and Soviet leader Mikhail Gorbachev, was one of the most far-reaching and successful nuclear arms reduction agreements in history. The treaty led to the verifiable elimination of nearly 2,700 US and Soviet ballistic and cruise missiles with ranges between 500 km and 5,500 km. The pact served as an important check on some of the most destabilizing types of nuclear weapons that the US and Russia could deploy. In recent years, Washington has repeatedly alleged that Russia was in breach of the agreement. Moscow forcefully rejected the charges and countered them with its own claims of non-compliance by the US.[70]

With the treaty's termination, each side is now free to develop, flight test, and possibly deploy previously banned INF systems in Europe and Asia. Without the INF Treaty, the potential for a new intermediate-range missile arms race in Europe and beyond becomes increasingly real. Furthermore, in the treaty's absence, the only binding, verifiable limits on the world's largest nuclear arsenals come from the New Strategic Arms Reduction Treaty (New START), which was due to expire in February 2021 unless the US and Russia agreed to extend it. The Trump administration's reluctance to extend the Treaty and failure to develop a coherent nuclear arms control strategy had been strongly criticized by experts in the field.[71] Fortunately, the Biden administration did not allow the New START to expire without a replacement treaty and in a last-minute agreement with Russia decided to extend the reduction treaty for another five years.[72]

Apart from the collapse of the INF Treaty, the nuclear non-proliferation and disarmament regime must also address other nuclear proliferation challenges, like the one progressing in North Korea and Iran's explicit threat to quit the NPT since the US withdrawal from the Joint Comprehensive Plan of Action (JCPOA).[73] The

70 Arms Control Association, 'The Post-INF Treaty Crisis: Background and Next Steps' (Arms Control Association, 7 August 2019) <https://www.armscontrol.org/issue-briefs/2019-08/post-inf-treaty-crisis-background-next-steps>; Greg Thielmann, Oliver Meier, and Victor Mizin, 'INF Treaty: Path to Renewal or the End of the Road?' Deep Cuts Brief, 8 May 2018. <https://deepcuts.org/files/pdf/Deep_Cuts_Issue_Brief_8-INF_Treaty_Compliance.pdf>; TASS, 'Russia Slams US Aegis Ashore Missile Deployment in Europe as Direct Breach of INF Treaty' (*TASS*, 26 November 2018) <https://tass.com/politics/1032585> all accessed 30 April 2022.

71 Daryl G Kimbel, 'Begin with New START, Not a New Arms Race' (*Arms Control Today*, June 2020) <https://www.armscontrol.org/act/2020-06/focus/begin-new-start-not-new-arms-race> accessed 30 April 2022.

72 Kingston Reif and Shannon Bugos, 'US, Russia Extend New START for Five Years' (*Arms Control Association*, March 2021) <https://www.armscontrol.org/act/2021-03/news/us-russia-extend-new-start-five-years> accessed 30 April 2022.

73 Kaveh Afrasiabi and Nader Entessar, 'Iran's Impending Exit from the NPT: A New Nuclear Crisis' (*Bulletin of the Atomic Scientists*, 28 January 2020) <https://thebulletin.org/2020/01/irans-impending-exit-from-the-npt-a-new-nuclear-crisis/> accessed 30 April 2022.

multilateral agreement signed in 2015 limited Iran's nuclear programme to block the development of nuclear weapons, in return for which Iran received relief from American and international sanctions. After the US withdrawal in 2018, the Trump administration reimposed and added new sanctions on Tehran, and Iran began breaching JCPOA restrictions. Taken as a whole, these developments represent a large step backward, imperilling international peace and security.

At the time of writing of this chapter, and just a few months before the NPT Review Conference is scheduled to take place, the situation regarding the NPT's credibility crisis is not showing any signs of improvement. Despite President Biden's pledge to return to the JCPOA, Iran has refused direct talks on resuming compliance in exchange for the lifting of US sanctions. It is unclear whether the indirect talks between the US and Iran, taking place in Vienna with representatives of Britain, China, France, Germany, Russia, and the EU, will culminate in a restoration of compliance with the JCPOA. The main differences exist over the pace of lifting of the US sanctions, the steps Iran must take to resume its obligations to restrict its nuclear programme, and how to sequence the process. Similar considerations will have to be taken into account in the current review of US policy towards North Korea. Some analysts suggest that the Biden administration should 'creatively engineer – and faithfully implement – incremental transactions that not only reduce security risks in the near term, but also pave the way for broader diplomatic solutions down the road'.[74]

6 Conclusion: the NPT's mid-life crisis and where we go from here

The roots of the NPT crisis lie in the origins of the treaty itself and the legal hierarchy between nuclear 'haves' and 'have-nots' enshrined in it. In particular, the vague formulation of Article VI and deep disagreements between nuclear and non-nuclear weapon States regarding the obligation and pace of nuclear disarmament could be regarded as the underlying causes of the erosion of the Treaty's normative authority. The normative order agreed upon in 1968 does not reflect the current interests, power structures, and technological features in place today. Out of nine countries with nuclear arsenals, four remain outside the NPT, and universalization of the regime remains elusive. Instead of disarmament, the ongoing modernization of nuclear arsenals as well as the development of new technologies and weapons are increasing the tensions between nuclear-armed States and the risk of the use of nuclear weapons.[75] Over the last couple of years there has been a strong sense among many non-nuclear-weapon State officials that the status quo cannot be

74 Christopher Lawrence, '"Transactional" Nuclear Diplomacy May Provide A Path Toward "Grand Bargains" with Iran and North Korea' (*Bulletin of the Atomic Scientists*, 29 April 2021) <https://bit.ly/3bMjPqo> accessed 30 April 2022.

75 Victor Gilinsky, 'Nuclear Risks Are Growing, and There's Only One Real Solution' (*Bulletin of the Atomic Scientists*, 10 December 2020) <https://bit.ly/3fIsVFT> accessed 30 April 2022.

allowed to stand. Against the backdrop of the receding nuclear arms control and disarmament and elevated nuclear threat levels, many countries concluded that new efforts were needed. The process leading to the negotiations over and adoption of the nuclear ban treaty provided a change of discourse and a new foundation for a future disarmament process. The TPNW constitutes a symbolic response to the nuclear-weapon States' apparent unwillingness to honour their end of the NPT grand bargain.[76]

The legitimacy crisis of the NPT reflects the broader legitimacy crisis of the United Nations and other global regimes established in the post-Second World War period.[77] 'Traditional' or 'hegemonic' multilateralism has always been under challenge because of its features, but the multilateral crisis of today needs to be put into perspective. Two major dynamics can be observed in the field of the nuclear non-proliferation regime. The first is a redefinition of security, including the call for human security, which found its expression in the change of discourse surrounding nuclear weapons. Calls for a 'humanitarian consequences' approach to disarmament – as opposed to national security, deterrence, and strategic stability – successfully mobilized the majority of the NPT member States to negotiate and adopt the TPNW. Despite enormous pressure from the nuclear powers, the non-nuclear weapons States normatively rejected the existing status quo and made nuclear weapons illegal under international law. The second dynamic and manifestation of the current crisis can be observed in the diversity of the actors involved in the process leading to the negotiation of the ban treaty. It is still too early to evaluate the role of particular players (civil society, international organizations, and States) in the process of establishing the prohibition of nuclear weapons, but the process has shown that it is time to make the nuclear non-proliferation and disarmament regime more inclusive and democratic. While the entry into force of the TPNW indicates a 'crisis of authority' in the existing multilateral order based on the NPT, it does not necessarily mean its collapse. The rules and institutions established during the Cold War remain in place. Support for the NPT is, in terms of membership, almost universal; and States continue to work together within the quintennial review process and the UN disarmament forums. The ban treaty is compatible with the NPT and its goal is to strengthen the disarmament obligation of the Article VI.

76 Kjolv Egeland, 'Introduction: Nuclear Ban Treaty as Negation of Negation' (2019) 7(1) Critical Studies Secur 69, 72.

77 Edward Newman, *A Crisis of Global Institutions? Multilateralism and International Security* (Routledge 2007); G John Ikenberry, *After Victory: Institutions, Strategic Restraint and the Rebuilding of Order after Major Wars* (Princeton UP 2000); G John Ikenberry, *Liberal Leviathan: The Origins, Crisis, and Transformation of the American World Order* (Princeton UP 2011); Robert Cox, 'Multilateralism and World Order' (1992) 18(2) Rev Int Stud 161; Edward Newman, Ramesh Thakur, and John Tirman, *Multilateralism Under Challenge: Power, International Order, and Structural Change* (UNUP 2006); Amitav Acharya, *The End of American World Order* (Polity Press 2014).

Therefore, what we witness is rather an evolution of multilateralism towards a more pluralistic, 'post-hegemonic' form.[78]

The latest developments in the field of nuclear non-proliferation and disarmament lead one to the conclusion that it is high time to reinvent nuclear disarmament.[79] The process should start as soon as the postponed NPT Review Conference can be convened. The postponement due to COVID-19 presents an opportunity to address the mounting pressures and polarization within the NPT regime.[80] The risks for the Conference, and ultimately for the Treaty itself, have been multiplying.[81] The war in Ukraine and an increased threat of nuclear weapons' use highlight the urgency of bringing Russia, Ukraine, and NATO member states to a negotiating table. It is up to the biggest defenders of the NPT – namely the nuclear-armed States – to show that the treaty is still relevant. One way of doing so is to make the negotiation process more inclusive and to reassure the non-nuclear weapon States that the disarmament obligations are being taken seriously.[82] When the world leaders will eventually be able to meet, everything might look different through the lenses of the war in Ukraine and COVID-19. Apart from the large list of worries and problems in the nuclear field, the pandemic raises new questions regarding the response capacity (or the lack thereof) to a global public health crisis. The pandemic, as well as climate change, require a deeper reflection about major threats and a reassessment of what constitutes State security. An evaluation of the place of nuclear weapons in a new concept of national and international security will be also necessary. If we hope to reverse the growing antagonisms between nuclear and non-nuclear weapon States, and prevent the *fin du regime*, substantial changes are essential at this stage.

78 Amitav Acharya, 'Post-Hegemonic Multilateralism' in Thomas Weiss and Rorden Wilkinson (eds), *Global Governance and International Organizations* (Routledge 2014) 192, 204; Amitav Acharya, 'Global Governance in a Multiplex World' EUI Working Paper no 2017/29 1, 17.

79 Nick Ritchie, 'Inventing Nuclear Disarmament' (2019) 7(1) Critical Studies Secur 73, 77; Tom Sauer, 'Crossroads: Why the Nuclear Non-proliferation Treaty Could Become Obsolete' (*The National Interest*, 8 December 2017) <https://bit.ly/3veakIe> accessed 30 April 2022.

80 Robert Einhorn, 'Covid-19 Has Given the 2020 NPT Review Conference a Reprieve. Let's Take Advantage of it' (*Bulletin of the Atomic Scientists*, 13 May 2020) <https://bit.ly/3uaBwpR>; Tariq Rauf, 'The Postponed NPT Review Conference: A Modest Proposal' (*Bulletin of the Atomic Scientists*, 2 June 2020) <https://bit.ly/2RDpFn3> both accessed 30 April 2022.

81 Pugwash Conferences on Science and World Affairs, 'The Postponement of the NPT Review Conference. Antagonisms, Conflicts and Nuclear Risks After the Pandemic' (*Bulletin of the Atomic Scientists*, 12 May 2020), <https://bit.ly/3vdvjuI> accessed 30 April 2022.

82 'Joint Statement from Civil Society to the States Parties of the Nuclear Non-Proliferation Treaty' (11 May 2020) <https://bit.ly/3uaBK0b> accessed 30 April 2022.

10 The Crisis of Multilateralism Through the Prism of the Experience of the International Criminal Court

Patrycja Grzebyk and Karolina Wierczyńska

1 Introduction

The need to establish a permanent international criminal court to prosecute individuals for international crimes was discussed in the United Nations (UN) Committee on the Progressive Development of International Law and its Codification, and later in the International Law Commission from the early days of their work.[1] However, the international community had to wait several decades to reach a consensus enabling the creation of the International Criminal Court (ICC).

The adoption of the Rome Statute in 1998[2] was regarded as a triumph of multilateralism in an area which is traditionally perceived as the exclusive remit of the sovereign powers of a State.[3] It seemed at the time that the international community had moved to the next level of cooperation, having in mind certain common interests which could not have been satisfied through unilateral policies, i.e. to put an 'end to impunity for the perpetrators' of the gravest international crimes and 'thus to contribute to the prevention of such crimes', and to 'guarantee lasting respect for and the enforcement of international justice' (Preamble of the Statute). The fact that the ICC was established on the basis of a multilateral treaty justified expectations that multilateralism was the way forward for the development of the new international criminal justice system.[4]

After almost two decades this initial enthusiasm has turned into wider disappointment, while calls for extensive reforms of the Court have become more frequent.[5] A hostile political offensive against the ICC has also

1 The subject was already debated before and during the Second World War. See 'Historical Survey of the Question of International Criminal Jurisdiction – Memorandum Submitted by the Secretary-General' (9 June 1949) UN Doc A/CN.4/7/Rev.1 19–25.
2 Rome Statute of the International Criminal Court (entry into force 1 July 2002) 2187 UNTS 3.
3 Cedric Ryngaert, *Jurisdiction in International Law* (2nd edn, OUP 2015) 5.
4 Philippe Kirsch QC and Valerie Oosterveld, 'Negotiating an Institution for the Twenty-First Century: Multilateral Diplomacy and the International Criminal Court' (2001) 46 McGill LJ 1141.
5 Richard H Steinberg (ed), *The International Criminal Court: Contemporary Challenges and Reform Proposals* (Brill 2020).

DOI: 10.4324/9781003312857-12

returned.[6] The ICC clearly appears to be in crisis, partly because of its geopolitical connections and partly because of its internal dysfunction.

Many discussions regarding the ICC, sometimes very heated,[7] concern the essence of multilateralism. This should not be surprising as the ICC is perceived as one of the 'independent international organizations'.[8] Analysing the challenges that the Court faces may therefore help in understanding the reasons behind the alleged crisis of multilateralism as a whole, and in identifying possible ways to strengthen the pro-multilateral approach.[9] This is also the focus of this chapter, which investigates how multilateralism fits into the idea of the international criminal justice system, in which the ICC plays a pivotal role, and how the crisis in multilateralism is manifested in the Court and its work. In this context, the chapter particularly takes a closer look at how the idea of multilateralism is mirrored in the structure and practice of the ICC, specifically how it is institutionalized, whether the rules and obligations are common and equal to all States, and whether they are equally applied. This perspective allows us to show that the ICC – as the product of multilateral cooperation – plays a twofold role in international relations. First, as an international organization, it enables discussion via the Assembly of States Parties (the Assembly or ASP) on international criminal justice – thus strengthening multilateral cooperation and supporting the idea of a fight against the impunity of perpetrators. Second, as a court fighting against impunity for international crimes, it acts as a suppliant requesting State cooperation and broader national engagement, thus pointing out the weaknesses of multilateral collaboration and the symptoms of the crisis. The chapter also pays a special attention to the consequences of the COVID-19 pandemic for the ICC, which has exposed the shortcomings of multilateral relations in the area of international criminal justice.

2 Multilateralism in theory

2.1 The ICC as an achievement of multilateralism

The idea of multilateralism is indirectly expressed in the preamble of the UN Charter, which refers to the establishment of 'conditions under which justice

6 See various US authorities' statements, e.g. John Bolton: 'we will let it die on its own' ('John Bolton Threatens ICC with US Sanctions' (*BBC*, 11 September 2018) <https://www.bbc.com/news/world-us-canada-45474864>); 'Pompeo on ICC: U.S. Won't Be Threatened by "Kangaroo Court"' (*Reuters*, 11 June 2020) <https://reut.rs/3fJpFLG> both accessed 15 May 2022.

7 See 'Remarks by President Trump to the 73rd Session of the United Nations General Assembly' (*The White House Office of the Press Secretary*, 25 September 2018) <https://bit.ly/3fJRJ16> accessed 15 May 2022.

8 Sasha Lüder, 'The Legal Nature of the International Criminal Court and the Emergence of Supranational Elements in International Criminal Justice' (2002) 84(845) IRRC 79, 84.

9 John O McGinnis, 'The Political Economy of Global Multilateralism' (2000) 1(2) Chi J Int L 381, 396–397.

and respect for the obligations arising from treaties and other sources of international law can be maintained', with the UN 'employ[ing] international machinery for the promotion of the economic and social advancement of all peoples'.[10] Consequently, the main aim of the organization is 'to achieve international co-operation in solving international problems of an economic, social, cultural, or humanitarian character, and in promoting and encouraging respect for human rights and for fundamental freedoms', and to 'be a centre for harmonizing the actions of nations in the attainment of these common ends' (Article 1).

The preamble of the Rome Statute directly reaffirms the objectives and principles of the UN Charter, and recognizes that 'grave crimes threaten the peace, security and well-being of the world' while at the same time emphasizing that the fight against impunity requires 'enhancing international cooperation'. The ICC is clearly an example of the multilateral approach to international problems – in this case, the impunity of perpetrators of the gravest crimes – which is consistent with the whole idea of the UN.

Multilateralism was perceived as a helpful panacea to rebuild the world after the atrocities of the Second World War. Engaging as many states as possible in multilateral treaties was intended to secure the stabilization of international relations. When the Cold War ended, international cooperation became possible in areas such as criminal justice, which had been protected until that point as exclusive sovereign domains.[11] Therefore, the relatively late establishment of the ICC was connected with the persistence of the Cold War, the end of which encouraged States to engage in multilateral treaties and consider punishment of perpetrators of the core crimes as a common obligation and interest. In addition, there was massive pressure on behalf of non-governmental organizations to establish a solid basis for the international criminal justice system. Those organizations (e.g. Amnesty International), which in some cases had greater legitimacy to speak in the name of victims than States did, were visibly involved in the process of negotiating the Statute (even if the final decisions were still taken by States).[12]

According to Robert Keohane, 'multilateralism can be defined as the practice of coordinating national policies in groups of three or more states,

10 Amendment to the Charter of the United Nations with the Statute of the International Court of Justice annexed thereto (17 December 1963) 557 UNTS 143.

11 John Peterson and Caroline Bouchard, 'Making Multilateralism Effective: Modernizing Global Governance' in Caroline Bouchard, John Peterson, and Nathalie Tocci (eds), *Multilateralism in the 21st Century: Europe's Quest for Effectiveness* (Routledge 2013) 13.

12 Zoe Pearson, 'Non-Governmental Organizations and the International Criminal Court: Changing Landscapes of International Law' (2006) 39(2) Cornell Int Law J 243, 254; John Washburn, 'The Negotiation of the Rome Statute for the International Criminal Court and International Lawmaking in the 21st Century' (1999) 11 Pace Int Law Rev 361; Marie Törnquist-Chesnier, 'How the International Criminal Court Came to Life: The Role of Non-governmental Organisations' (2007) 21(3) Glob Soc 449.

through ad hoc arrangements or by means of institutions'.[13] Caroline Bouchard and John Peterson similarly point out that multilateralism means: 'Three or more actors engaging in voluntary and (essentially) institutionalised international cooperation governed by norms and principles, with rules that apply (by and large) equally to all states'.[14] Based on these definitions, one may mention some general features of such multilateral engagements, such as: (1) institutionalization, and (2) sharing the same principles and rules, which in consequence means applying unified norms equally to all State Parties so everyone has the same rights and obligations. Both elements are reflected in the Rome Statute.

2.2 Institutionalization

In 1995, the Ad Hoc Committee on the Establishment of an International Criminal Court briefly noted in its report presented to the International Law Commission that:

> There was broad recognition that the establishment of an effective and widely accepted international criminal court could ensure that the perpetrators of serious international crimes were brought to justice and deter future occurrences of such crimes. The remark was made that the establishment of a single, permanent court would obviate the need for setting up ad hoc tribunals for particular crimes, thereby ensuring stability and consistency in international criminal jurisdiction.[15]

The lesson learnt from the controversies surrounding the creation of the International Criminal Tribunals for the former Yugoslavia and for Rwanda, which were established by UN Security Councils resolutions,[16] the need to gain the support of as many States as possible in order to achieve universal recognition of the new tribunal, and the general conviction about the significance of the statutory obligations were all decisive factors in the choice of the way (i.e. as an international treaty negotiated outside the UN framework) the permanent, independent court was established. The ICC is criticized for many different reasons, but not for the manner of its establishment.

13 Robert O Keohane, 'Multilateralism: An Agenda for Research' (1990) 45(4) Int J 731.

14 Peterson and Bouchard (n 11) 18.

15 United Nations 'Report of the Ad Hoc Committee on the Establishment of an International Criminal Court' (6 September 1995) UN Doc A/50/22 [12].

16 UN Security Council (SC) Res 827(1993) (25 May 1993) UN Doc S/RES/827 (1993); UNSC Res 955(1994) (8 November 1994) UN Doc S/RES/955 (1994). See also Antonio Cassese, *Cassese's International Criminal Law* (OUP 2008) 260. The legality of the ad hoc tribunals was challenged in a few cases before those institutions, for example: *Prosecutor v Dusko Tadić* (Decision on The Defence Motion for Interlocutory Appeal on Jurisdiction) IT-94–1-AR72 [14]-[25]; *Prosecutor v Kanyabashi* (Decision on Defence Motion on Jurisdiction) ICTR-96–15-T [27].

The strong legitimization of the new international criminal institution was supposed to be reinforced by the relatively high number of ratifications required for the entry into the force of the Statute, a fact that is clearly evidenced in the *travaux préparatoires.*[17] It is quite clear that the drafters perceived the broad acceptance of the Court by States as a *conditio sine qua non* for enhancing the future effectiveness of the newly-created institution. In consequence, Article 126 of the Statute requires 60 ratifications of the Statute in order for it to enter into force. This number was achieved on 11 April 2002 when ten States simultaneously deposited instruments of ratification, by which they brought the number of ratifications to 66 (among those States there were also representatives of those who abstained during the final vote in Rome, e.g. Trinidad and Tobago). Consequently, the Statute entered into force on 1 July 2002.

In the first years after its adoption the number of ratifications steadily increased (with a booster effect from the ratifications by France and the UK in 2000 and 2001 respectively), and only after 2011 did the pace of ratification significantly slow down to one per year, and this regress was deepened by the withdrawals of Burundi (notified on 27 October 2016) and of the Philippines (notified on 17 March 2018).[18] This regression was not stopped by such encouragements in the Statute such as the possibility of depositing a declaration accepting the jurisdiction of the ICC in a particular situation by non-State Parties, which were supposed to result in closer cooperation and as a next step – ratification of the Statute by those States (this path was followed by Palestine and Côte d'Ivoire).

A small (or non-existent) number of new ratifications is considered natural when more than 20 years have passed since the adoption of the treaty, as States who were in favour of adoption of the treaty would be expected to have ratified it already. Nevertheless, there is a significant group of States which signed the treaty but have not yet ratified it (Algeria, Angola, Armenia, Bahamas, Bahrain, Cameroon, Egypt, Eritrea, Guinea-Bissau, Haiti, Iran, Israel, Jamaica, Kuwait, Kyrgyzstan, Monaco, Morocco, Mozambique, Oman, Russia, São Tomé and Principe, Solomon Islands, Sudan, Syria, Thailand, Ukraine, United Arab Emirates, the USA, Uzbekistan, Yemen, and Zimbabwe). This could suggest that expectations for the greater universalization of the Statute are justified.[19] While the current (as of 15 May 2022) number of 123 State Parties is a notable figure, it

17 United Nations (n 15) 3 ('[it] was suggested that a relatively high number of ratifications and accessions, for instance 60, should be required for the entry into force of the treaty, as a way of ensuring general acceptance of the regime').

18 In addition, The Gambia and South Africa announced their will to withdraw, but after fierce national and international debate. See Desmond Tutu, 'In Africa, Seeking a License to Kill' *The New York Times* (10 October 2013) <https://nyti.ms/3vbH8Az> accessed 15 May 2022, both States resigned from this step. See also Chapter 6 in this volume.

19 However, some of those states like Russia (30 November 2016), Sudan (26 August 2008), and the US (6 May 2002) have already communicated that they do not intend to become a party to the treaty. Not surprisingly, those statements were related to a threat of prosecution of their citizens by the ICC.

might appear low when compared to the number of ratifications of the Geneva Convention on the Protection of War Victims of 1949 (196),[20] the Convention on Prevention and Punishment of Genocide of 1948 (153),[21] the International Covenant on Economic, Social and Cultural Rights (ICESCR) of 1966 (171),[22] the International Covenant on Civil and Political Rights (ICCPR) of 1966 (173),[23] and the Convention against Torture and Other Cruel, Inhuman or Degrading Treatment or Punishment (UNCAT) of 1984 (173).[24] At the same time, this comparatively low number of ratifications cannot be explained by the date of adoption of the Rome Statute if we consider that, for example, the Convention on the Rights of Persons with Disabilities (CRPD) of 2006[25] has already reached 185 ratifications. However, instead of comparing the Rome Statute's level of recognition to typical international humanitarian law (IHL) or human rights law (HRL) treaties, composed mainly of conduct/substantive rules, one should rather scrutinize the level of acceptance of other institutions tasked with the execution of substantive rules. Therefore, the most appropriate comparison would be with other treaties with similar characteristics, i.e. consisting of mainly procedural rules.

Consequently, 123 ratifications seems to be an impressive number in comparison to the 117 States Parties to the Optional Protocol to the ICCPR of 1966;[26] 26 to the Optional Protocol to the ICESCR of 2008;[27] 48 to the Optional Protocol to the Convention on the Rights of the Child on a communications procedure of 2011;[28] 91 to the Optional Protocol to the UNCAT of 2002;[29] 100 to the Optional Protocol to the CRPD of 2006[30] or the 73 declarations recognizing the jurisdiction of the International Court of Justice (ICJ) as compulsory.[31] As a result, the scope of ratifications of the Rome

20 Geneva Convention for the Amelioration of the Condition of the Wounded and Sick in Armed Forces in the Field (entry into force 21 October 1950) 75 UNTS 31 (First Geneva Convention).

21 Convention on the Prevention and Punishment of the Crime of Genocide (entry into force 12 January 1951) 78 UNTS 277.

22 International Covenant on Economic, Social and Cultural Rights (entry into force 3 January 1976) 993 UNTS 3.

23 International Covenant on Civil and Political Rights (entry into force 23 March 1976) 999 UNTS 171.

24 Convention Against Torture and Other Cruel, Inhuman or Degrading Treatment or Punishment (entry into force on 26 June 1987) 1465 UNTS 85.

25 Convention on the Rights of Persons with Disabilities (entry into force on 3 May 2008) 2515 UNTS 3.

26 Optional Protocol to the International Covenant on Civil and Political Rights (entry into force on 23 March 1976) 999 UNTS 171.

27 UNGA Report of the Human Rights Council (28 November 2008) A/63/435.

28 UNGA Res 66/138 (27 January 2012) A/RES/66/138.

29 Optional Protocol to the Convention against Torture and Other Cruel, Inhuman or Degrading Treatment or Punishment (adopted on 18 December 2002, entered into force on 22 June 2006) 2375 UNTS 237.

30 Optional Protocol to the Convention on the Rights of Persons with Disabilities (entry into force on 3 May 2008) 2518 UNTS 283.

31 ICJ, 'Declarations Recognizing the Jurisdiction of the Court as Compulsory' <https://www.icj-cij.org/en/declarations> accessed 15 May 2022.

Statute could be considered as proof of the growing acceptance by States of the enforcement of international responsibility. It should be also stressed that the fact that some major powers (i.e. permanent members of the Security Council (SC), further P-5) are not parties to the Statute does not undermine the idea of multilateralism as such. Multilateralism can be developed without the engagement of the P-5. Moreover, without claims of special privileges for the P-5, multilateralism can work even more effectively as the absolute equality and unity of rights and obligations are accepted.[32]

2.3 Equality of rights and obligations

As has already been stressed, multilateralism requires application of the same rules to all parties, so in consequence all participants have the same (equal) rights and obligations. In line with this idea, the Statute did not allow for any reservations to be made to its provisions (Article 120). Any amendments could refer only to the provisions of an institutional nature (Article 122), and a review of a statute demands a conference be convened under the auspices of the Assembly of States Parties (Article 123). Therefore, despite the massive pressure on behalf of the US, a two-tiered system of justice, so characteristic of a 'victor's justice', was rejected as incompatible with the multilateral approach.[33]

The only departure from the equal rules for all Member States was introduced in Article 124 – a State becoming a new State Party could declare that for a period of seven years after the entry into force of the Statute for the State concerned it did not accept the jurisdiction of the ICC with respect to war crimes referring to the territory of that state or its nationals. At any time, a State could withdraw a declaration made based on Article 124 (France used this opportunity in 2008). In 2015, the ASP adopted an amendment according to which Article 124 should be deleted. Therefore, the above-mentioned derogation will be withdrawn when the required number of ratifications is achieved (Article 124(4)), which, however, is not expected to happen soon, taking into account that seven-eighths of State Parties (so currently 108 states) must deposit their instruments of ratification and at this point only 18 States have done so.

The Rome Statute introduced an amendment procedure which deviates from the Vienna Convention on the Law of Treaties of 1969 (Articles 40–41).[34] According to the Statute, the adoption of an amendment at a meeting

32 From P-5 only the UK and France are parties to the Rome Statute. However, in recent decades they did not overuse their veto power (the last time they used a veto was in 1989). Significantly, both States withstood the pressure put on them by the US in order to block crime of aggression-related amendments.

33 Diane F Orentlicher, 'Unilateral Multilateralism: United States Policy toward the International Criminal Court' (2004) 36(3) Cornell Int Law J 415, 428. Cf Eric P Schwartz, 'The United States and the International Criminal Court: The Case for "Dexterous Multilateralism"' (2003) 4(1) Chi J Int Law 223, 231.

34 Vienna Convention on the Law of Treaties (entry into force 27 January 1980) 1155 UNTS 331. The Convention states that 'The amending agreement does not

of the ASP or at a Review Conference requires a two-thirds majority of States Parties (consensus is preferable) (Article 121(3)), and the amendment will enter into force for all (!) States Parties one year after the instruments of ratification or acceptance have been deposited by seven-eighths of them (Article 121(4)). The only option for a State which does not accept a particular amendment is to withdraw from the Statute with immediate effect. This amendment procedure was supposed to secure the unity of States Parties and equal rights and obligations.

Unfortunately, some exceptions were introduced to the rules mentioned above. In the case of amendments concerning the definitions of international crimes (Articles 5–8), an amendment enters into force (one year after the deposit of a ratification instrument) only for those States which have accepted the amendment (Article 121(5)). This means that the Statute was contaminated with the threat of diversified regimes, a threat which deepened with the adoption of the crime of aggression-related amendments, for which States opted for a different amendment regime (with the option of the opt-out declaration), which in turn raised questions about its consistency with the whole amendment procedure regime, a concern which heightened when ASP decided to further amend adopted amendments.[35]

Moreover, with the newly adopted amendments on the crime of aggression, States introduced different rules concerning jurisdiction in comparison to other crimes. Genocide, war crimes, and crimes against humanity can be prosecuted when they are committed on the territory of a State Party or by a citizen of a State Party – which means that also crimes of citizens of a non-State Party are covered by the jurisdiction of the Court if they were committed on the territory of a State Party (or on the territory of a State whose situation was submitted by the SC to the ICC or a non-State Party accepting the Court's jurisdiction). In the case of the crime of aggression, both States – the aggressor and the victim of aggression – must ratify the Rome Statute with the relevant amendments (although, SC still may refer a situation involving a crime of aggression committed on the territory of a non-State Party). In addition, the impact of the SC on the proceeding is different, as in cases of, e.g., war crimes, the opinion of the SC whether war crimes were committed or not is irrelevant, while in cases of the crime of aggression, the prosecutor 'shall first ascertain whether the SC has made a determination of an act of aggression committed by the State concerned'. It could be argued that there is no 'one-size-fits-all' solution for all crimes which are or which could be covered by the jurisdiction of the ICC. Therefore, the alteration of the ICC's rules in the case of the crime of aggression is a natural process. However, the

bind any State or international organization already a party to the treaty which does not become a party to the amending agreement' (Article 40(4)).

35 Andreas Zimmermann, 'Amending the Amendment Provisions of the Rome Statute: The Kampala Compromise on the Crime of Aggression and the Law of Treaties' (2012) 10(1) JICJ 209.

differences introduced by amendments on the crime of aggression reopen the discussion on the principles of the ICC and support arguments concerning the violation of the principle *pacta tertiis nec nocent nec prosunt*, or the possible politicization of the Court.[36]

The threats related to regime diversification within the ICC could be reduced if the amendments had achieved either a high level of ratifications or none. This is not the case. The amendments broadening the definition of war crimes applied in non-international armed conflicts attained a low number of ratifications (those concerning poison weapons, poisonous gases, or bullets expanding or flattening easily in a human body, reached 43 ratifications; but those concerning biological weapons reached only 12 ratifications and those concerning weapons whose primary effect is to injure by fragments which in the human body escape detection by X-rays and laser weapons – only 10 ratifications). Amendments concerning the crime of aggression were ratified by 43 States. This can be interpreted as a signal of the mistrust of multilateralism in international criminal law. Even if some obligations are considered binding (like the prohibition of aggression or prohibition of certain weapons), states are reluctant to broaden the ICC's possibilities to scrutinize their respect for certain prohibitions. Consequently, the existence of a few different regimes within the Statute means that not every individual and State Party covered by the Court's jurisdiction (taking into account their obligations towards the Court) has the same rights and obligations. Obviously, this could cause controversies between States when further developing the rules of the Statute. As a consequence of the adoption of amendments, a unified approach to prosecuting international crimes is undermined.

The Statute had to be negotiated and adopted outside the UN, both in order to avoid guarantees of privileges for the permanent members of the SC and to emphasize the equality of rights and obligations of all State Parties. However, the special role of the SC permanent members within international law was not disregarded. The SC can submit a situation to the ICC (but the Court is free to decide whether the situation requires the investigation of particular cases – Article 13(b)), and defer the investigation for one year (this decision cannot be ignored by the Court – Article 16). This power of the SC was much criticized, but practice so far has demonstrated that it is not being overused. As an example, despite strong claims on behalf of African States, the SC did not use its competence to defer the investigation of Uhuru Kenyatta (the president of Kenya accused of committing crimes against humanity).[37]

The spirit of multilateralism, i.e. the equality of rights and obligations, is visible in the procedure for the nomination and election of the Court's judges. For instance, each State Party may present one candidate for the position of

36 Harold H Koh and Todd F Buchwald, 'The Crime of Aggression: The United States Perspective' (2015) 109 AJIL 257.

37 UNSC Res 660 (2013) (15 November 2013) S/2013/660 (2013).

judge (a candidate has to be a citizen of one of the State Parties) and there can be only one national judge from one State. During the selection of judges, State Parties are obliged to consider fair regional representation, representation of principal legal systems, and gender balance (Article 36(8)).

One might, however, observe that not all State Parties are equally represented in the ICC. There are only 18 judges, which means that not every country has its own judge. Moreover, a State can have no judge for decades, as there are no provisions in the Statute restricting the election of judges from individual countries. In the case of other staff members (including internees), they represent several dozen countries and several continents,[38] although an imbalance in geographical representation, and that of women in senior levels has been noted ('81 % of female staff hold lower grade levels').[39] The situation in the ICC is, however, better than in the ICJ or International Tribunal for the Law of the Sea, where the gender imbalance and scarcity of staff members coming from the Global South are striking.[40]

The equality of States is secured in the composition of the ASP. According to Article 112 of the Statute, every State has one participant in the ASP and every State Party has only one vote. Equal voting rights can only be limited when a State is in arrears in the payment of its fees to the Court. Additionally, the Assembly should try to reach decisions by consensus, and only when a consensus cannot be reached does the Statute provide for another way of reaching decisions (majority voting of 2/3).

The Statute secured many competences for the Assembly, which significantly impacts the functioning of the Court. Through the actions of the Assembly, State Parties influence the staffing of judges, the staffing of the prosecutor's office, decide budgetary issues, and can consider the question of lack of cooperation on the part of states (Article 112(2)). The Assembly can also be competent and may seek to settle a dispute between States Parties relating to the application and interpretation of the Statute (Article 119). Moreover, the ASP dynamically responds to emerging questions related to international criminal justice. For example, in the context of threats from the US towards the Court, the ASP expressed its solidarity with the actions of the Court, creating a counterweight to the populism and critical views of the Trump administration.[41]

38 In July 2021, the Court had almost 500 professional posts, comprised of 92 different nationalities, 24 nationalities represented by nationals from non-state parties; see Assembly of State Parties, 'Report of the Bureau on equitable geographical representation and gender balance in the recruitment of staff of the International Criminal Court' (29 November 2021) ICC-ASP/20/29, 4.

39 Ibid.

40 Viviana Kristicevic, 'Gender Equality in International Tribunals and Bodies: An Achievable Step With Global Impact' (*GQUAL*, 14 September 2015) <https://bit.ly/3vL8AGv> accessed 15 May 2022, also Stéphanie Hennette Vauchez, 'Gender Balance in International Adjudicatory Bodies', MPEIL, July 2019.

41 Assembly of State Parties, 'ASP President, O-Gon Kwon, Reaffirms Unwavering Support for the ICC' (25 March 2020) ICC-ASP-20200325-PR1521 <https://

The Assembly may also establish subsidiary bodies (Article 112(4)), and until now has used this opportunity several times, establishing *inter alia* the Committee on Budget and Finance; the Independent Oversight Mechanism (IOM); the Working Group on Amendments, and the Special Working Group on the Crime of Aggression. This can again be perceived as giving States yet another opportunity to engage in works concerning the functioning of the Court. In fact, the IOM is an additional tool in the hands of States to maintain the Court's credibility and effectiveness.

The participation of States in the work of the ASP is supposed to assure the transparency of proceedings and subsequently enhance the credibility and moral authority of the Court. It also proves that multilateralism is secured in many stages in the rules concerning the functioning of the Court.

3 Multilateralism in practice

3.1 Cooperation with States

In order to secure States' cooperation with the ICC, which must include the possibility of exercising independent investigations, the Agreement on the Privileges and the Immunities of the International Criminal Court of 2002 should have been ratified by all State Parties.[42] This is not the case, however, as only 79 States deposited their ratification instruments. Moreover, the number of cooperation agreements between the ICC and States is very small.[43] Agreements on the enforcement of sentences have been concluded between the ICC and only 13 States. The ICC has managed to sign several agreements with international organizations, e.g. in 2006 with the European Union,[44] but not with the African Union (the majority of situations investigated by the Court took place in Africa).

This is a clear signal that States are not consistent in their pro-multilateral approach to the international criminal justice system. They ignore the obligation stemming from Article 86 of the Statute, which emphasizes the obligation of State Parties to 'cooperate fully with the court in its investigations and prosecution' of crimes covered by the jurisdiction of the ICC. The role of

www.icc-cpi.int/Pages/item.aspx?name=pr1521>; Assembly of State Parties, 'ASP President O-Gon Kwon Rejects Measures Taken Against ICC' (11 June 2020) ICC-ASP-20200611-PR1527 <https://www.icc-cpi.int/Pages/item.aspx?name=pr1527> both accessed 15 May 2022.

42 Agreement on the Privileges and Immunities of the International Criminal Court (entry into force 22 July 2004) 2271 UNTS 3.

43 Cooperation agreements address all aspects of the Court's activities under the Rome Statute, including but not limited to the protection of victims and witnesses, enforcement of sentences, interim release, and release of persons. See International Criminal Court, 'Cooperation Agreements' <https://www.icc-cpi.int/sites/default/files/Cooperation_Agreements_Eng.pdf> accessed 15 May 2022.

44 Agreement between the International Criminal Court and the European Union on cooperation and assistance (28 April 2006) L115 50.

cooperation cannot be overestimated, as the Court does not have any enforcement mechanism;[45] hence it is completely dependent on cooperation at every stage of the proceedings. This starts with information concerning the admissibility of the case. The Court acts based on the principle of complementarity (Article 1), so the Court must determine whether a case is being or has been investigated or prosecuted by a state (Article 17)), and examine the collection of evidence, surrender of suspects, and execution of sentences. Obviously, good relations with States Parties are necessary for the Court to exist as a functioning body, as without such cooperation the Court is not able to function at all.

The Statute does not oblige non-States Parties to cooperate with the Court, although they are encouraged to do so.[46] However, if the SC triggers the Court's jurisdiction over a given situation (Article 13(b)), the duty to cooperate binds the relevant UN Members, regardless of whether or not they are State Parties to the Rome Statute (this can be derived from Articles 24–25 and 103 of the UN Charter). The SC also emphasized that the most interested States must cooperate with the Court, as was stressed in the resolutions referring the situations in Darfur (Sudan)[47] and Libya.[48] The SC urged all other States to cooperate fully with the Court.[49] It must be added that in relation to the ICC, the SC has proven to be an extreme hypocrite, as it issued a reminder about the obligations of States towards the ICC while at the same time refusing – despite its obligations (Article 115 of the Statute) – to finance the proceedings conducted on its request.

The lack of cooperation between States Parties and non-Parties was most visible in case of the non-execution of arrest warrants against Omar Al-Bashir, who was accused of the crime of genocide and crimes against humanity. Following the SC resolution, the ICC issued two arrest warrants for Al-Bashir.[50] Neither Sudan (which is not a party to the Rome Statute) nor any other State arrested and surrendered Al-Bashir to the ICC. Al-Bashir freely visited both State and non-States Parties. Not one State Party, although they are bound by Article 27 of the Statute (stating that immunities are not a

45 Annalisa Ciampi, 'Legal Rules, Policy Choices and Political Realities in the Functioning of the Cooperation Regime of the International Criminal Court' in Olympia Bekou and Daley Birkett (eds), *Cooperation and the International Criminal Court: Perspectives from Theory and Practice* (Brill 2016) 16.
46 William A Schabas, 'The International Criminal Court and Non-Party States' (2010) 28(1) Windsor Yearbook of Access to Justice 1, 12.
47 UNSC Res 1593(2005) (31 March 2005) UN Doc S/RES/1593 (2005).
48 UNSC Res 1970(2011) (26 February 2011) UN Doc S/RES/1970 (2011).
49 It is, however, questionable how to interpret the obligation 'to cooperate fully', see Alexander Galand, *UN Security Council Referrals to the International Criminal Court: Legal Nature. Effects and Limits* (Brill 2018) 187.
50 Case Information Sheet, 'Situation in Darfur, Sudan, *The Prosecutor v. Omar Hassan Ahmad Al Bashir* ICC-02/05–01/09–267' (International Criminal Court, April 2018) <https://www.icc-cpi.int/CaseInformationSheets/AlBashirEng.pdf> accessed 15 May 2022.

bar to exercise the jurisdiction by the Court), cooperated with the ICC in order to surrender Al-Bashir, referring instead to his immunity as head of state. This lack of cooperation from State Parties was referred to the SC many times[51] and non-compliance by Jordan was discussed in one decision and a judgement of the ICC, which addressed the scope of State obligations vis-à-vis the ICC Statute,[52] emphasizing that such cooperation cannot be restricted by immunities.[53] In the meantime, Al-Bashir lost his power, but still has not been surrendered to the ICC.

Currently, over a dozen arrest warrants had been issued by the ICC, majority of persons mentioned there had not been surrendered to the Court. It is quite a paradox that one of surrender of an accused individual, i.e. Ali Muhammad Ali Abd-Al-Rahman (known as Ali Kushayb), was not the result of cooperation with States but due to his voluntary surrender to the ICC.[54]

As the Court noted in its report on cooperation:

> The pending arrest warrants are an unfortunate testament to the challenges the Court faces in terms of cooperation. The ICC will not be able to fully exercise its mandate without arrests and/or surrenders, as court proceedings cannot commence without the presence of the suspect(s).[55]

The case of Al-Bashir shows that cooperation with the Court is not dependent on being a State Party to a Statute. State Parties try to avoid cooperation when it is politically uncomfortable and involves possible economic losses.

The issue of cooperation is also a key element when it comes to the payment of membership fees. According to the report presented during the Assembly of the State Parties in December 2021, as of October 2021, only 88 State Parties were fully settled (about 72 per cent), 26 had outstanding contributions for 2021 (about 21 per cent), and 9 (about 7 per cent) were in arrears (according to Article 112(8) of the Statute, this occurs when the

51 Decision on the Cooperation of the Democratic Republic of the Congo Regarding Omar Al Bashir's Arrest and Surrender to the Court (9 April 2014) ICC-02/05–01/09–195 [29]; *The Prosecutor v Omar Hassan Ahmad Al Bashir* (Pre-trial Chamber II Decision) ICC-02/05–01/09–267 (11 July 2016).

52 Decision under Article 87(7) of the Rome Statute on the non-compliance by Jordan with the request by the Court for the arrest and surrender of Omar Al-Bashir (Pre-trial Chamber II Decision) ICC-02/05–01/09–309 (11 December 2017); *The Prosecutor v Omar Hassan Ahmad Al Bashir* (The Appeals Chamber Judgement) ICC-02/05–01/09 OA2 (6 May 2019).

53 Hanna Kuczyńska and Karolina Wierczyńska, 'Head of State Immunity in Triangular Relations. The Case of Al-Bashir before the ICC' (2019) 10 CYIL 47, 51.

54 ICC, 'Situation in Darfur (Sudan): Ali Kushayb is in ICC Custody' (ICC Press Release ICC-CPI-20200609-PR1525, 9 June 2020) <https://www.icc-cpi.int/Pages/item.aspx?name=PR1525> accessed 15 May 2022.

55 International Criminal Court Assembly of the State Parties, 'Report of the Court on Cooperation' (ICC-ASP/19/25, 20 October 2020) <https://asp.prod.icc-cpi.int/sites/asp/files/asp_docs/ASP19/ICC-ASP-19-25-ENG-Cooperation-Report-%2028oct20-1830.pdf, par. 27.

amount of fees exceeds the amount of contributions due from this state for the two preceding full years, in which case the State has no vote in the ASP).[56]

The delay related to fees may be justified by the situations of States, but it undoubtedly does not apply to all of the nearly 30 per cent of countries which in some way have delayed payments. Whether this can be considered as proof of a lack of will to cooperate with the Court and/or a general negative approach to the idea of multilateralism in international criminal justice is questionable, especially given that the current ICC budget crisis could be compared to the prolonged crisis of UN finances. In the case of the UN, as of 10 May 2022, only 99 Members had paid their regular budget assessment in full (so only 51%!).[57] Additionally, in the case of the UN it is not so important *how many* States have not paid, but *which* States have not. President Trump refusal to pay its debts towards the UN was a budgetary nightmare, as the US is responsible for 22 per cent of the UN's total budget (fortunately, President Biden declared the will to fully meet US obligations to the UN).[58] Such a situation is not possible within the ICC, as the US is not a State Party to the Statute. Consequently, it can be assumed that the ICC situation is better than that of the UN.

3.2 Expectations of States and reality

The international community definitely has high expectations of the ICC. Nevertheless, the Court cannot open an investigation in every possible case; not without reason its jurisdiction is limited by gravity requirements (Articles 17 and 53), which must be verified in each situation and at every stage of the proceedings. Put bluntly, not every core crime is worthy of investigation by the Court. This conclusion could be shocking for victims, but this is a reality of the Court, which operates with extremely limited resources. The mere comparison of the budget of the ICC (approximately €154,855,000. in 2022)[59], and the estimated appropriation for International Residual Mechanism for Criminal Tribunals for 2021 ($97,194,000)[60] shows that while the ICC could, in theory, possess global jurisdiction (taking into account the SC's competences), its budget is totally inadequate. Economics, however, cannot explain

56 ICC-ASP/20/27, 30 November 2021 [9]. This is still a significant improvement in comparison to situation in 2019 when only 76 states were fully settled, ICC-ASP/18/34, 30 November 2019 [9].

57 UN Committee on Contributions, 'Contributions Received for 2022 for the United Nations Regular Budget' <https://www.un.org/en/ga/contributions/honourroll.shtml> accessed 15 May 2022.

58 Council on Foreign Relations, *Funding the United Nations: How Much Does the U.S. Pay?*, 4 April 2022, <https://www.cfr.org/article/funding-united-nations-what-impact-do-us-contributions-have-un-agencies-and-programs> accessed 15 May 2022.

59 ICC-ASP/20.Res.1, 9 December 2021.

60 A/RES/75/249, 8 January 2021.

every decision to start or close an investigation, and while each of the decisions is open to criticism, some of them are clearly more so than others. An instructive example is the decision concerning crimes committed in relation to the conflict in Afghanistan, when the ICC initially rejected opening an investigation in April 2019 because it was not in the interests of justice and 'pursuing an investigation would inevitably require a significant amount of resources'.[61]

Even if the ICC has limited resources and struggles with securing appropriate premises, its achievements, when measured in terms of the numbers of convictions and sentences, are not satisfactory. Up to 15 May 2022, the ICC had convicted only four individuals for the core crimes (Al Mahdi, Katanga, Lubanga, Ntaganda); and four others (Bemba Gombo, Ngudjolo Chui, Gbagbo, and Ble Goude) were acquitted. This result is not impressive. The International Criminal Tribunal for the former Yugoslavia (ICTY) convicted 99 persons and acquitted 19 (over 160 were charged) during its 24 years of existence.[62] The International Criminal Tribunal for Rwanda (ICTR), during its 21 years of activity, convicted 62 persons and acquitted 14. This data explains the growing disillusionment with the ICC and with the multilateral approach to the fight against impunity for the gravest crimes.

The ICC, like the other international courts, struggles with the length of proceedings, which is particularly outrageous in cases where they end with an acquittal after the accused has spent 10 years in custody (the case of Bemba Gombo). While it can be noted that Ante Gotovina waited almost 7 years before final acquittal while under arrest by the ICTY (similarly in the case of Ramash Haradinaj), nevertheless it seems damning that the ICC cannot meet even the ICTY's low standards. One has to agree that the fairness of trials by the ICC might be assessed by acquittals and not by convictions, but the question remains as to why some proceedings took such an extreme length of time to conclude. At the same time, we are aware that the comparison of the ICC with ad hoc tribunals is not necessarily a fair one. Both the ICTY and ICTR were supported by the UN economically, politically, and legally. The ICC has never achieved such assistance.

The credibility of a court is often measured by the public perception of its staff. Unfortunately, the ICC is not free from scandals, including the

61 *Decision Pursuant to Article 15 of the Rome Statute on the Authorisation of an Investigation into the Situation in the Islamic Republic of Afghanistan* (Pre-trial Chamber II Decision) ICC-02/17–33 (12 April 2019) [90]-[95], however, on 5 March 2020, the Appeals Chamber overturned the decision and authorized the prosecutor to launch an investigation, *Judgment on the Appeal against the Decision on the Authorisation of an Investigation into the Ssituation in the Islamic Republic of Afghanistan*, ICC-02/17-138.

62 United Nations International Criminal Tribunal for former Yugoslavia, Infographic, 'ICTY Facts & Figures' <https://www.icty.org/en/content/infographic-icty-facts-figures> accessed 15 May 2022.

appointment of incompetent judges,[63] the unjustified (at least, in light of budgetary constraints) complaints of some judges about salary,[64] and allegations of corruption against the ICC's main officers.[65]

4 The impact of the COVID-19 pandemic

The COVID-19 pandemic, which emerged in 2020, could be the first of many pandemics which humanity will have to struggle against, therefore its impact on multilateral relations and international institutions is worth assessing.

Many institutions were forced to conduct their work remotely, including the ICC,[66] which, however, can pose a fundamental question, namely: how can a fight for global justice be conducted remotely? The Court introduced some technical guidelines concerning organization of the work of Chambers on 23 June 2020.[67] According to those Guidelines, 'the applicable Chamber may decide independently whether required hearings should be conducted physically, remotely or as a combination of both'. Consequently, the Chamber can decide that witnesses can be heard remotely, with due respect for all the rights and protections as guaranteed in the regulations of the Court. This solution could be the only option to avoid further delays, and as was indicated above, the length of proceedings in the ICC can and must be criticized. Remote hearings are nothing new in the ICC, as there had previously been Skype sessions with Uhuru Kenyatta, although these were considered an extraordinary measure. If the current remote sessions are considered by judges to be reliable and satisfying, perhaps remote hearings could become a standard procedure, which would help reduce the costs. However, the Court cannot avoid the criticism – mostly on behalf of the accused – that remote hearings impact their rights and undermine fair trial standards. Therefore, the Court must be extremely cautious in its implementation of the guidelines and profoundly justify each of its decisions.

Unfortunately, the guidelines will not prevent the prolongation of proceedings. Prosecutors have complained that the Court does not have enough courtrooms, and in consequence even if the trial is ready to be heard, the

63 Open Society Justice Initiative, 'Raising the Bar: Improving the Nomination and Election of Judges to the International Criminal Court' (2019) Open Society Foundation.

64 *H and others v ICC* (ILOAT, Judgment No. 4354) <https://www.ilo.org/dyn/triblex/triblexmain.fullText?p_lang=fr&p_judgment_no=4354&p_language_code=EN> accessed 15 May 2022.

65 EIC Network, 'Secrets of the International Criminal Court Revealed' (*The Black Sea*, 29 September 2017) <https://theblacksea.eu/stories/secrets-of-the-international-criminal-court-revealed/> accessed 15 May 2022.

66 See, generally, Hirad Abtahi, 'The International Criminal Court during the COVID-19 Pandemic' (2020) 18(5) J Int Crim Justice 1069.

67 ICC, 'Guidelines for the Judiciary Concerning the Holding of the Court Hearings During the Covid-19 Pandemic' (23 June 2020) <https://bit.ly/3ceoUYu> accessed 15 May 2022.

Chamber must wait for months to proceed with a hearing as there is no appropriate room available.[68] The Guidelines emphasize that 'the capacity of conducting hearings is limited to 1 hearing per day, consisting of 3 sessions of 1 hour maximum, with 2 breaks of 45 minutes in between'. These limitations severely restrict the possibilities for Chambers to conduct proceedings at the standard (pre-COVID) speed, and in addition require further expenditures.[69]

However, COVID-19 has impacted to a greater extent the work of prosecutors, whose ability to collect evidence (including travel to the places of the commission of alleged crimes) has been reduced or in some cases eliminated entirely. This is extremely dangerous with respect to investigations, as time plays a crucial role in the collection of evidence, and any delays (as they allow cover-ups and/or the loss of evidence) can undermine the credibility of the evidence presented in the Court afterwards. The Court must, therefore, more than at any time before, rely on local resources – hence cooperation with States' organs must be strengthened. This can help develop mutual trust and new procedures for the collection of evidence. In many cases, close cooperation can also help with the sharing of technical knowledge.

In the context of this discussion, it must be stressed that multilateral relations became an element of the public debate, and the value of multilateralism, in terms of cooperation in the fight against disease, has been emphasized. However, the pandemic shapes the classification of the main existing international threats, and justice is not at the top of the list, with the focus being on the non-military elements of security – health, climate change, and nuclear weapons.[70] If the pandemic helps to shift the focus from State security to human security and emphasises security's non-military aspects, the international criminal justice system should benefit from such a paradigm change. On 2 April 2020, the UN General Assembly approved a resolution (74/270) calling for 'international cooperation' and 'multilateralism' in the fight against COVID-19. At the same time, the resolution stresses the need for full respect of human rights. The right to justice (including the right to clarify the circumstances of deaths, and to receive a remedy for violations of IHL and HRL) is a human right and the concept of reconciliation is a component of the notion of human security.[71] If the focus is on human security and HRL, then international justice problems should not disappear from the radar of the international community. However, this optimism must be tamed

68 Statements of Fabricio Guariglia (Director of the Prosecution Division, International Criminal Court) during the Nuremberg Forum 2018: 20th Anniversary of the Rome Statute: Law, Justice and Politics, 19 October 2018.

69 International Criminal Court Assembly of the State Parties 'Report of the Committee on Budget and Finance on the Work of its Thirty-Fourth Session' (ICC-ASP/19/5/AV, 1 July 2020) [26].

70 Patrycja Sasnal, 'Konsekwencje pandemii Covid-19 dla stosunków międzynarodowych' (PISM 2020) 26.

71 Commission on Human Security, 'Human Security Now' (2003) <https://bit.ly/3vQXhge> accessed 15 May 2022, 60, 65.

as – despite statements by different UN organs and agencies, reminding us of the value of human rights in times of pandemic – those rights are restricted, and the pandemic argument is overused to justify abuses of State power.

In the pandemic times, the heaviest burdens are put on States. States as decisive authorities are left to decide what is good or bad for a given community, with varying results. The pandemic has already strengthened visible trends in international relations; trends which are not in favour of strong international communities and organizations, but instead support national movements. In this respect, Bertram Schmitt – a German judge on the ICC – noted that: 'Nationalism and ruthless enforcement of national interests seem to be predominant'.[72]

Some of the consequences of COVID-19 for States or international organizations are at the moment invisible. It may take some time before one can assess which freedoms have been irretrievably lost, and how far authoritarian State policy has gone in the name of the fight against the virus. It is very likely that current political solutions and restrictions enacted by States because of the pandemic might lead to grave violations which can even be qualified as crimes against humanity.[73] As a result, in the near future., situations referred to the Court may be associated with the commission of crimes against humanity in times of peace. This could constitute a challenge for the ICC.

COVID-19 has once again proven how important is the role of civil society. Non-governmental organizations (NGOs) are monitoring States' responses to the crisis caused by COVID-19 in order to report and avoid violations of basic human rights.[74] Tellingly, the same NGOs are active supporters of the ICC. From the very beginning they have participated in the ASP annual meetings, although in 2020 they did so virtually.[75] Even if they criticize the Court, they never undermine its usefulness and they undertake campaigns to strengthen it (e.g. by broadening its material jurisdiction, as recently happened in case of the criminalization of starvation in non-international armed conflicts). NGOs (as well as other forms of representation of victims) scrutinize the work of the prosecutor, putting immense pressure on her/him, much

72 Bertram Schmitt, 'The International Criminal Court After 20 Years: The Possible Way Ahead' in Gerhard Werle and Andreas Zimmermann (eds), *The International Criminal Court in Turbulent Times* (Springer 2019) x.

73 Article 7(1)(k) of the Rome Statute: 'the inhumane acts of a similar character intentionally causing great suffering …' could be qualified as the crime against humanity if committed 'as part of a widespread or systematic attack directed against any civilian population, with knowledge of the attack'.

74 Amnesty International, 'COVID-19: How Human Rights Can Help Protect Us' (20 March 2020) <https://bit.ly/3wSuk3l>; Human Rights Watch, 'Human Rights Dimensions of Covid-19 Response' (19 March 2020) <https://www.hrw.org/news/2020/03/19/human-rights-dimensions-covid-19-response> both accessed 15 May 2022.

75 Human Rights Watch, 'International Criminal Court's Decisive Moment' (14 December 2020) <https://bit.ly/3vLH2kk> accessed 15 May 2022.

greater than the pressure national prosecutors struggle with. This means not only high demands concerning the opening of an investigation, but also concerning respect for the rights of the suspect/accused. In the COVID-19 era, the role of civil society to alert the prosecutor and monitor the situation can be expected to be even more.

Because of the pandemic, some international organizations have been accused of serving particular global powers (as was the case of the World Health Organization vis-à-vis China). In addition, they need to struggle with disinformation, e.g. concerning their role in the crisis. However, this kind of situation is nothing new for the Court. The ICC has experience in responding to disinformation orchestrated by some States. It was falsely accused by the African Union of being in the hands of Western powers (namely the EU), and for being racist. The ICC – and the ASP in particular – dealt with this problem through open debates, showing its transparency and preventing further hostile actions. COVID-19 has proven that cooperation and open information are of great value and the exclusion of some big powers (namely the US, China, and Russia) might actually be beneficial for the organization, as the discussion can be more merit-based.

The pandemic had impact on the economy of some regions in a more severe way – in particular, the Global South States.[76] As this same category of States has also delayed payments to the ICC budget, the liquidity crisis in the ICC will definitely not be resolved in the near future.

5 Conclusion

The ICC is a product of multilateralism, and currently shapes the scope of and hopes for multilateralism in the area of criminal justice for international crimes. At the same time, the example of the ICC indicates that multilateralism is easier in theory than in practice, as some States – despite adopting the Statute – deny the Court full cooperation. Additionally, the divergent regimes introduced into the Statute (for example, referring to the definition of aggression) have resulted in differing rights and obligations vis-à-vis States members. This solution is in contradiction to one of the main principles of multilateralism – equality (in law and before the law) of rights and obligations.

The existence of different regimes, and consequently different treatments, can discourage States from effective cooperation, paying membership fees, or executing arrest warrants. Additionally, some States have their own interests which prevent them from supporting or cooperating with the ICC, regardless of their obligation to do so by an international treaty. International 'condemnation' is less severe than the risk of destroying bilateral relations.

76 World Bank, 'The Global Economic Outlook During the COVID-19 Pandemic: A Changed World' (8 June 2020) <https://bit.ly/3wR2pkq> accessed 15 May 2022.

If multilateralism is currently under attack on the part of some States (i.e. the US, which under the Trump Administration preferred bilateral rather than multilateral approaches), the ICC can be attacked as just another expensive international institution threatening sovereignty. If States refrain from paying their membership fees to the UN and other institutions, it is hardly surprising that they will also reduce their payments to the ICC. Mistrust of international cooperation in general also restricts cooperation with the ICC, especially when the Court comes to be seen as another ineffective organization (if measured by the number of completed cases and the length of proceedings in comparison to other international and national tribunals). As can be observed, the crisis of multilateralism can be manifested similarly in different institutions, including the ICC.

As to the ICC, however, one can observe that States are not willing to broaden their multilateral approach to include international criminal justice. This is proven by the lack of new ratifications of the Statute in recent years; current withdrawals, and attempts to withdraw from the Statute; communications of a lack of intention to become a party to the treaty; the low number of ratifications of amendments and other agreements facilitating the work of the Court; the reluctance to include other crimes (such as drug trafficking or terrorism); and limited cooperation with the Court.

Seen from the perspective of human rights or the experience of other international institutions (such as the UN), one has to admit that there is nothing new or specific about the multilateral crisis at the ICC. States are always trying to avoid making international commitments, especially related to human rights' responsibilities. China, Russia, or the US are known for their conservative policies concerning new multilateral commitments.[77] However, unilateral multilateralism (i.e. the selective support for multilateral institutions in order to pursue national interests),[78] combined with hostile actions against the Court, have (or will have) detrimental effects for those States.[79] It is worth keeping in mind that no State can afford a complete inability and unwillingness to react against grave violations as such violations threaten world peace and security.

Multilateralism brings concrete benefits, which in the context of institutionalized international criminal justice include common shared rules and principles, comprehensive dialogue, a common fight against international crimes, fair procedures, equal treatment, and non-discrimination. However, if the Court's rules are inconsistent, the selection of cases not always transparent, and the credibility of the main officers of the ICC is under attack, then States may choose national jurisdictions to deal with international crimes. For them, catalysing domestic accountability processes is exactly the option preferred

77 Louis Henkin, 'That "S" Word: Sovereignty, and Globalization, and Human Rights, Et Cetera' (1999) 68 Fordham L Rev 1, 5.

78 Orentlicher (n 33) 416.

79 Ibid 429.

from the beginning of the adoption of the Rome Statute. As expressed a long time ago: 'the success in one sense would be no cases prosecuted',[80] as this would mean that States themselves are dealing with prosecution of international crimes. However, the ICC acts based on the principle of complementarity, therefore States are more than welcome to prosecute international criminals, and only if they are not carrying out prosecutions, or are unable or unwilling to do so, do they then have the Court at their disposal. Paradoxically the establishment of the Court should be mutually beneficial for States and the Court. It is time to acknowledge and learn from the fact that the Statute was not drafted to put the Court and States in a competition for criminal jurisdiction. The Statute, by giving priority to the jurisdiction of States, strengthened their jurisdiction. Therefore, it can be assumed that the Statute is prepared for the current rise of the unilateral (nationalistic) approach to criminal jurisdiction. Now, taking into account the experience gained and the current state of multilateral relations, the ICC (especially including the Office of the Prosecutor) could engage in more active support for national courts by, e.g. the organization of training, advisory services, development of a monitoring system of national proceedings with the aim to advise and not to 'name and shame'. Sooner or later States would then remind themselves that the fight against impunity for international crimes – the main aim of the creation of the ICC – cannot be won alone.

80 Iain Cameron, 'Jurisdiction and Admissibility Issues under the ICC Statute' in Dominic McGoldrick, Peter Rowe, and Eric Donnelly (eds), *Permanent International Criminal Court: Legal and Policy Issues* (Hart 2004) 91.

11 Global Governance Crises and Rule of Law

Lessons from Europe's Multilevel Constitutionalism

Ernst-Ulrich Petersmann

1 Introduction

Similar to the disruption of the first economic globalization brought about by the First World War and by the post-war political, health, and economic crises (1919–1945), the incoherent responses to the global health, economic, and environmental emergencies in 2020 once again risk undermining the global trading, investment, financial, and health systems. The trade wars waged by the US Trump administration disrupted the WTO legal and dispute settlement systems and peaceful cooperation in protecting global public goods (PGs), such as climate change mitigation, rule of law, and the de-nuclearization of Iran. 'America first', Brexit, and trade wars with China illustrate how the diverse – neo-liberal, mercantilist, ordo-liberal, state-capitalist and 'third world' – conceptions of economic regulation risk destroying the post-1945 systems of world trading and investment.

This contribution discusses the need for rule of law as an essential building-block for the multilevel governance of interdependent PGs, such as public health, environmental protection, and mutually beneficial trade and investment systems. Section 2 recalls that human rights require protecting the rule of law and judicial remedies as legal constraints on the multilevel governance of 'aggregate PGs', such as the above-mentioned mutually beneficial trading, investment, public health and environmental protection systems. Section 3 explains why – both within the European Union (EU) and in the EU's external relations – investor-State arbitration (ISA) procedures are being transformed into public law adjudications aimed at protecting human and constitutional rights more effectively. Section 4 argues that restoring the WTO appellate review system – following its arbitrary destruction by the US Trump administration in December 2019 – remains of systemic importance for rules-based responses to the crises in global economic, health, and environmental governance. Section 5 discusses the German Constitutional Court judgment of 5 May 2020 confirming constitutional complaints that the European Central Bank (ECB) and the Court of Justice of the European Union (CJEU) exceeded their limited powers by not examining whether the ECB's monetary policy powers disproportionately encroached on the economic and fiscal

DOI: 10.4324/9781003312857-13

policy competences of EU Member States (e.g. by lacking 'proportionality justification' and due respect for the national 'constitutional identities'). Section 6 concludes that multilevel governance of PGs loses its democratic legitimacy and support if multilevel governance institutions exceed their limited delegation of powers and disregard constitutional rights and the principles of subsidiarity, proportionality, democratic governance, rule of law, and respect for 'constitutional pluralism'.

2 From 'rule by law' to 'rule of law' through democratic constitutionalism

All human societies use law as an instrument of social ordering and governance. And in all human societies, abuses of 'rule by law' have led to 'struggles for justice' aimed at limiting abuses of power through 'rule of law'. Aristotle, in his books on *Politics* and on the *Constitution of Athens*, explained why 'the rule of law is preferable to that of any individual'; 'even if it be better for certain individuals to govern, they should be made only guardians and ministers of the law'.[1] Centuries later, Cicero's books on *The Republic* and on *The Laws* emphasized the need for rule of law in the Roman republic.[2] The *Magna Carta* of 1215 and the recognition of *habeas corpus* (as a judicial remedy against unlawful detention) in England during the thirteenth century; the English Bill of Rights of 1689; and the democratic US and French Constitutions and Bills and Declarations of Rights of the eighteenth century constituted other historical milestones on the way to the 1948 Universal Declaration of Human Rights (UDHR) and its recognition of the need to protect 'inalienable' human rights by 'rule of law'. Article 1 UDHR codified the recognition by all UN Member States that 'All human beings are born free and equal in dignity and rights. They are endowed with reason and conscience and should act towards one another in a spirit of brotherhood'. Yet, the Preamble to the UDHR also recalls that the human tragedies which took place through 'disregard and contempt for human rights have resulted in barbarous acts which have outraged the conscience of mankind', like the two World Wars and the Holocaust. The Preamble draws two conclusions from this 'human condition':

1. 'it is essential, if man is not to be compelled to have recourse, as a last resort, to rebellion against tyranny and oppression, that human rights should be protected by the rule of law';
2. 'recognition of the inherent dignity and of the equal and inalienable rights of all members of the human family is the foundation of freedom, justice and peace in the world'.

1 Aristotle, *The Politics, and the Constitution of Athens* (Stephen Everson ed, Stephen Everson tr, CUP 1996) 88.
2 See Brian Z Tamanaha, *On the Rule of Law: History, Politics, Theory* (CUP 2004) 11ff.

Since the adoption of the UDHR, all 193 UN Member States have reconfirmed these 'constitutional principles' in dozens of worldwide and regional human rights conventions and hundreds of UN resolutions. Successful 'rebellions' led to worldwide decolonization and the incorporation of human rights into the national constitutions of most UN Member States. The WTO Agreement is committed to 'sustainable development, seeking both to protect and preserve the environment', as well as to 'raising standards of living, ensuring full employment and a large and steadily growing volume of real income and effective demand'.[3] Yet unlike the 2030 UN Sustainable Development Goals, it neither refers to human rights nor offers solutions to respond to global emergencies like the COVID-19 pandemic or climate change. Proposals for redefining international law as the multilevel governance of PGs for the benefit of peoples and citizens and their 'inalienable' human rights,[4] and for a 'systemic interpretation' which reinterprets international economic law (IEL) as the 'international law of states, peoples and citizens' committed to sustainable development as recognized by all UN and WTO (World Trade Organization) Member States,[5] continue to be ignored by most diplomats, for instance, by insisting on 'member-driven WTO governance' without any references to human rights. Also international lawyers proudly demonstrate why 'idealistic-deductive' interpretations of indeterminate international law rules are so often rejected as 'utopian' and as lacking state consent.[6] Even if they admit that 'constitutional' and 'systemic interpretations' of regional economic and human rights treaties – like the EU treaties and the European Convention of Human Rights – have succeeded in protecting human rights and other PGs more effectively than 'realist interpretations' of UN and WTO law, they rarely support 'constitutional interpretations' of UN/WTO law and of multilevel governance of global PGs.[7]

Albert Einstein defined 'madness' as doing the same thing over and over again in the hope of attaining different results. It is usually impossible to resolve problems using the same methods used in creating these problems, like power-oriented failures to protect human rights and rule of law for the benefit

3 Marrakesh Agreement Establishing the World Trade Organization (entry into force 1 January 1995), 1867 UNTS 154, Preamble.

4 See Ernst-Ulrich Petersmann, *Multilevel Constitutionalism for Multilevel Governance of Public Goods: Methodology Problems in International Law* (Hart Publishing 2017).

5 See Ernst-Ulrich Petersmann, *International Economic Law in the 21st Century: Constitutional Pluralism and Multilevel Governance of Interdependent Public Goods* (Hart Publishing 2012).

6 See Martti Koskenniemi, *From Apology to Utopia: The Structure of International Legal Argument* (2nd edn, CUP 2006).

7 See Martti Koskenniemi, *The Politics of International Law* (Hart Publishing 2011); among his 14 articles re-published in this book, only one – on pp. 238ff – seems to acknowledge that 'constitutional approaches' to interpretation and development of treaty systems can protect human rights and community interests more effectively.

of citizens. Sections 2–4 of this chapter explain why the 'judicialization' and 'constitutionalization' of international trade and investment law have proven more effective in protecting transnational rule of law for the benefit of European citizens than the 'realist', power-oriented approaches of diplomats and governments. This 'bounded rationality' on the part of many legal practitioners (such as diplomats, investment arbitrators, investors) prioritizes self-interested utility maximization rather than an 'inclusive, public reason' which accepts moral responsibility for reconciling all public and private interests on the basis of mutually agreed 'principles of justice'. Democratic constitutions, human rights law, and UN law include agreements on procedural and substantive 'principles of justice' which limit the selfish maximization of personal gains. They also prescribe procedures for 'institutionalizing' and progressively clarifying 'public reason', for instance, through democratic legislation and administration, and adjudication interpreting and clarifying constitutional principles and international agreements using a 'systemic interpretation' 'in conformity with the principles of justice and international law', including also 'human rights and fundamental freedoms for all', as prescribed in the Vienna Convention on the Law of Treaties (VCLT) (Preamble and Article 31).[8] In order to justify the 'basic structures' of national and international legal systems and judicial dispute settlements, 'courts of justice' in international trade and investment law rely more on 'systemic interpretations' and agreed-upon 'principles of justice' than on UN human rights, the legal scope and interpretation of which remain contested.[9] Sections 3–5 illustrate how the indeterminacy of many international law rules often leads to challenges to the independence, impartiality, and 'constitutional mindsets' of 'courts of justice' by complainants and defendants in trade and investment disputes, rejecting judicial deductions by inductive claims of lack of state consent, thereby reinforcing adversarial legalism and the dialectic evolution of IEL. Reconciling IEL more clearly with the UN's sustainable development agenda would strengthen cooperation and synergies, leading to better responses to the global regulatory challenges, geopolitical rivalries, and legitimate expectations of citizens all over the world.

3 From 'constitutionalism 1.0' to investor-State arbitration and multilevel investment adjudication

Much like medicines were developed as rational remedies for the weaknesses and failures of the human organism, so too constitutionalism emerged – since the ancient democratic Constitution of Athens and the republican

8 For more on 'constitutional treaty interpretation' and the diverse principles of procedural, constitutional, distributive, corrective, and commutative justice and equity, see Petersmann (n 4) 76ff.

9 For more on the lack of citizen-oriented theories of justice in most textbooks on IEL, and the lack of references to human rights in WTO dispute settlement reports, see Petersmann (n 5) 43–209.

Constitution of Rome more than 2400 years ago – as the most important 'political remedy' for political failures of the human mind in protecting social justice. For example, in response to its past 'constitutional failures', post-1945 Germany recognized – in its constitutional commitments to human dignity, human rights, and constitutional democracy (e.g. Articles 1, 20, 79 of the German Basic Law) – a constitutional right to democratic self-determination (based on Article 38.1 in conjunction with Article 20 Basic Law), which citizens increasingly invoke in the German Constitutional Court to hold the German Parliament and Government accountable for delegating only limited powers to international organizations, and for democratically controlling the exercise of such delegated powers. Such constitutional self-limitation of powers over both domestic and foreign policy ('Constitutionalism 1.0') has a long tradition in Kantian legal theory, which underlies Germany's constitutional commitments to human dignity and maximum equal freedoms in Articles 1 and 2 of the German Basic Law. It also contributed to Germany's 'exportation of principles of justice', since 1959, through more than 135 bilateral investment treaties (BITs) protecting foreign direct investments through reciprocal guarantees of non-discrimination, full protection and security, fair and equitable treatment, access to judicial remedies and other legal protection standards.[10] 'Multilevel constitutionalism' is encouraged in the German Basic Law (e.g. in Articles 23–25) based on republican conceptions of law, as explained by Kant.[11] This 'open constitutionalism' was influenced by Kant's proposals in *Perpetual Peace: A Philosophical Sketch* (1795): in order to institute lasting peace among rational egoists with limited reasonableness and 'unsocial sociability' (Kant), 'all men who can at all influence one another must adhere to some kind of civil constitution' promoting national, transnational and international cooperation:

1 a constitution based on the civil rights of individuals within a nation (*ius civitatis*);
2 a constitution based on the international rights of states in their relationships with one another (*ius gentium*);
3 a constitution based on a cosmopolitan right, in so far as individuals and states, coexisting in an external relationship of mutual influence, may be regarded as citizens of a universal state of mankind (*ius cosmopoliticum*).

10 For more on the use of Kantian legal theory and human rights as 'principles of justice' in IEL, see Petersmann (n 5) 160ff, 407ff, 456ff. The early German BITs did not provide for ISA.

11 Article 2.1 of the Basic Law protecting equal basic freedoms of 'every person' reflects Kant's definition of law as 'the sum total of those conditions within which the will of one person can be reconciled with the will of another in accordance with a universal law of freedom'; see Immanuel Kant, 'The Metaphysics of Morals', in Hans S Reiss (ed), *Kant: Political Writings* (CUP 1977) 133. It follows from Kant's moral 'categorical imperative' that 'every action which by itself or by its maxim enables the freedom of each individual's will to co-exist with the freedom of everyone else in accordance with a universal law is *right*' (ibid).

> This classification, with respect to the idea of a perpetual peace, is not arbitrary, but necessary. For if even one of the parties were able to influence the others physically and yet itself remained in a state of nature, there would be a risk of war, the avoidance of which is precisely the aim of the above articles.[12]

This Kantian conception of multilevel constitutionalism as a morally necessary 'categorical imperative' for protecting human dignity and the equal freedoms of individuals in all their social interactions – in national, transnational, and international relations – reflects not only moral self-limitation by rules of a higher rank. Kantian multilevel constitutionalism also rests on Kant's insight that – since rules cannot specify all the conditions of their own application – the application of every rule requires the interposition of an authority determining what the rule should mean in a particular situation, and whether applying the rule might be better than resorting to an exception. Transnational legal systems require institutional 'checks and balances' necessary for their legislative, administrative, judicial, and private enforcement; the nationalist disregard by the Trump administration for multilateral trade and environmental rules illustrates why, as explained by Kant, the 'problem of establishing a perfect civil constitution is subordinate to the problem of a law-governed external relationship with other states, and cannot be solved unless the latter is also solved'.[13] Kant's proposals for separating and limiting representative legislative, executive, and judicial powers by multilevel constitutional restraints were aimed at institutionalizing and promoting 'public reason'. Kant expected that it is only through antagonistic, historical learning processes that individuals and States can progressively transform the lawless state of nature into law-governed national, transnational, and international relations protecting 'conditions under which the choice of one can be united with the choice of another in accordance with a universal law of freedom'.[14] The history of international law confirms this dialectic evolution of legal systems, the normative orders of which are constantly challenged by legal practices. Multilevel constitutional restraints – based on agreed-upon constitutional restraints on 'rule by law' – promote 'rule of law' and mutual coherence among fragmented, legal regimes by requiring individuals and law-appliers to interpret and apply indeterminate rules in reasonable ways, which respect equal freedoms and humanistic, universal 'principles of justice'.

Constitutional democracies protect equal private autonomy rights also in the field of commercial arbitration, subject to the proviso that national courts (e.g. if requested to enforce private commercial arbitration awards) must

12 See Immanuel Kant, 'Perpetual Peace: A Philosophical Sketch' in Hans S Reiss (ed), *Kant: Political Writings* (CUP 1977) 98.

13 See Immanuel Kant, 'Idea for a Universal History with a Cosmopolitan Purpose' in Hans S Reiss (ed), *Kant: Political Writings* (CUP 1977) 47.

14 Kant (n 10).

review the legal consistency of the awards with the 'public policy' and constitutional law in the country where the complainant seeks recognition and enforcement of the award. Due to the worldwide recognition of human rights, 'public policy' considerations are increasingly recognized as also including procedural human rights of access to justice, and substantive (e.g. *jus cogens*) human rights guarantees. Following the conclusion of BITs aimed at protecting foreign investments in less-developed host countries, the 1966 Convention establishing the International Centre for the Settlement of Investment Disputes (ICSID) provided a multilateral, procedural framework for ISA and for the judicial enforcement of arbitration awards, which today includes 163 ICSID Member States. The more than 775 ICSID investor-state arbitration proceedings (by 2019), as well as the numerous additional ISA procedures modelled on commercial arbitration have come under increasing criticism, for instance, on the grounds that BITs, ISA, and commercial arbitrators privilege foreign investor rights without adequate regard for the regulatory duties of host states to protect the human and constitutional rights of all citizens by reconciling investment regulation with all other economic and non-economic public interest regulations.[15]

The 2018 *Achmea* judgment of the CJEU[16] – according to which ISA in relations among EU Member States is inconsistent with the EU constitutional law guarantees of the autonomy of EU law; the exclusive jurisdiction of the CJEU over the interpretation of EU law; and with the multilevel judicial protection of individual rights and judicial remedies by the CJEU in cooperation with national courts – illustrates how Europe's multilevel constitutionalism has imposed constitutional restraints on path-dependent conceptions of commercial autonomy and state sovereignty. The CJEU continues to recognize private party autonomy to submit private and commercial law disputes to private arbitration. Yet according to the Achmea judgment, both private legal autonomy and the national sovereignty of EU Member States have become limited by the autonomy of EU constitutional law to the effect that more than 200 intra-EU BITs among EU Member States can no longer justify ISA in view of the EU Treaty provisions reserving the multilevel judicial protection of EU law, individual rights, and non-discriminatory treatment to national courts and European courts.[17] In January 2019, the EU Member States adopted three Declarations committing themselves to the following:

15 See Sergio Puig, 'Debiasing International Economic Law' (2020) 30 EJIL 1339.
16 Case C-284/16 *The Slovak Republic v Achmea BV* [2018] ECLI:EU:C:2018:158.
17 See ibid, referring especially to Article 18 of the Treaty on the Functioning of the European Union (TFEU) (prohibition of discrimination), 19 of the Treaty on European Union (TEU) (judicial protection of rule of law in the EU), 267 TFEU (preliminary rulings reference procedure), 344 TFEU (exclusive jurisdiction of the CJEU for interpreting EU law), to 'the preservation of "the particular nature" of EU law' and of the 'EU principle of mutual trust'. The judgment did not review the compatibility of the substantive clauses of *intra*-EU BITs with EU law.

1 the termination of their intra-EU BITs before the end of 2019;
2 requesting all courts to set aside arbitration awards based on intra-EU BITs;
3 informing ISA tribunals in all pending cases about the legal consequences of the *Achmea* judgment.[18]

According to the EU Commission, the legal reasoning of the *Achmea* judgment – which concerned an intra-EU BIT providing for ISA governed by the UN Commission for International Trade Law (UNCITRAL) arbitration procedures, with EU law being part of the applicable law – applies also to ISA governed by the Energy Charter Treaty (ECT) and by ICSID procedures; it requires a 'modernization' of the ECT and ICSID procedures for ISA similar to the EU initiatives for a new 'investment court system' in EU trade and investment agreements with third countries (like Canada, Mexico, Singapore, and Vietnam). Accordingly, a subsequent agreement on the termination of BITs among 23 EU Member States of 6 May 2020 confirmed the incompatibility with EU law of ISA among EU Member States, including the 'sunset clauses' in such BITs. As a result, all related investment disputes must now be decided by domestic courts in the EU Member States, in conjunction with preliminary rulings by the CJEU, as appropriate.[19] Yet many legal questions regarding the relationships between intra-EU arbitration awards based on the ECT or ICSID procedures and enforcement actions by national courts inside EU Member States remain controversial.[20] Opinion 1/17, in which the CJEU interpreted the ISA provisions in the EU-Canada Comprehensive Economic and Trade Agreement as being consistent with EU law,[21] could suggest that the CJEU may support the view of the EU Commission that ECT and ICSID arbitration procedures need to be 'modernized' in order to make them compatible with EU constitutional law principles.

Based on the Lisbon Treaty's conferral of exclusive EU competence for the common commercial policy, including foreign direct investment, the EU

18 For a detailed analysis of these Declarations and of the legal consequences of the *Achmea* judgment on ISA proceedings and on *intra*-EU BITs, see Maria Fanou, 'The EU as an Actor Shaping the Future of ISDS: Unveiling the Interplay Between the Clash of Two Autonomies and the Reform of Investor-State Arbitration' (DPhil thesis, European University Institute 14 February 2020).

19 See Matteo Fermeglia and Alessandra Mistura, 'Killing All Birds with One Stone: Is This the End of Intra-EU BITs?' (*EJIL: Talk!*, 26 May 2020) <https://www.ejiltalk.org/killing-all-birds-with-one-stone-is-this-the-end-of-intra-eu-bits-as-we-know-them/> accessed 30 April 2022.

20 See *Micula et alii v Romania* (2013) ICSID Case No ARB/05/20. The tribunal ordered Romania to pay compensation for the revocation of state aid that had been found by the EU Commission to violate EU state aid prohibitions. The investors successfully challenged in the EU General Court the European Commission's decision to block the enforcement of the award. See also Cases T-624/15, T-694/15 and T-704/15 *Micula and Others v Commission* [2019] ECLI:EU:T:2019:423 (the appeal by the Commission is pending before the CJEU).

21 Case C-1/17 *Accord ECG UE-Canada* [2019] Avis 1/17, Opinion of AG Bot.

Commission continues to pursue international negotiations aimed at transforming ISA into multilateral investment court systems, for instance, by modernizing the UNCITRAL, ECT, and ICSID arbitration procedures and ISA provisions in EU trade and investment agreements with third States. It remains uncertain how the ongoing reform negotiations will respond to the widespread criticism of traditional ISA – for instance, its lack of an appeal mechanism; insufficient transparency and the incoherence of ISA jurisprudence; the inadequate independence and impartiality of arbitrators; pro-investor biases threatening the regulatory powers of host States; limiting access to justice; burdening tax-payers and undermining the legitimacy of ISA – and improve the UNCITRAL, ICSID, and other ISA procedures and protection standards. If economic efficiency is determined not only by cost-benefit analyses, but also by voluntary compliance with democratically agreed-upon rules protecting informed preferences and the basic needs of citizens, the progressive replacement of FDI privileges by more inclusive investment rules and investment court procedures protecting all affected citizens' interests offers social, democratic, and legal advantages which also enhance 'economic efficiency' and the 'rule of law'.

4 'Constitutionalism 2.0': multilevel judicial protection of rule of law in international trade

Constitutionalism 2.0 refers to multilateral treaty 'constitutions' establishing organizations for the multilevel governance of PGs, like the constitutions (*sic*) establishing the International Labour Organization (ILO), the World Health Organization (WHO), the Food and Agriculture Organization (FAO), and UN Educational, Scientific and Cultural Organization (UNESCO).[22] Each of these UN Specialized Agencies is embedded in the broader UN system (establishing global security, human rights, and development systems) and justifies its mandate to protect 'aggregate PGs' in terms of labour rights (ILO), health rights (WHO), rights to food (FAO), and rights to education and participation in the benefits of science and cultural development (UNESCO). The GATT/WTO were deliberately kept outside of the UN system. Yet, it was only the WTO that succeeded in establishing multilevel, compulsory dispute settlement systems aimed at protecting the rule of law in international trade at the national and international levels.[23] The 316 disputes under GATT 1947 and the 1979 Tokyo Round Agreements,[24] and the more

22 For more on the historical development from 'constitutionalism 1.0' to 'constitutionalism 4.0', see Petersmann (n 4) 321ff.

23 For more on the multilevel guarantees in GATT/WTO law of access to domestic courts and to (quasi-)judicial remedies in GATT/WTO bodies, see Ernst-Ulrich Petersmann, *The GATT/WTO Dispute Settlement System: International Law, International Organizations and Dispute Settlement* (Brill/Nijhoff 1997) 23.

24 See World Trade Organization, *GATT Disputes 1948–1995*: vol 1 and vol 2 (WTO 2018).

than 600 formal dispute settlement proceedings under the WTO Agreement (1996–2020), protected – for the first time in world history – transnational rule of law in trade relations among the 164 WTO members. The complex GATT/WTO jurisprudence approved by GATT/WTO members clarified the rights and duties under international trade law with due regard to general international law and the more than 400 free trade agreements concluded among GATT/WTO members (often providing for additional judicial remedies). As more than 85 per cent of the more than 500 GATT/WTO dispute settlement findings were approved and implemented by GATT/WTO members, the GATT/WTO dispute settlement system was the most frequently used and successful worldwide dispute settlement system in the history of international law. Even if most GATT/WTO members did not allow for the 'direct application' and judicial enforcement of GATT/WTO obligations in their domestic jurisdictions, many GATT/WTO disputes were preceded or followed by domestic court proceedings (e.g. challenging illegal trade remedies). The global 'interpretive community' of trade lawyers, academics, and judges analysing and developing GATT/WTO law and the jurisprudence resulting therefrom strengthened this 'international trade law culture', institutionalizing 'public reason' (e.g. in the sense of shared systems of public justification of multilevel trade rules and of their decentralized enforcement), thus providing 'security and predictability to the multilateral trading system' (Article 3 of the Understanding on rules and procedures governing the settlement of disputes, DSU)[25] and reducing transaction costs in the global division of labour.

The 1979 GATT and 1994 WTO agreements on trade remedies and trade-related intellectual property rights extended the 'neo-liberal, regulatory capture' in the US trade policies to the worldwide trading system. This contributed to increasing controversies within the WTO regarding WTO disputes on anti-dumping measures, countervailing duties, safeguard measures, and intellectual property rights. At the insistence of US trade negotiators, the DSU provisions limited 'due process of law' in unreasonable ways, for instance, by adjusting DSU deadlines for appellate review within 60–90 days to those imposed in US trade remedy laws. The trade policies of the Trump administration were dominated by former US trade remedy lawyers (like Robert Lighthizer) and other former US lobbyists (like WTO ambassador Dennis Shea), who progressively attacked and ignored WTO rules and jurisprudence (e.g. WTO constraints on trade remedies and on 'bilateral trade deals' exploiting US power vis-à-vis other WTO members). In addition, China's totalitarian, state-capitalist trading practices, and the unwillingness of less developed WTO countries (like India) to engage in reciprocal trade liberalization/regulation, further undermined US support for the WTO system. The legal justifications offered by the Trump administration for their illegal

25 Understanding on rules and procedures governing the settlement of disputes, Annex 2 of the WTO Agreement (entry into force 1 January 1995) 1869 UNTS 401.

'blocking' of WTO Appellate Body (AB) nominations were based on (and insisted on) US interpretations of WTO rules and US criticism of AB findings, without any evidence that the legal interpretations by the AB violated the customary rules of treaty interpretation or the (quasi-)judicial AB mandate for impartial, independent, and prompt third-party adjudication through quasi-automatic adoption of the WTO panel and AB reports by the Dispute Settlement Body (DSB). The 2020 USTR (United States Trade Representative) Report – notwithstanding its valid criticism of some WTO rules and dispute settlement practices (e.g. that the AB no longer consulted with the parties when deciding to disregard the Article 17.5 deadline) – revealed systemic biases and incorrect claims by the US, such as:

- the US denial of the (quasi-)judicial functions of WTO third-party adjudication, even though numerous WTO publications and WTO dispute settlement reports over more than 20 years acknowledged the (quasi-) judicial mandates of WTO dispute settlement bodies (i.e. WTO panels, the AB, and the quasi-automatic adoption of their reports by the DSB);
- the US disregard for judicial AB arguments in the performance of the DSU's mandate 'to clarify the existing provisions of those agreements in accordance with customary rules of interpretation of public international law' (Article 3 DSU), for instance, whenever the AB found that compliance with the time limit of 90 days (Article 17.5 DSU) – which was imposed by US negotiators in 1993 notwithstanding the widespread criticism that no other court seemed to be subject to such an unreasonably short time limit – was impossible to reconcile with the other AB tasks (e. g. due to illegal US blocking of the filling of AB vacancies);
- contradictory USTR claims that AB legal findings against the US violated the DSU's prohibition to 'add or diminish the rights and obligations in the covered agreements' (Article 3.2 DSU) – even if the AB had justified these legal findings on the basis of the customary rules of treaty interpretation and its (quasi-)judicial mandate – notwithstanding the USTR's regular support of AB reports accepting 'creative WTO interpretations' advocated by the USTR as a legal complainant;
- the US description of US 'zeroing practices' as a 'common-sense method of calculating the extent of dumping'[26] even if their biases had been consistently condemned by the AB and DSB as violations of the WTO obligations of 'fair price comparisons' (which are barely mentioned in the USTR report);
- a one-sided focus on WTO texts as interpreted by US negotiators without regard to the customary law and DSU requirements to clarify the meaning of the often-indeterminate WTO provisions with due regard also to

26 United States Trade Representative, 'Report on the Appellate Body of the WTO' (Washington, DC, February 2020) <https://bit.ly/3fexUPk> accessed 30 April 2022, 2.

WTO legal texts revealing the 'context, object and purpose' of WTO provisions and the explicitly recognized 'systemic character' of what the WTO Agreement calls 'this multilateral trading system' (Preamble) and its 'dispute settlement system' (Article 3 DSU);

- the denigration of AB members as 'three unelected and unaccountable persons'[27] whose 'overreaching violates the basic principles of the United States Government' (USTR Report, Introduction), notwithstanding the election of AB members through consensus decisions of the 164 DSB member governments (including the US), their (quasi-)judicial mandate, and the approval of WTO agreements (including the DSU) by the US government and US Congress;
- insulting claims that the AB Secretariat has weakened the WTO dispute settlement system by not respecting WTO rights and obligations.[28]

The USTR Report acknowledges that its purpose 'is not to propose solutions'.[29] It repeated what the US ambassador had been stating in DSB meetings since 2017: 'WTO Members must come to terms with the failings of the Appellate Body set forth in this Report if we are to achieve lasting and effective reform of the WTO dispute settlement system.'[30] Yet nothing suggests that – even if WTO members were to accept the false US claims of the AB's 'persistent overreaching … contrary to the Appellate Body's limited mandate', and 'the Appellate Body's failure to follow the agreed rules' – the US would be willing to comply with its DSU obligation of filling AB vacancies 'as they arise' (Article 17.2) and return to the WTO's third-party adjudication, appellate review, customary rules of treaty interpretation, and 'judicial interpretations' for the 'prompt settlement' of WTO disputes, as prescribed in the DSU. Past WTO members' 'appeasement' of false USTR claims (e.g. in Ambassador Walker's informal mediation proposal of October 2019 for overcoming the WTO dispute settlement crisis) never changed the USTR's refusal to return to WTO third-party adjudication as prescribed in the DSU. Since the mandates of two AB judges expired on 10 December 2019, the AB was reduced to one single judge and can no longer accept new appeals.

The 'Economic and Trade Agreement' signed by China and the US on 15 January 2020 confirmed the Trump administration's preference for power-oriented rather than judicial settlement of disputes. It provides for discriminatory Chinese commitments to buy US products and discriminatory US import tariffs and trade restrictions (e.g. targeting Chinese technology companies), without third-party adjudication. This bilateral 'opt-out' – by the two largest trading nations – from their WTO legal and dispute settlement obligations seems to be

27 Ibid 8, 13.
28 Ibid 120.
29 Ibid 121.
30 Ibid 1.

the policy option preferred by USTR officials prioritizing 'bilateral US trade deals' and their unilateral enforcement. The US invocation of the 'security exception' in GATT Article XXI (e.g. imposing import restrictions on steel and aluminium) illustrates how the Trump administration circumvented WTO rules (e.g. GATT Articles I, II, and XIX) and dispute settlement procedures whenever it suited the American political interests and US interest group politics. 'Constitutionalism 2.0' seems to continue only in the European Economic Area (EEA), with its multilevel judicial protection of rule of law among the 30 EEA member countries.

5 'Constitutionalism 3.0': multilevel judicial governance inside the EU and its constitutional limits

All UN Member States have accepted, for example, in their UN Declaration on the 'Rule of Law at National and International Levels' of November 2012, that:

- 'human rights, the rule of law and democracy are interlinked and mutually reinforcing and that they belong to the universal and indivisible core values and principles of the United Nations';
- 'the advancement of the rule of law at the national and international levels is essential for sustained and inclusive economic growth, sustainable development, the eradication of poverty and hunger and the full realization of all human rights and fundamental freedoms'.[31]

The history of democratic constitutionalism confirms that the limitation of abuses of majoritarian governance powers must be complemented by non-majoritarian institutions (such as courts of justice, independent central banks, and competition policy institutions) that are needed to protect PGs. Multilevel judicial governance requires 'comity' and cooperation among domestic and international courts of justice in their joint task of protecting the rule of law at the national and international levels. The progressive transformation of European integration into a multilevel constitutional order was driven by the jurisprudence of the CJEU (e.g. on legal primacy, direct effect, the direct applicability of EU law, judicial protection of human and constitutional rights, and implied EU powers) and its acceptance and enforcement inside the EU Member States. Successive treaty reforms (e.g. introducing direct elections of the European Parliament and its co-decision powers) and independent EU institutions (such as the EU Commission and the ECB) promoted the progressive 'constitutionalization' of the EU's micro-economic 'common market

31 UN General Assembly (UNGA), 'Declaration of the High-level Meeting of the General Assembly on the Rule of Law at the National and International Levels' (30 November 2012) UN Doc A/RES/67/1 5, 7. See also UNGA, 'Report of the Secretary-General' (2012) UN Doc A/66/49.

constitution', macro-economic 'monetary constitution', and multilevel 'foreign policy constitution'.[32]

The constitutional complaints initiated in 2015 in Germany's Federal Constitutional Court (FCC) on behalf of more than 1700 citizens contended, *inter alia*, that the ECB decisions introducing the Public Sector Asset Purchase Programme (PSPP) and the Corporate Sector Purchase Programme constituted *ultra vires* acts violating the EU prohibition of monetary financing (Article 123(1) TFEU) and the principle of conferral of limited EU powers (Article 5(1) TEU in conjunction with Articles 119, 127ff TFEU). The complainants asserted violations of their constitutional rights to democratic self-determination and of the constitutional identity enshrined in Germany's Basic Law to the extent that the ECB programmes infringed on the budgetary powers of the German *Bundestag*. They sought a judicial declaration from the FCC that the Federal Government and the Bundestag violated their constitutional responsibilities with respect to European integration. In 2017, the second senate of the FCC suspended the proceedings and referred a number of related questions to the CJEU for a preliminary ruling pursuant to Article 267(1) TFEU. The CJEU responded, in its judgment of 11 December 2018,[33] that its consideration of the questions from the FCC had disclosed no factor of such a kind as to affect the validity of the ECB decisions concerned. The FCC judgment of 5 May 2020[34] declared the constitutional complaints 'well-founded to the extent that they challenge the omission on the part of the Federal Government and the Bundestag to take suitable steps to ensure that the ECB, by means of purchasing securities under the PSPP, does not exceed its monetary policy competence and encroach upon the economic policy competence of the Member States' (para 97).

This finding was based, *inter alia*, on the following conclusions:

- 'The democratic legitimation by the people of public authority exercised in Germany belongs to the essential contents of the principle of the sovereignty of the people and thus forms part of the Basic Law's constitutional identity protected in Art. 79(3) GG; it is therefore beyond the reach of European integration in accordance with Art. 23(1) third sentence in conjunction with Art. 79(3) GG' (para 101).
- 'The Basic Law … prohibits conferring upon the European Union the competence to decide on its own competences (Kompetenz-Kompetenz) … [D]ynamic treaty provisions must be subject to suitable safeguards that enable the German constitutional organs to effectively exercise their responsibility with regard to European integration' (para 102).

32 See Petersmann (n 4) 151ff; Kaarlo Tuori, *European Constitutionalism* (CUP 2015).

33 C-493/17 *Weiss and others* [2018] ECLI: EU:C:2018:1000 (GC).

34 BVerfG, Judgment of the Second Senate (2 BvR 859/15, 5 May 2020) 1–237 <https://bit.ly/3wySXBU> accessed 30 April 2022.

- 'It is for the German Bundestag, as the organ directly accountable to the people, to take all essential decisions on revenue and expenditure; this prerogative forms part of the core of Art. 20(1) and (2) GG, which is beyond the reach of constitutional amendment … [A] transfer of sovereign powers violates the principle of democracy at least in cases where the type and level of public spending are, to a significant extent, determined at the supranational level, depriving the Bundestag of its decision-making prerogative' (para 104).
- 'Where measures taken by institutions, bodies, offices and agencies of the European Union exceed the limits of the European integration agenda (*Integrationsprogramm*) in a manifest and structurally significant manner, it is incumbent upon the Federal Government and the Bundestag to actively address the question how the order of competences can be restored and to make a positive determination as to which course of action to pursue' (para 109).
- 'While the Federal Constitutional Court must review substantiated *ultra vires* challenges regarding acts of institutions, bodies, offices and agencies of the European Union, the Treaties confer upon the CJEU the mandate to interpret and apply the Treaties and to ensure uniformity and coherence of EU law (cf. Art. 19(1) subpara 2 TEU, Art. 267 TFEU); it is imperative that the respective judicial mandates be exercised in a coordinated manner … [T]he Member States remain the "Masters of the Treaties" and the EU has not evolved into a federal state' (para 111).
- 'The *ultra vires* review must be exercised with restraint, giving effect to the Constitution's openness to European integration … The methodological standards recognized by the CJEU for the judicial development of the law are based on the (constitutional) legal traditions common to the Member States (cf. also Art. 6(3) TEU, Art. 340(2) TFEU), which are notably reflected in the case-law of the Member States' constitutional and apex courts and of the European Court of Human Rights … [T]he mandate conferred in Article 19(1) second sentence TEU is exceeded where the traditional European methods of interpretation or, more broadly, the general legal principles that are common to the laws of the Member States are manifestly disregarded' (para 112).
- 'If the CJEU crosses the limit set out above, its actions are no longer covered by the mandate conferred in Article 19(1) second sentence TEU in conjunction with the domestic Act of Approval; at least in relation to Germany, its decision then lacks the minimum of democratic legitimation necessary under Art. 23(1) second sentence in conjunction with Article 20 (1) and (2) and 79(3) GG' (para 113).
- 'Where such acts of institutions, bodies, offices and agencies of the European Union give rise to effects that bear on Germany's constitutional identity enshrined in Art. 1 and 20 GG, they exceed the limits of open statehood set by the Basic Law … This concerns the protection of the human dignity core enshrined in fundamental rights under Art. 1 GG …

as well as the basic tenets that inform the principles of democracy, the rule of law, the social state and the federal state within the meaning of Art. 20 GG. With a view to the principle of democracy enshrined in Art. 20(1) and (2) GG, it must *inter alia* be ensured that the German Bundestag retains for itself functions and powers of substantial significance … and that it remains capable of exercising its overall budgetary responsibility' (para 115).

- 'Based on these standards, the Federal Government and the German Bundestag violated the rights of the complainants … by failing to take suitable steps challenging that the ECB, in Decision (EU) 2015/774 as amended … [N]either assessed nor substantiated that the measures provided for in these decisions satisfy the principle of proportionality. In light of this, Decision (EU) 2015/774 and amending Decisions … constitute a qualified, i.e. manifest and structurally significant, exceeding of the competences assigned to the ECB in Art. 119, Art. 127 *et seq.* TFEU and Art. 17 *et seq.* ECB Statute. The differing view of the CJEU set out in its Judgment of 11 December 2018 does not merit a different conclusion, given that on this point, the judgment is simply not comprehensible so that, to this extent, the judgment was rendered *ultra vires* … Nevertheless, it cannot be definitively determined whether the ECB decisions at issue satisfy the principle of proportionality.'[35]

Arguably, German constitutional law, the Lisbon Treaty, and the multilevel judicial application of EU law illustrate 'systemic constitutional problems' in the multilevel governance of 'aggregate PGs' (such as transnational economic markets, rule of law, and democratic governance) that are of importance also in the multilevel governance of global PGs (e.g. in the WTO) and related challenges of 'judicial overreach' in the AB, ISA, the CJEU, and the FCC.

6 Policy conclusions

This chapter has briefly discussed the rule of law crises in WTO law, investment law, and European law and adjudication. In each jurisdiction, claims of judicial 'overreach' were related to the constitutional principles of limited delegation of powers, democracy, and the judicial administration of justice. As recalled in Section 2, democratic constitutionalism and republican constitutionalism were invented in the ancient Athenian democracy and Italian city republics and further developed through democratic revolutions in Europe and North America. Also 'multilevel constitutionalism' for the multilevel governance of transnational PGs was a 'European invention', based on humanistic insights into the moral, psychological, political, and constitutional

35 These very incomplete excerpts from the long FCC judgment are sufficient for the limited purposes of this chapter, which does not allow a more complete summary and criticism of the reasoning of the FCC.

advantages of 'reasonable self-limitations' of public and private abuses of power, which are a challenge for all legal systems. Even though all UN Member States have adopted written or unwritten national constitutions, their actual 'constitutionalization' of legislative, political and judicial powers and multilevel protection of human rights often remain underdeveloped, especially outside Europe's multilevel constitutionalism. Hence, the 'normative pull' of UN human rights and of the universally agreed-upon 'sustainable development goals' remains weak in many States due to their insufficient 'normative push' through democratic legislation, administration, judicial remedies, and domestic enforcement of international treaties. Human rights require respect for democratic diversity and constitutional pluralism. Yet, the 'political lessons' from European constitutionalism discussed in this chapter refer to political and human problems existing in all societies due to the 'bounded rationality' of human beings.[36]

6.1 Limited delegation of powers

All international organizations operate on the basis of a limited delegation of powers by Member States. As emphasized by the FCC in the above-mentioned judgment on *ultra vires* acts of EU institutions, democracies do not confer on international organizations the competence to enlarge their own limited powers by imposing new obligations without the consent of Member States. For instance, the WTO DSU acknowledges that: 'Recommendations and rulings of the DSB cannot add to or diminish the rights and obligations provided in the covered agreements' (Article 3.2). This provision, introduced during the Uruguay Round negotiations at the request of the US delegation, was construed in conformity with the recognition by Member States that the DSU 'serves to preserve the rights and obligations of Members under the covered agreements, and to clarify the existing provisions of those agreements in accordance with customary rules of interpretation of public international law'. The WTO, ISA, and EU judicial bodies apply the customary rules of treaty interpretation common to the Member States. According to the AB, WTO legal interpretations clarifying WTO provisions in conformity with the customary rules of treaty interpretation cannot simultaneously violate the DSU prohibitions against 'add[ing] to or diminish[ing] the rights and obligations provided in the covered agreements' (Articles 3.2 and 19.2 DSU).[37] Yet, as emphasized in the *Achmea* judgment, the EU constitutional principles and judicial remedies prevail over the applicable law in ISA against EU Member States. And, as emphasized by the FCC, the EU Member States and their

36 See Ernst-Ulrich Petersmann, 'Lessons from European Constitutionalism for Reforming Multilevel Governance of Transnational Public Goods in Asia?' in Julien Chaisse (ed), *Sixty Years of European Integration and Global Power Shifts: Perceptions, Interactions and Lessons* (Hart Publishing 2020) 217, 237.

37 See Appellate Body Report, *Chile-Alcoholic Beverages* (13 December 1999) WT/DS87/AB/R, WT/DS110/AB/R [79].

national 'constitutional identities' are protected by EU law against unjustified (e.g. disproportionate) interferences by EU institutions. Article 5(1) TEU, for instance, clarifies the 'principle of conferral' by specifying that: 'The use of Union competences is governed by the principles of subsidiarity and proportionality.' In its judicial examination of whether the contested ECB decisions and the related CJEU judgment are consistent with the 'proportionality principle', the FCC criticized both the ECB decisions and the related judgment of the CJEU for failing to examine whether the ECB's use of monetary policy instruments disproportionately affected the economic and fiscal policy competences of EU Member States. According to the FCC, they 'manifestly fail[ed] to give consideration to the importance and scope of the principle of proportionality (Art. 5(1) second sentence and Art. 5(4) TEU), which also applies to the division of competences'.[38]

6.2 Democratic constitutionalism

Western democracies are based on the recognition of human rights, rule of law, and democracy as the three core principles of democratic constitutionalism. Yet their national constitutions, democratic legislation, administration and jurisprudence differ, depending on their diverse histories and democratic preferences. For instance, the German Basic Law's protection of judicially enforceable, constitutional rights to democratic self-determination, including the parliamentary prerogative of taking all essential decisions on revenue and expenditure as an indispensable element of constitutional democracy in Germany, differs from the constitutional traditions in other EU Member States. This diversity of democratically defined 'national identities' must be respected by the law of international organizations, as explicitly prescribed in Article 4 TEU and explained in the German FCC judgment of 5 May 2020:

> The democratic legitimation by the people of public authority exercised in Germany belongs to the essential contents of the principle of the sovereignty of the people and thus forms part of the Basic Law's constitutional identity protected in Art. 79(3) GG; it is therefore beyond the reach of European integration in accordance with Article 23(1) third sentence in conjunction with Art. 79(3) GG.[39]

But democracy as a constitutional constraint on the multilevel governance of PGs applies only to 'constitutional democracy' rather than merely 'majoritarian views'.

In its 2020 Report on the WTO AB, the USTR complains of 'persistent overreaching' by the AB in its interpretation of WTO rules, and claims that:

38 BVerfG (n 34) 119.
39 Ibid 101.

> [T]his overreaching also violates the basic principles of the United States Government. There is no legitimacy under our democratic, constitutional system for the nation to submit to a rule imposed by three individuals sitting in Geneva, with neither agreement by the United States nor approval by the United States Congress.[40]

Yet at the same time the very long USTR Report identifies no AB interpretation that could not be justifiable based on the (quasi-)judicial DSU mandate 'to clarify the existing provisions of those agreements in accordance with customary rules of interpretation of public international law' for the 'prompt settlement' of disputes (Article 3 DSU). Nor does the Report identify any US constitutional law provision prohibiting US consent to international third-party adjudication. As both the US government and the US Congress approved the WTO Agreements and the DSU provisions (including Article 17 on the establishment of the AB), and the US government consented to the appointment of each AB member, the USTR claims are factually wrong – like so many other 'populist claims' of the US Trump administration. Such claims by majoritarian government institutions cannot justify non-compliance with democratically approved treaty obligations, such as the illegal US 'blocking' of AB nominations in violation of Article 17.2 DSU. The democratic approval of the WTO Agreement by parliaments confers limited, democratic legitimacy also on the AB as long as it operates within its legal constraints and respects the 'subsidiarity principle', for instance by choosing judicial interpretations that respect legitimate 'constitutional pluralism' in the interpretation of the 'general' and 'security exceptions' in WTO law (e.g. on sovereign rights to protect public morals, public order, and 'essential security interests').

6.3 Multilevel judicial protection of the rule of law

This chapter has described the emergence of multilevel judicial protection of the rule of law before discussing the recent claims of 'judicial overreach' in ISA (e.g. inside the EU), in the WTO appellate system, and in the EU's multilevel judicial governance. It has argued that inasmuch as international organizations do not have the competence to enlarge their own competence, disagreements over *ultra vires* acts of international institutions (like the CJEU, the ECB, ISA, or the WTO AB) must be resolved through multilevel judicial cooperation or agreed-upon compromises among governments, with due respect for legitimate 'constitutional pluralism' and for constitutional law principles common to the Member States concerned. 'Manifest' and 'structurally significant' *ultra vires* acts, as criticized in the German FCC judgment of 5 May 2020, remain very rare and contested in the evolution of international law and jurisprudence. The FCC rightly emphasizes that – as Member States remain the 'masters of the treaties', and the EU has not evolved into a

40 USTR Report (n 26) 3.

federal state – such conflicts 'must be resolved in a cooperative manner, in keeping with the spirit of European integration, and mitigated through mutual respect and understanding'.[41] The compromise proposal by the WTO Facilitator Ambassador Walker for resolving the WTO AB crisis,[42] the EU initiative for a plurilateral agreement on using 'appellate arbitration' based on Article 25 DSU as an interim solution pending the illegal US blocking of AB nominations,[43] and the EU initiatives for transforming ISA into a multicourt system inside the EU as well as in the context of external EU trade and investment agreements, all offer reasonable, political responses to the ongoing challenges of the WTO and ISA jurisprudence.

This chapter has emphasized that the global economic, health, environmental, and political crises cannot be resolved in coherent and legitimate ways without the multilevel legal and judicial protection of transnational rule of law. The international community's inability to prevent, or effectively address, global environmental problems (such as climate change, biodiversity losses, or the pollution of the oceans) confirms the need for interpreting the WTO's 'objective of sustainable development' in conformity with the UN's 2030 Agenda for Sustainable Development in order to make it clear for citizens, democratic institutions, and governments all over the world that the UN's 17 'sustainable development goals' protecting citizens and their human rights (e.g. to health and environmental protection) cannot be realized without WTO law and WTO third-party adjudication protecting the rule of law in the application of trade policy instruments (such as, for example, non-discriminatory access to vaccines and medical equipment, non-discriminatory border adjustments of national carbon taxes aimed at reducing greenhouse gas emissions) to the regulatory challenges of the global health, environmental, economic and rule of law crises. The 'regulatory competition' among WTO members with mutually inconsistent neo-liberal, state-capitalist, ordo-liberal constitutional or 'third world' conceptions of economic regulation likewise requires a strong WTO dispute settlement system preventing 'trade wars', promoting independent judicial rule-clarifications and third-party adjudication, and assisting UN and WTO members in realizing their universally agreed-upon sustainable development goals.[44]

41 BVerfG (n 34) 111.

42 See WTO General Council, 'Informal Process on Matters Related to the Functioning of the Appellate Body – Report by the Facilitator, H.E. Dr. David Walker (New Zealand)' (15 October 2019) JOB/GC/222.

43 See WTO, 'Statement on Mechanism for Developing, Documenting and Sharing Practices and Procedures in the Conduct of WTO Disputes' (30 April 2020) JOB/DSB/1/Add.12.

44 See Ernst-Ulrich Petersmann, *Transforming World Trade and Investment Law for Sustainable Development* (OUP 2022).

12 We Have Never Been 'Multilateral'

Consensus Discourse in International Trade Law

Jessica C Lawrence

1 Introduction

In international economic law circles, it has become common to speak of a 'crisis of multilateralism' and of the threatened collapse of the post-World War II international consensus on trade policy. Amrita Narlikar, for example, recently wrote that 'trade multilateralism faces a crisis of existential proportions today'.[1] Ernst-Ulrich Petersmann lamented 'US President Trump's attack on the multilateral trading system,' which precipitated 'the WTO's biggest "governance crisis' since the entry into force of the 1994 Agreement establishing the WTO'.[2] And Michael Hahn has analysed the EU's counter-reaction to 'the scepticism of the Trump administration towards the multilateral liberal order, including … the WTO' which has led Europe to 'engage in multiple efforts to strengthen the rules-based approach to international economic governance'.[3]

As is evident from the above quotes, talk of the 'crisis of multilateralism' has been precipitated most directly by the United States' (US) rebellion against the World Trade Organization (WTO) system, which the Trump administration saw as hostile to US interests.[4] Perhaps the best-known part of this insurrection is the ongoing 'Appellate Body crisis'. Citing concerns regarding judicial overreach,[5] the US has refused to agree to the appointment

1 Amrita Narlikar, 'Trade Multilateralism in Crisis: Limitations of Current Debates on Reforming the WTO and Why a Game-Changer is Necessary' in Teddy Soobramanien, Brendan Vickers, and Hilary Enos-Edu (eds), *WTO Reform: Reshaping Global Trade Governance for 21st-Century Challenges* (The Commonwealth 2019) 21.

2 Ernst-Ulrich Petersmann, 'How Should WTO Members React to Their WTO Crises?' (2019) 18 WTR 1, 1.

3 Michael Hahn, 'We'll Always Have Geneva: The Existential Crisis of the US-led Multilateral Trading System and EU Reactions' in Inge Govaere and Sacha Garben (eds), *The Interface Between EU and International Law: Contemporary Reflections* (Hart Publishing 2019) 271.

4 Carol Schaeffer, 'Donald Trump Tells Aides He Wants to Withdraw US from WTO, Reports Say' *Independent* (29 June 2018) <https://bit.ly/3bpbvN6> accessed 30 April 2022.

5 See United States Trade Representative (USTR), 'Report on the Appellate Body of the WTO' (February 2020) <https://bit.ly/3gTgt7N> accessed 30 April 2022.

DOI: 10.4324/9781003312857-14

of new members to the WTO's Appellate Body since 2017, leading to that Body's ceasing to be quorate in December 2019, and endangering the overall system of WTO dispute settlement.[6]

As explained in Section 2, however, the Appellate Body crisis is only one of the many challenges that currently threaten the multilateral system of trade governance; the latest in a long line of crises that have plagued the WTO since it came into being in 1995. Between the US actions, the calls for WTO 'modernization' collectively made by states in the Global North, and the willingness of powerful economies to take unilateral action to protect their interests, this is a difficult time for the WTO, and it is easy to see why this moment could be viewed as an 'existential crisis' that threatens the unraveling of the multilateral system. In this sense, the integrity of the multilateral trade system in its current form is certainly under threat.

But this chapter argues that describing this moment as a 'crisis of multilateralism' does more than simply signify the collective political and economic forces that are currently pulling at the seams of the WTO. It also constructs a discourse that actively works to shape our understanding of the world – and a highly political and partial one at that. In effect, the 'crisis of multilateralism' discourse depicts the WTO as the institutional embodiment of an imagined past in which there was broad consensus on how to manage the international economy for the good of all (i.e. a past in which 'multilateralism' existed), in contrast with a present in which fragmentation reigns, rogue actors flout collective norms in pursuit of their own self-interests, and the WTO is ineffective in reining in their behavior. As Mazaka and Bishop write:

> [A]ssertions about the end of trade multilateralism often operate as *political narratives* that, despite their specificities, rely on an artifice that depicts and romanticizes – whether explicitly or implicitly – the multilateralism of the past as having been operational, but currently under threat.[7]

Far from being an institution formerly characterized by multilateral consensus that has now fallen into crisis, however, the WTO has been plagued by deep disputes and continual disruptions since its earliest days.[8] Moreover, despite the catechistic references of trade enthusiasts to Smith, Ricardo, and the theory of comparative advantage, there has never been consistent agreement among policymakers, scholars, or the wider public on either the ends or means of trade policy.

This chapter seeks to highlight the political effects of the 'crisis of multilateralism' discourse, and to challenge the implied narrative that there was

6 See Chang-fa Lo, Junji Nakagawa, and Tsai-fang Chen (eds), *The Appellate Body of the WTO and Its Reform* (Springer 2020).

7 Valbona Mazurka and Matthew L Bishop, 'Doha Stalemate: The End of Trade Multilateralism?' (2015) 41 Rev Int Stud 383, 385.

8 See Section 2.

ever a time in which states had turned away from bilateralism, rejected 'self-help', or achieved consensus around a set of universal values in the world of trade policy. Instead, it argues that the 'crisis of multilateralism' narrative papers over a history filled with contestation and resistance – a whitewashing that serves the interests of those who wish to perpetuate a hegemonic vision of the global economic order. This universalist rhetoric obscures the strong disagreement that has always existed regarding the substantive content of international economic norms and throws a cloak of legitimacy over rules designed to further particular, contestable interests.[9]

Diving into the history of the modern WTO, Section 2 contextualizes the current 'crisis of multilateralism' in terms of broader institutional reform efforts and the history of crises dating back to the founding of the organization in 1995. Section 3 then analyses the discourse of multilateralism as it applies to international trade governance, identifying three distinct ways in which the term is deployed: (1) multilateralism as opposed to regionalism or bilateralism; (2) multilateralism as opposed to unilateralism; and (3) multilateralism as policy consensus. Section 4 tackles each of these meanings in turn, demonstrating that – contrary to implicit claims of the 'crisis' discourse – there was never a time when multilateralism supplanted regionalism; there was never a time when unilateralism and self-help were eliminated; and there was never a time when consensus on core substantive issues of economic policy was achieved. Section 5 concludes by returning to the political function of the claim that we are currently facing a 'crisis of multilateralism' at the WTO, emphasizing the ideological role played by this discourse and the need to reconsider our assumptions about the past and present of public international trade law.

The idea of an idyllic trade policy past characterized by consensus and mutual support is an illusion. In practice, global trade governance is, and always has been, a partial system that was designed to meet the needs and demands of its architects, and that has served some actors far better than others. As it has evolved, the WTO rulebook has been held together not by consensus on trade issues, by instead by the strategic use of loopholes, agreements to disagree, temporary workarounds, and conflicting interpretations. The 'crisis' the WTO faces today is not the result of 'the end of multilateralism', but is rather the consequence of a changing global economic and geopolitical landscape. It is no coincidence that as new alignments of states have begun to gain ground and pursue their own economic interests within the WTO (in particular, larger economies like India and China), this has caused the more established powers – like the US and the European Union (EU) – to find the system less to their liking, and to pull away from or seek to revise a set of rules and practices that no longer seem to suit their interests. The 'crisis of multilateralism' discourse hides all of this, erasing the ways in which trade governance has always been a site of contestation and resistance,

9 See Section 4 of this chapter.

built by and for a particular set of actors with specific economic and political goals in mind.

2 A history of crises

The current claims of a 'crisis of multilateralism', as noted above, have been precipitated most immediately by the breakdown of the WTO's Appellate Body caused by the US refusal to endorse the appointment of new members. However, the US blockage of appointments to the Appellate Body is only one of the many challenges facing the WTO.

To begin with, in parallel with its moves against the Appellate Body, the Trump administration championed the return of self-help in the trade arena. During his time in office, President Trump made heavy use of tariff policy to correct perceived trade imbalances, famously declaring that '[t]rade wars are good and easy to win',[10] and imposing duties on imports from China, the EU, and others as part of his 'America First' trade strategy. At one point, the US even went as far as threatening a total exit from the WTO, which President Trump called a 'disaster' that was 'designed by the rest of the world to screw the United States'[11] – this despite the fact that, as Gregory Shaffer, Manfred Elsig, and Mark Pollack calculate, the US has a higher 'win rate' as both a claimant and respondent than all other major users of the dispute settlement system.[12]

This revolt by one of the world's biggest economies – and one of the original driving forces behind the creation of the multilateral trade regime – seriously rattled the WTO and has worried those who study it. And while there is some hope that the Biden administration will back away from the most egregious of these attacks on the system, many of the US complaints pre-date the Trump era,[13] and US efforts to reform the WTO and willingness to take unilateral actions are unlikely to cease altogether.

Indeed, the US is not alone in feeling that the WTO no longer serves its interests and is thus in need of reform. Two issues in particular have risen to the fore in recent debates regarding WTO 'modernization'. First, the EU,[14]

10 'Trump Tweets: "Trade Wars Are Good, and Easy to Win"' (*Reuters*, 2 March 2018) <https://reut.rs/3h3so1N> accessed 30 April 2022.

11 Schaeffer (n 4).

12 Gregory Shaffer, Manfred Elsig, and Mark Pollack, 'The Slow Killing of the World Trade Organization' *Huffington Post* (17 November 2017) <https://bit.ly/2SRAQJ5> accessed 30 April 2022.

13 The unilateral attempt by the Obama administration to unseat Appellate Body Member Seung-wha Chang in May 2016. See Sung-jin Choi, 'US Set to Oust Korean Judge from WTO Appellate Body' *The Korea Times* (1 June 2016) <https://www.koreatimes.co.kr/www/tech/2020/09/693_206012.html> accessed 30 April 2022.

14 European Commission, Director General for Trade, 'Concept Paper on WTO Modernisation' 2018 <https://trade.ec.europa.eu/doclib/docs/2018/september/tradoc_157331.pdf> accessed 30 April 2022.

Australia,[15] and other wealthy economies have joined the US[16] in arguing that China, India, and other emerging markets should be stripped of their self-declared 'developing country' status at the WTO, as they believe that it is unfair to continue granting them special and differential treatment when their economies are among the world's largest (notwithstanding the fact that per capita income in these states remains relatively low).[17] Second, the EU, Japan, and others have also joined the US in voicing concerns regarding developing states' use of subsidies, proposing new punitive measures for countries that fail to properly notify their subsidies to the WTO,[18] and arguing that the WTO's current rules are out of date and inadequate for reining in China and other states that make extensive use of implicitly subsidized state-owned enterprises.[19] In addition to these two 'big-picture' criticisms, complaints are continually raised regarding the WTO's failure to prevent developing states from violating intellectual property rights to the detriment of Western companies (China's technology transfer practices have come under particular fire in this regard).[20]

The US is also not the only country that has turned to unilateral action and self-help in order to protect its domestic interests. For example, following the US decision to impose tariffs on steel and aluminum products in 2018, the EU and Canada both retaliated immediately, without waiting for a ruling from the WTO's dispute settlement system as to whether their retaliation was justified.[21] And as part of the EU's efforts to set up an alternate WTO dispute settlement mechanism that could arbitrate trade disputes among like-minded WTO Members while the Appellate Body is inoperative, the European Commission released a proposal to amend its trade Enforcement Regulation to permit the use of unilateral unauthorized countermeasures in cases where a WTO Panel ruled in the EU's favor but the decision could not be adopted or

15 Prime Minister Scott Morrison, 'Speech at Chicago Council on Global Affairs' (23 September 2019) <https://www.pm.gov.au/media/chicago-council-global-affairs> accessed 30 April 2022.

16 Presidential Documents, 'Reforming Developing-Country Status in the World Trade Organization' Federal Register Vol 84 No 147 (26 July 2019) <https://www.govinfo.gov/content/pkg/FR-2019-07-31/pdf/2019-16497.pdf> accessed 30 April 2022.

17 European Commission (n 14) 1.

18 Procedures to Enhance Transparency and Strengthen Notification Requirements under WTO Agreements (1 November 2018) JOB/GC/204/Rev.1 <https://bit.ly/33FxmLS> accessed 30 April 2022.

19 European Commission (n 14) 4.

20 This was a major subject of both the US and EU bilateral negotiations with China, and a subject of discussion during the trilateral talks between the US, the EU, and Japan.

21 Specifically, they did not wait for the WTO to rule on whether or not the US's action was a national security measure, as claimed by the US, or whether it was a safeguard measure, as the EU and Canada maintained. See Marianne Schneider-Petsinger, 'Stretching the Rules Will Not Save Global Trade' *Financial Times* (9 October 2019) <https://on.ft.com/3gU5smN> accessed 30 April 2022.

enforced due to the other party appealing the decision 'into the void'.[22] While these unilateral actions have been taken largely in response to US behavior, they nevertheless indicate that even the biggest champions of 'multilateralism' are willing to work outside of the system when they feel that their interests demand it.[23]

The Appellate Body crisis, the calls for WTO reform, and the turn to unilateralism by the US and others have certainly made this a challenging moment for the WTO. But they are also only the latest in a long series of perceived existential threats to the multilateral system of trade governance in the years since the WTO was founded in 1994. The WTO is no stranger to crisis.

Even before these latest developments, the WTO had been in the midst of a 'legislative crisis', with entrenched disagreements on policy issues among various member governments having led to a near-total standstill in the process of negotiating further liberalization. The Doha Development Round, the first negotiating round under the WTO initiated in 2001, had barely recovered from a collapse in the mid-2000s that '[left] global multilateralism in a parlous state', according to former WTO Director General Peter Sutherland.[24] These failures seemed even more ominous in the aftermath of the global financial crisis of 2008, leading many to question whether the WTO was the right tool for the job of managing global market integration. Recognizing these concerns, in 2012, the WTO itself convened a prescient public forum entitled 'Is Multilateralism in Crisis?' in which Director General Pascal Lamy addressed the organization's struggles to maintain multilateralism and global cooperation.[25] Today, the Doha Round continues to limp along with no end in sight and few major results achieved (with the notable exception of the Trade Facilitation Agreement).[26] The biennial Ministerial Conference held in Buenos Aires in 2017 failed to produce any significant outcomes, and concluded without a Ministerial Declaration for the first time in WTO history – a breakdown due in no small part to disagreements between the US and India

22 European Commission, 'Proposal for a Regulation of the European Parliament and of the Council Amending Regulation (EU) No 654/2014 of the European Parliament and of the Council Concerning the Exercise of the Union's Rights for the Application and Enforcement of International Trade rules' COM (2019) 623 final.

23 See Mike Smith, 'The EU, the US and the Crisis of Contemporary Multilateralism' (2018) 40 J Eur Integr 539; Christian Leffler, 'Championing Multilateralism' in Martin Westlake (ed), *The European Union's New Foreign Policy* (Springer 2020).

24 Alan Beattie, 'WTO Faces an Uncertain Future as its Negotiating System Seizes Up' *Financial Times* (25 July 2006).

25 Pascal Lamy, 'Multilateralism Is Struggling' (*WTO*, 24 September 2012) <https://www.wto.org/english/news_e/sppl_e/sppl244_e.htm> accessed 30 April 2022.

26 WTO, 'Protocol Amending the Marrakesh Agreement Establishing the World Trade Organisation' (28 November 2014) WT/L/940 <https://bit.ly/3eLa0Lf> accessed 30 April 2022.

over agricultural stockpiles and fishing subsidies.[27] Now the 2019 Nur-Sultan Conference, already postponed once to June 2020, has been pushed back again as a result of COVID-19.[28]

The 'legislative crisis' was itself taking place against the background of another 'crisis of multilateralism' caused by WTO Members' continued turn to bilateral, regional, and mega-regional trade agreements as the primary negotiating forums for deepening trade governance. This 'spaghetti-bowl crisis', which had been ongoing for the past two decades, had already spurred rafts of commentary about whether or not these individually-tailored treaties were 'termites in the trading system' that would fatally undermine multilateral trade governance, or whether instead they would deepen integration incrementally, ultimately leading to further multilateral trade liberalization.[29] For pessimists, the US negotiation of the mega-regional Trans-Atlantic Trade and Investment Partnership and the Trans-Pacific Partnership – which seemed *faits accomplis* in 2017 before the Trump administration surprised the world by pulling out of the deals – appeared at the time to be further nails in the multilateral coffin. Nor was the US the only 'culprit': other countries, too, have been pushing ahead with integration projects outside of the WTO, with major economic agreements like the African Continental Free Trade Agreement, the Eurasian Economic Union, ASEAN, and the China-led Belt and Road Initiative, among others, creating new dispersed centers of economic governance outside of direct Western control.

And all of this is not to mention the 'legitimacy crisis', which threatened the multilateral order in the late 1990s, and came to a head following the collapse of the Seattle Ministerial in 1999.[30] That crisis stemmed from the

27 'A Shameful Failure to Tackle Overfishing' *The Economist* (19 December 2017) <https://econ.st/3gQOqpw> accessed 30 April 2022.

28 WTO, 'Twelfth WTO Ministerial Conference' (*WTO*, undated) <https://bit.ly/3vTCmbv> accessed 30 April 2022.

29 Jagdish Bhagwati, *Termites in the Trading System: How Preferential Agreements Undermine Free Trade* (OUP 2008). See Sungjoon Cho, 'Defragmenting World Trade' (2006) 27 Nw J Int L & Bus 39; Stephen Joseph Powell and Trisha Law, 'Is the WTO Quietly Fading Away?: The New Regionalism and Global Trade Rules' (2011) 9 Geo J L & Pub Policy 261; Arie Reich, 'Bilateralism versus Multilateralism in International Trade Law: Applying the Principle of Subsidiarity' (2010) 60 UTLJ 263; Thomas Renard, 'Partnerships for Effective Multilateralism? Assessing the Compatibility between EU Bilateralism, (Inter-) Regionalism and Multilateralism' (2016) 29 Camb Rev Int Aff 18; Thomas Rixen and Ingo Rohlfing, 'The Institutional Choice of Bilateralism and Multilateralism in International Trade and Taxation' (2007) 12 Int Negot 389; Tamar Megiddo, 'Beyond Fragmentation: On International Law's Integrationist Forces' (2019) 44 Yale J Int L 115.

30 See Manfred Elsig, 'The World Trade Organization's Legitimacy Crisis: What Does the Beast Look Like?' (2007) 41 JWT 75; Daniel C Esty, 'The World Trade Organization's Legitimacy Crisis' (2002) 1 WTR 7; Rorden Wilkinson, 'The WTO in Crisis: Exploring the Dimensions of Institutional Inertia' (2001) 35 JWT 397.

deep divide between developed and developing country preferences on issues such as the expansion of the WTO's mandate into investment, procurement, and competition policy; whether environmental and labor issues should be brought onto the organization agenda; and the institution's insufficient focus on development – issues that to this day have still not been put to rest.[31]

It is plain to see from this litany of crises that there has never been a time when the WTO has been free of disagreement or contestation. Thus far, none of the 'crises of multilateralism' have actually resulted in the dissolution of the post-1994 system of trade governance. The WTO and its covered agreements have endured, despite these challenges, and the organization continues its work as the most important multilateral hub for trade negotiation and dispute settlement, even during the current difficulties. Given this history of persistent and endemic crisis, it may therefore be that those who speak of the 'crisis of multilateralism' continue to do so partially because they use the term 'multilateralism' to refer to much more than the bare survival of the WTO as a functioning organization, as Section 3 will now explore.

3 The meaning of multilateralism in public international trade law

'Multilateralism' can mean many different things, and *does in fact* mean many different things in the context of public international trade law. In the narrowest sense, 'multilateralism' may refer to nothing more than what Robert Keohane, in a famously descriptive definition in 1990, called 'the practice of co-ordinating national policies in groups of three or more states'.[32] Trade governance generally, and the WTO specifically, are certainly 'multilateral' according to this bare-bones definition: the WTO and its covered agreements coordinate policies among a large number of states (currently 164). As described in Section 2, the WTO has proven quite resilient as an organization, and its existing covered agreements continue to set the global baseline for trade policymaking. Even the (likely temporary) loss of the Appellate Body and the US turn to self-help during the Trump era have not put the WTO in serious jeopardy as a multilateral forum for the coordination of trade policy – they have, instead, spurred talks on how to reform, augment, or shift the system in response. It would be hard to find an institution or legal framework *anywhere* that did not have to contend with disagreement and rule-breaking to one degree or another, and even the exit of a powerful player would not necessarily mean the end of multilateral cooperation among the remaining members. The 'crisis of multilateralism' must therefore mean more than simply a danger to the nominal existence of the WTO and its covered agreements as mechanisms for coordinating international economic policy.

31 See Rorden Wilkinson, *Multilateralism and the World Trade Organisation: The Architecture and Extension of International Trade Regulation* (Routledge 2006).

32 Robert Keohane, 'Multilateralism: An Agenda for Research' (1990) 45 Int J 731.

Instead, 'multilateralism' in international economic law indicates a set of broader qualitative and substantive concerns regarding the political choice for peaceful, cooperative, and consultative trade relations, in contrast with economic policies characterized by conflict, self-help, and narrow self-interest. Common uses of 'multilateralism' can be roughly subdivided into three categories: (1) multilateralism as opposed to regionalism or bilateralism; (2) multilateralism as opposed to unilateralism; and (3) multilateralism as policy consensus.

First, the term 'multilateralism' is often heard in international economic policy discussions in the context of the turn to bilateralism and regionalism. Here, 'multilateralism' refers concretely to whether states choose to conduct economic policy negotiations at the 'multilateral' WTO, or instead within fragmented bilateral or regional groups. The 'crisis' of multilateralism in this sense refers to the fear that the WTO's role will be undermined as states turn to other forums to accomplish their trade policy goals. This was the subject of the 'spaghetti bowl' 'regionalism crisis' discussed in Section 2. Debates over whether regional and bilateral agreements are 'building blocks' or 'stumbling blocks' to further integration in the multilateral system are at this point well known.[33]

Second, 'multilateralism' is also used in contrast to unilateralism, as indicating a preference for institutionalism and mediated dispute settlement rather than self-help. Here, 'multilateralism' means a willingness to deal with trade policy and trade disputes through the diplomatic and quasi-judicial mechanisms provided by the WTO (either in addition to, or instead of, regional and bilateral trade agreements), rather than via unilateral actions: to 'jaw jaw' rather than 'war war' in Churchill's famous phrase. The 'crisis of multilateralism' in this context refers to the danger of states taking matters into their own hands, and using their economic power to coerce one another into altering their trade policies. This problem is also well known and well explored: the tendency for states to resort to unilateral action, political arm-twisting, and economic blackmail when they feel it is in their interest to do so is neither novel nor unexpected.

These two more functionalist definitions are complemented by (and interwoven with) a third use of the term 'multilateralism' in international economic law discourse – as a concept indicating not only multinational coordination or a preference for global (rather than regional) institutionalism and negotiated dispute settlement, but also as consensus on a set of normative principles. This is the most expansive sense of 'multilateralism' in the trade context, encompassing substantive norms as well as processes and practices. John Ruggie has called this the 'qualitative dimension' of multilateralism, arguing in response to Keohane's bare-bones definition that 'what is distinctive about multilateralism is not merely that it coordinates national

33 Jagdish Bhagwati, *The World Trading System at Risk* (Princeton UP 1991) 77; see further the works cited in (n 29).

policies in groups of three or more states … but that it does so on the basis of certain principles of ordering relations among those states'.[34] In his words, these principles are 'generalized principles of conduct … which specify appropriate conduct for a class of actions, without regard to the particularistic interests of the parties or the strategic exigencies that may exist in any specific occurrence'.[35] Providing examples from the realm of international economic law, he argued that such substantive principles include 'the norm of MFN [most favored nation] treatment, corresponding rules about reciprocal tariff reductions and the application of safeguards, and collectively sanctioned procedures for implementing the rules'.[36] The idea that 'multilateralism' has substantive semantic content is evident in international economic law discussions. For example, James Bacchus, former member of the WTO Appellate Body, has written of the need for 'a way back to multilateralism in trade' as both an antidote to unilateralism and as a remedy for 'protectionism' – the idea that countries should not protect their markets through tariffs, unnecessary or discriminatory regulations, or other measures at the expense of their neighbors.[37] Daniel Chow similarly contrasts multilateralism with both 'vicious nationalism' and 'protectionism'.[38]

Each of these definitions of multilateralism is used at various times in discussions of international trade law. When they are used in the context of the crisis narrative, they all share a common feature: they contrast an imagined past in which multilateral cooperation existed with a present day in which regionalism, unilateralism, and dissensus are on the rise. What's more, each of them carries within it strong normative policy preferences: for centralized trade governance, institutionalized dispute settlement, and substantive norms, such as MFN treatment, the desirability of tariff reductions, the illegitimacy of protectionism, and abolition of 'unnecessary' barriers to trade.

4 The myth of 'multilateralism' in the WTO

The trouble with the 'crisis of multilateralism' is that the image of the past on which it relies is a false one – or is at least incomplete. In terms of the three specific meanings of multilateralism outlined above: there was never a time when multilateralism supplanted regionalism; there was never a time when unilateralism and self-help were eliminated; and there was never a time when consensus on core substantive issues of economic policy was achieved.

34 John G Ruggie, 'Multilateralism: The Anatomy of an Institution' (1992) 46 Int Organ 561, 567.

35 Ibid 571.

36 Ibid.

37 James Bacchus, 'We Need a Way Back to Multilateralism in Trade' (*Cato At Liberty*, 16 July 2019) <https://bit.ly/3eHvTeh> accessed 30 April 2022.

38 Daniel Chow, 'U.S. Trade Infallibility and the Crisis of the World Trade Organization' (2020) Mich St L Rev 4.

4.1 Multilateralism versus regionalism

The idea that the current trade landscape is dominated by 'regionalism' whereas the past was an era of 'multilateralism' is questionable. It is indisputable that there are *more* regional and bilateral agreements today than ever before. As of 20 September 2020, there were 306 such agreements in force and notified to the WTO.[39] However, regional and bilateral agreements pre-date and have always coexisted with the WTO. The General Agreement on Tariffs and Trade (GATT) of 1947 recognized and provided exceptions for regional integration, even referring to regional agreements as affirmatively *desirable*,[40] and the WTO continued this tradition.[41] Some 39 such agreements had entered into force prior to the WTO's birth in 1995;[42] indeed, the Organization came onto the scene in the midst of the so-called 'second wave' of regional treaties that began in the early 1990s following the end of the Cold War and the opening of previously closed economies to wider international trade. Despite the attempt by the GATT and GATS to impose certain requirements for regional and bilateral agreements to benefit from the MFN exemption, no agreement has ever been found inconsistent with the multilateral regime, and WTO Members seem content to continue on this path. Taking all of this into account, Alberta Fabbricotti has argued that 'the axiom of the WTO universality is tenable only considering the twofold essence of this international organization, within which the two paradigms of multilateralism and regionalism coexist'.[43]

Second, viewing the WTO as a multilateral system in this sense papers over an important aspect of its governance: that though WTO commitments are multilateralized and apply on an MFN basis once they are approved, the negotiation of these commitments largely takes place bilaterally or within groups. This is true of both individual members' commitments, as well as of ongoing negotiations as part of the single undertaking. The reciprocity principle sits at the core of the WTO legal system. New candidates for WTO membership must negotiate their schedules of concessions with current members, a process that most often takes place on a state-to-state bilateral basis.

39 WTO, 'Regional Trade Agreements' (*WTO*, undated) <https://www.wto.org/english/tratop_e/region_e/region_e.htm> accessed 30 April 2022.

40 'The contracting parties recognize the *desirability* of increasing freedom of trade by the development, through voluntary agreements, of closer integration between the economies of the countries parties to such agreements' GATT Article XXIV (4) (emphasis added).

41 GATS Article V; Decision on Differential and More Favourable Treatment, Reciprocity and Fuller Participation of Developing Countries (1979) ('Enabling Clause').

42 WTO, 'Regional Trade Agreements Database' (*WTO*, undated) <http://rtais.wto.org/UI/PublicAllRTAList.aspx> accessed 30 April 2022.

43 Alberta Fabbricotti, 'Universalism and Regionalism in International Trade Law: Is the WTO a Truly Universal International Organization?' in *Scritti in Memoria di Maria Rita Saulle*, Vol I (Editoriale Scientifica 2014) 559, 573.

In the words of the Appellate Body: 'Tariff negotiations are a process of reciprocal demands and concessions, of "give and take"'.[44] Concessions create rights and obligations between individual members, and dispute resolution regarding breaches of those obligations thus takes place *inter partes* rather than *erga omnes*. Indeed, WTO dispute settlement does not speak of 'breach' but rather of the 'nullification or impairment of benefits' to the complaining member, and any authorization of retaliation is granted on a bilateral basis and to a degree reflecting only the bilateral damage. Moreover, renegotiations of trade concessions can take place among subsets of members with substantial trade interests in the sector concerned: no collective consultation is required.[45] Thus, as Joost Pauwelyn has argued, despite the multilateral framework of the WTO, members' commitments are essentially of an individualized and bilateral character.[46]

Third, bilateral and plurilateral negotiations are the norm during liberalization discussions at the WTO, despite the multilateral framework in which they take place. It is well known that the difficulties posed by consensus decision-making are a major challenge for the WTO.[47] Because of the WTO's consensus rule, the members have made extensive use of informal processes in which smaller groups of countries conduct pre-negotiation sessions to come to agreements amongst themselves prior to multilateral talks. Before the collapse of the Seattle Ministerial, the so-called 'green room' practices had already led to accusations that the WTO was essentially a 'rich man's club' dominated by the Quad (Canada, the EU, the US, Japan), who acted as 'deal-makers' while the remainder of the states were relegated to being 'deal-takers'. Despite the extension of the Quad to the G-6 and other formations in more recent years, the consensus decision-making practices at the WTO continue to favor plurilateral negotiations among the more powerful states – suggesting that 'multilateralism' may often be simply plurilateralism in disguise. Indeed, one of the most common explanations for the turn to bilateral and regional agreements as the primary forums for further negotiations is that the major economies can no longer get what they want at the WTO, as developing countries have refused to take on new issues within the multilateral framework until the Doha Development Round has been completed, and they have achieved some of their own trade policy goals.

44 Appellate Body Report, *European Communities – Customs Classification of Certain Computer Equipment* (5 June 1998) WT/DS62/AB/R, WT/DS67/AB/R, WT/DS68/AB/R [109].

45 GATT Article XXVIII, GATS Article XXI.

46 Joost Pauwelyn, 'A Typology of Multilateral Treaty Obligations: Are WTO Obligations Bilateral or Collective in Nature?' (2003) EJIL 907.

47 This was the major result of the so-called 'Sutherland Report' in 2004. See 'Report by the Consultative Board to the Director-General Supachai Panitchpakdi' in WTO, *The Future of the WTO: Addressing Institutional Challenges in the New Millennium* (WTO 2004).

All of this leads to the conclusion that the multilateral WTO has always existed alongside, through, in concert with, as well as in tension with, multiple forms of bilateralism, regionalism, and plurilateralism. There is not now, and never has been, a time when WTO-based multilateralism or collective action supplanted these other forms of economic integration *tout court*.

4.2 Multilateralism versus unilateralism

The idea that there has been a turn to 'unilateralism' that upsets a 'multilateral' past also needs to be reconsidered. It is certainly true that the US and other countries have in recent years resorted to using unilateral self-help measures in pursuit of their trade policy goals without regard to the rules and procedures of the WTO. But this, too, is not a new development. Despite the availability of the WTO's negotiation, conciliation, and dispute settlement mechanisms, countries have never ceased to employ unilateral means to try to influence the behavior of their trading partners. As a case in point, the US's Section 301 unilateral tariff sanctions policy has been the subject of perennial complaints since the GATT days. Even at what was arguably the high-water point of international trade multilateralism – the conclusion of the Marrakesh Agreement and the birth of the WTO in 1995 – the Japan-US dispute over autos saw the US mobilizing Section 301, rather than the newly formed WTO dispute settlement system, to threaten a 100 percent tariff on imports of Japanese luxury cars in order to pressure Japan to do away with perceived unfair trade practices in the auto parts market.[48] Indeed, the US pursued unilateral action in this case despite the fact that the EU and Japan had consented to the WTO's more highly judicialized dispute settlement mechanisms partially in exchange for reassurances that the US would begin using the WTO dispute settlement system instead of its own domestic 301 process as a first port of call for dispute resolution.[49]

Perhaps more novel from this perspective is the weakening of the WTO as an institution, most particularly by the US refusal to support the appointment of new members to the Appellate Body. One of the goals of the WTO is to reduce unilateral action and avoid the possibility of trade wars by channeling conflicts through the WTO's third-party dispute settlement system.[50] This function is seriously impeded by the Appellate Body's ceasing to function, leading to real questions about the effective enforcement of the covered agreements pending Appellate Body reform.

48 See Jay L Eizenstat, 'The Impact of the World Trade Organization on Unilateral United States Trade Sanctions under Section 301 of the Trade Act of 1974: A Case Study of the Japanese Auto Dispute and the Fuji-Kodak Dispute' (1997) 11 Emory Int L Rev 137.

49 William J Davey, 'The WTO and Rules-Based Dispute Settlement: Historical Evolution, Operational Success, and Future Challenges' (2014) 27 JIEL 679, 686.

50 Article III:3 of Marrakesh Agreement Establishing the World Trade Organization.

However, the 'crisis of multilateralism' narrative hides something here, too: that the US defection from the WTO dispute settlement system is directly related to the fact that this system has, over time, become less biased in its favor. As Gregory Shaffer explains, at the birth of the WTO in 1995, the US and the EU[51] were in a uniquely privileged position in terms of public and private legal resources, giving them a major institutional advantage in dispute settlement.[52] What's more, the fact that enforcement of disputes ultimately relies on retaliation – with the winning party being authorized to suspend trade concessions granted to the losing party in an amount equivalent to the injury – means that larger economies are favored over smaller ones.[53] In terms of cost, access to legal resources, and ability to retaliate, then, the US and the EU were for some time at a significant structural advantage in WTO dispute settlement.

Today, things have changed. Access to justice has improved through the establishment of the Advisory Centre on WTO Law, which provides legal assistance to developing countries pursuing dispute settlement claims and has become a significant player in trade disputes.[54] Emerging economies – China, in particular – have become regular participants in WTO dispute settlement, holding the US and the EU to account for their application of anti-dumping policies, countervailing duties, safeguards, sanitary and phytosanitary standards, and other rules in an unbiased and non-protectionist way.[55] Though the US still has a much higher 'win rate' than China in these disputes (with the US winning every one of its cases against China, while China's cases see more mixed success),[56] it has increasingly seen the WTO as constraining its policy freedom in a way that it had not initially anticipated.

51 The term the EU is used throughout this contribution for the purpose of clarity, despite the fact that in some instances – here included – the term European Communities would be historically appropriate.

52 See Gregory C Shaffer, *Defending Interests: Public-Private Partnerships in WTO Litigation* (Brookings Institution Press 2003).

53 See Hakan Nordstrom and Gregory Shaffer, 'Access to Justice in the World Trade Organization: The Case for a Small Claims Tribunal?' (2008) 7 WTR 587.

54 See Advisory Centre on WTO Law <https://www.acwl.ch/> accessed 30 April 2022.

55 See e.g. Appellate Body Report, *US – Definitive Safeguard Measures on Imports of Certain Steel Products* (10 November 2003) WT/DS248/AB/R, WT/DS249/AB/R, WT/DS251/AB/R, WT/DS252/AB/R; WT/DS253/AB/R, WT/DS254/AB/R, WT/DS258/AB/R, WT/DS259/AB/R; Panel Report, *US – Certain Measures Affecting Imports of Poultry from China* (29 September 2010) WT/DS392/R; Panel Report, *US – Anti-Dumping Measures on Certain Shrimp and Diamond Sawblades from China* (8 June 2012) WT/DS422/R/Add.1; Appellate Body Report, *US – Countervailing and Anti-Dumping Measures on Certain Products from China* (7 July 2014) WT/DS449/AB/R.

56 Jeffrey J Schott and Euijin Jung, 'In US-China Trade Disputes, the WTO Usually Sides with the United States' (*Peterson Institute for International Economics*, 12 March 2019) <https://bit.ly/3h1Mr0H> accessed 30 April 2022.

Just as there was no past historical moment when multilateralism eliminated unilateralism and self-help from the world of international economic policy, there was also no time when the WTO dispute settlement system was a model of multilateralism based on the rule of law, free from systemic bias and institutional lopsidedness. The past was not egalitarian – it was one in which the US and other big economies had numerous structural advantages that gave them outsized power in the WTO system, and in which powerful states continued to engage in strong-arm self-help tactics in order to achieve their economic goals despite the availability of WTO dispute settlement. Now that China has joined the WTO and emerging economies have begun to use the WTO to their advantage, it is worth considering whether the US has ramped up its use of self-help measures and sabotaged the Appellate Body in order to *preserve* the unilateral power *it has always had* in trade disputes. Once again, the 'crisis of multilateralism' discourse encourages a manufactured nostalgia for a 'fair and cooperative' past that never truly existed: unilateral action was never entirely supplanted by the multilateral WTO system, and the big players always had an unfair advantage in trade disputes.

4.3 Multilateralism as consensus

The vast majority of the world's states are members of the WTO – 164 at the current count, representing 98 percent of global trade.[57] However, this widespread *participation* ought not be mistaken for *consensus* on the contours of economic law as a constitutionalist or cosmopolitan project. In the words of Laurence Boisson de Chazournes: the 'ambition to create a global public order … has not prospered in international economic law'.[58]

Despite the hegemonic rhetoric that liberalized trade policy is an unqualified good, the modern history of international economic governance has been characterized not by consensus, but rather by disagreement and partiality, both in theory and in practice. Indeed, none of the core normative principles of WTO law are or were apolitical, without distributional consequences, or universally agreed upon.

Take, for example, the central principle of non-discrimination in the application of trade rules. Post-World War II trade policy was shaped by the GATT drafters' common experience of protectionism during the inter-war period, leading to some concurrence on non-discrimination as the backbone of international economic policy. However, even the non-discrimination principle was more advantageous for some than others: it was adopted after a targeted campaign by the US to end the UK's preferential arrangements with

57 WTO, 'WTO in Brief' (*WTO*, undated) <https://bit.ly/3dc0e3n> accessed 30 April 2022.

58 Laurence Boisson de Chazournes, 'International Economic Law and the Quest for Universality' (2019) 32 LJIL 401, 402.

its current and former colonies, which the US saw as threatening its commercial interests.[59]

Tariff reduction, too, was designed to further the interests of the original GATT drafters. The focus on lowering tariffs and eliminating protectionism was linked, as Ha-Joon Chang argues, to protecting the interests of developed economies who no longer needed to make use of interventionist industrial policies such as infant industry protection – the 'free trade' approach was not devised with the needs of diverse or developing states in mind, but rather with an eye to providing markets for the competitive industries of the Global North.[60] What's more, the free trade agenda always targeted some tariffs while leaving aside others. The notable exclusion of developed country agricultural quotas from the GATT's liberalization agenda was a case in point, as was the sheltering of developed country textile industries under the Multi-Fibre Arrangement. While developing countries were generally not required to make substantial concessions in pre-Uruguay Round trade negotiations, they were also unable to pressure the developed world to open markets in key sectors. It was in fact the ineffectiveness of the early GATT in addressing these concerns that led to the establishment of the UN Conference on Trade and Development in 1964, which was intended as a forum where the economic needs of the developing world would receive greater attention.[61] The rhetoric of free trade coupled with the reality of selective tariff liberalization skewed the benefits of trade in favor of some countries and some industries while ignoring or undermining the needs of others, contradicting the narrative of consensus on the 'universal good' of across-the-board tariff reductions.

The establishment of the WTO in 1994 came at the height of the 'Washington Consensus' era, a moment when policy concurrence around a (neo-)liberal economic model was imagined to have been achieved, at least by its cheerleaders in the District of Columbia. The WTO brought new disciplines in a host of areas and deepened the existing rules on trade in goods while strengthening the dispute settlement mechanism, pushing the 'rules-based system' of trade governance farther than it had ever gone before. But here, too, the triumphalist assertions of the 'end of history'[62] belied the internal dissent and contestation that accompanied the birth of the organization.

To give only the most obvious example, the new areas over which the WTO gained authority were selectively chosen and their benefits were far from evenly distributed. The focus on intellectual property protection and the liberalization of services trade (at least in the modes of cross-border provision and investment) strongly favored the interests of the US, the EU, and other

59 Dani Rodrik, *The Globalization Paradox: Why Global Markets, States, and Democracy Can't Coexist* (OUP 2011) 70.

60 Ha-Joon Chang, *Kicking Away the Ladder: Development Policy in Historical Perspective* (Anthem Press 2002).

61 Constantine Michalopoulos, *Developing Countries in the WTO* (Palgrave Macmillan 2001) 27.

62 Francis Fukuyama, 'The End of History?' (1989) The National Interest 3.

services hubs and capital exporters, with developing countries agreeing to these disciplines only as part of a bargain whereby developed states would later begin phasing out textile and agricultural controls.[63] This selectivity was a direct cause of the 'legitimacy crisis' that reached a critical peak in 1999, when developing countries who felt they had not reaped the results of the Uruguay Round refused to enter into negotiations about further liberalization of procurement, competition, investment, and other areas pushed by the developed world until they saw some movement on issues relevant to them. The opening of the Doha Development Round – which, as noted above, is essentially moribund – was the response to these demands.

The point of these few examples is simply to demonstrate what should be obvious to any critical observer: that there was no point at which the WTO or its covered agreements represented a policy consensus. At best, they represented partial and contextual agreements to work together on issues of international economic governance *despite* deep and continued divergence on fundamental issues. Robert Hudec referred to this tension as the 'political theatre' dimension of international economic law, and described it in the following terms:

> The international agreements in this area, like international agreements generally, are frequently documents which claim to solve problems, but in fact merely paper over conflicting national positions without resolving them. The normal way of doing this is to create legal documents embroidered with elegant ambiguities, but the same result can be achieved whenever agreements simply declare divergent understandings about clear texts.[64]

The WTO's covered agreements are full of such 'elegant ambiguities', postponements, and divergences. They are and were contingent agreements to cooperate on certain aspects of trade policy in exchange for certain benefits in terms of market access, dispute settlement, and so on – *not* fully formed consensus-based programs with universal validity. Indeed, portraying WTO rules as representing multilateral consensus – as the crisis narrative implicitly does – elevates their status from 'contingent agreements' to 'universal truths' and thus grants them an aura of incontestability. The 'crisis of multilateralism' discourse, in this sense, fits Koskenniemi's description of an international order in which 'the winners have consolidated their victory by the institutions they rule' and use the language of expertise, universalism, and reason to advance projects that serve their particular interests, and not some idealized conception of an agreed common good.[65]

63 Michalopoulos (n 61).

64 Robert E Hudec, 'International Economic Law: The Political Theatre Dimension' (1996) 17 U Pa J Int Econ L 9, 9.

65 Martti Koskenniemi, 'International Law and the Far Right: Reflections on Law and Cynicism' (2019) Fourth Annual TMC Asser Lecture at 6.

5 Conclusion: multilateralism as political discourse

The challenges that the WTO faces today are serious ones: the rebellious US that during the Trump administration sabotaged the Appellate Body and ramped up its use of punitive tariffs as tools of economic policy; a negotiating deadlock that has seen a near-total failure to achieve further liberalization of trade rules in the post-1994 era; the (related) turn to bilateralism and regionalism as alternative forums for trade policy negotiations; and the push by the 'West' for WTO 'modernization', to name just a few. These are, indeed, tough days for the organization, and it is easy to see why commentators would speak of a 'crisis of multilateralism' in this context. The WTO, a multilateral organization in Keohane's sense above, seems to be struggling to fulfill its function.

This chapter has argued, however, that the 'crisis of multilateralism' rhetoric should be scrutinized rather more closely. While on its face it appears to be merely a neutral descriptive phrase that sums up the challenges facing the WTO, it is in fact much more than this: it is an unacknowledged political discourse that invites us to imagine the world in accordance with its underlying presumptions. Specifically, it assumes, implies, and in some cases directly articulates an imagined past in which cooperation, community, and consensus were the order of the day, in contrast with a present characterized by regionalism, unilateralism, and disagreement.

But this imagined 'multilateral' past never really existed: multilateral negotiations never supplanted bilateral and regional economic cooperation (or coercion); countries have never stopped using unilateral measures to achieve their economic policy goals (including by leveraging their economic power *within* WTO dispute settlement); and there was never a time when the substantive content of trade governance was anywhere near uncontested or universally agreed upon. Instead, the history of trade governance in general and the WTO in particular has been one filled with inequality, partiality, contestation, and resistance – in addition to agreement. It is a history of 'political theatre' and power politics and contingency – in addition to cooperation.

The 'crisis of multilateralism' discourse papers over the disagreements, power struggles, and inequality that have characterized trade governance. In doing so, it promotes a hegemonic vision of a global economic order to which the only alternatives are unreasonable, short-sighted, or 'populist'. But this consensus-based understanding of trade policy is demonstrably false, and opposition to a partial and contingent system is not, in itself, illegitimate.

Martti Koskenniemi recently cautioned that

> international lawyers ought to re-examine their commitment to present global institutions. Like all institutions, they operate under ideas and assumptions that are contestable and revisable but that tend to be taken as natural and obvious by the people who work in them.[66]

66 Ibid 7.

The idea that the WTO represents a triumph of multilateralism – in any sense other than the most mundane – is one such assumption that ought to be revisited. Re-examining this ‘multilateral’ institution in light of the current crises it faces may cause us to come to some very different conclusions than those suggested by the ‘crisis of multilateralism’ discourse: that perhaps the US is going rogue in order to *preserve* an unequal status that it long held *within* the system; that perhaps the Doha Round negotiations have failed because the promise of focusing on developing countries’ needs is *incompatible* with the interests protected by the covered agreements (that is to say, the interests of the rich); that perhaps the rhetoric of ‘multilateralism’ should be recognized as a *political* discourse – not a historical fact.

13 The EU's Reform of the Investor-State Dispute Resolution System

A Bilateral Path towards a Multilateral Solution

Ewa Żelazna

1 Introduction

Since the entry into force of the Treaty of Lisbon,[1] the European Union (the EU or the Union) has become the champion of reforms in international investment law[2] and its common international investment policy has given a new impetus to the process of multilateralization in the field. The Union has begun to replace the bilateral investment treaties (BITs) previously concluded by the Member States, consolidating the existing network of agreements. Additionally, the EU has been spearheading the initiative to establish a Multilateral Investment Court during the negotiations of the UNCITRAL Working Group III.

The Union is required in its external action to adhere to the principles that inspired its creation as well as promote multilateral solutions to common problems.[3] In this regard, the Treaty on European Union (TEU) provides the foundations for value-based leadership by the EU on the international plane, which could positively contribute to the process of constitutionalisation in international economic law (IEL). The EU's ultimate ambition is to incorporate an agreement on investment protection into the framework of the World Trade Organization (WTO).[4] However, several attempts to conclude a multilateral investment treaty have failed in the past and, as a new actor in the

1 The Treaty of Lisbon amending the Treaty on European Union and the Treaty Establishing the European Community [2007] OJ C 306/1. The Treaty of Lisbon expanded the EU's external competences, in particular, the scope of the common commercial policy in Article 207 TFEU to incorporate foreign direct investment (FDI), which has enabled the Union to develop a comprehensive policy on investment protection.

2 European Commission, 'Communication from the Commission to the Council, the European Parliament, the European Economic and Social Committee and the Committee of Regions: Towards a Comprehensive European International Investment Policy' COM (2010) 343 final; European Commission, 'Trade for All: Towards a More Responsible Trade and Investment Policy' (October 2015) <https://bit.ly/3cHTKsR> accessed 30 April 2022.

3 Article 21 of the Consolidated versions of the Treaty on European Union and the Treaty on the Functioning of the European Union [2012] OJ C 326/13.

4 European Commission ('Trade for All') (n 2).

DOI: 10.4324/9781003312857-15

field, the EU has faced an uphill battle to build support for its reform proposals. Drawing on the lessons of the past, the Union has therefore adopted a unique approach to use its bilateral treaties with third countries[5] as building blocks of a systemic reform in the field of investment law.[6]

This chapter evaluates the EU's bilateral path towards establishing a Multilateral Investment Court. Section 2 discusses the interaction and the relationships between the bilateral and multilateral approaches to the development of IEL from a theoretical perspective, drawing on the legal and economic literature. Section 3 outlines the evolution of the EU's approach in its bilateral treaty-making practice and evaluates the Investment Court system incorporated in the EU's investment treaties, which is intended as a stepping-stone towards the establishment of the multilateral dispute resolution body. Section 4 looks at the negotiating progress of the UNCITRAL Working Group III, focusing on the question whether the EU's bilateral and multilateral actions have been mutually reinforcing thus far, and identifying improvements that could be made in the future.

2 Bilateralism versus multilateralism?

Multilateralism as an approach to organising international economic relations between States has enjoyed a degree of success in the post-war era. The General Agreement on Tariffs and Trade (GATT) 1947 and the subsequently-created WTO have achieved significant reductions of tariffs and non-tariff barriers to trade and established an institutional framework for the peaceful resolution of trade disputes.[7] However, the slow progress of the latest WTO negotiating round and the institutional crisis caused by the United States (US) during the Trump Administration have increased States' reliance on bilateral treaties.[8] While the WTO Agreements recognise that preferential trade agreements can contribute to the goal of trade liberalisation, hence in certain circumstances their conclusion is permitted,[9] some economists have

5 Countries that are not members of the EU.

6 Council of the European Union, 'Negotiating Directives for a Convention Establishing a Multilateral Court for the Settlement of Investment Disputes' (20 March 2018) 12981/17 ADD 1 DCL.

7 Robert E Baldwin, 'The Case for a Multilateral Trade Organization' in Martin Daunton, Amrita Narlikar, and Robert M Stern (eds), *The Oxford Handbook of the World Trade Organisation* (OUP 2012).

8 WTO, 'World Trade Report 2011, The WTO and Preferential Trade: From Co-existence to Coherence' (WTO Publications 2011) <https://www.wto.org/english/res_e/publications_e/wtr11_e.htm>; UNCTAD, 'World Investment Report 2015. Reforming International Investment Governance' (United Nations Publications 2015) <https://unctad.org/system/files/official-document/wir2015_en.pdf> both accessed 30 April 2022. See also Chapters 11 and 12 in this volume.

9 Article XXIV of the General Agreement on Tariffs and Trade 1994, Marrakesh Agreement Establishing the World Trade Organization, Annex 1A (entry into force 1 January 1995) 1867 UNTS 187; Article V of the General Agreement on

demonstrated that such an approach is not welfare-enhancing and preferential trade agreements should be regarded as stumbling, rather than building, blocks to international free trade.[10] Bilateralism has also faced criticism from international lawyers, who have pointed out that such a practice undermines international solidarity and fails to provide an adequate response to common challenges, such as the accelerating anthropocentric global warming, environmental degradation, or world peace.[11] Nonetheless, bilateral treaties continue to lure States by their reputation of being the 'workhorse of international law', which carries a promise of achieving quick results.[12]

During these challenging times for the international community, the EU has tried to fill the leadership vacuum left by the US and preserve the multilateral legal order. The most notable effort has been the plurilateral agreement that ensures the continued availability of the dispute resolution procedure at the WTO.[13] The EU's approach can be regarded as symptomatic of a growing tendency to use routes other than traditional multi-party negotiations to advance multilateral objectives (e.g. the liberalisation of free trade or institutional reforms). Other strategies, labelled 'multilateralising bilateralism', are not uncommon and may include extending existing preferential arrangements to encompass additional parties through the most favoured nation provisions, geographical expansion of free trade agreements (FTAs), or regulatory harmonisation.[14]

In the field of international investment law, which comprises thousands of BITs, a certain degree of multilateralisation has been observed.[15] In this context, the multilateralisation has been conceptualised, thus far, as a normative

Trade in Services, Marrakesh Agreement Establishing the World Trade Organization, Annex 1B (entry into force 1 January 1995) 1869 UNTS 183.

10 Jacob Viner, *The Customs Union Issue* (Paul Oslington ed, OUP 2014); Jagdish Bhagwati, 'Regionalism versus Multilateralism' (1992) 15(5) World Econ 535; Richard E Baldwin, 'Multilateralising Regionalism: Spaghetti Bowls as Building Blocks on the Path to Global Free Trade' (2006) 29(11) World Econ 1451; Jagdish Bhagwati, *Termites in the Trading System* (OUP 2008).

11 Bruno Simma, 'From Bilateralism to Community Interest in International Law' (1997) 250 RCADI; José E Alvarez, 'Multilateralism and Its Discontents' (2000) 11(2) EJIL 393; Philip Allott, 'Making the New International Law: Law of the Sea as Law of the Future' (1985) 40(3) Int J 442.

12 The expression was first coined by Simma and later repeated by Schill. See Simma (n 11) 323; Stephan W Schill, *The Multilateralization of International Investment Law* (CUP 2009).

13 Elisa Baroncini, 'Saving the Right to Appeal at the WTO: The EU and the Multi-Party Interim Appeal Arbitration Agreement' (*Federalismi.it*, 22 July 2020) <https://bit.ly/35g0Lgj> accessed 30 April 2022; Multi-Party Interim Appeal Arbitration Agreement Pursuant to Article 25 of the DSU (27 March 2020) JOB/DSB/1/Add.1 2.

14 Richard Baldwin, Simon Evenett, and Patrick Low, 'Beyond Tariffs: Multilateralizing Non-tariff RTA Commitments' in Richard Baldwin and Patrick Low (eds), *Multilateralizing Regionalism: Challenges for the Global Trading System* (CUP 2012).

15 Schill (n 12).

convergence, with many bilateral treaties containing either identical or very similar provisions.[16] This phenomenon has challenged the conception of bilateral and multilateral actions of States on the international scene as being mutually exclusive. The need for a paradigm shift in the thinking about the relationship between bilateralism and multilateralism has been highlighted in the legal and economic literature.[17] In this regard, Bhagwati, a proponent of multilateralism, stated: '[t]hose who think of the two as alternatives are prisoners of defunct modes of thinking, based on the days when protection was a different beast'.[18] Therefore the modern approach is to regard the bilateral undertakings of States as a way towards a gradual multilateralisation of the rules governing a particular field, in line with the ideas that have been advanced by economists like Baldwin[19] and lawyers like Schill.[20]

The emergence of the EU as an actor in international investment law has facilitated the process of multilateralisation in the field[21] consistently with the conceptual framework advanced by Baldwin. This is due to the fact that the transfer of competences from the Member States to the Union has resulted in the consolidation of the existing network of BITs.[22] In this regard, the Union's new investment agreements have replaced those of individual Member States, while in the *Achmea* case, the Court of Justice of the European Union (CJEU) ruled that all intra-EU BITs should be terminated.[23] Moreover, in accordance with Article 21 TEU, the EU has the obligation to promote multilateral solutions to common problems and an international system based on stronger multilateral cooperation.[24] The EU law principles that govern the exercise of its external competences, such as sincere cooperation, solidarity, and unity in external representation, could further contribute to multilateral progress by ensuring the unequivocal support of the Member States, thus strengthening the EU's bargaining power in international negotiations.[25]

In external relations, the EU regards itself as a normative power and the 'Trade for All' strategy has further developed the Union's identity around this

16 Ibid.

17 Arie Reich, 'Bilateralism Versus Multilateralism in International Economic Law: Applying the Principle of Subsidiarity' (2010) 60(2) UTLJ 263.

18 Bhagwati ('Regionalism') (n 10) 547.

19 Baldwin, Evenett, and Low (n 14); Baldwin (n 10); Schill (n 12).

20 Schill (n 12).

21 Baldwin (n 10).

22 Regulation (EU) 1219/2012 of the European Parliament and the Council of 12 December 2012 establishing transitional arrangements for bilateral investment agreements between Member States and third countries [2012] OJ L351/40.

23 Ibid; C-284/16 *Slowakische Republik v Achmea BV* [2018] ECLI:EU:C:2018:158; Agreement for the Termination of Bilateral Investment Treaties between the Member States of the European Union [2020] OJ L169/1.

24 Article 21 TEU.

25 Marise Cremona (ed), *Structural Principles of EU External Relations Law* (Hart 2018).

concept.[26] Since the entry into force of the Treaty of Lisbon, the EU has been implementing changes in the system of international investment protection and embarked upon the ambitious task of leading the establishment of a Multilateral Investment Court. Despite the EU's strong geo-political position, the Commission – a body that sets the Union's international trade and investment strategies – has envisaged serious difficulties associated with negotiating proposals at multilateral fora. Therefore, after a period of deliberation, the Commission proposed an interim change to the investor-State dispute settlement process that would be implemented in the EU's new bilateral treaties, which would serve as building blocks for a new multilateral court.

The proposed solution develops, in an innovative way, the idea that bilateralism can lead to the gradual multilateralisation of the legal framework that governs international relations between States by applying it not only to the extension of preferential treatment but also to influence an institutional change. Section 3 describes the path that led the EU to the development of this approach, providing the background to the critical evaluation of the Commission's strategy in the subsequent parts.

3 The development of EU's policy on investment protection

Despite the initial uncertainty about the scope of the EU's new FDI competence,[27] the Commission announced its intentions to develop a policy on international investment protection soon after the entry into force of the Treaty of Lisbon.[28] While the first Communication, which broadly outlined the objectives of the Union's actions in the area, included hints of the

26 European Commission ('Trade for All') (n 2); Ian Manners, 'Normative Power Europe: A Contradiction in Terms?' (2002) 40(2) J Com Mar St 235; Ernst-Ulrich Petersmann, 'How to Evaluate the European Union as a Normative Power in Multilevel Governance of Public Goods? Methodological Pluralism and its Constitutional Limits in European Governance', in Christine Kaddous (ed), *The European Union in International Organisations and Global Governance: Recent Developments* (Hart 2001).

27 Marc Bungenberg, 'The Division of Competences between the EU and Its Member States in the Area of Investment Politics' in Marc Bungenberg, Joern Griebel, and Steffen Hindelang (eds), *International Investment Law and EU Law* (Springer 2011) 29–42; Markus Krajewski, 'The Reform of the Common Commercial Policy' in Andrea Biondi, Piet Eeckhout, and Stefanie Ripley (eds), *EU Law After Lisbon* (OUP 2012) 292–311; Julien Chaisse, 'Promises and Pitfalls of the European Union Policy on Foreign Investment – How Will the New EU Competence on FDI Affect the Emerging Global Regime?' (2012) 15(1) JIEL 51; Wenhua Shan and Sheng Zhang, 'The Treaty of Lisbon: Halfway Toward a Common Investment Policy' (2010) 21(4) EJIL 1049; Anna De Luca, 'New Developments on the Scope of the EU Common Commercial Policy under the Lisbon Treaty: Investment Liberalisation vs. Investment Protection?' (2012) Yb Int L & Pol 165.

28 European Commission ('Communication') (n 2).

Commission's plans to reform the system of investor–State arbitration, the scale of its ambition was not immediately apparent.[29] The Commission's initial proposals were limited to strengthening the commitment to transparency in arbitration proceedings, as well as improving the consistency and predictability of arbitral awards by introducing 'quasi-permanent arbitrators' and, potentially, an appellate mechanism.[30] Nonetheless, at the time investor-State arbitration was considered an important legacy of the Member States and, in the light of the Commission's limited experience in the field, only modest changes were expected to the status quo.[31]

The early negotiating efforts of the Commission confirmed these expectations, as the initial drafts of the Comprehensive Economic and Trade Agreement (CETA) and the EU–Singapore FTA incorporated the traditional mechanism for resolving disputes between investors and States, which closely followed the established practice of the EU Member States.[32] Nevertheless, some innovations were introduced, one of which was a roster of arbitrators which was to be deployed if the disputing parties failed to decide on the composition of their tribunal,[33] and the code of conduct for adjudicators.[34] Both agreements also made small steps towards establishing an appellate system, by requiring treaty committees to consider the feasibility of pursuing this option in the future.[35] While at the time the EU's contribution to the field of international investment protection law seemed minor, it transpired later that these incremental developments were laying the foundations for future systemic reform.[36]

29 Ibid.
30 Ibid.
31 Emanuel Castellarin, 'The Investment Chapter in the New Generation of the EU's Economic Agreements' (2013) 2 TDM 1; Catherine Titi, 'International Investment Law and the European Union: Towards a New Generation of International Investment Agreements' (2015) 26(3) EJIL 639; Luca Pantaleo and Mads Andenas, 'Introduction: The European Union as a Global (Legal) Role Model for Trade and Investment?' (2017) 28(2) Eur Bus L Rev 99; N Jansen Calamita, 'The Making of Europe's International Investment Policy: Uncertain First Steps' (2012) 39(3) LIEI 329, 301.
32 Draft Comprehensive Economic and Trade Agreement (CETA) between Canada and the European Union, Consolidated Text (26 September 2014), Chapter 10; Draft version of the Free Trade Agreement between the European Union and the Republic of Singapore (October 2014), Chapter 9.
33 Article X.25 of the Comprehensive Economic and Trade Agreement (CETA) between Canada, of the one part, and the European Union and its Member States, of the other part [2017] OJ L11/23; Article 9.21 of the Free Trade Agreement between the European Union and the Republic of Singapore [2019] OJ L 294/3.
34 Article X.42 CETA; Annex 9-B of the EU–Singapore FTA.
35 Article X.42 CETA; Article 9.33 of the EU–Singapore FTA.
36 Martins Paparinskis, 'International Investment Law and the European Union: A Reply to Catherine Titi' (2015) 26(3) EJIL 663; Christian J Tams, 'Procedural Aspects of Investor-State Dispute Settlement: The Emergence of a European Approach' (2014) 15(3–4) JWIT 585, 611; Szilárd Gáspár-Szilágyi, 'Quo Vadis

The commencement of negotiations on the Transatlantic Trade and Investment Partnership (TTIP) Agreement with the US was an important catalyst for change in the EU's approach.[37] The decision to include the investment protection chapter in the agreement brought issues concerning investment arbitration to the forefront of the public debates and added to the discontent that was already apparent in some Member States.[38] The Eurobarometer data, collected in autumn 2014, indicated that the majority of citizens in Austria, Germany, and Luxembourg opposed the free trade and investment agreement between the EU and the US.[39] An application was made to register a European Citizens' Initiative (ECI), the aim of which was to pressure the EU institutions to cancel the negotiating mandate for the TTIP and not to conclude the CETA.[40] The 'Stop TTIP' ECI collected over three million signatures, but was registered only after a legal battle with the Commission was won in the CJEU.[41] In addition to concerns over lowering employment, social, environmental, privacy, and consumer standards, the citizens opposed the investor-State dispute resolution mechanism. The signatories expressed their fears that giving large corporations an option to challenge policy decisions before international tribunals, without the involvement of national courts, gave the multinational companies too much power and posed a threat to both democracy and the rule of law.[42]

The Commission acknowledged the 'vigorous public debate' concerning the TTIP and organised a public consultation on the EU's approach to investment protection.[43] With regard to the dispute resolution procedure, the proposed text included an innovative provision for establishing the appellate mechanism for investor-State cases.[44] The largest number of replies were

EU Investment Law and Policy? The Shaky Path Towards the International Promotion of EU Rules' (2018) 23(2) Eur Foreign Aff Rev 167, 186.

37 Council of the European Union, 'Directives for the Negotiation on the Transatlantic Trade and Investment Partnership between the European Union and the United States of America' (17 June 2013) 11103/13 DCL 1.

38 Alexsia T Chan and Beverly K Crawford, 'The Puzzle of Public Opposition to TTIP in Germany' (2017) 19(4) Bus Polit 683, 708.

39 European Commission, 'Autumn 2014 Standard Eurobarometer: Confidence in the European Union Is Increasing' (*European Commission*, 17 December 2014) <https://bit.ly/3giwVye> accessed 30 April 2022 at 32.

40 European Citizens' Initiative, 'Stop TTIP Commission Registration Number: ECI (2017)000008' (*European Union*, 10 June 2017) <https://bit.ly/3d9mOtG> accessed 30 April 2022.

41 Case T-754/14 *Michael Elfer and Others v European Commission* [2017] ECLI: EU:T:2017:323.

42 Ibid.

43 European Commission, 'Staff Working Document, Report: Online Public Consultation on Investment Protection and Investor-to-State Dispute Settlement (ISDS) in the Transatlantic Trade and Investment Partnership Agreement (TTIP)' SWD (2015) 3 final.

44 European Commission, 'Public Consultation on Modalities for Investment Protection and ISDS in TTIP' (27 March 2020) 41–44.

submitted by citizens in countries where the TTIP faced the strongest opposition, including the United Kingdom (UK), Austria, and Germany.[45] A majority of participants considered that the EU's approach did not make sufficient improvements to the existing system.[46] However, some support was expressed for the establishment of the appellate mechanism, including at the multilateral level.[47]

The widespread opposition of civil society to the existing regime of investment protection, and in particular its enforcement mechanism, gave the Commission a mandate to adopt a bolder position on the international scene. The EU's rhetoric changed significantly in the 'Trade for All' policy document, released in October 2015, where it stated that the question was not whether the system of investor-state arbitration should be changed, but how this should be done.[48] Moreover, the EU declared that it was prepared to lead global reforms in the area,[49] reinforcing its post-Lisbon character as the normative power in international economic relations.[50] Consistent with Article 21 TEU, which requires the EU external action to promote multilateral solutions to common problems and strengthen the international system based on multilateral cooperation, the 'Trade for All' policy document proposed the establishment of an International Investment Court and, in the long term, incorporation of investment protection rules into the WTO legal framework.[51]

However, international negotiations on investment protection rules had proven contentious in the past, and several attempts to agree on multilateral rules in the field had failed. The first effort dates back to the 1950s and the Abs-Shawcross Convention, which remained a draft.[52] In 1998, the Organisation for Economic Co-operation and Development (OECD) abandoned its plans for the Multilateral Agreement on Investment, which did not obtain the necessary support of States.[53] Finally, attempts to incorporate investment rules in the WTO system came to a halt in 2004.[54] A number of reasons have been put forward to explain the past failures, such as the protectionist attitudes, complex negotiating tactics deployed across different areas at the WTO, the diverging interests of capital-exporting and capital-importing States, as well as the opposition from the developing countries, who feared that the multilateral rules on investment would unduly restrain their freedom to regulate.[55]

45 Ibid 10.
46 Ibid 28.
47 Ibid 24.
48 European Commission ('Trade for All') (n 2) 21.
49 Ibid.
50 Manners (n 26).
51 European Commission (n 3).
52 Christoph Schreuer, 'Investments, International Protection' in *Max Planck Encyclopedia of Public International Law* (OUP 2013) 11.
53 Ibid.
54 Ibid.
55 Ibid; Pierre Sauvé, 'Multilateral Rules on Investment: Is Forward Movement Possible?' (2006) 9(2) JIEL 325, 355.

4 A bilateral path towards the multilateral reform

Recognising the complexity of the task, the EU decided to implement systemic changes in the field of investment protection in an incremental way, through its bilateral treaty-making practice. The strategy has had a number of advantages, enabling the Commission to develop capacity, as well as test and refine its solutions in negotiations with more experienced treaty-partners. Moreover, the EU's actions gave a new momentum to the debates at the multilateral level about the need for a change in the investment-protection regime, creating conditions for a future convergence of standards. In 2015, the United Nations Conference on Trade and Development (UNCTAD) published its annual World Investment Report, which acknowledged that there was a 'pressing need to reform the global IIAs [International Investment Agreements] regime' and provided a range of recommendations on how the existing system could be improved, some of which coincided with the EU's proposals.[56]

The first building block of the EU's reform was supposed to be the TTIP. The concept paper entitled 'Investment in TTIP and beyond – the path for reform' marked a considerable leap in the evolution of the EU's approach.[57] The most radical changes that were proposed therein included breaking the link between the disputing parties and investment tribunals and establishing an appellate mechanism.[58] An Investment Court System, introduced in the TTIP, was based on the principle that members of both the first instance and the appellate tribunals were selected by the parties to the treaty.[59] The tribunals' presidents were to assign adjudicators to specific cases randomly and on a rotation basis, giving everyone an equal opportunity to serve.[60] The amendments significantly modified the nature of investor-State dispute resolution by weakening the position of investors, who in a traditional model of investment treaty arbitration are able to influence the composition of tribunals.[61] The assumption behind the EU's proposal was that aligning the way in which an investor-State dispute resolution mechanism operates with the traditional model of a court system would

56 UNCTAD (n 8) xi.

57 European Commission, 'Concept Paper: Investment in TTIP and Beyond – the Path for Reform' (September 2015) <https://trade.ec.europa.eu/doclib/docs/2015/may/tradoc_153408.PDF> accessed 30 April 2022.

58 Ibid.

59 European Commission, 'Resolutions of Investment Disputes and Investment Court System, Transatlantic Trade and Investment Partnership' (12 November 2015) <https://bit.ly/3cEVGm1> accessed 30 April 2022, Section 3, Articles 9 and 10.

60 Ibid Articles 9(7) and 10(9).

61 Christoph H Schreuer and others, *The ICSID Convention: A Commentary* (CUP 2009) 475–476; Stephan Wilske, Geetanjali Sharma, and Raeesa Rawal, 'The Emperor's New Clothes: Should India Marvel at the EU's New Proposed Investment Court System?' (2017) 6 Indian J Arb L 79, 97; Charles N Brower and Charles B Rosenberg, 'The Death of the Two-Headed Nightingale: Why the Paulson-van den Berg Presumption that Party-Appointed Arbitrators Are Untrustworthy Is Wrongheaded' (2013) 29(1) Arbitr Int 7.

positively impact on the legitimacy of the investment regime and improve its public perception.[62]

Although the TTIP was not successfully concluded, other countries, such as Viet Nam,[63] Canada,[64] Singapore,[65] and Mexico[66] were amenable to the EU's proposals, which has kept the EU's reform proposals alive. The negotiations with the US, however, have revealed some challenges relating to the establishment of an Investment Court System on a bilateral basis.

First, the implementation of the system to date has highlighted that the maintenance of an elaborate network of tribunals could unduly burden the EU's budget, as cumulatively the Investment Courts established pursuant to the aforementioned agreements envisage the appointment of 39 adjudicators. The number is expected to increase as the EU's bilateral negotiations progress, with the Commission planning to incorporate its new dispute resolution mechanism in around 20 international agreements.[67] The first-tier tribunals of the Investment Court System vary in size depending on the EU's negotiating partner, comprising from 6 up to 15 adjudicators.[68] The appeal tribunals in all bilateral agreements consist of 6 members.[69] All appointees are entitled to a monthly retainer fee in order to ensure their availability, which is paid in addition to fees and expenses for services provided in specific cases.[70] The Commission estimates that the average annual fixed costs of a single, inactive Investment Court System will be at around EUR 400,000 per treaty party,[71] albeit in agreements with less prosperous countries, such as Viet Nam and

62 European Commission (n 57) 4, 7.

63 European Commission, 'Investment Protection Agreement Between the European Union and Its Member States, of the One Part, and the Socialist Republic of Viet Nam on the Other Part' COM (2018) 692 final (EU–Viet Nam Investment Agreement 2018).

64 Chapter 8 of the CETA.

65 European Commission, 'Investment Protection Agreement Between the European Union and Its Member States, of the One Part, and the Republic of Singapore, of the Other Part' COM (2018) 194 final (EU–Singapore Investment Agreement 2018).

66 Modernisation of the Trade Part of the EU–Mexico Global Agreement, Agreement in Principle of 21 April 2018 (EU–Mexico Global Agreement 2018).

67 European Commission, 'Staff Working Document: Impact Assessment: Multilateral Reform of Investment Dispute Resolution' SW (2017) 302 final 21.

68 Article 3.38(2) of the EU-Viet Nam Investment Agreement 2018; Article 8.27(2) CETA; Article 3.9(1) of the EU–Singapore Investment Agreement 2018; Article 11(2) of the EU-Mexico Global Agreement 2018.

69 Article 3.39(2) of the EU-Viet Nam Investment Agreement 2018; Article 3.10(2) of the EU-Singapore Investment Agreement 2018; Article 12(2) of the EU-Mexico Global Agreement 2018; Article 2 of the Draft Decision of the CETA Joint Committee Setting out the Administrative and Organisational Matters Regarding the Functioning of the Appellate Tribunals, 7 May 2020.

70 Article 3.38 and 3.39 of the EU-Viet Nam Investment Agreement 2018; Article 8.27 and 8.28 CETA; Articles 3.9 and 3.10 of the EU-Singapore Investment Agreement 2018; Article 11 and 12 of the EU-Mexico Global Agreement 2018.

71 European Commission (n 67) 37.

Mexico, the EU made a commitment to bear a higher proportion of fixed costs.[72] Additionally, the system will generate administrative expenses, as the management of the network of tribunals will require the commitment of human and financial resources.[73]

In the medium term, the EU's intention is to replace the Investment Court System with a multilateral institution,[74] which presents itself as a more sustainable option for managing costs, as less adjudicators will be appointed and administrative expenses will be distributed among multiple parties. However, given the complex nature of multilateral negotiations, an international court may not be an option that is readily available, and the longer the period required for its establishment, the less effective the EU's bilateral solution becomes. The problem is not only the burden on the EU's budget, which is expected to substantially increase over time, but also the capability of the Investment Court System to achieve the main objectives of the reform, thus delivering value for money. The European Commission admitted that the bilateral solution is unlikely to substantially improve the overall predictability of investment awards and a large number of Investment Court Systems would negatively impact the interpretative consistency sought by the institutionalisation of investor–State dispute resolution.[75] This raises the question whether it is justified to commit a considerable amount of public funds to the establishment of the new interim dispute resolution mechanism, which, according to the Commission's own estimates, generates higher per case costs than the traditional ad hoc investor state arbitration.[76]

Another serious challenge relating to the establishment of the Investment Court System is the availability of appropriately qualified adjudicators, particularly if diversity in the tribunals' compositions is to be promoted.[77] Following the idea that the traditional courts' system provides a blueprint for improving the credibility of investor-State dispute settlement, the provisions of the aforementioned investment treaties stipulate that a tribunal's member should possess qualifications required for appointment to a judicial office or be a jurist of recognised competence.[78] Additionally, individuals need to

72 Ibid 18, 37, 92; the Commission estimates the yearly EU expenditure on the Investment Court system under the EU-Viet Nam FTA at EUR 700,000 plus administrative costs (European Commission, 'Proposal for a Council Decision on the Conclusion of the Investment Protection Agreement between the European Union and its Member States, of the One Part, and the Socialist Republic of Viet Nam, of the Other Part', COM (2018) 693 final).
73 European Commission (n 67) 17–18, 21, 34, 39.
74 Council of the European Union (n 6).
75 European Commission (n 67) 21.
76 Ibid 102–104. John Veeder, 'What Matters – About Arbitration' (2016) 82 Int J of Arb Med & Disp Manag 153, 157.
77 Sir Michael Wood, 'Choosing between Arbitration, and a Permanent Court: Lessons from Inter-State Cases' (2017) 32(1) ICSID Rev 1, 14.
78 Articles 3.38(4) and 3.39(7) of the EU-Viet Nam Investment Agreement 2018; Article 8.27(4) CETA; Articles 3.9(4) and 3.10(4) of the EU-Singapore

demonstrate expertise in public international law, international investment law, international trade law, and international dispute resolution.[79] While such elaborate criteria may ensure the highest level of expertise, they may also reinforce the existing paradigms in the appointment of arbitrators and have an unintended consequence of undermining diversity in terms of age and gender among them.[80] A comparison of empirical data on appointments to the WTO dispute resolution bodies and to investor-State tribunals led Pauwelyn to recommend that the latter system should focus on ensuring inclusivity and representation in order to improve its public perception.[81]

Appointments to tribunals of the Investment Court System could also be seen as an opportunity to expand and diversify the pool of available adjudicators. However, the current strict criteria and the lack of a legally binding commitment to ensuring fair gender representation in the EU's agreements may hinder the attainment of these objectives. The recent selection of individuals to a roster of arbitrators for State-to-State disputes under the CETA gives cause for concern. While Article 29.8 CETA imposes laxer appointment criteria in comparison to the analogous provisions on the Investment Court System, only 4 out of 15 individuals on the roster were women and only one of them was nominated by the EU.[82] Improving diversity in appointments to investment tribunals, where experienced individuals with requisite qualifications to large extent display similar characteristics in terms of age, gender, and ethnicity, could thus prove challenging under the current conditions in the EU's agreements.[83] The EU should be mindful of this issue, given its normative power in international economic relations and since the Investment Court System is intended as a building block of a future multilateral institution.

In addition to establishing the Investment Court System, all the EU's bilateral treaties contain separate provisions intended to facilitate the establishment of the Multilateral Investment Court. The strongest commitments

Investment Agreement 2018; Articles 11(4) and 12(7) of the EU-Mexico Global Agreement 2018.

79 Ibid.

80 Filippo Fontanelli and others, 'Lights and Shadows of the WTO-Inspired International Court System of Investor- State Dispute Settlement' (2016) 1(1) Eur Invest L Arbit Rev 205, 207.

81 Joost Pauwelyn, 'The Rule of Law without the Rule of Lawyers? Why Investment Arbitrators Are from Mars, Trade Adjudicators from Venus' (2015) 109(4) AJIL 761, 805.

82 Council Decision (EU) 2019/2226 on the position to be taken on behalf of the European Union in the CETA Joint Committee as regards the adoption of the List of Arbitrators pursuant to Article 29.8 of the Agreement [2019] OJ L 336/288.

83 Berwin Leighton Paisner, 'International Arbitration Survey: Diversity on Arbitral Tribunals. Are We Getting There?' BLP 2017 <https://bit.ly/35lyepG> accessed 30 April 2022; 'Report of the Cross-Institutional Task Force on Gender Diversity in Arbitral Appointments and Proceedings' The ICCA Report No 8 (2020) 43, 57.

towards this goal are present in the CETA and the EU–Mexico Global Agreement 2018, which provide that the parties to the treaties shall actively support the initiative and when the new international court is established, it is to replace the Investment Court System.[84] Clauses in the EU-Singapore and EU-Viet Nam investment treaties provide the parties with more flexibility by leaving the final decision on whether to adhere to the jurisdiction of a multilateral dispute resolution mechanism to the joint treaty committees.[85] This creates a possibility for the Investment Court System and the Multilateral Investment Court to coexist in the future, depending on the preferences of the EU's negotiating partner. However, such an option would considerably increase the costs of the reforms for the Union.

Similar provisions supporting the establishment of the Multilateral Investment Court have appeared in a few recent BITs of the EU Member States.[86] Strong commitments to the jurisdiction of the Multilateral Investment Court, stipulating that the institution would replace the traditional arbitration mechanism, can be found, for example, in the investment agreements between Hungary and Cabo Verde, as well as Slovakia and Iran.[87] The Slovakia and United Arab Emirates BIT leaves open a possibility for the contracting parties to incorporate new developments in investor-State dispute settlement into the agreement.[88] Since the Treaty of Lisbon, the Member States may conclude BITs only if expressly authorised by the EU.[89] The process of authorisation is governed by Regulation 1219/2012, which states the European Commission may require that a Member State includes a particular clause in its BIT in order to ensure its consistency with the EU's investment policy.[90] The

84 Article 8.29 CETA; Article 14 of the EU-Mexico Global Agreement 2018.

85 Article 3.41 of the EU-Viet Nam Investment Agreement 2018; Art. 3.13 of the EU-Singapore Investment Agreement 2018.

86 See Article 15 of the Netherlands Model Investment Agreement (*Investment Policy Hub UNCTAD*, 22 March 2019) <https://bit.ly/3vs3i1I>; Article 21 of the Belgium-Luxembourg Economic Union Model BIT 2019 (*Investment Policy Hub UNCTAD*, 28 March 2019) <https://bit.ly/3voADuk>; Article 28 of the Slovak Republic Model BIT (*Investment Policy Hub UNCTAD*, 2019) <https://bit.ly/35lrNmO>; Article 8(17) of the Czech Republic Model BIT 2016 (*Investment Policy Hub UNCTAD*, 28 December 2016) <https://bit.ly/3zpng09> all accessed 30 April 2022.

87 Article 9(11) of the Agreement between the Government of Hungary and the Government of the Republic of Cabo Verde for the Promotion and Reciprocal Protection of Investments (*Jus Mundi*, 28 March 2019) <https://bit.ly/3xiPZC6>; Article 24(4) of the Agreement between the Slovak Republic and the Islamic Republic of Iran for the Promotion and Reciprocal Protection of Investments (*Investment Policy Hub UNCTAD*, 20 August 2017) <https://bit.ly/3pSjGr1> both accessed 30 April 2022.

88 Article 26(4) of the Agreement between the Slovak Republic and the United Arab Emirates for the Promotion and Reciprocal Protection of Investments (*Investment Policy Hub UNCTAD*, 5 February 2018) <https://bit.ly/3xq5M29> accessed 30 April 2022.

89 Article 2 TFEU.

90 Article 9 of Regulation (EU) 1219/2012.

framework, therefore, provides an opportunity for the EU to use its Member States' bilateral treaty-making practice in order to build broader international support for its reform proposals.

While the multilateral institution obtained some backing from the EU Member States, the Investment Court System has not been incorporated into their treaty-making practice. Nonetheless, it is noteworthy that the 2019 Dutch Model BIT breaks the link between disputing parties and the composition of arbitral tribunals, which is broadly in line with the EU's idea for improving the legitimacy of investor-State dispute settlement. The Dutch solution appears to be more cost-effective than that of the EU, as instead of establishing a new institution it uses the existing appointing authorities.[91]

5 Multilateral progress

As the EU was rolling out its Investment Court System, multilateral debates about the reform of the legal framework governing the protection of international investment started at the UNCITRAL.[92] In 2017, Working Group III was assigned the task of identifying key problems with the current mechanism of investor-State dispute resolution, evaluating whether a reform was necessary, and developing relevant solutions.[93] The commencement of this work has provided an important counterweight to the crises that were ongoing elsewhere in IEL, namely in the WTO, and injected new energy into multilateral relations. It was greeted with enthusiasm in academic circles, where it was recognised that the initiative to reform investment protection law had the potential to be a 'constitutional moment in international economic governance'.[94]

While the process at the UNCITRAL provides good guarantees of legitimacy, the decision-making by consensus can be cumbersome and requires a considerable commitment of time and resources, not to mention the diplomatic skills necessary to persuade all the parties, which normally display strong nationalistic sentiments in negotiations rather than offering a commitment towards the 'community interests.'[95] It has been apparent from the outset of the UNCITRAL process that a considerable distance has existed between the positions adopted by different States and the EU in relation to the multilateral investment court. Notably, one of the views recorded during the 50th meeting of the UNCITRAL Commission in 2017 was that 'the [current] diversity in approaches to investor-State dispute settlement reflected

91 Article 20 of the Netherlands Model Investment Agreement.

92 UN, 'Report of the United Nations Commission on International Trade Law' (Forty-ninth Session 27 June–15 July 2016) UN Doc A/71/17 [187]-[194].

93 UN, 'Report of the United Nations Commission on International Trade Law' (Fiftieth Session 3 July 2017–21 July 2017) UN Doc A/72/17 [264].

94 Stephan W Schill, 'Investor-State Dispute Settlement Reform at UNCITRAL: A Looming Constitutional Moment?' (2018) 19(1) JWTI 1.

95 Alvarez (n 11).

thoughtful decisions by sovereign States on what approach best suited their particular legal, political, and economic circumstances'.[96]

In the past, the success of multilateral negotiations often depended on the support of a powerful State, like the US, which possessed sufficient political and economic capital to set the tone in international relations. On the flip side, multilateral negotiations were easily derailed by political changes in those countries that are the key players, which the history of the International Trade Organization clearly demonstrates.[97] The EU has led the initiative to establish the Multilateral Investment Court, filling the leadership gap in international economic relations left by the Trump administration. However, as an organisation of conferred powers and a new actor in the field, the EU has had to overcome unique obstacles to establish itself as the leader of the reform in international investment law. First, the Union has lacked the requisite experience, being granted the competence to engage in matters concerning the protection of international investment relatively late, when most States had already established their approaches to the protection of FDI. Second, the Union is not formally a member of the UNCITRAL Commission, and in the Working Group III it only enjoys an enhanced observer status, which enables it to be involved in the deliberations, but without the right to vote.[98]

In spite of its peculiar position, however, the EU as an aggregate has considerable influence, as 12 of its Member States participate in the negotiations at the Working Group III.[99] EU Member States are bound to fully coordinate their positions with that of the Union and act in its interests where measures adopted by an international body may directly impact the EU's *acquis*.[100]

96 UN (n 93) [244].

97 Richard Toye, 'The International Trade Organization' in Martin Daunton, Amrita Narlikar, and Robert M Stern (eds), *The Oxford Handbook of the World Trade Organization* (OUP 2012).

98 UN General Assembly (UNGA), Resolution 65/276: Participation of the European Union in the work of the United Nations (3 May 2011) UN Doc A/RES/65/276. For more on the subject of the EU's participation in the UN, see Mariangela Zappia, 'The United Nations: A European Union Perspective' in Christine Kaddous (ed), *The European Union in International Organisations and Global Governance: Recent Developments* (Hart 2017) 24–32.

99 These are: Austria (2022), Belgium (2025), Croatia (2025), Czechia (2025), Finland (2025), France (2025), Germany (2025), Hungary (2025), Italy (2022), Poland (2022), Romania (2022), Spain (2022); UNGA, 'Report of Working Group III (Investor-State Dispute Settlement Reform) on the Work of its Thirty-eighth Session' (Vienna, 14–18 October 2019) UN Doc A/CN/1004 5. Only certain states are members of the Working Group III and they are selected for a term. The numbers in the brackets indicate when their term expires.

100 Article 218(9) TFEU; Case C-399/12 *Germany v Council* [2014] ECLI:EU:C:2014:2258 [49], [52]–[55], [63]–[64]; Case C-45/07 *Commission v Greece* [2009] ECLI:EU:C:2009:81 [30]–[31]; Opinion 2/91 *Convention No 170 of the International Labour Organization Concerning Safety in the Use of Chemicals at Work* [1993] ECLI:EU:C:1993:106 [5]; Council of the European Union (n 6) 1.

Moreover, some of the EU's third country partners who have supported the institutionalisation of the investor-State dispute resolution mechanism in their bilateral treaties, such as Canada, Mexico, Singapore, and Viet Nam, also take part in the deliberations, which improves the Union's position.[101] It is worth noting that ahead of the 40th Session of the Working Group III, Canada issued a statement in favour of the creation of a permanent two-tier investment court on a multilateral or plurilateral basis.[102]

However, large economies, such as China and Russia, have opposed the idea of breaking the link between the disputing parties and tribunals.[103] Their objection may be difficult to overcome, as it pertains to the central principle of the proposal to institutionalise the investor-State dispute settlement mechanism.[104] This could cause the negotiations to stall in the future, a risk that is inherent in multilateral negotiations, as currently demonstrated by the Doha Round of negotiations at the WTO, which have been ongoing since 2001. This threat has been recognised in the deliberations of the Working Group III and several possible ways to reach a compromise have been identified.

One of them is to establish an appeals mechanism, which could be superimposed on the existing structure of the BITs that subscribe to ad hoc arbitration in the first instance.[105] The paper prepared by the UNCITRAL Secretariat has outlined a number of design possibilities, including the option where the disputing parties do not have the power to appoint members of the appellate tribunals.[106] For the international community, this solution would be a step towards the institutionalisation of investor-State dispute settlement. Taking into account the ongoing pandemic, it seems sensible to take an incremental approach to the implementation of reforms in international investment law, which currently may not be a priority for many States. Furthermore, even before the outbreak of COVID-19, some countries had expressed reservations about the resource-intensive nature of the task of establishing a multilateral court, and asked for a flexible and incremental approach to the implementation of the systemic reform.[107]

101 UNGA (n 98) [5].

102 UNGA, 'Possible Reform of Investor-State Dispute Settlement (ISDS): Appellate Mechanism and Enforcement Issues. Communication by Canada' A/CN.9/WG.III/WP.

103 UNGA, 'Possible Reform of Investor-State Dispute Settlement (ISDS): Submission from the Government of China' A/CN.9/WG.III/WP.177 [4]; UNGA, 'Possible Reform of Investor-State Dispute Settlement (ISDS): Submission from the Government of the Russian Federation' A/CN.9/WG.III/WP.188/Add.1.

104 UNGA (n 99) 103–104.

105 UNGA 'Possible Reform of Investor-State Dispute Settlement (ISDS): Appellate and Multilateral Court Mechanism. Note by the Secretariat' A/CN.9/WG.III/WP.185.

106 Ibid.

107 UNGA, 'Possible Reform of Investor-State Dispute Settlement (ISDS): Submission from the Government of Thailand' A/CN.9/WG.III/WP.162; UNGA, 'Submission from the Governments of Chile, Israel and Japan' A/CN.9/WG.III/WP.163; UNGA, 'Submission from the Government of Costa Rica' A/CN.9/WG.

Another possibility debated at the UNCITRAL has been a multilateral convention that offers a multitude of options for investor-State dispute settlement and allows States to opt into the mechanism that meets their needs.[108] This 'open architecture' of the multilateral instrument was suggested in the EU's original proposal and has some advantages.[109] First, it would enable a group of like-minded states to lead the reform and create conditions for a gradual convergence of positions on a multilateral basis. Second, the establishment of a permanent court that replaces the Investment Court System would make it possible to rationalise the number of appointed adjudicators and the costs to the taxpayer could be further reduced if user fees were implemented.

These proposals are, however, two out of the many reform options that are being considered by the Working Group III.[110] The multitude of possible solutions have made it difficult to find agreement on the best way forward in the multilateral negotiations, which led to the decision that the Working Group III would develop all solutions simultaneously in the third phase of the deliberations.[111] While this inclusive approach may be conducive to consensus-building in the long term, it is unlikely to result in the creation of a new institution any time soon. The EU's own experience with the Unified Patents Court highlights that it could take even a decade to establish the Multilateral Investment Court.[112]

In the light of this, the EU should rethink the way that it uses BITs to influence the wider reform. For the moment, their main benefit is derived from the clauses that commit the EU's trading partners to actively support the creation of the international investment court. However, the Investment

III/WP/164; UNGA, 'Possible Reform of Investor-State Dispute Settlement (ISDS): Submission from the Government of Columbia' A/CN.9/WG.III/WP.173.

108 UNGA, 'Possible Reform of Investor-State Dispute Settlement (ISDS): Multilateral Instrument on ISDS Reform. Note by the Secretariat' A/CN.9/WG.III/WP.194; Stephan W Schill and Geraldo Vidigal, 'Cutting the Gordian Knot: Investment Dispute Settlement à La Carte', Geneva, International Centre for Trade and Sustainable Development' (ICTSD & IDB November 2018); Anthea Roberts and Taylor St John, 'UNCITRAL and ISDS Reform: Visualising a Flexible Framework' (*EJIL: Talk!*, 24 October 2019) <https://bit.ly/2SzooxF> accessed 30 April 2022.

109 UNGA, 'Possible Reform of Investor-State Dispute Settlement (ISDS): Submission from the European Union and Its Member States' A/CN.9/WG.III/WP.159/Add.1.

110 Ibid 43–45; UNGA, 'Possible Reform of Investor-State Dispute Settlement (ISDS): Appellate Mechanism and Enforcement Issues' A/CB.9/WG.III/WP [42]-[56].

111 Ibid [25]; UNGA, 'Report of Working Group III (Investor-State Dispute Settlement Reform) on the work of its Thirty-seventh Session' (New York, 1–5 April 2019) UN Doc A/CN.9/970, [62]-[85].

112 Jacopo Alberti, 'New Developments in the EU System of Judicial Protection: The Creation of the Unified Patent Court and Its Future Relations with the CJEU' (2017) 24(1) Maast J Eur & Comp L 6, 24.

Courts System itself constitutes an unstable foundation for the new multilateral institution. Its main disadvantage is its costly institutional design, with its disproportionately large number of salaried adjudicators compared to the number of cases that are likely to be heard pursuant to the individual investment treaties. In that context, Baldwin's approach of 'multilateralising bilateralism' could provide inspiration to the EU. Building on the idea that FTAs' geographical coverage could be gradually expanded, the Union could establish a single institutional structure for a two-tier tribunal and expand its membership through bilateral negotiations.

Baldwin's concept provides a theoretical framework for a more cost-effective institutional design, reducing the number of adjudicators and spreading the costs among multiple parties. This bottom-up approach towards establishing a multilateral institution would allow the EU to lead by example, while at the same time removing the risk that no consensus can be reached, which frequently materialises in the multilateral process. It does not depend on the support of states such as China, Russia, or the US and makes it possible to test different solutions as the institution expands over time. If it is effectively implemented, it could ensure a dynamic and incremental development of the international governance framework even in times of crisis.

6 Conclusion

The initiative of establishing the Multilateral Investment Court has in theory the potential to bring the much-needed momentum to multilateral cooperation in IEL, the development of which has been stalled for a number of years. In practice, however, progress in deliberations at the Working Group III seems to be hindered by the same challenges that usually arise at multilateral fora. Thus, it is unlikely that the current ongoing negotiations will provide the next 'constitutional moment' in the field. While they may deliver some incremental changes, such tinkering without a commitment to a structural reform could further increase the complexity of the already chaotic system of international investment protection and deepen the crisis of public perception.

The approach of 'multilateralising bilateralism', which has been embraced by the EU since the entry into force of the Treaty of Lisbon, provides alternative tools to ensure a gradual and dynamic development of the international governance framework. This thinking highlights that bilateral treaties can be used in a deliberate manner as a remedy to a crisis, and in the long term can be a way to enhance coherence in international law. While sometimes multilateralisation can occur spontaneously, as the evolution of the network of BITs demonstrates, institutional change frequently requires a leader that can implement the systemic thinking in the bilateral treaty-making practice. The EU, consistent with the principles that guide its external action, has tried to adopt this position in international investment law.

Since the 'Trade for All' policy, the Union has used its bilateral treaties as the building blocks of a multilateral reform in international investment law.

Through the implementation of this strategy, the Union has been able to gain experience, develop its reform proposal, build broader political support, and create a new momentum in international debates. However, to date, the EU has not used the full potential of bilateral treaties. The main obstacle has been the flawed design of the Investment Court System, which does not present itself as an economically viable option, even in the interim period before the establishment of the Multilateral Investment Court. To remedy this problem, the EU could consider replacing the multitude of dispute resolution tribunals with a single institutional structure, membership in which can be gradually extended through the EU's bilateral treaties, in a similar manner that preferences in FTAs can be extended to third countries, as suggested by Baldwin. This approach, which is functional in nature and requires fewer resources than the current Investment Court System, would allow support among states to develop in an organic manner, and provide an indication whether the Multilateral Investment Court is the initiative that is needed to end the crisis of multilateralism in IEL.

14 Challenges to Multilateralism at the World Health Organization

Margherita Melillo

1 Introduction

Health cooperation is one of the oldest forms of international collaboration between States, but also one that has traditionally attracted little attention. For most of its life, the World Health Organization (WHO) has been a low-profile organization, in contrast to the highly political discussions that take place in other multilateral organizations such as the United Nations (UN).[1] Health cooperation, with its own achievements and failures, has for a long time been sheltered from intense public scrutiny.[2]

The COVID-19 pandemic abruptly changed that. In the span of a few weeks, the WHO found itself at the centre of a global crisis, with its Member States asking for guidance on how to face the crisis. This alone has been a mammoth task, which has exposed the WHO to substantial criticism.[3] The WHO's job has been also made harder by the existing geopolitical landscape, as the WHO's political leadership has found itself pressed between China and the United States (US).[4] The two superpowers have acted as 'playground bullies', advancing opposing narratives on the pandemic and launching reciprocal attacks.[5]

It is now well known that the WHO and public health experts had been insisting for years that States ought to prepare for the likely risk of a

1 Kelley Lee, *The World Health Organization (WHO)* (Routledge 2008) 10.

2 Yves Beigbeder, *The World Health Organization: Achievements and Failures* (Routledge 2017); Marcos Cueto, Theodore M Brown, and Elizabeth Fee, *The World Health Organization: A History* (CUP 2019).

3 Lukasz Gruszczynski and Margherita Melillo, 'The Uneasy Coexistence of Expertise and Politics in the World Health Organization: Learning from the Experience of the Early Response to the COVID-19 Pandemic' IOLR (published online ahead of print 2022) <https://doi.org/10.1163/15723747-20220001>.

4 Kate Kell and Stephanie Nebehay, 'Caught in Trump-China Feud, WHO Leader under Siege' (*Reuters*, 15 May 2020) <https://www.reuters.com/investigates/special-report/health-coronavirus-who-tedros/> accessed 30 April 2022.

5 'In Hunt for Virus Source, W.H.O. Let China Take Charge' *The New York Times* (2 November 2020) <https://www.nytimes.com/2020/11/02/world/who-china-coronavirus.html> accessed 30 April 2022.

DOI: 10.4324/9781003312857-16

respiratory-borne pandemic.[6] Although the International Health Regulations (IHR) were adopted in 2005[7] exactly for this purpose, none of the previous outbreaks (i.e. the swine flu, Zika, or Ebola) which were declared Public Health Emergencies of International Concern (PHEICs) had ever reached the massive dimensions of COVID-19. Hence, the potential of the IHR to respond to a global health emergency of this scale had not yet been fully tested.[8] The problem is partially a structural one: it is hard to anticipate all the possible variables of an event as extraordinary as a pandemic. Or to put it another way: you cannot know how your parachute will work until you jump and pull the cord.

The events surrounding the WHO's response to the COVID-19 pandemic have spurred intense debates over the WHO's powers in global health cooperation[9], as well as on whether and how they should be strengthened.[10] Aside from the normative dimension of these debates, however, the COVID-19 pandemic also offers an opportunity to reflect on the limits inherent in multilateral cooperation in global health. Accordingly, this chapter investigates the challenges to multilateralism that have emerged in the WHO during the pandemic (approximately from January 2020 until early 2021). While it is undeniable that the pandemic has been a dramatic stress test for the WHO, it would be mistaken to conclude that it *caused* the crisis of global health multilateralism. This chapter argues that the pandemic rather has exacerbated the structural problems in the field. It shows that global health has a long and difficult history of multilateral cooperation. Some of the contradictions which have always animated the WHO have simply become more visible during the COVID-19 pandemic. In this respect, it seems that the pandemic has mostly *aggravated* existing challenges at the WHO.

Against this background, Section 2 of this chapter illustrates the challenges inherent in global health multilateralism. In particular, it notes that while health cooperation is one of the oldest forms of international cooperation, the WHO has, since its inception, struggled to live up to its broad and ambitious

6 David P Fidler and Lawrence O Gostin, 'The WHO Pandemic Influenza Preparedness Framework: A Milestone in Global Governance for Health' (2011) 306 JAMA 200; Bill Gates, 'The Next Epidemic – Lessons from Ebola' (2015) 372 N Engl J Med 1381.

7 International Health Regulations (2005) (entry into force 15 June 2007) 2509 UNTS 79.

8 David P Fidler and Lawrence O Gostin, 'The New International Health Regulations: An Historic Development for International Law and Public Health' (2006) 34 J Law Med Ethics 85; Lawrence O Gostin, Mary C DeBartolo, and Eric A Friedman, 'The International Health Regulations 10 Years on: The Governing Framework for Global Health Security' (2015) 386 The Lancet 2222.

9 Eyal Benvenisti, 'The WHO – Destined to Fail?: Political Cooperation and the COVID-19 Pandemic' (2020) 114 AJIL 588.

10 Steven Erlanger, 'World Leaders Call for an International Treaty to Combat Future Pandemics' *The New York Times* (30 March 2021) <https://nyti.ms/2RV8Vrz> accessed 30 April 2022.

mandate due to several structural limitations. Section 3 turns to the current events and reviews how the WHO has managed the COVID-19 pandemic. It shows how the previous challenges that the WHO was facing made it harder for the organization to exercise its role as an expert authority and global health leader. The chapter concludes by arguing that the COVID-19 crisis has revealed the inherent contradictions existing within the WHO. Therefore, the challenges that the global health multilateralism are undergoing today are not new, but rather the result of decades of unaddressed problems.

Before proceeding, a word of caution is in order. This chapter is written at a time when the COVID-19 pandemic has not yet come to an end. We do not yet have a full picture of the events, and thus of the WHO's actions. In particular, it is not yet possible to conclusively assess whether the WHO's COVID-19 response was ineffective or flawed. However, without attempting to draw any final conclusions in this regard, it is already possible to address a more modest, yet important question, which is how the WHO's pre-existing limitations have impacted its pandemic response, and thus revealed the limits inherent in the currently functioning global health multilateralism.

2 The mixed record of global health and multilateralism

International cooperation in global health has a long history, and for good reasons. In the fight against epidemics, international cooperation is not only desirable: it is necessary. Infectious agents are unaware of national borders. They have always travelled swiftly across countries and continents.[11] Modern globalisation has made the need for global health cooperation even more critical, as the hectic movement of goods and people has made the spread of infections even more rapid.[12]

Despite having a long tradition and a solid rationale for its existence, global health cooperation is far from being an ideal prototype of successful multilateral cooperation. The following two subsections first briefly review the history of global health multilateralism (Section 2.1), and then assess the major challenges that the WHO was facing even before the COVID-19 pandemic struck (Section 2.2).

2.1 A brief history of global health multilateralism

The first 'International Sanitary Conference' was held in 1851 at the initiative of the French Government. The focus was on cholera, or better put, on how to harmonize quarantine and similar measures among countries so as to

11 Peter Frankopan, *The Silk Roads: A New History of the World* (Vintage 2017) 187–192.

12 David P Fidler, 'The Globalization of Public Health: Emerging Infectious Diseases and International Relations' (1997) Indiana J Glob Leg Stud 11.

prevent outbreaks while not unnecessarily restricting trade.[13] It took six more conferences and 40 years, but eventually the participating States managed to agree to the first International Sanitary Convention in 1892, and then new Conventions in 1893, 1894, 1897, and 1903 (with the last one consolidating the previous ones).[14] In parallel, the first international organizations dealing with public health (the Pan American Sanitary Bureau and the Office International d'Hygiène Publique) were established in 1902 and 1907, respectively.[15]

The outcome of the International Sanitary Conferences was limited and inadequate to fully tackle infectious diseases. In spite of their shortcomings, however, David Fidler has pointed out the importance of the conferences in raising European countries' awareness that the fight against infectious diseases was something that required collective action.[16] At the time of the first conferences, the aetiology and the mode of spread of cholera were not yet clear, but many doctors already believed that it was a contagious disease, somehow able to travel from one country to another.[17] The first International Sanitary Conferences reinforced this idea, and the subsequent developments in epidemiology confirmed it.

International cooperation on global health matters progressively strengthened over the course of the twentieth century with the establishment of the Health Section of the League of Nations in 1922.[18] The adoption of multiple disease-specific conventions, however, had made the international legal framework for health cooperation a complex and inefficient 'patchwork' of different treaties.[19]

It is against this backdrop that the post-war architects of the international legal order decided to establish a multilateral organization tasked with the surveillance and the management of global health.[20] The WHO was thus born in 1948. The WHO Constitution conferred a special authority on the World Health Assembly (WHA) – the assembly of State Parties – giving it the power to adopt regulations to prevent the international spread of diseases.[21] This power is different from the traditional law-making powers of

13 Norman Howard-Jones and WHO, *The Scientific Background of the International Sanitary Conferences, 1851–1938* (WHO 1975).
14 WHO, 'Origin and Development of Health Cooperation' (*WHO*, undated) <https://www.who.int/global_health_histories/background/en/> accessed 30 April 2022.
15 Ibid.
16 David P Fidler, 'From International Sanitary Conventions to Global Health Security: The New International Health Regulations' (2005) 4 Chin J Int Law 325, 329.
17 Howard-Jones and WHO (n 13) 25.
18 WHO, 'Archives of the League of Nations, Health Section Files' (*WHO*, undated) <https://www.who.int/archives/fonds_collections/bytitle/fonds_3/en/> accessed 30 April 2022.
19 Fidler (n 16) 332.
20 Ibid 330–331.
21 Articles 21(1)(a) and 22 of the Constitution of World Health Organization (entry into force 7 April 1948) 14 UNTS 185.

international organizations, insofar as the WHO Constitution stipulates that the regulations are binding on State Parties, *unless* they opt out.[22] Accordingly, the first International Sanitary Regulations were adopted in 1951, and were replaced in 1969 by the IHR and further updated in the following years. However, with the exception of the IHR, the WHO has not often resorted to its law-making powers.[23] It has mostly eschewed formal law-making, preferring to exercise its authority through technical standards regulations.[24]

The pre-Second World War International Sanitary Conventions did not establish any coherent or effective regime. Remarkably, however, they laid the foundations of the main features of global health cooperation against infectious diseases, providing some elements that are still at the core of the IHR: a system of notification of new diseases or outbreaks; and rules concerning the application of restrictions to trade and travel.[25]

2.2 *The challenges of global health multilateralism*

The history of global health multilateralism described thus far could mislead some to conclude that this is an area where international cooperation has proved quite successful. That is not the case. In one way or another, all international organizations suffer from structural limitations that derive from their intergovernmental nature, and their agent/principal relationship.[26] However, even compared to other international organizations the WHO suffers from some structural limitations that particularly constrain its work.[27]

The first limitation lies in its organizational structure. Like many international organizations, the WHO is often considered a slow-moving and rigid bureaucratic organization that is not suited to addressing the challenges of the twenty-first century.[28] That is arguably true, but it is also the case that the WHO's structure that makes the organization particularly complex and inefficient. The WHO is divided into six regional offices, which are 'unique within

22 José E Alvarez, *International Organizations as Law-makers* (OUP 2006).

23 Another exception, albeit pertaining to a different area of health cooperation, is the Framework Convention on Tobacco Control, adopted in 2003 pursuant to Article 19 of the WHO Constitution.

24 Jan Klabbers, 'The Normative Gap in International Organizations Law: The Case of the World Health Organization' (2019) 16 Int Organ L Rev 272.

25 David P Fidler, 'Emerging Trends in International Law Concerning Global Infectious Disease Control' (2003) 9 Emerg Infect Dis 285.

26 Roland Vaubel, 'Principal-Agent Problems in International Organizations' (2006) 1 Rev Int Organ 125.

27 Lee (n 1); Theodore M Brown and Marcos Cueto, 'The World Health Organization and the World of Global Health' in Richard Parker and Marni Sommer, *Routledge Handbook of Global Public Health* (Routledge 2010); Lawrence O Gostin, *Global Health Law* (Harvard UP 2014); Beigbeder (n 2).

28 Liliana B Andonova, *Governance Entrepreneurs, International Organizations and the Rise of Global Public-Private Partnerships* (CUP 2017) 7–12; Kelley Lee and Julianne Piper, 'The WHO and the COVID-19 Pandemic: Less Reform, More Innovation' (2020) 26 Glob Governance 523, 527.

the UN system in their degree of independence and decision-making power'.[29] This decentralized structure creates an additional level of complexity, undermining effectiveness and the global coherence of its initiatives.[30] In spite of calls for reforms since at least the 1990s,[31] the WHO's working structure and methods have remained *grosso modo* unchanged.

The second of the WHO's limitations is the contradiction enshrined in its mandate. The WHO Constitution entrusts the organization with a very utopian objective, but no resources or powers to achieve it. It declares that the WHO's objective is 'the attainment by all peoples of the highest possible level of health', with health defined as 'a state of complete physical, mental and social well-being and not merely the absence of disease or infirmity'.[32] However, the WHO's budget does not allow it to carry out even a fraction of the activities that would be necessary to fulfil such a broad mandate.[33] The WHO's financial challenges became particularly visible in the 1990s, when Member States declared their dissatisfaction with the WHO's work and froze its regular budget to 'zero nominal growth'.[34] Today, the WHO receives half of its funds from non-state actors,[35] but in spite of these additional resources the organization's capabilities remain severely constrained. As Lee and Piper have described, the WHO is 'trapped in a perpetual cycle … of not having sufficient resources to effectively achieve objectives, and donors viewing these unmet objectives as disincentives for increasing funding'.[36] In the past few months, it has become commonplace to describe these difficulties by highlighting that the WHO's budget is comparable to that of a 'large U.S. hospital'.[37]

The challenges of implementing the WHO's mandate lie not only in its broad formulation and financial constraints, but also in the limited powers that the WHO actually possesses. The WHO is meant to carry out its mandate by acting as an expert authority in the field of global health, providing scientific or technical support to governments in their actions and carrying out some of the actions by itself.[38] Yet there is now a growing awareness that

29 Lee (n 1) 31.
30 Ibid 33.
31 Voldemar Ermakov, 'Reform of the World Health Organization' (1996) 347 The Lancet 1536.
32 WHO Constitution, Article 1 and preamble respectively.
33 Lee (n 1) 38–44.
34 Srikanth K Reddy, Sumaira Mazhar, and Raphael Lencucha, 'The Financial Sustainability of the World Health Organization and the Political Economy of Global Health Governance: A Review of Funding Proposals' (2018) 14 Glob Health 119.
35 Kristina Daugirdas and Gian Luca Burci, 'Financing the World Health Organization: What Lessons for Multilateralism?' (2019) 16 Int Organ L Rev 299.
36 Lee and Piper (n 28) 529.
37 Pien Huang, 'Trump and WHO: How Much Does the U.S. Give? What's the Impact of a Halt in Funding?' (*NPR*, 15 April 2020) <https://n.pr/3fxdSzG> accessed 30 April 2022.
38 WHO Constitution, Article 2.

a purely medical or technical approach is not sufficient to tackle global health problems. Science, including medical science, is not separate from society. Many scholars have shown that science is essentially a social activity, with embedded values and limits.[39] In parallel, modern thinking in public health has demonstrated that many of the threats to healthy living come from inequalities and inadequate living conditions[40] – the so-called 'social determinants of health'.[41] It follows that global health cannot be significantly improved without making important changes to our political, economic, and social structures.[42] Naturally, as an international organization the WHO has only a limited power to influence these types of reforms.

It is no coincidence that the field where the WHO supposedly exercises its authority has been renamed 'global health law'. This term was introduced at the beginning of 1990s to mark the passage from a more 'intergovernmental' view of international health law – in which almost all the prerogatives remain in the hands of governments – to a more 'global' view of the field, with non-state entities assuming a more prominent role in managing public health problems.[43] In fact, today more than ever in history, much of the work in the promotion of global health is carried out by non-governmental organizations (NGOs), alone or in partnership with national governments and international organizations.[44] The change of the name of the field to 'global health law' has validated the status of the WHO as an important actor, but not the protagonist, of global health law.

The WHO's limitations are also visible in the framework for fighting infectious diseases, that is the IHR. After the SARS epidemic of 2003–2004, it became obvious that the IHR was not an effective instrument in coordinating action against infectious diseases.[45] A new IHR was adopted in 2005 and entered into force in 2007. The current text is an improved version of the previous one, but as has become evident during the COVID-19 pandemic (and as discussed below), it is still imperfect, and most notably it lacks the 'teeth' to ensure that the WHO or any Member

39 Sheila Jasanoff, *The Fifth Branch: Science Advisors as Policymakers* (Harvard UP 1990); Sheila Jasanoff, *States of Knowledge: The Co-Production of Science and the Social Order* (Routledge 2004).

40 Michael Marmot, *The Health Gap: The Challenge of an Unequal World* (Bloomsbury 2015).

41 WHO, 'Social Determinants of Health' (*WHO*, undated) <https://www.who.int/westernpacific/health-topics/social-determinants-of-health> accessed 30 April 2022.

42 Lawrence O Gostin and Benjamin M Meier (eds), *Foundations of Global Health & Human Rights* (OUP 2020).

43 Theodore M Brown, Marcos Cueto, and Elizabeth Fee, 'The World Health Organization and the Transition from "International" to "Global" Public Health' (2006) 96 AJPH 62.

44 Chelsea Clinton and Devi Sridhar, *Governing Global Health: Who Runs the World and Why?* (OUP 2017).

45 Fidler and Gostin (n 8).

State enforces its provisions. Ultimately, the indirect proof that the IHR is not a powerful instrument is reflected in the little consideration that it has so far enjoyed in international law. The niche status that global health law has had is proof of what scholars have long affirmed: traditionally, there is little appreciation for international law at the WHO.[46] I would add that the feeling is probably mutual. Many international lawyers had never heard of the IHR before the COVID-19 pandemic broke out, or knew very little about it.

In conclusion, this brief review of the global health multilateralism and of the challenges that the WHO faces demonstrates that in spite of all the old and new attempts to forge treaties and institutions, cooperation in the field has always been substantially underdeveloped.

3 The WHO on trial during the COVID-19 pandemic: unveiling the structural problems

The WHO has been hyperactive since the outbreak of the novel coronavirus epidemic was notified by China on 31 December 2019. The COVID-19 timeline prepared by the WHO describes all the organization's main actions, dividing them in six categories: (1) information; (2) science; (3) leadership; (4) advice; (5) response; and (6) resourcing.[47]

Although there is not much indication as to where these categories are drawn from and what they exactly mean, we can presume that the first five approximately correspond to some of the main WHO objectives as spelled out in the WHO Constitution: (1) 'to provide information, counsel and assistance in the field of health';[48] (2) 'to promote and conduct scientific research';[49] (3) 'to act as the directing and co-ordinating authority on international health work';[50] (4) 'to furnish appropriate technical assistance';[51] (5) 'in emergencies, [to provide] necessary aid upon the request or acceptance of Governments'.[52] The sixth area of work (resourcing, consisting mostly of fundraising work) is not included in the WHO Constitution, probably because at that time it could not be anticipated that the WHO would suffer from such severe financial constraints.

Despite all the efforts, however, the inherent limits of the WHO became apparent during the COVID-19 pandemic, sometimes leading to confusion and to increased tensions among governments. In this context, it should be

46 David P Fidler, 'International Law and Global Public Health' (1999) 48 U Kan L Rev 1, 15.
47 WHO, 'Timeline: WHO's COVID-19 Response' (*WHO*, undated) <https://bit.ly/3c13nT1> accessed 30 April 2022.
48 Article 2(q) of the WHO Constitution.
49 Ibid Article 2(n).
50 Ibid Article 2(a).
51 Ibid Article 2(d).
52 Ibid Article 2(d).

noted that the WHO's response has sparked criticism not only from the former US administration but also across a broad spectrum of commentators and experts.[53]

Against this backdrop, this section investigates the WHO's actions during the COVID-19 pandemic by focusing on two areas. The first, described in Section 3.1, reviews the fulfilment of objectives 1, 2, 4, and 5 described above, jointly considered as expressing the WHO's 'expert authority'. The second area of investigation, illustrated in Section 3.2, covers objective no 3, dubbed 'the WHO as a global health leader'. While these sub-sections do not attempt to be comprehensive or conclusive, they aim to show how the WHO's pandemic response was affected by the structural limits of the WHO and by the general geopolitical background.

3.1 The WHO as an expert authority

As has been shown above, the WHO is meant by design to act as an expert authority in the field of global health, providing technical support, advice, and promoting scientific research. This is not surprising. Much of the capacity of international organizations to influence global affairs is based on the possession of specific technical knowledge and expertise.[54]

The conception of the WHO as an expert authority is also embedded in the IHR (2005). Indeed, the most significant of the powers granted to the Director-General in the event of a public health emergency of international concern is the authority to issue temporary recommendations to States on health or other measures to be implemented.[55] It is clearly stated that such measures should be issued on the basis of the advice of a committee of experts to the Director-General.[56]

Accordingly, providing technical advice has been one of the main activities of the WHO during the COVID-19 pandemic. The WHO describes this work as a careful and comprehensive process, whereby 'the experts review reports,

53 Thomas J Bollyky and David P Fidler, 'It's Time for an Independent Coronavirus Review' *Foreign Affairs* (24 April 2020) <https://fam.ag/3fZfpgS>; Thomas R Pickering and Atman M Trivedi, 'The International Order Didn't Fail the Pandemic Alone' *Foreign Affairs* (14 May 2020) <https://fam.ag/2RVCb1m>; Lois Parshley, 'The WHO Isn't to Blame for Trump's Disastrous Coronavirus Response' (*Vox*, 15 April 2020) <https://bit.ly/3wHZBG5> all accessed 30 April 2022.

54 Ernst B Haas, *When Knowledge Is Power: Three Models of Change in International Organizations* (University of California Press 1990); Michael Barnett and Martha Finnemore, *Rules for the World: International Organizations in Global Politics* (Cornell UP 2004); Frank Biermann and Bernd Siebenhüner (eds), *Managers of Global Change: The Influence of International Environmental Bureaucracies* (MIT Press 2009); Guy Fiti Sinclair, *To Reform the World: International Organizations and the Making of Modern States* (OUP 2017).

55 Article 15 IHR (2005).

56 Ibid Articles 17, 48 and 49.

studies, presentations by countries, they analyse trends, consult further expert groups and then agree on the best approach'.[57] Between January and July 2020, for example, the WHO estimates that it published more than 50 detailed technical documents on COVID-19 testing, tracing, prevention of transmission, and on many other topics related to the pandemic.[58] In about the same time span, the WHO also held 90 media press briefings and 28 briefings for its Member States.[59] Finally, it convened an indeterminate number of meetings of scientists and scientific networks.[60]

Although to the best of my knowledge nobody has objected to the notion that the WHO ought to act as an expert authority in the event of a pandemic, strong disagreement has emerged with respect to the few but very critical recommendations issued by the WHO. I submit that, for the most part, this disagreement finds its origin in the narrow understanding of the technical and medical guidance that the WHO is supposed to provide – one of the WHO's pre-existing limitations identified above.[61] As noted above, the WHO is an organization with a very limited budget. It does not have the resources to carry out or finance all sorts of research activities, and most of its job consists in talking to scientists and reviewing existing studies. This task is already enormous with respect to medical science, but it becomes even trickier with respect to societal measures such as facemasks or travel restrictions. These measures, in fact, require taking into account social and economic considerations that the WHO is not necessarily able – and perhaps not even best placed – to provide.

The first and most notable case of disagreement over the WHO's recommendations during the COVID-19 pandemic concerned the issue of facemasks. For several months at the beginning of the pandemic, the WHO continued to recommend the use of facemasks only in medical settings and by sick people.[62] Conversely, their widespread use by the general population was not endorsed by the organization. The recommendation on facemasks was

57 WHO, 'A Guide to WHO's Guidance on COVID-19' (*WHO*, undated) <https://www.who.int/news-room/feature-stories/detail/a-guide-to-who-s-guidance> accessed 30 April 2022. An updated guide on the WHO's guidance has not been released, but the number of technical documents has undoubtedly grown.

58 Ibid. As above, an updated guide on the WHO's guidance has not been released, but the WHO has continued to hold press conferences on a regular basis.

59 WHO, 'Listings of WHO's Response to COVID-19' (*WHO*, undated) <https://www.who.int/news/item/29-06-2020-covidtimeline> accessed 30 April 2022.

60 Ibid.

61 On this point, see also: Lukasz Gruszczynski and Margherita Melillo, "The uneasy coexistence of expertise and politics in the World Health Organization: Learning from the experience of the early response to the COVID-19 pandemic" *International Organizations Law Review 1* (2022), 1–31; Margherita Melillo, 'When a Delay Is a Denial: The Role of Scientific Evidence in the World Health Organization's Response to the Covid-19 Pandemic' in Shinya Murase and Suzanne Zhou (eds), *Epidemics and International Law* (Brill, 2021).

62 WHO, 'Advice on the Use of Masks in the Community, during Home Care, and in Health Care Settings in the Context of COVID-19: Interim Guidance' (19 March 2020) WHO/2019-nCoV/IPC_Masks/2020.2.

eventually changed in June 2020 to include such widespread use by the general population.[63] However, this change amounted to an acknowledgement of the existing situation, as by that time many States or local governments were already recommending or even requiring their citizens to wear facemasks outdoors or in social situations. By choosing to err on the side of caution on the issue of facemasks, the WHO effectively chose to be silent on one of the most topical issues of this pandemic. What is even worse, however, is that the long delay may have affected the organization's standing as an expert authority.

The reason why the WHO hesitated for so long to change its recommendation on facemasks was simple: there was no evidence that they could be effective.[64] At the beginning of the pandemic, there was very little understanding about the modes of transmission of the novel coronavirus, namely pre- and asymptomatic transmission (i.e. transmission from a person that is infected but has not yet developed symptoms, or may never develop them)[65] and airborne transmission (i.e. transmission through small droplets that can remain suspended in the air).[66] At the same time, there was no evidence that the widespread use of facemasks could slow the transmission of the novel coronavirus.[67] This evidence is only emerging now.[68]

It is undoubtedly hard to reach a scientific consensus in a short amount of time on scientific questions concerning a new virus, and we could not reasonably expect the WHO to have had ready-made solutions. In choosing not to recommend the use of facemasks by the general population, the WHO took a decision based on a strict assessment of the existing medical and technical knowledge. The decision was not incorrect *per se* (assessed against the knowledge available at that time), but it was probably influenced by the medical culture of the WHO.[69] The governments which recommended the use

63 WHO, 'Advice on the Use of Masks in the Context of COVID-19' (5 June 2020) WHO/2019-nCoV/IPC_Masks/2020.4.

64 Larry D Curtis, 'WHO: There Is No Evidence Wearing a Mask in Public Setting Prevents COVID-19 Infection' (*2KUTV*, 7 April 2020) <https://bit.ly/3p36pvv> accessed 30 April 2022.

65 Sarah Boseley, 'WHO Expert Backtracks after Saying Asymptomatic Transmission "Very Rare"' *The Guardian* (9 June 2020) <https://bit.ly/3wKoiC4>; WHO, 'Coronavirus Disease (COVID-19): How Is It Transmitted?' (*WHO*, 13 December 2020) <https://www.who.int/news-room/q-a-detail/coronavirus-disease-covid-19-how-is-it-transmitted> both accessed 30 April 2022.

66 Reuters Staff, 'WHO Says No Change to COVID-19 Transmission Guidance after U.S. Draft Change' (*Reuters* 21 September 2020) <https://reut.rs/3p5oLvV> accessed 30 April 2022.

67 Danielle Renwick, 'Face Masks: Can They Slow Coronavirus Spread – and Should We Be Wearing Them?' *The Guardian* (2 April 2020) <https://www.theguardian.com/world/2020/apr/02/face-masks-coronavirus-covid-19-public> accessed 30 April 2022.

68 Lynne Peeples, 'Face Masks: What the Data Say' (2020) 586 Nature 186.

69 Zeynep Tufekci, 'Why Did It Take So Long to Accept the Facts About Covid?' *The New York Times* (7 May 2021) <https://www.nytimes.com/2021/05/07/opinion/coronavirus-airborne-transmission.html> accessed 10 May 2022.

of facemasks by the general population did not have more or better technical or medical knowledge than the WHO did. Rather, they made a precautionary choice in deeming that wearing masks was a beneficial cost-effective intervention, with few potential drawbacks and many potential advantages.[70] What the WHO missed, hence, was an appreciation of the social and economic considerations that led many States to recommend the wearing of facemasks.

A similar dynamic can be observed with respect to the recommendations against travel restrictions which were issued by the WHO at the beginning of the pandemic.[71] While almost every country in the world has adopted some form of travel restrictions at some point during the COVID-19 pandemic,[72] the WHO's recommendations sparked less interest in the media and among the public, possibly because travel restrictions soon became a *fait accompli*, with little room for debate. Nevertheless the dissatisfaction was probably noted by the WHO, as a slightly modified recommendation was eventually issued (recognizing that States could consider travel restrictions based on public health considerations).[73]

Again, the problem with travel restrictions was mainly a problem of evidence and its appreciation. The WHO considered that it did not have enough evidence on the effectiveness of travel restrictions.[74] The reality seems to be that such evidence is hard to obtain, as closing the border is a measure that is rarely adopted in isolation, and hence it plays along with many other variables. However, the governments which adopted travel restrictions did consider these measures to be potentially effective measures, or at least compatible with the same logic of domestic lockdowns. Strictly speaking, the adoption of travel restrictions was not based on evidence. It was rather based on a broad consideration of social factors and circumstances that the WHO apparently did not consider, or weighted differently.

More than one year into the pandemic, almost all countries in the world maintain some form of such restrictions.[75] Moreover, the preliminary evidence suggests that border closures helped slow down the COVID-19 pandemic.[76] Like the recommendations on facemasks, the WHO's recommendations constituted

70 Renwick (n 67).

71 WHO, 'Updated WHO Recommendations for International Traffic in Relation to COVID-19 Outbreak' (20 February 2020) <https://bit.ly/2RVTDCW> accessed 30 April 2022.

72 'Policy Responses to the Coronavirus Pandemic – Statistics and Research' (*Our World in Data*) <https://ourworldindata.org/policy-responses-covid> accessed 30 April 2022.

73 Armin von Bogdandy and Pedro Villarreal, 'Critical Features of International Authority in Pandemic Response: The WHO in the COVID-19 Crisis, Human Rights and the Changing World Order' MPIL Research Paper 2020–16.

74 WHO (n 71).

75 International Air Transport Association, 'International Travel Document News' (*IATA*, 30 April 2021) <https://www.iatatravelcentre.com/world.php> accessed 30 April 2022.

76 Matteo Chinazzi and others, 'The Effect of Travel Restrictions on the Spread of the 2019 Novel Coronavirus (COVID-19) Outbreak' (2020) 368 Science 395.

another missed opportunity for the WHO to prove its role as a global expert authority. In the event of a future epidemic, which country will heed any WHO recommendation against travel bans?

The fact that the WHO was not able to lead as an expert authority with regard to the issues of facemasks and travel restrictions does not imply, however, that it has not been able to do so with respect to other issues. These examples rather show how the WHO's response to the COVID-19 pandemic was affected by one of its pre-existing structural limitations; namely by the fact that, like all decision-makers, even the most technical of WHO's decisions involve normative (political) considerations. They need to be recognized and properly managed rather than ignored.

3.2 The WHO's global health leadership

Expertise is not the only type of authority that international organizations exercise. By virtue of their mandate and their impartiality, international organizations also enjoy a type of more subtle authority, which has sometimes been referred to in the literature as 'moral authority'.[77] While this term may be defined in different ways, for the purposes of this chapter I interpret it as the capacity to fully and effectively implement the objective provided in the WHO Constitution 'to act as the directing and co-ordinating authority on international health work'.[78]

Despite this strong mandate, the WHO is further than ever from being the coordinating authority in global health. This chapter has already discussed how, because of its structural limitations, the WHO is only one actor, and not the protagonist, of the global health landscape. The COVID-19 pandemic could have been an opportunity for the WHO to show its leadership, or at least its leadership potential, to assume a coordinating role in global health. Instead, the pandemic has only unveiled the reality of an organization that struggles to live up to its mandate.

The WHO's difficulties in being a global health leader have been particularly evident with respect to two issues: the geopolitical struggle between the US and China; and the plans for a global vaccine distribution. The problem with geopolitical struggles is well known. The former US President Donald Trump repeatedly and vocally accused not only China of being responsible for the spread of the novel coronavirus, but also the WHO of being complicit by helping China to disguise its real role.[79] He did not stop at verbal accusations,

77 Barnett and Finnemore (n 54) 23.
78 Article 2(a) of the WHO Constitution.
79 Donald G McNeil Jr and Andrew Jacobs, 'Blaming China for Pandemic, Trump Says U.S. Will Leave the W.H.O.' *The New York Times* (29 May 2020) <https://www.nytimes.com/2020/05/29/health/virus-who.html>; Rick Gladstone, 'Trump Demands U.N. Hold China to Account for Coronavirus Pandemic' *The New York Times* (22 September 2020) <https://nyti.ms/3fz5eAV> both accessed 30 April 2022.

but chose to 'punish' the WHO by first suspending its US funding, and later withdrawing the US from the organization altogether.[80] Fortunately, the advent of a new government has led the US to recently restore its ties with the WHO.[81] However, this recent change seems more one of tone than of substance. The new US government, in fact, continues to be very critical of the treatment that the WHO afforded to China, with recent criticism being directed at the report on the origins of the SARS-CoV-2 virus.[82] In the meantime, the attacks that the WHO has suffered will hardly be forgotten anytime soon by either the general public or by other governments. Perhaps even more importantly, while China and the US were skirmishing, the WHO's leadership was very much sidelined at the very moment when it was most needed.

It seems very hard to believe that the WHO intended in any way to support or favour China. While it is true that it has refrained from criticizing China for not sharing important information, many believe that it has done so as part of an effort to guarantee smooth cooperation in order to obtain as much information as possible about the virus during the initial phase of the epidemic.[83] As an investigation recently reported, while, in public, WHO officials were admiring China for being transparent and effective in responding to the outbreak, in private settings they expressed frustration at China's delays in releasing information.[84] On other issues, such as praise for their strict lockdown, it is conceivable that the WHO's assessment was – to the extent possible – objective. Von Bogdandy and Villarreal, for example, believe that 'the WHO's positive assessments of Chinese measures are due to the fact that many of them are acceptable in scientific terms'.[85]

While in many ways the so-called 'New Cold War' between the US and China made the confrontation hard for the WHO to eschew,[86] at the same time we should nevertheless refrain from considering any of these events as inevitable. An additional pinch of sensitivity towards diplomatic affairs could have allowed the WHO to avoid at least some of the polemics. Was it really

80 Gian Luca Burci, 'The USA and the World Health Organization: What Has President Trump Actually Decided and What Are Its Consequences?' (*EJIL: Talk!*, 5 June 2020) < https://bit.ly/2RVa5Dr> accessed 30 April 2022.

81 Christina Morales, 'Biden Restores Ties with the World Health Organization That Were Cut by Trump' *The New York Times* (21 January 2021) <https://www.nytimes.com/2021/01/20/world/biden-restores-who-ties.html> accessed 30 April 2022.

82 'Trump's Gone, but China, U.S. Still at Odds over Coronavirus Origins Ahead of WHO Report' (*NBC News*, 16 February 2021) <https://nbcnews.to/3p3F10k> accessed 30 April 2022.

83 Kell and Nebehay (n 4); Gian Luca Burci, 'EJIL: The Podcast! WHO Let the Bats Out?' (*EJIL: Talk!*, 6 May 2020) <https://www.ejiltalk.org/ejil-the-podcast-who-let-the-bats-out/> both accessed 30 April 2022.

84 'China Delayed Releasing Coronavirus Info, Frustrating WHO' (*AP NEWS*, 2 June 2020) <https://apnews.com/3c061794970661042b18d5aeaaed9fae> accessed 30 April 2022.

85 von Bogdandy and Villarreal (n 73) 26.

86 Robert D Kaplan, 'A New Cold War Has Begun' (*Foreign Policy*, 7 January 2019) <https://foreignpolicy.com/2019/01/07/a-new-cold-war-has-begun/> accessed 30 April 2022.

necessary to repeatedly praise China, not only for sharing information but also for enforcing a strict lockdown that severely limited people's freedoms and privacy? Could any informal contacts on the part of the WHO have moderated the US's irritation with its praise of China? We do not fully know what really happened in those days, nor what the WHO tried, didn't try, or tried *not* to do. However, viewed from the outside, the WHO's actions seem to have been at the very least quite *maladroit*. The overall picture that emerges from the WHO's COVID-19 response seems to be that the organization was ill-equipped to exercise its role as global health leader.

The second issue where the WHO faced difficulties in assuming the role of leader concerns global vaccine distribution. As we are now witnessing, vaccines are being rolled out, but in a very unequal way among countries.[87] From the inception of the pandemic, wealthy States have rushed to conclude advance purchase agreements with pharmaceutical companies, leading to an inequitable and unhealthy competition among countries, which many have dubbed as 'vaccine nationalism'.[88] This is certainly not a novel development in global health. Similar events have occurred even during less important pandemics, such as the 2009 H1N1, and many experts had warned that something similar was doomed to happen again.[89]

In order to try to anticipate and resolve many of the envisioned problems, a multi-partner initiative called 'COVAX' was created in April 2020.[90] The aim of this initiative is to function as a platform to support the development and manufacture of COVID-19 vaccines, while at the same time ensuring that all participating States can equally access them.[91] The COVAX is best described as 'a network of different legal agreements', where at one end are the States, at the other end the pharmaceutical companies, and in the middle several organizations mediating between them.[92]

The mediating organizations are of different natures and carry out different tasks and functions. The most important ones are two longstanding public-private partnerships: the Global Alliance for Vaccines and Immunisations (GAVI); and the Coalition for Epidemic Preparedness Innovations (CEPI). These two organizations are, along with the WHO, 'co-convenors' of COVAX.[93] In fact, they play a

87 'Coronavirus (COVID-19) Vaccinations - Statistics and Research' (*Our World in Data*) <https://ourworldindata.org/covid-vaccinations> accessed 30 April 2022.

88 Lukasz Gruszczynski and Chien-huei Wu, 'Between the High Ideals and Reality: Managing COVID-19 Vaccine Nationalism' (2021) 12(3) EJRR 711.

89 Margherita Melillo, 'COVID-19 Symposium: The Right to Enjoy the Benefits of Scientific Progress at the Time of the COVID-19 Pandemic' (*Opinio Juris*, 6 April 2020) <https://bit.ly/3fAVPZK> accessed 30 April 2022.

90 Armin von Bogdandy and Pedro Villarreal, 'The Role of International Law in Vaccinating Against COVID-19: Appraising the COVAX Initiative' (2021) 81 ZaöRV 89.

91 Seth Berkley 'COVAX Explained' (*Gavi*, 3 September 2020) <https://www.gavi.org/vaccineswork/covax-explained> accessed 30 April 2022.

92 von Bogdandy and Villarreal (n 90) 26.

93 WHO, 'COVAX' (*WHO*, undated) <https://www.who.int/initiatives/act-accelerator/covax> accessed 30 April 2022.

very important role in COVAX, as their Board Chairs are the co-chairs of the COVAX Coordination Meeting, the body directing and coordinating COVAX.[94] The legal administrator of COVAX is GAVI, and its office is located within the GAVI Secretariat.[95] Other organizations, government officials, and experts are involved in the management of COVAX. Among the international organizations, one can find members of the World Bank and of the United Nations International Children's Emergency Fund (UNICEF, the main delivery partner of COVAX[96]). Among the non-governmental organizations one can find representatives of long-standing actors in global health such as Médecins Sans Frontières and the Bill & Melinda Gates Foundation.[97]

Given that so many actors are involved, one may wonder: What is the WHO's role in COVAX? WHO officials participate in all the meetings of COVAX.[98] The WHO, moreover, provides COVAX with guidance on 'vaccine policy, regulation, safety, R&D, allocation, and country readiness and delivery'.[99] This work relies, once again, on the technical and medical expert authority of the WHO, as it is carried out mostly through expert bodies such as the Strategic Advisory Group of Experts.[100]

Despite being an essential actor, it is difficult to avoid the impression that (as some authors have already noted) the WHO is merely a 'partner', and not the 'coordinator', in the operations of COVAX.[101] The reason is very practical: vaccine development and distribution are a money- and labour-intensive business, and even before COVID-19, leadership in the field of vaccine development and distribution was already not in the hands of the WHO, but rather in those of wealthier organizations. In this respect, the development of COVAX has merely consolidated the existing power structures.

As of June 2021, COVAX has managed to mobilize an impressive amount of resources, and it has delivered almost 80 million vaccine doses to 129 different countries.[102] Nevertheless, overall, COVAX is certainly not working as much or as fast as some would like it to.[103] It will take a long time before we

94 WHO, 'COVAX: The Vaccines Pillar of the Access to COVID-19 Tools (ACT) Accelerator' (*WHO*, 9 November 2020) 6 <https://bit.ly/3p37gMJ> accessed 30 April 2022.

95 Ibid 13.

96 WHO (COVAX) (n 93).

97 WHO (ACT Accelerator) (n 94).

98 Ibid.

99 WHO, 'COVAX Reaches over 100 Economies, 42 Days after First International Delivery' (*WHO*, 9 April 2021) <https://bit.ly/3i0F2Ri> accessed 30 April 2022.

100 Ibid.

101 Tine Hanrieder, 'Priorities, Partners, Politics: The WHO's Mandate beyond the Crisis' (2020) 26 Glob Governance 534, 541.

102 GAVI, 'Covax Vaccine Roll-Out' (*GAVI*, updated as of 3 June 2021) <https://www.gavi.org/covax-facility> accessed 3 June 2022.

103 Ann Danaiya Usher, 'CEPI Criticised for Lack of Transparency' (2021) 397 The Lancet 265; 'Almost One Billion Doses of Covid-19 Vaccines Have Been

will be able to assess whether the programme can be actually considered a successful experiment, and how it could have been improved. But for the time being, it already seems possible to affirm that the WHO has been relegated to the role of supporting actor.

Similarly as in the sub-sections above, the two examples presented here do not imply that the WHO has been unable to show any leadership at all in the COVID-19 pandemic response. However, they do show that the WHO's actions have been severely constrained by its pre-existing limitations.

4 Conclusion

The COVID-19 pandemic represented a critical moment for the WHO to show its authority in global health. By focusing on four examples (i.e. the recommendation on facemasks; the recommendation against travel restrictions; the China-US feud; and the COVAX initiative), this chapter has shown how pre-existing challenges in global health cooperation have considerably limited the WHO's ability to respond to the current pandemic. The WHO's actions have been particularly hampered by a lack of resources, a contradictory mandate, as well as by limitations arising from its over-emphasis on technical and medical expertise.

The good news that emerges from this picture is that despite what many may think, the WHO is no more in crisis today than it was ten or five years ago. While it is too early to draw any firm conclusions on the WHO's response as a whole, it is worth noting that those who know the organization well believe that, considering all the existing constraints, the WHO has overall done a good job.[104]

Paradoxically, the WHO may be also in a better position today than it was before the pandemic. Its relevance has never seemed greater, and there are already several initiatives in place pushing for reform.[105] As a result of all the criticism and pressures it received from many stakeholders, in May 2020, the WHA decided to launch an independent evaluation of the WHO's COVID-19 response.[106] Following on the WHA's mandate, in July 2020, the WHO Director General appointed Ellen Johnson Sirleaf and Helen Clark as co-chairs of the newly established Independent Panel for Pandemic Preparedness

Produced' *The Economist* (3 April 2021) <https://econ.st/3c75DbH>; Michael Safi and Ashley Kirk, 'Revealed: Big Shortfall in Covax Covid Vaccine-Sharing Scheme' *The Guardian* (22 April 2021) <http://www.theguardian.com/world/2021/apr/22/revealed-big-shortfall-in-covax-covid-vaccine-sharing-scheme> both accessed 30 April 2022.

104 'Tedros Adhanom Ghebreyesus: The Ethiopian at the Heart of the Coronavirus Fight' (*BBC News*, 7 May 2020) <https://www.bbc.com/news/world-africa-51720184> accessed 30 April 2022.

105 Stephanie Nebehay, 'WHO Needs Reforms, While Preserving "Political Independence": Panel' (*Reuters*, 5 November 2020) <https://www.reuters.com/article/us-health-coronavirus-who-idUSKBN27L1WA> accessed 30 April 2022.

106 World Health Assembly, Resolution, 'COVID-19 response' (19 May 2020) WHA73.1 [9]-[10].

and Response.[107] In parallel, a Review Committee on the Functioning of the International Health Regulations (2005) during the COVID-19 response was also launched.[108] In May 2021, both mechanisms published their final reports, where they identified many areas for improvement, both in terms of national preparedness and in international cooperation during the pandemic response.[109] The WHA endorsed the reports, and held a special session in November–December 2021, where it adopted a resolution establishing an Intergovernmental Negotiating Body to Strengthen Pandemic Prevention, Preparedness and Response (INB).[110]

It is too soon to predict whether the attempts to develop a new treaty will succeed or what the final text might look like. However, the decision of the WHA to establish an INB already shows that, despite all the difficulties encountered in the COVID-19 pandemic response discussed above, States have not lost faith in global health multilateralism, and are interested in learning and understanding how cooperation can be improved to prevent, or at least better manage, a future pandemic. Overall, the mere existence of these efforts shows that the concept of global health multilateralism is far from *passé*.

107 Independent Panel for Pandemic Preparedness and Response, 'Terms of Reference' <https://bit.ly/3p6tk9q> accessed 30 April 2022.

108 WHO, 'Review Committee on the Functioning of the International Health Regulations (2005) during the COVID-19 Response' <https://www.who.int/teams/ihr/ihr-review-committees/covid-19> accessed 30 April 2022.

109 WHO, 'Report of the Review Committee on the Functioning of the International Health Regulations (2005) during the COVID-19 Response' (5 May 2021) A74/9 Add.1; The Independent Panel for Pandemic Preparedness and Response, 'COVID-19: Make It the Last Pandemic' (12 May 2021) <https://bit.ly/2RhrFRW> accessed 30 April 2022.

110 World Health Assembly, 'The World Together: Establishment of an Intergovernmental Negotiating Body to Strengthen Pandemic Prevention, Preparedness and Response' (1 December 2021) SSA2(5).

15 The Council of Europe and Russia

Emerging from a Crisis or Heading Towards a New One?

Szymon Zaręba

1 Introduction

Founded in 1949, the Council of Europe (CoE) – an international organisation which promotes peaceful cooperation between its members, democracy, human rights, and the rule of law – remains one of the cornerstones of European multilateralism. While undoubtedly it has been crucial to the promotion of these principles in Europe for years, recently it has been increasingly struggling with enforcing the compliance of some of its Member States with these principles. One of the most instructive cases in this regard is the way the organisation has handled the crisis over participation of the Russian delegation in the works of one of its primary organs – the Parliamentary Assembly of the Council of Europe (PACE). This case, discussed in detail below, may serve as an example of the type of crisis that multilateral institutions have been facing recently – the clash between an organisation and one of its powerful Members; one which does not shy away from using various means of exerting pressure (political, economic, etc.) to evade compliance or force concessions.[1]

The following analysis seeks to demonstrate that the failure of an organisation to stick to its own fundamental principles and to resist giving in to demands has, in the described instances, made other Members frustrated with the functioning of the organisation, as it fails to deliver on its declared goals. Consequently, the steps taken to accommodate the demands of the powerful Member (Russia), if insufficiently justified in the light of the organisation's law and practice, may undermine the legitimacy of the organisation in the eyes of its less powerful Members. The unwelcome result is an erosion of trust in multilateral solutions and a reduced incentive to comply with the rules set by an organisation.

This chapter proceeds as follows: Section 1 summarises the origins of the crisis in question, its development, and the remedies implemented by the organisation to address it. Section 2 presents Thomas Franck's concept of

1 As regards the pressure to force concessions, see, for example, the actions of the United States (US) during Donald Trump's term of office, e.g. with respect to the Universal Postal Union or the World Health Organization.

DOI: 10.4324/9781003312857-17

legitimacy in the international system. Section 3 examines the impact of the measures taken by the CoE to restore Russian representation in the PACE on the legitimacy of the organisation and its enforcement system. The final section offers some more general conclusions.

2 The crisis: origins, development, and remedies

The origin of the crisis in question dates back to 10 April 2014. In response to the Russian occupation of Ukrainian Crimea, the subsequent annexation of the peninsula and 'threats of military actions in the rest of Ukraine's territory' (shortly thereafter realised in Eastern Ukraine),[2] the PACE imposed sanctions on the Russian delegation to the Assembly. Russia, it argued, had seriously violated the basic principles of the CoE, set out in Article 3 and the preamble to its Statute,[3] as well as the commitments it undertook upon accession. Therefore, under Article 8 of its Rules of Procedure, the PACE deprived the Russian representatives of the right to vote and take part in the works of the main organs of the Assembly (the Bureau, the Presidential Committee, and the Standing Committee) and election observation missions.[4] It also called on Russia to de-escalate the situation and reverse the annexation of Crimea. This was the first of several resolutions issued in connection with the conflict in Ukraine. In January 2015, the PACE again limited the Russian delegation's rights in the Assembly, thereby affecting the right of Russian representatives to be appointed rapporteurs, to become members of ad hoc committees on the observation of elections, and to represent the Assembly both within the CoE and externally. The new resolution further called on the Russian authorities to, e.g. withdraw their troops from Ukrainian territory; cease support

2 On 24 February 2022, Russia launched another aggression against Ukraine, this time on a much larger scale. Hostilities of varying degrees of intensity covered not only Eastern Ukraine, but in fact the entire territory of the state, in particular the Eastern and Southern regions (oblasts) and the Kyiv, Chernihiv, and Sumy oblasts in the North. These actions were met with a much stronger CoE response, briefly outlined in n 81.

3 Article 3 specifically states that every Member of the Council of Europe must accept the principles of the rule of law and of the enjoyment by all persons within its jurisdiction of human rights and fundamental freedoms, and collaborate sincerely and effectively in the realisation of the aim of the Council which is, *inter alia*, the realisation of the ideals of the CoE. According to the preamble, one of these ideals is the 'pursuit of peace based upon justice and international co-operation' (see Statute of the Council of Europe (entry into force 3 August 1949) 87 UNTS 103).

4 Resolution 1990 (2014) 'Reconsideration on Substantive Grounds of the Previously Ratified Credentials of the Russian Delegation' 10 April 2014. It needs to be underscored that this was not equivalent to non-ratification of the credentials of the Russian delegation, see Andrew Drzemczewski, 'The (Non-)Participation of Russian Parliamentarians in the Parliamentary Assembly of the Council of Europe: An Overview of Recent Developments' (2020) 1 Europe des droits & libertés 7, 7–8.

for the separatists in Eastern Ukraine; and stop human rights violations of ethnic Ukrainians and Tatars in Crimea.[5] Regrettably, these calls were ignored.

Faced with the possibility that its delegation would become the object of further sanctions – as limitations on the rights of PACE delegations may be introduced or renewed each year in January, when the PACE ratifies credentials for a new session – from 2016, Russia decided to forego sending a delegation to the Assembly.[6] Its officials announced that Russian representatives would not return as long as there was a risk the PACE would not allow them to participate fully in the works of the body. They considered the PACE's previous actions as an encroachment on the rights of the Russian delegates in violation of the CoE Statute.[7] By refusing to send its delegates, Russia effectively excluded itself from the PACE, significantly losing influence over the activities of the CoE. In an attempt to exert pressure on the organisation to change its policy, in June 2017, Russia suspended the payment of its membership fees (about 7 per cent of the organisation's annual budget).[8] Some of its politicians even threatened to leave the CoE if steps were not taken to fully and unconditionally restore the rights of Russia's PACE delegation.

These actions provoked a swift response on the part of the CoE: by October 2017, the PACE had set up an ad hoc Working Group and initiated a process to ensure that all members of the CoE would be 'fully represented' in both statutory organs.[9] Certain officials, such as the Secretary General Thorbjørn Jagland, began to voice concerns over a possible Russian withdrawal from the organisation, highlighting that over 140 million Russians would not have recourse to the European Court of Human Rights (ECtHR). Still, the pace of the process envisaged by the PACE was slow, and another two years passed without Russia sending a delegation to the Assembly in an attempt to avoid possible sanctions. Over time, key CoE political figures such as Jagland, then-Chairman of the Committee of Ministers Timo Soini, and

5 Resolution 2034 (2015) 'Challenge, on substantive grounds, of the still unratified credentials of the delegation of the Russian Federation' 28 January 2015.

6 European Stability Initiative, 'Negotiating with a Pointed Gun. Sanctions, Appeasement and the Role of Russia in the Council of Europe' 8 October 2018 <https://bit.ly/2RXEaSI> accessed 30 April 2022.

7 See e.g. a statement by Mr Sergey Lavrov, the Minister of Foreign Affairs, who also called this encroachment 'illegitimate', in Drzemczewski (n 4) 7–8. A more detailed explanation of the view can be found in, e.g. Antonino Ali, 'The Parliamentary Assembly of the Council of Europe and the Sanctions Against the Russian Federation in Response to the Crisis in Ukraine' (2018) 27(1) Ital Yb Int L 77, 88–90.

8 'Russia Evades Exclusion from Council of Europe' *The Moscow Times* (16 May 2019) <https://bit.ly/2S27iIH> accessed 30 April 2022.

9 Resolution 2186 (2017) 'Call for a Council of Europe Summit to Reaffirm European Unity and to Defend and Promote Democratic Security in Europe' 11 October 2017.

the President of the Parliamentary Assembly Liliane Maury Pasquier,[10] increasingly emphasised that the CoE was suffering from an unprecedented political, institutional, or perhaps even financial crisis, which needed to be promptly resolved.[11] In 2018 and 2019, the Russian authorities suggested that Russia might leave the CoE if its delegates were not allowed to participate in the election of the new Secretary-General and the judges of the ECtHR,[12] scheduled for 26 June 2019.[13] On 17 May 2019, the Committee of Ministers adopted a decision calling on the PACE to ensure that all CoE Members (including Russia) could take part in the PACE summer session on 24–28 June. Discussion in the Committee was heated, with some States, particularly the Baltic states (Lithuania, Latvia, Estonia), Georgia, and Ukraine strongly opposing this recommendation. However, they were outvoted.

On 24 June 2019, a vote concerning the proposed resolution to remove the rules allowing the application of the most important sanctions previously imposed on Russia (i.e. sanctions on the ability to speak, vote, and be represented in the Assembly and its bodies) from the PACE's Rules of Procedure, took place – this time in the PACE.[14] In a tense atmosphere, a large majority of delegates from France, Spain, Germany, Turkey, Italy, and others approved the removal of said rules, while representatives from Georgia, Lithuania, Latvia, Estonia, Poland, Sweden, Ukraine, and the UK voted

10 See 'Secretary General of Council of Europe Speaks about the Crisis in PACE Due to the Conflict with Russia' (*UA Wire*, 23 January 2019) <https://bit.ly/3p97Kkp>; 'Addressing the Council of Europe crisis requires constructiveness from all parties, says Timo Soini' (*Council of Europe*, 8 April 2019) <https://bit.ly/3i9CUH5>; Liliane Maury Pasquier, 'Speech at the Opening of the 3rd part of the 2019 Ordinary Session' (*Council of Europe*, 24 June 2019) <https://bit.ly/3yUssJn> all accessed 30 April 2022.

11 See e.g. a quote from Jagland's speech: 'depriving the Russian delegation of the right to vote in this assembly has not led to the return of Crimea to Ukraine or improved the human rights situation in the Russian Federation. It has created a crisis within this organisation instead' (Alexandra Stiglmayer, 'The Council of Europe's Surrender to Russia' (*EU Observer*, 27 June 2019) <https://euobserver.com/opinion/145282> accessed 30 April 2022).

12 See 'Foreign Minister Sergey Lavrov's Interview with Euronews' (*Ministry of Foreign Affairs of the Russian Federation*, 16 October 2018) <https://bit.ly/2TyxjQg>. See also a statement by the head of the Russian Senate's International Relations Committee, Konstantin Kosachev, that Russia 'entertained a possibility of leaving the Council of Europe' – 'Ruxit' would be a 'blow' similar to Brexit – Council of Europe chief (*RT*, 7 April 2019) <https://www.rt.com/news/455807-russia-leave council-europe-brexit/> both accessed 30 April 2022.

13 Interestingly, under the CoE statute, July 2019 would mark the date from which Russia's right to participate in the work of PACE and the second main CoE body, the Committee of Ministers, could be suspended due to a two-year delay in paying contributions. That would have deprived it of all influence on the organisation's activities, but was highly improbable at the time.

14 See Resolution 2287 (2019) 'Strengthening the Decision-Making Process of the Parliamentary Assembly Concerning Credentials and Voting' 25 June 2019 [10].

against.[15] In addition, the PACE declared its intention to implement a new joint reaction procedure[16] for future systematic and flagrant violations of the organisation's basic principles in order to improve the existing sanction system for the enforcement of the CoE's fundamental rules. On the same day, the PACE adopted another resolution which accepted the credentials of the Russian delegation without further conditions, although calling for, e.g. the immediate payment of Russia's overdue CoE contributions and release of the Ukrainian seamen captured during the so-called Kerch incident in November 2018.[17] These two June 2019 resolutions allowed the Russian delegation to once again participate in the PACE without restriction.

These developments were met with positive reactions from some Western States, particularly France and Germany, which argued that upholding the pan-European character of the organisation and the continued protection of Russian citizens via the ECtHR marked a success. Russia, obviously, also welcomed them. However, Ukraine, which insisted on maintaining the possibility of applying sanctions because of ongoing Russian aggression and the occupation of part of its territory, recalled its CoE representative for consultations, and revoked its invitation for CoE observers to monitor the elections on 21 July 2019. Its delegation withdrew from further participation in the PACE's summer session and called on the Ukrainian president to consider whether the country should remain in the CoE. In a gesture of solidarity, delegates from Georgia, Lithuania, Latvia, Estonia, Poland, and Slovakia also left the session. Together with the representatives of Ukraine, they issued a joint declaration stating that Russia's return to the PACE despite continuing serious violations of CoE resolutions was in conflict with the basic principles of the organisation and its statute.[18]

In early September 2019, Russia finally cleared its outstanding payments for 2017 and 2018, totalling about EUR 55 million. However, Ukraine declared that its representatives would not participate in the Autumn session of the Assembly and the celebrations marking the 70th anniversary of the CoE in October 2019.[19] Latvia followed suit. Other countries, such as Lithuania, Estonia, Georgia, and Poland, announced they would boycott the

15 The results were: 118 voting in favour, 62 against, 10 abstaining, see 'Vote on Resolution' (*European Council Parliamentary Assembly*, 24 June 2019) <https://bit.ly/3fWkCpS> accessed 30 April 2022.

16 Also labelled the 'joint procedure of reaction' or the 'joint response mechanism'.

17 One should mention, however, that the PACE invited its Monitoring Committee to present a report on the honouring of obligations and commitments by Russia no later than in April 2020. See of Resolution 2292 (2019) 'Challenge, on Substantive Grounds, of the Still Unratified Credentials of the Parliamentary Delegation of the Russian Federation' 26 June 2019 [14].

18 'Estonian Delegation Leaves PACE Session in Protest' (*ERR News*, 27 June 2019) <https://bit.ly/3g4oYwm> accessed 30 April 2022.

19 'Statement by VRU Delegation on Participation in PACE' (*Verkhovna Rada of Ukraine*, 24 September 2019) <https://iportal.rada.gov.ua/en/news/News/181782.html> accessed 30 April 2022.

official events marking CoE's anniversary in protest against Russia's return to the body.[20] Lithuania, Latvia, and Estonia, together with Georgia and Ukraine, created the Baltic Plus alliance, aiming to oppose the decision by PACE, which they regarded as an unconditional surrender to Russian economic blackmail and political pressure. They also expressed their concerns over the proposed joint response mechanism as unsatisfactory and ineffective.[21]

These steps did not lead to any noticeable change. Moreover, the absence of the Ukrainian and Latvian delegates diminished the number of those opposing the Russian return to the PACE and those supporting a robust mechanism of enforcement of the CoE principles. Having realised that, in mid-January 2020, the Ukrainian parliament instructed its delegation to return to the PACE.[22] The Latvian parliament followed suit. During the PACE winter session on 27–31 January, the Baltic Plus group tried to challenge the credentials of the Russian delegation on both material and procedural grounds,[23] but ultimately they failed.[24] The initiatives were mostly supported by PACE Members from the Baltic Plus states[25] and Poland, Sweden, and the UK.[26] Interestingly, the introduction of the new mechanism of response to serious violations of the CoE Statute, ultimately called the 'complementary joint

20 'Poland Joins Boycott of 70th Anniversary of PACE' (*112 Ukraine*, 1 October 2019) <https://bit.ly/3vAL4fk> accessed 30 April 2022.

21 'Latvian Delegation to the PACE Reiterates Its Protest Against Restoring the Voting Rights of Russia' (*Latvijas Republikas Saeima*, 30 September 2019) <https://bit.ly/3yPQ161> accessed 30 April 2022.

22 'Parliament in Ukraine Approves Return of Country's Delegation to PACE' (*Unian Information Agency*, 16 January 2020) <https://bit.ly/3fzohLj> accessed 30 April 2022.

23 Pointing out, respectively, that Russia continued to violate the most fundamental CoE obligations (Lithuanian MP), and that the Russian delegation included two people elected with the votes of the people of illegally occupied Crimea and sanctioned by the EU for their support of Crimea's annexation (Latvian MP). See 'Authorities of Russian Delegation Litigated in PACE' (*112 Ukraine*, 27 January 2020) <https://bit.ly/3ca8vod>; and respectively, 'PACE Ratifies the Credentials of the Russian Federation' (*Council of Europe*, 29 January 2020) <https://bit.ly/3caA7th> and 'Challenges, on Procedural Grounds, to the Credentials of the Spanish, Moldovan and Russian Delegations' (*Council of Europe*, 29 January 2020) <https://bit.ly/3caAdkD> all accessed 30 April 2022.

24 In the meantime, Russian delegates warned they would leave PACE if their rights were restricted, evoking the nightmares of the recent past. See Leonid Slutskiy, 'Any Secondary Sanctions Against the Russian Delegation to PACE Will Again Make Us Leave the Assembly' (*Russian State Duma*, 28 January 2020) <http://duma.gov.ru/en/news/47639/> accessed 30 April 2022.

25 With the exception of Estonia's representatives who did not vote.

26 'Consequences of Russia's Restored Rights in PACE' (*Euromaidan Press*, 7 February 2020) <https://bit.ly/3fCWwBE>. See also 'The Members of National Delegations Signing This Declaration Regret the Approval, by the Assembly, of the Credentials Submitted by the Russian Federation' (*Council of Europe*, 31 January 2020) <https://pace.coe.int/en/files/28586> both accessed 30 April 2022.

procedure',[27] met with mixed reactions. Representatives of Ukraine voted against it, arguing it would be hard to initiate, slow and not effective.[28] Lithuanian, Latvian and the majority of Swedish representatives abstained and the ones from Estonia did not vote – all without providing an explicit reason. Those from Georgia, Poland, and some from Sweden supported the new procedure, as did the vast majority of other delegations.[29] On 5 February 2020, the procedure was adopted by the Committee of Ministers, with only Ukraine reportedly voting against and several other states abstaining.[30] These different approaches were most probably due to the varying assessments of the new procedure.[31] Ukraine believed that the CoE would simply use it as an excuse to avoid taking any meaningful action against Russian violations of Article 3 of the CoE Statute. The majority of other states and NGOs saw it as an opportunity to engage Russia in a dialogue that could somewhat improve the human rights situation, even if over a much longer timeframe.

3 The concept of legitimacy

As seen above, a considerable number of CoE Members repeatedly voiced concerns regarding the approach of the CoE towards Russia in 2019, including concerns about the credibility of the organisation and/or its system of sanctions after PACE's votes in June 2019.[32] At first glance these allegations

27 See Committee of Ministers, Decision CM/Del/Dec(2020)1366/1.7-app, 5 February 2020 <https://rm.coe.int/1366d01-7app/16809a59c4> accessed 30 April 2022; Resolution 2319 (2020) 'Complementary Joint Procedure Between the Committee of Ministers and the Parliamentary Assembly in Response to a Serious Violation by a Member State of Its Statutory Obligations' 29 January 2020.

28 Surprisingly, Russian delegates also either voted against or abstained, claiming their amendments had not been adopted; see 'Russian Delegation to PACE Opposed the Resolution Regulating the Restriction of Rights of National Delegations' (*Russian State Duma*, 31 January 2020) <http://duma.gov.ru/en/news/47668/> accessed 30 April 2022.

29 'Vote on Resolution 2319 (2020)' (*PACE*, 29 January 2020) <https://bit.ly/3fGo0q5> accessed 30 April 2022.

30 'Russia's Occupation of Crimea, Donbas War Not "Serious Violations" in Council of Europe's New Sanctions Procedure' (*Euromaidan Press*, 8 February 2020) <https://bit.ly/3i3IZ7P> accessed 30 April 2022.

31 The procedure involves PACE, the Committee of Ministers and the Secretary General. It includes an assessment of the situation, the creation of a roadmap containing actions to be taken by the Member State concerned, and a dialogue aimed at implementation of this roadmap (see Resolution 2319 (2020)).

32 See the concerns over diminished PACE legitimacy by an Ukrainian MP – Oleksiy Goncharenko, 'PACE Risks Becoming a Watchdog with No Bite' (*Atlantic Council*, 27 January 2020) <https://bit.ly/3fVBCwx>. Also interesting is a summary of the EU-Russia Legal Dialogue Symposium, which indicates that the word 'crisis' was used by many participants, either lawyers or NGO workers, in connection with the recent situation within the CoE, and that the Russia's delegation's exclusion from or return to the PACE were mentioned as one of its major reasons. See Mikhail Kaluzhsky, 'The Future of Human Rights and the

might seem to be of little importance from a legal perspective, belonging rather to the realm of ethics or political science. This does not hold true, however, if one looks at the wider consequences of this disappointment, namely the possibly diminished legitimacy of the organisation as a multilateral institution and of its sanctions system. Since such a situation could increase the risk of non-compliance with the law established by the organisation, it thus seems necessary to evaluate the effects of the decisions taken by the PACE in light of the appropriate criteria.

In order to assess the impact on the legitimacy of the CoE and its sanctions system, one must first reflect on what 'international legitimacy' effectively means. Although there are many competing theories in the literature,[33] the analysis below will be based on the understanding of the term proposed by late Thomas Franck.[34] There are several reasons for this. First, Franck remains a key figure in the debate on legitimacy in international law, and his seminal work is considered the mainstream view.[35] Second, his approach is positivist in its focus on State consent and the rule of recognition[36] as a tool to identify the international legal obligations,[37] and aligns with the methodological approach of the author of this chapter. Third, Franck's theory is centred around the social aspects of compliance with law.[38] This is in line with the stated objective of this text, which is to show how the failure of a multilateral institution to live up to its own principles undermines the trust of other actors involved and may diminish their willingness to obey its rules.

Franck defines legitimacy as:

> a property of a rule or rule-making institution which itself exerts a pull toward compliance on those addressed normatively, because those

Council of Europe: The Need for a Reset' (*Legal Dialogue*, 13 February 2020) <https://bit.ly/3uCgzEp> both accessed 30 April 2022.

33 For an overview, see Daniel Bodansky, 'Legitimacy in International Law and International Relations' in Jeffrey L Dunoff and Mark A Pollack (eds), *Interdisciplinary Perspectives on International Law and International Relations: The State of the Art* (CUP 2013) 321–342; Rüdiger Wolfrum and Volker Roeben (eds), *Legitimacy in International Law* (Springer-Verlag 2008).

34 Thomas M Franck, *The Power of Legitimacy Among Nations* (OUP 1990).

35 Mohsen Al Attar and Edward Miller, 'Rethinking Legitimacy in International Law' in Thomas Muhr (ed), *Counter-Globalization and Socialism in the 21st Century* (Routledge 2013) 82.

36 The rule of recognition is a secondary, meta-rule, which in essence makes a legal system of a set of rules, particularly by identifying which of those rules are valid and which are not. The concept has been put forward by one of the most influential positivist writers, Herbert Hart. See Herbert LA Hart, *The Concept of Law* (Clarendon Press 1978) 97–107. Franck's fourth criterion of legitimacy, 'adherence' (soon to be discussed below), largely corresponds with this concept.

37 Jutta Brunnée and Stephen J Toope, *Legitimacy and Legality in International Law: An Interactional Account* (CUP 2010) 52–53.

38 Ibid 53; Harold H Koh, 'Why Do Nations Obey International Law?' (1997) 106 (8) Yale L J 2599, 2628, 2635, and 2642.

> addressed believe that the rule or institution has come into being and operates under accepted principles of right process.[39]

In the passage just quoted, he speaks about 'rules' and not 'law'. The reason he does so is because he believes that international law cannot be considered as law proper, but rather as a body of 'rules applicable among states'.[40] In his view, this is because the obligations imposed are not enforced by a centralised coercive power.[41] Even if one disagrees with this opinion, Franck's observations and conclusions on legitimacy remain pertinent. An institution or a rule is legitimate, he argues, if it exerts a 'compliance pull', i.e. makes its addressee feel obligated by it and compelled to behave in a given way.[42] Neither the pull to compliance nor the legitimacy are dummy variables; they come in shades. The higher the former, the higher the latter. States, he believes, tend to obey the rules or institutions they perceive as having a high degree of legitimacy,[43] while much more frequently avoiding or ignoring those less legitimate ones.

According to Franck, there are four factors that need to be taken into account when assessing the degree of legitimacy and resulting compliance pull: (1) determinacy; (2) symbolic validation; (3) coherence; and (4) adherence. Determinacy means that the rule or institution must indicate what is permitted and what is not in a clear and determinate way.[44] This refers not only to its textual clarity but also, or even primarily, to the message it conveys. The less ambiguous it is, the harder it is for a state to justify non-compliance. The second factor, symbolic validation, focuses on the use of ritual, pedigree, or both, as – in Franck's own words – 'cues to secure compliance'. This means that a rule or rule-making authority is seen as more legitimate if it is perceived as established and deeply rooted because of its historical continuity (pedigree) or is accepted through a specific ceremony (ritual),[45] such as a vote. The third indicator of legitimacy, coherence, requires the rules to be applied equally unless they provide for exceptions, which ought to be based on objective, generally applicable, rational grounds and accepted by all parties involved as justifying the inconsistent treatment.[46] Coherence must also be considered when symbolic validation is evaluated – if the rule or institution is to be legitimate, the reality to which the ritual or pedigree refers should not be plainly false, e.g. an inter-state organisation should not admit as its member state an entity which manifestly fails to fulfil the criteria of statehood.[47] The next, and final, factor which according to Franck's theory allows

39 Franck (n 34) 24.
40 Ibid 24.
41 Ibid 38–39.
42 Ibid 26, 42, 44.
43 Ibid 150.
44 Ibid 52–57.
45 Ibid 92–94.
46 Ibid 138–139, 144–148, 153.
47 Ibid 111–112, 136–138.

for the assessment of legitimacy is adherence, which demands that a rule adheres to a hierarchy of secondary rules which govern how the sources of rules are identified, made, interpreted and applied.[48] This means that in order to exert a considerable compliance pull, it should not be an ad hoc arrangement but rather a rule which is 'systemically based', i.e. established within an organised community consisting of interdependent members, such as the one of States. Only then is its observance of concern not only for those directly involved, but for other members of the community as well, since violation of such a rule or rules affects the stability of the entire system of rules to be applied and obeyed.

4 PACE's decisions and their legitimacy

Assessed using the criteria described above, PACE's decisions to let the Russian delegation unconditionally return to the Assembly and change its Rules of Procedure appear controversial. Their consequences related to the legitimacy of the CoE as a multilateral institution and of its system of enforcement of fundamental rules will now be discussed.

The PACE's sanctions on Russia were imposed in 2014 and 2015 to express disapproval over Russian violations of Ukrainian sovereignty and territorial integrity, considered by the Assembly as 'a flagrant violation' of a CoE Member State's 'obligations and commitments'.[49] These violations had not ceased by the June 2019 votes. In fact, between 2014 and 2019, they were followed by numerous other violations of human rights in Crimea and Eastern Ukraine. This makes the reasoning underlying PACE's June 2019 resolutions – not only to let Russian delegates return to PACE but also to make the easy reimposition of sanctions against them impossible in the future through the change of its own Rules of Procedure[50] – disturbing. The CoE Member States might reasonably wonder whether the grounds on which the Russian delegation had been deprived of its PACE rights in 2014 and 2015 constituted a 'serious violation of the basic principles of the Council of Europe' in the first place, as required by Rule 8.2.a. of the PACE Rules of Procedure and Article 3 of the CoE Statute.

Since Russia failed to bring itself into compliance with PACE's resolutions before June 2019, and PACE's Rules of Procedure were nevertheless changed according to Russia's wishes,[51] one may infer that Russia's actions must not have been serious enough to justify even the possibility of the reimposition of the sanctions on its PACE delegation. But if that was the case, then it is hard

48 Ibid 184–191.
49 Resolution 1990 (2014) 'Reconsideration on Substantive Grounds of the Previously Ratified Credentials of the Russian Delegation' (10 April 2014).
50 See Resolution 2287 (2019) [10].
51 This remark refers to para 10 of the Resolution 2287 (2019), not para 7, providing for a derogation that allowed Russia to present the credentials of its representatives in June 2019.

to imagine what the Article 3 requirements mean in practice. As a result, one can conclude that the decision of PACE has negatively affected the determinacy of Article 3 of the Statute as grounds for CoE sanctions. The rule has become less clear, and doubts have arisen over what this provision really means. Had PACE not imposed sanctions in 2014, or had Russia fulfilled at least part of the demands contained in Ukraine-related resolutions before the June 2019 votes, this problem would not have existed.

Russia's return to the CoE – without any substantial improvement in its observance of the norms it had been accused of violating – also watered down the determinacy of the values defended by the organisation, at least in the opinion of some of its Member States. By giving way to Russian demands and changing PACE's Rules of Procedure to reflect Russian expectations, while faced with a considerable financial crisis provoked in essence by the Russian decision to withhold paying its member fees, the CoE seemed to have yielded to economic pressure. This was reflected in the accusations by some Member States and civil society representatives that the CoE was trading its values for money.[52] Some Member States even expressed confusion over what these values were, since they allowed the return to PACE of a state which had not only manifestly violated the territorial integrity and political independence of another Member State, but also committed serious human rights violations, stopped payment of its membership dues, and ignored all resolutions issued by PACE in this respect.[53]

But the problem does not end with determinacy. The decision to allow Russia's delegation to return to the PACE without any Russian concessions to alleviate the situation also greatly undermined the coherence – in Franck's understanding of the term – of the CoE sanctions system. The measures imposed against Russia in 2014 and 2015 were nothing extraordinary in PACE's practice. There have been two cases of CoE Member States facing even more stringent sanctions following internal political crises or coups which led to massive human rights violations, i.e. the refusal to ratify the credentials of their delegates – Greece in 1969[54] and

52 See e.g. 'Council of Europe's Parliamentary Assembly Cannot Exchange Its Values for Money – Libina-Egnere' *The Baltic Times* (6 June 2019) <https://bit.ly/3p6fLql> accessed 30 April 2022.

53 See a quote by Andreas Kubilius, former Lithuanian Prime Minister and former candidate for the post of the Secretary General of the CoE, 'The crisis of the Council of Europe is not functional or financial, it is a deep crisis of values and is related to Russia and its behaviour in the European continent' Andrius Kubilius, 'Saving the Council of Europe' *The Lithuania Tribune* (3 July 2019) <https://lithuaniatribune.com/saving-the-council-of-europe/> accessed 30 April 2022.

54 See Recommendation 547 (1969) 'Situation in Greece' (30 January 1969). The text of the recommendation leaves no doubt that the Assembly decided not to recognise the credentials of Greek delegates if submitted before; freedom of expression is restored, and a free and representative parliament is elected in Greece'. Moreover, in 1969, the Assembly even recommended that the Committee of Ministers suspend Greece's right of representation in the CoE as a whole, in accordance with Article 8 of the Statute. In turn, Greece decided to withdraw

Turkey in 1981.[55] In these cases, the delegations of the respective Member States were only allowed to once again take part in the works of the Assembly after democratic changes took place and fundamental rights and freedoms were restored.[56]

This means that in the case at hand, there was a blatant exemption from an established (and arguably, reasonable) practice and rule that sanctions should remain in force (or, to be more precise, be periodically reimposed) until the CoE Member in question improved its conduct. By changing its Rules of Procedure and stripping itself of the ability to impose certain sanctions,[57] the PACE in fact made it virtually impossible to apply them to the Russian delegation for ongoing violations.[58]

However, as stated above, an exception is not necessarily inconsistent with the principle of coherence if it is rationally and objectively explained and accepted by all members of the community (here the CoE). Regretfully, in the case in question, these requirements were not fulfilled. The main argument for the decision taken by the PACE, repeated over and over again, was that without any action Russia could have left the CoE altogether – as it threatened to do – which would have left its nationals and other people affected by the violations it committed without recourse to the ECtHR. However, the previous and very similar case of Greece (mentioned above) was handled in a totally different manner – the PACE did not refrain from recommending even more far-reaching measures to exert more pressure for compliance. As a result, at the time, Greece indeed left the CoE, but within a few years it returned as a democratic state.

Even more unsettling, Russia's national delegation to the PACE had already been temporarily deprived of some rights in the past (in April 2000) and was treated by the Assembly then in a manner similar to the way the

from the CoE. See Philip Leach, 'The Parliamentary Assembly of the Council of Europe' in Stefanie Schmahl and Marten Breuer (eds), *The Council of Europe: Its Law and Policies* (OUP 2007) 192. The Greek delegation returned to PACE only in 1974, when Greece rejoined the CoE after the fall of the dictatorship there.

55 See Order 392 (1980) 'Members of the Turkish Delegation to the Parliamentary Assembly' (1 October 1980), and Order 398 (1981) 'Term of Office of the Turkish Parliamentary Delegation' (14 May 1981). The non-recognition of the Turkish delegation's credentials was a consequence of the repression of human rights following a military coup d'état. The Turkish delegation was not allowed to return to the Assembly until 1984, when the free elections were held. See Leach (n 54) 192–193. See also Council of Europe 'Statement by the Secretary General of the Parliamentary Assembly' (19 October 2018) <https://bit.ly/3wTP0rZ> accessed 30 April 2022.

56 See Michel Waelbroeck, 'PACE Resolution to Lift Sanctions on Russia "Strategic Defeat for Human Rights Defenders" – Professor of European Law' (*Euromaidan Press*, 15 June 2019) <https://bit.ly/3g1YKJB> accessed 30 April 2022.

57 That is, rights to vote, to speak, and to be represented in the Assembly and its bodies.

58 The imposition of such measures would be possible only after a reversal to the previous version of Rule 10 of the PACE Rules of Procedure.

recent case has been handled. The reason for suspension of its rights at the time was Russia's most serious violations of fundamental human rights, such as the right to life, the right to liberty, and the right to security – violations committed through its indiscriminate and disproportionate use of force against the civilian population in Chechnya. In that case, some slight and superficial progress (such as the creation of a joint CoE-Russia working group on Chechnya) was used as the basis for the revocation of the suspension of the Russian delegation's voting rights after just a few months, i.e. in January 2001.[59] In fact however, grave violations of human rights in this part of Russia continued for years, as evidenced by, e.g., a report by the PACE of 2005[60] – and even in 2019 the situation remained far from perfect.

What is also important is that Russia's behaviour in recent years in general makes it a difficult task to justify its return to the PACE in 2019. Up until June 2019 (and in fact at present as well), Russia was still refusing to fully implement a large majority of ECtHR judgments (only paying compensation);[61] had legally sanctioned the possibility of refusing to enforce those judgments found to be incompatible with the Russian Constitution by its Constitutional Court;[62] and actively supported separatist groups or regimes in

59 Surprisingly, it is impossible to find the document suspending the voting rights of the Russian delegation. Still, one may find the information that this indeed happened in other CoE documents, see PACE Committee on Rules of Procedure and Immunities, 'Tabling and Adoption of Amendments and Sub-Amendments. Report' (7 February 2002) <https://bit.ly/3yWPqzF>. See also e.g. Eckhart Klein, 'Membership and Observer Status' in Stefanie Schmahl and Marten Breuer (eds), *The Council of Europe: Its Law and Policies* (OUP 2007) 90, Florence Benoît-Rohmer and Heinrich Klebes, *Council of Europe Law: Towards a Pan-European Legal Area* (Council of Europe Publishing 2005) 43.

60 See e.g. the quote: 'There is no end to gross human rights abuses in Chechnya, in the form of murder, enforced disappearance, torture, hostage-taking, and arbitrary detention. In addition, the climate of impunity is spreading further' PACE Committee on Legal Affairs and Human Rights, 'Human rights violations in the Chechen Republic: The Committee of Ministers' responsibility vis-à-vis the Assembly's concerns. Report' (21 December 2005) <https://bit.ly/3wTU13N> accessed 30 April 2022.

61 See Veronika Fikfak, 'Changing State Behaviour: Damages before the European Court of Human Rights' (2018) 29(4) EJIL 1115, who calls Russia 'one of the worst systemic violators of the ECHR' and emphasises that little progress has been made there with respect to addressing the underlying causes of violations. See also Rene Provost, 'Teetering on the Edge of Legal Nihilism: Russia and the Evolving European Human Rights Regime' (2015) 37(2) HRQ 289, 311 (quoting Y. Lapitskaya: 'Russia's Payments Mask the Ways the Russian Government Has Ignored or Even Actively Undermined the Goals of the ECHR').

62 Based on this law, Russia has refused to execute e.g. the judgments in *Anchugov and Gladkov v Russia* (App no 11157/04, 15162/05 (ECtHR, 4 July 2013)), regarding Russia's ban on the voting rights of all convicted prisoners serving prison sentences (this case was later settled by the Committee of Ministers, see Resolution CM/ResDH(2019)240 of 25 September 2019); and in *Yukos v Russia* (App 14902/04 (ECtHR, 31 July 2014)), ordering a payment of EUR 1.9 billion in compensation to the shareholders of the Yukos group, which was essentially

several CoE Member States, including Georgia and Moldova, as confirmed by several ECtHR judgments which found Russia responsible for violations of human rights committed by these groups.[63] These factors, combined with a continuous assault on human rights defenders, independent journalists, and NGOs,[64] earned it the reputation of a Member State adopting an 'à la carte approach' to human rights protection.[65] Most human rights experts agree that 'the overall human rights situation in Russia has become worse [in recent years] and legislative amendments have been used to tighten the screws'.[66] Therefore, it would not have been easy to provide a convincing rational explanation of why Russia's expectations deserved to be met. Given that, in the interest of legitimacy of the organisation it might have been better to not take any decision at all than to take one which turned out to be so divisive.

There was also another argument put forward by some members of the Assembly and other CoE officials before the June 2019 votes: that the CoE suffered from an institutional and/or political crisis because some Member States were not represented in the Assembly. Legal opinions were provided which argued that all members should be equally represented in both main organs of the organisation, i.e. the PACE and the Committee of Ministers, and that PACE had suspended the Russian delegation's rights to vote, to speak, and to be represented in the Assembly and its bodies in violation of the CoE Statute.[67] These conclusions were, once again, manifestly inconsistent with the organisation's established practice. There have been several cases where CoE Member States have been excluded from participation in the

expropriated by the government. Similar cases are not numerous though; see Maria Smirnova, 'Russia', in Fulvio M Palombino (ed), *Duelling for Supremacy: International Law vs. National Fundamental Principles* (CUP 2019) 310–317.

63 One could obviously add to this list also the ongoing Russian full-scale military aggression against Ukraine mentioned in n 2 but see n 81 for further developments.

64 One of the most recent and highly publicised instances was the poisoning of Alexei Navalny, an opposition leader and anti-corruption activist, in August 2020. PACE has even appointed a special rapporteur to look into the case, see 'Special Rapporteur on Alexei Navalny Poisoning: We Bet on Russia's Cooperation' (*Deutsche Welle*, 29 October 2020) <https://bit.ly/3uQwf7r> accessed 30 April 2022. Among others, one can mention the assassination of the liberal politician Boris Nemtsov and the murder of journalist Anna Politkovskaya. Russian authorities deny any involvement but at the same time refuse to cooperate with international organisations such as the CoE or other states to investigate the circumstances of these cases.

65 Petra Roter, 'Russia in the Council of Europe: Participation à la carte' in Lauri Mälksoo and Wolfgang Benedek (eds), *Russia and the European Court of Human Rights: The Strasbourg Effect* (CUP 2017) 29–30, 51.

66 Lauri Mälksoo, 'Introduction' in Lauri Mälksoo and Wolfgang Benedek (eds), *Russia and the European Court of Human Rights: The Strasbourg Effect* (CUP 2017) 6.

67 John Dalhuisen, 'What Is the Council of Europe for?' (*openDemocracy*, 27 June 2019) <https://www.opendemocracy.net/en/odr/what-council-europe/> accessed 30 April 2022.

works of the PACE while retaining their seat and rights in the Committee of Ministers. One should mention here the case against Cyprus which lasted for 19 years (1964–1983)[68] – or the case regarding Malta in the early 1980s.[69] This begs the question of why the illegality of such actions was not noticed and eliminated much earlier.[70] Once again, there was no proper explanation put forward why the CoE had tolerated this practice for so many years before concluding that it was not in line with its Statute. On the other hand, there were also no reasons provided as to why the Committee of Ministers could not change its own procedural rules instead, to give itself the ability to deprive its own members of the right to representation or vote in cases of grave violations of the CoE principles.[71] That would also lead to participation on an equal basis in the CoE's Committee of Ministers and the PACE.

It can be inferred from the above that the treatment of the case in question was inconsistent with established CoE practices, because the PACE Rules of Procedure concerning sanctions already in place had never previously been changed under pressure from the sanctioned state. At the same time, this move was inadequately justified by rational, general principles of distinction. As such, it undermined the equality of treatment of the Members of the organisation regarding sanctions, and in doing so also undermined the coherence of the system of enforcement of CoE's rules. This was the first time the rules were changed to accommodate the needs of a Member State facing a genuine threat that it would be sanctioned again. It is therefore not surprising that delegates from several CoE Member States voted against the proposed changes in June 2019, and that some of them did not support the establishment of the 'complementary joint procedure' in January 2020. The organisation's main bodies did not seek consensus on the matter, ignoring the voices of states neighbouring Russia and not attempting to address their justifiable concerns.

One also needs to note with regret that the decision of the PACE to change its Rules of Procedure and eliminate the possibility of imposing certain sanctions raises doubts – because of its inconsistency with past practice – about whether there were some other ulterior motives. Among the ones most frequently mentioned by the representatives of states or delegates opposed to such a decision are: surrendering to Russia's economic blackmail; the overriding desire of the CoE bureaucracy and some State leaders to show

68 See PACE Committee on Rules of Procedure, Immunities and Institutional Affairs, 'Strengthening the Decision-Making Process of the Parliamentary Assembly Concerning Credentials and Voting. Report' (21 September 2018) <https://bit.ly/3ccIu7B> accessed 30 April 2022, [22] and [32].

69 Leach (n 54) 192. As regards Cyprus, credentials were refused by the Assembly at least at the beginning of the period; later Cyprus declined to submit them.

70 This has been pointed out even in one of the Assembly's reports, see PACE Committee on Rules of Procedure, Immunities and Institutional Affairs (n 68) [29].

71 Or even use its already present extensive powers to achieve such an effect.

organisational unity for its 70th anniversary; or grand policy considerations, such as the need to not 'push Russia away from Europe', as doing so might provide a valuable political ally to a rising China[72] or an unpredictable US (i. e. under then-President Donald Trump).[73] These once again confirm that the CoE – meaning both the PACE and the Committee of Ministers – did not provide a sufficiently justified explanation (if one were even possible) of Russia's differential treatment which could have successfully convinced all its Member States to accept this exception. As a result, the crisis over Russia's return to the PACE has negatively affected the coherence of the image of the CoE as a guardian of common European values and fundamental rights and freedoms.

Finally, the June 2019 resolutions of the PACE also dealt a blow to the symbolic validation of the CoE's system of sanctions for grave violations of human rights or of the organisation's statute. Here one may note with astonishment all the inexplicable steps taken. First, the PACE changed a rule with a considerable pedigree, one which had been applied for years against states violating the most fundamental rights and freedoms,[74] claiming that it had been inconsistent with the Statute throughout this entire period. Second, it announced the creation of a new system of sanctions, but simultaneously made it impossible to impose several of them which had been available up to that point[75] and could have been applied to one of the Member States (i.e. Russia),[76] thus creating an inexplicable void in accountability. It could have devised new measures first and then repealed the existing ones, but it decided to get rid of them altogether instead. This is even more significant in light of the fact that it appears unlikely – considering both the prevailing attitude towards Russia in the PACE and the possible legal objections, e.g. of retroactivity[77] – that the CoE will initiate the complementary procedure adopted

72 James Nixey and Mathieu Boulègue, 'On Russia, Macron Is Mistaken' (*Chatham House*, 5 September 2019) <https://www.chathamhouse.org/expert/comment/russia-macron-mistaken> accessed 30 April 2022.

73 Jean-Luc Mounier, 'Russia's Undiplomatic Return to the Council of Europe' (*France24*, 28 June 2019), <https://bit.ly/3uIXGzE> accessed 30 April 2022.

74 See Resolution 2287 (2019) [10]

75 See e.g. Silvia Steininger, 'An Internal Safety Net for the Council of Europe?' (*Verfassungsblog*, 28 December 2019) <https://verfassungsblog.de/an-internal-safety-net-for-the-council-of-europe/> accessed 30 April 2022; Drzemczewski (n 4) 15, particularly fn 41.

76 From a purely technical point of view, through the change of its Rules of Procedure PACE made it a lot harder to deprive a CoE member of its rights to vote and representation in the Assembly while voting on credentials Such an action is currently impossible unless the whole change of said Rules is reversed. Due to the fact that Russia decided not to send its representatives to PACE in 2017 and 2018, in practice there were no sanctions in place against it. Still, there was a real risk that its delegation would not be allowed to vote in the Assembly, etc. again. So, effectively, the change of the PACE's Rules of Procedure eliminated the threat of further imposition of those sanctions.

77 It is unclear, however, whether these would be rejected or not, if raised.

in 2020 against Russia in order to address the ongoing violations which had formed the basis for the previous measures enacted against the Russian delegation. So, in the end, the PACE to a large extent nullified what Franck called the 'ritual' of imposing sanctions, showing that in fact the organisation could get rid of some measures it used with no meaningful explanation.

Finally, by allowing the Russian delegation to participate in the works of the Assembly after changing its Rules of Procedure, the PACE has given it the opportunity to take part in creating a new, revised system of sanctions against states facing a serious possibility of being sanctioned for flagrant violations of CoE Member States' obligations. The Russian delegation indeed tried to dilute its effectiveness as much as possible. Though its efforts were ultimately unsuccessful, the whole idea contributed to the 'demystification' of the 'ritual' of the imposition of sanctions and negatively affected its symbolic validation.

The only one of Franck's criteria of legitimacy which appears to have been fulfilled in the case under consideration seems to be that of adherence, which demands a rule to be established within an organised community and an already established legal framework, and not ad hoc. As the respective documents adopted within the organs of the CoE are generally in accordance with their procedural rules, the requirement of adherence seems to have been satisfied.

5 Conclusion: another crisis?

The above analysis shows that while trying to address one crisis, the CoE bodies have created another one. The initial crisis – an institutional, political, and to a large extent also a financial one[78] – was in fact caused mainly by Russia's actions. They can be viewed as a continuum, starting with the annexation of Crimea and through to its decision to withhold the CoE membership fees and cease participation in the works of the PACE and continuing to refuse to heed most of the calls contained in subsequent resolutions of the Assembly. The latter is a crisis of legitimacy. Although some may be eager to blame the Baltic Plus group for not being flexible enough to accept what they consider the lesser of two evils (i.e. Russia returning to the PACE vs Russia leaving the CoE), the concerns of these States should not be ignored. In the end, it is they who were appealing to what is (or ought to be) the most important element for an international organisation such as the CoE: its most basic rules and values.

One needs to note with regret that the complementary joint procedure established by the CoE has not been initiated so far with respect to Russia for

78 As noted above, some of Russia's representatives such as Mr Lavrov also claimed that the actions of PACE were illegitimate. Even if so (which is debatable), there was no explanation provided by the CoE about why it took into account the perception of legitimacy by just one of its Member States as opposed to several others.

those violations which formed the basis for the previous measures against its delegation. If it were, such a move could serve as a strong indication that the changes to the CoE sanctions system analysed above were not motivated by an intention to pursue a policy of 'business as usual' towards Russia, but by a genuine desire to make the response of the CoE to violations of the principles expressed in Article 3 of its Statute more flexible and better tailored to the existing challenges. This could alleviate the objections to the legitimacy of the CoE and its sanction system put forward by the Baltic Plus group. It remains to be seen whether and how the CoE will address these objections. Since March–April 2020, the CoE Member States have been mainly focused on dealing with the acute public health crisis caused by the COVID-19 pandemic, and on addressing its grim economic consequences. But this does not mean that concerns over the legitimacy of the CoE's actions regarding Russia, or with respect to the whole organisation and its sanctions system, have been forgotten. One can look, for example, to the July 2020 declaration of the foreign ministers of Lithuania, Poland, and Ukraine expressing their opposition to the Russian aggression in Ukraine and the need to uphold international law (and also, arguably, respect for human rights in the occupied territories) within international organisations such as the CoE.[79] As long as Russia continues to consider Crimea a part of its territory and support the separatist groups in Eastern Ukraine in violation of the PACE resolutions, the end to this recent crisis of legitimacy is nowhere in sight.[80] Unfortunately, what seems to be the most probable outcome is that the situation will remain as it is, and the feeling of injustice on the part of the states opposing the lenient handling by the CoE of Russia's actions with respect to Ukraine will deepen, eroding their trust in this very important multilateral institution. The diminished legitimacy of the CoE and its sanction system may further reduce the compliance pull exerted on Member States of the organisation, thus jeopardising the effectiveness of its efforts with respect to human rights protection.[81]

79 'Joint Declaration of Foreign Ministers of the Republic of Poland, the Republic of Lithuania and Ukraine on Establishing Lublin Triangle' (*Ministry of Foreign Affairs of the Republic of Lithuania*, 28 July 2020) <https://bit.ly/3wL3wSz> accessed 30 April 2022.

80 The whole issue may become another prolonged dispute, such as the Cypriot-Turkish one.

81 In the end, it turned out that even the compliance pull on Russia was so weakened that the Russian government was not deterred from invading Ukraine again – in 2022 (see n 2). Just one day after this recent aggression began, on 25 February 2022, the Committee of Ministers decided to immediately suspend Russia from its rights of representation in the CoE (both in PACE and the Committee itself). Since it did not cease its aggression, the Committee decided on 16 March, following an unanimous opinion of the PACE, that Russia should cease to be a member of the CoE as from that day. Both decisions were made pursuant to Article 8 of the CoE Statute. See Council of Europe 'The Russian Federation Is Excluded from the Council of Europe' (16 March 2022) <https://

The case under consideration suggests that the failure of an international organisation to meaningfully address the objections of Member States to some of its actions which have sparked controversy may undermine the legitimacy of the organisation as a whole and its procedures in the eyes of these members. The problem is particularly acute if the interests of a major power and less powerful states are involved and in opposition. The result may be a feeling of injustice on the part of the smaller nations and an increased scepticism towards multilateralism as a way of addressing the challenges they are facing. This may lead to various adverse consequences, such as reduced compliance with the rules set by the organisation they are part of, or seeking other methods instead of multilateral ones for resolving disputes (e.g. appealing for help to major powers). To prevent crises, multilateral institutions must ensure equal treatment of both the powerful and those less so.

Acknowledgements

I would like to express thanks to Professor Andrew Drzemczewski for his insightful comments on the earlier drafts of this chapter. The usual disclaimers apply.

bit.ly/3lwh68Z> accessed 15 May 2022. With these decisive steps, the CoE can be said to have at least partially retrieved its legitimacy in the eyes of its members, but nevertheless the mistakes it previously made were irreparable. The wrong signals it sent to Russia through its earlier lenient approach clearly had a negative impact on the CoE's compliance pull on that country.

16 Conclusion

Paolo Davide Farah, Marcin J Menkes, Lukasz Gruszczynski and Veronika Bílková

Are we witnessing a severe crisis of the multilateral international order? If so, what is its nature? Are the disturbing events simply natural setbacks – similar to those in the past – of progressive multilateralization? Or are they perhaps aftershocks of deeper, tectonic shifts in the world order that are currently taking place?

The first difficulty in answering these questions relates to the fact that multilateralism is an elusive concept. As we highlighted in Chapter 1 (the Introduction) multilateralism can be seen in purely quantitative terms as a form of international cooperation among three or more States. Neither the nature of such cooperation nor the rules regulating it are important – what matters is the existence of a triangular (at least) relationship among States. But multilateralism may be also conceptualized differently, in a way that combines both quantitative and qualitative elements, with the latter implying that the process of organizing relations among three or more States must be based on generalized principles of conduct, understood as 'principles which specify appropriate conduct for a class of actions, without regard to the particularistic interests of the parties or the strategic exigencies that may exist in any specific occurrence.'[1] Depending on the specific conceptualization applied, one will get a completely different picture of the world and the processes that are currently going on.

As explained at the beginning of this volume, we gave freedom to our contributing authors to choose their understanding of the concept. Eventually, all of them opted for a mixed approach, combining quantitative and qualitative components. Many authors have also connected it with a liberal vision of international relations. In other words, what they have discussed is specific form of multilateralism that can be labelled liberal multilateralism i.e. characterized by the rejection of power politics and an emphasis on international cooperation through international institutions, liberalization of economic relations among States, promotion of democracy as a preferable political model, and the central position of human rights.[2] This should come as no surprise, as the current

1 John G Ruggie, 'Multilateralism: The Anatomy of an Institution' (1992) 46 Int Organ 561, 571.

2 Eric Shiraev and Vladislav Zubok, *International Relations* (OUP 2014) 78–90; see also Tanja A Börzel and Michael Zürn, 'Contestations of the Liberal

DOI: 10.4324/9781003312857-18

institutional and normative architecture of the international order is based on liberal ideals. Consequently, the crisis of multilateralism – in terms of its institutions, norms, and new initiatives – can indeed be seen as a crisis of the international multilateral liberal order.

While this unintended consensus among the contributing authors has improved the overall coherence of the book, it has also created a second, paradoxical, difficulty. It thus assumes that there is some set of universally shared principles underpinning the (currently threatened) global order. However, this creates the danger of imposing – by way of acknowledgement – such a moral consensus, which becomes self-defeating if it undermines the balance of power.[3] An example of this risk is the scale of the problems of the European Union, the Council of Europe, or the World Trade Organization with countries that have joined the organizations and, by contesting the rule of law (Poland and Hungary), human rights (Russia), or the free market (China), are currently undercutting their foundations. Removal of such members (irrespective of whether that is technically possible) would reveal the scale of the dissonance. At the same time, their continued membership is a threat to the survival of the organization. These three organizations have, in effect, fallen into their own trap by limiting their ability to ensure respect for the principles which they have believed to be universally accepted. At the same time, imposing a balance of power without a moral consensus has always turned out to be self-defeating as well. A recent example of this was the pace of the Taliban's takeover of Afghanistan, treading on the heels of the retreating US forces. Leaving aside the complexities associated with the failure of the so-called War on Terror, the externally imposed order collapsed as the power ratio changed.

These two conflicting needs for stability and freedom explain the cyclical expansion and contraction of state powers.[4] According to the late sociologist Zygmunt Bauman, the pendulum swinging between the longing for freedom and the longing for security is the fundamental dilemma of the (post)modern world.[5] During periods of deregulation, insecurity reigns. At times of regulation, there is resistance to overly restrictive laws, which are deemed to encroach on individual freedom. The difficulty in striking the proper balance between freedom and security is equally challenging at the international, heterogeneous stage, where States struggle to address common challenges without excessively curbing their own sovereignty.[6] Following the end of the Cold War, and even more so during the Arab Spring, the Western world equated the victory of democracy and a free-market economy with a universal

International Order: From Liberal Multilateralism to Postnational Liberalism' (2021) 75(2) Int Organ 282.

3 See e.g. Henry Kissinger, *Diplomacy* (Simon & Schuster 1994).

4 Erich Fromm, *Escape from Freedom* (Holt Paperbacks 1994).

5 Zygmunt Bauman, *Ponowoczesność jako źródło cierpień* [Postmodernity as a source of suffering] (Sic! 2000).

6 Henry Kissinger, *World Order* (Penguin Books 2014).

consensus on these concepts, which were deemed to be a crowning political evolution.[7] However, while democracy and the free market continue to be the organizing principles of international organizations and shape the thinking of key decision-makers, it is only now becoming clear that their importance in international relations reflects more the power of inertia than a universal consensus.

As a result, the dynamics of international cooperation, and the divisions, reinforced during the COVID-19 pandemic, raise the question of whether the existing tensions actually pose a threat to multilateralism, or whether the reconstruction of the multilateral order reflects a belated adaptation of multilateralism to the diverse expectations of various decision-making centres: global, regional and local. Assessments of the genesis, essence, and consequences of the crisis vary widely, depending on the lens through which they are viewed. In some areas of international relations and law, the crisis of multilateralism is revealing itself forcefully. In others, the alarmist tones seem exaggerated. Finally, there are areas where it is fair to question whether multilateralism ever existed. The crisis of multilateralism does not therefore manifest itself equally across international law.

In the immanently subjective context of consensus formation, a third general observation emerges. The starting point for reflection was the recognition of common challenges – in particular, environmental degradation and climate change, global security, the arms race, and threats to public health – which have greater unifying power across political systems than any abstract concept. At the same time, however, this book is written and compiled at a very particular time, when information societies are proving vulnerable to the achievements of technological progress.[8] Changes in the way we communicate have caused societies to break down into 'one-person worlds', created according to the preferences of the people who inhabit them.[9] As a result, without a common set of facts, it is increasingly difficult to have a public debate even at the level of States, let alone the whole world, while the companies that manage the flow of information have gained unprecedented public control.[10] In this sense, the world order is currently suffering the simultaneous impact of powerful forces, both centrifugal and centripetal.

7 See generally Francis Fukuyama, *The End of History and the Last Man* (Reissue, Free Press 2006); see also Robert Kagan, *The Return of History and the End of Dreams* (Vintage 2009); Alex Hochuli, George Hoare, and Philip Cunliffe, *The End of the End of History: Politics in the Twenty-First Century* (Zero Books 2021).

8 Jeff Orlowski (dir), *The Social Dilemma* (Netflix 2020).

9 Marc Dugain and Christophe Labbé, *L'homme nu - La dictature invisible du numérique* (Plon 2016).

10 Robert H Frank and Philip J Cook, *The Winner-Take-All Society: Why the Few at the Top Get So Much More Than the Rest of Us* (Reprint edition, Penguin Books 1996).

In contrast to past eras, when unifying and decentralizing tendencies resulted in the relocation of decision-making centres,[11] we are now observing the co-functioning of ever more parallel orders. This fact will have an obvious impact on the fate of multilateralism (at least in its liberal, Western-based form) in the coming future.

***

Multilateralism rests on the premise that a superior international order is needed to address existing global challenges (one may also argue that since these challenges tend to increase, multilateralism is needed now more than ever before). Yet, this superior and, in theory, independent system has to distance itself from the egoisms of its constituent members and their destructive behaviour and antagonisms in order to be effective. The conceptualization of sovereignty, the normative contents of foundational principles, the effectiveness and legitimacy of international law, as well as the allocation of power among various international actors, should therefore be the central focus of any and all attempts at reform. While these issues may be addressed from different research perspectives, we believe that international law can play an important role here. In particular, it may shed light on such fundamental problems as the nature of the (greatly multilateralized) international legal order, the structural tensions that are emerging within it, and the impact of geopolitics on the system as a whole. Legal analysis may also provide interesting empirical insights into the state of play in specific areas of international law, making it possible to test certain general claims on the ground.

This book thus built on the causes, dynamics, and implications of the crisis of multilateralism in international legal order. The contributing authors have identified the following normative trends:

1 Multilateralism (at least in its liberal form) is a cultural product of specific times, shaped by the dominant narratives, the actors involved, and the relevant international geopolitical settings. Since the current form of multilateralism is based on liberal foundations, changes to these elements can have a profound impact on the operation of the entire system and/or its specific components.[12]
2 International institutions, while playing an important role in promoting multilateralism, can also weaken the system (e.g. by taking ineffective, unprincipled, or contradictory actions). They also often remain heavily constrained by States unwilling to limit their sovereign powers. Consequently, their operational effectiveness is limited.[13]

11 Douglass C North and Robert P Thomas, *The Rise of the Western World* (CUP 1973).
12 See Oleksandr Vodiannikov (Chapter 2), Sean Butler (Chapter 3), Maria Varaki (Chapter 4), and Jessica Lawrence (Chapter 12).
13 See Patrycja Grzebyk and Karolina Wierczyńska (Chapter 10), Margherita Melillo (Chapter 14), and Szymon Zaręba (Chapter 15).

3 Numerous non-state actors also have a positive impact on the shape of multilateral arrangements, and their inclusion in the international legal framework could give the global community a new multilateral impetus.[14]
4 Trust is a crucial element of multilateralism. Once it diminishes, States tend to take unilateral actions based primarily on political power and/or political objectives. Restoring trust is therefore a prerequisite for any successful multilateral reforms.[15]
5 Multilateral institutions and arrangements show a significant level of resilience, which appears to be crucial for the long-term prospects of multilateralism.[16]
6 The inherent contradictions of multilateralism stem, at least in part, from the structural primacy of the international order over the group of hegemonic actors that rely on the Westphalian notion of sovereignty. Thus reinvigorating multilateralism may require rethinking and reconceptualizing the concept of sovereignty, which in turn will entail structural reform of the entire legal system.[17]
7 Multilateral regionalism (or regional multilateralism), the return to fundamental principles (including the rule of law), and experimenting with new governance formats and institutional reforms can help achieve the goals of the international community and enhance its ability to address global challenges in a meaningful manner.[18]

At the granular level, Oleksandr Vodiannikov conceptualizes the crisis as a consequence of the inherent limits of multilateralism. He claims that multilateralism requires a 'trusting relationship' resulting from the 'conjunction of ignorance and faith that is possible in a community with a history(-ies) built up of actors sharing "practices" that incrementally build upon the experiences of interaction'. However, ever-growing doubts about the sources of legitimacy in world politics have entailed a twofold crisis in the nature of multilateralism. At the same time, *the* crisis can be also seen as a *process* within the international organization (understood as a process in which relations among players in the international environment are arranged), as the gaps between individual expectations and the conceptualizations of multilateralism and its

14 See Maria Varaki (Chapter 4), Mary Footer (Chapter 5), Vassilis Pergantis (Chapter 8), and Patrycja Grzebyk and Karolina Wierczyńska (Chapter 10).
15 See Oleksandr Vodiannikov (Chapter 2), Sean Butler (Chapter 3), and Vassilis Pergantis (Chapter 8),
16 See Mary Footer (Chapter 5), Christopher Lentz (Chapter 6); Vassilis Pergantis (Chapter 8), and Margherita Melillo (Chapter 14).
17 See Maria Varaki (Chapter 4), Ernst-Ulrich Petersmann (Chapter 11), and Jessica Lawrence (Chapter 12).
18 See Mary Footer (Chapter 5), Malgosia Fitzmaurice (Chapter 7), Agnieszka Nimark (Chapter 9), Ernst-Ulrich Petersmann (Chapter 11), Ewa Żelazna (Chapter 13), and Margherita Melillo (Chapter 14).

practice keep growing. As a result, narratives and ways of framing the crisis can become self-fulfilling prophecies.

Trust is also the central concept for Vassilis Pergantis' analysis of the state of affairs among the State parties to the European Convention of Human Rights (ECHR). He argues that the recent backlash against the rule of law and the rise of authoritarian moods throughout Europe undermine the very foundations of the ECHR system. However, rather than focusing on the rebuilding of trust, Pergantis first considers the inherent limitation of law as a trust-building tool, and, second, suggests the need for a critical reappraisal with regard to judicial cooperation.

For Sean Butler, the recognition of the crisis is predetermined by the starting assumptions regarding the nature of sovereignty and the structure of the world order. Whether the current situation is a crisis of multilateralism depends on the perception that the international community is based on a shared normative vision that can override individual preferences for the sake of universal common goals (such as human rights or democracy). However, this is not the case in a society of mutual interests built on the foundations of the principle of sovereignty. The two possibilities, though, are not dichotomous. In essence, we are facing the waning of the US normative hegemony, and the resulting reduced appeal of the conditional variant of sovereignty. Yet this does not undermine the central role of Westphalian sovereignty, which is poorly suited to the demands of multilateralism. The zero-sum tension between sovereignty and the requirements of international public order may lead to three possible scenarios: adaptation, frustration, or a dysfunctional re-ordering. The most problematic feature is that the ongoing changes may be a result of inertia. On the one hand, the conditional and Westphalian variants of sovereignty may no longer be acceptable. On the other, any alternative requires a hardly imaginable universal consensus that would resolve the central tension between universal interests and sovereign concerns.

Unlike, for instance, Vodiannikov and Butler, several chapters focus on the static, constructivist perception of multilateralism (and the resulting acknowledgement, or rejection, of the *crisis*), and frame the crisis dynamically, as a process.

Maria Varaki focuses on the crisis as a process that can rejuvenate international law. She emphasizes that the development of international law has not been linear, but is a history of tides and waves, and thus the crisis, if such exists, is by no means a 'current' event. Accordingly, she explores the cathartic potential of the current pushback against multilateralism, whereby this opportunity can be tapped for a critical discussion and fine-tuning of existing arrangements.

The systemic embeddedness of multilateralism is also considered by Ernst-Ulrich Petersmann, who scrutinizes the role of the rule of law as a building block of international economic law. The examples of the pushback against investor-State arbitration (ISDS), the WTO dispute settlement system, or even of Europe's 'integration through law' are used as an opportunity to draw lessons from and responses to the 'systemic crises' of the multilateral legal order.

Jessica Lawrence draws conclusions similar to Maria Varaki regarding the perceived nature of multilateralism (and its crisis). To her, the current situation merely reflects the 'collective political and economic forces that are currently pulling at the seams of the WTO [World Trade Organization]'. It is a constructivist narrative that shapes perception of the social world rather than a description of empirical facts. Similar to Varaki's non-linear characterization of the history of international law, Lawrence points to WTO Members' cyclical progress in forging normative consensus, interrupted by recurring backtracking in cooperation. Such an approach allows her to capture the ideological role played by the discourse of a 'crisis of multilateralism', and ultimately to call for a reconsideration of the fundamental assumptions about the past and present of public international trade law. The crisis is serious, but the crisis narratives hinder understandings of its true causes and dynamics.

The cyclical element of international law history also resonates in Chapter 15 on the participation of the Russian Federation in the works of the Parliamentary Assembly of the Council of Europe. Szymon Zaręba concludes that while solving its political and financial crisis, the Council of Europe has been plunged into a legitimacy crisis. While his analysis is one of the more fatalistic accounts of the current state of affairs in the Council of Europe, in the long term it does not necessarily mean that the CoE is doomed.

Mary Footer also acknowledges the decline in multilateralism in the international order and the atomization of the international stage (i.e. beyond a state-centric system). However, she argues that while the post-Second World War international order is in decline, this does not mean that multilateralism as such is ending. Instead, she posits that we may be witnessing the birth of 'multi-stakeholderism', and while it does not necessarily solve the crisis in the international order, it may spur the extension and development of international cooperation in new areas. However, this potential can only be realized in combination with the adequate accountability of the new stakeholders.

Whereas the above authors consider whether the 'crisis' should be conceptualized statically or dynamically, and to what extent its existence is subjective or objective, Christopher Lentz shows that – at least with regard to the jurisdiction of international adjudicative bodies – the broad perception of 'crisis' is empirically questionable. Although instances of States' withdrawals from dispute settlement clauses (treaties) tend to resonate widely, the number of adhering states is greater than those withdrawing from this institutional pillar of the multilateral order.

Even more promising than the absence of crisis is finding and developing new areas with hopeful prospects for the development of international law. This, according to Malgosia Fitzmaurice, is the case of international environmental protection. She traces important developments with respect to communitarian interests and, more specifically, the *locus standi* of States to enforce them, most importantly through creative combination-synergies between international environmental law and human rights law.

Similarly promising, even if not fully satisfactory, conclusions are drawn by Margherita Melillo, who analyses how the World Health Organization dealt with the COVID-19 pandemic. While the health crisis exacerbated the institutional limitations of the organization, at the same time the inescapable sense of reality of the global challenge raised awareness of the need for global health multilateralism. Thus, the dramatic public health crisis also gives hope for the advancement of international law.

A very particular image results from the analysis of the nuclear non-proliferation regime on its 50th anniversary presented by Agnieszka Nimark. She highlights the split between the normative convergence of the non-nuclear states, on the one hand, and those actually threatening global security, on the other. She argues that this 'mid-life crisis' echoes the broader legitimacy crisis of the United Nations and the post-Second World War order, which makes it part of a broader transition from a 'hegemonic' order towards a more pluralistic one.

Patrycja Grzebyk and Karolina Wierczyńska also paint a similar split image with respect to the International Criminal Court. They argue that the International Criminal Court plays a twofold role in international relations. It both strengthens multilateralism by performing an enabling function within the Assembly of State Parties, and exacerbates its weaknesses when the Court is forced to act as a 'supplicant' requesting State cooperation.

Finally, another surprising pattern emerges from the analysis of international investment arbitration (ISDS). Following scrutiny of the EU's agenda for the reform of ISDS, Ewa Żelazna concludes that we are currently witnessing the forging of a new multilateral approach to foreign investment protection; one which is transcending its atomized nature and is being achieved through a series of streamlined bilateral agreements.

Given the variety of assessments of various situations and the relevant recommendations, it is appropriate at this point to return to the two initial questions of this volume about the nature, and the dynamics and implications, of the crisis. The answer to the second question is a function of the first answer. The answer to the first question is that the crisis is both present and absent, depending on the perspective of the inquirer and the social world to which one refers. As disappointing as this may be with respect to achieving the primary research objective of this book, it has quite important legal implications. Since the essential function of law is the construction and implementation of rules of social coexistence beyond family and tribal ties of trust,[19] the concomitant atomization of societies, together with global challenges, make international law the best instrument we know for working for the common good.

19 Piotr Sztompka, *Zaufanie. Fundament Społeczeństwa* (Znak 2007).

Index

Page numbers followed by 'n' refer to notes.